ACCA

Applied Skills

Financial Management (FM)

Practice & Revision Kit

For exams in September 2023, December 2023, March 2024 and June 2024

First edition 2007

Sixteeth edition February 2023

ISBN: 9781 0355 0112 0

Previous ISBN: 9781 5097 4759 7

e-ISBN: 9781 0355 0116 8

Cataloguing-in-Publication Data

A catalogue record for this book is available from the British Library

Published by

BPP Learning Media Ltd

BPP House, Aldine Place

London W12 8AA

learningmedia.bpp.com

Printed in the United Kingdom

Your learning materials, published by BPP Learning Media Ltd, are printed on paper obtained from traceable, sustainable sources.

We are grateful to the Association of Chartered Certified Accountants for permission to reproduce past examination questions. The suggested solutions in the Practice & Revision Kit have been prepared by BPP Learning Media Ltd, except where otherwise stated.

A note about copyright

Contents

Question index

	Marks	Time allocation (mins)	Page number	
			Questions	Answers
Section B questions				
286-290 Rose Co (amended) (June 2015)	10	18	109	286
291-295 Edwen Co (pilot exam)	10	18	110	287
296-300 Zigto Co (amended) (June 2012)	10	18	112	288
301-305 Marigold Co (Sep/Dec 2020)	10	18	113	289
306-310 Peony Co (March/June 2019)	10	18	115	290
Mock Exams				
Mock exam 1 (September 2016)			295	309
Mock exam 2 (Specimen exam)			323	339
Mock exam 3 (December 2016)			355	371
Mock exam 4 (including ACCA Sep/Dec 2022 Section C exam questions)			387	401

Question index

The headings in this checklist/index indicate the main topics of questions, but questions sometimes cover several different topics. The dates indicate the timing of past real exam questions eg March/June 2021 is a past question from the sample questions published by the ACCA for the March and June 2021 exams.

Topic index

Listed below are the key *Financial Management* (FM) syllabus topics and the numbers of the questions in this Kit covering those topics.

If you need to concentrate your practice and revision on certain topics or if you want to attempt all available questions that refer to a particular subject, you will find this index useful.

Syllabus topic	Question numbers	Workbook chapter
Asset replacement decisions	126, 133–134, 143–144, 156, 165	8
Business valuation	187, 209, 224–232, 238–240, 242, 243–245, 247–250, 253–261, 263–267	13
Capital rationing	129–131, 135, 141–142, 156–157, 159–160	8
Capital structure	197–206, 218	12
Cash management	56–58, 82, 87, 89	4
Cash operating cycle	41, 85, 88	3
Cost of capital	188–196, 207–208, 213–218, 220–221, 251–252	11
Dividend policy	172–176, 213d, 214b, 218, 221, 262	10
Economics	21–25, 32, 36–40, 162	2
Financial intermediaries and markets	24, 26–33, 33–35	2
Financial management	2, 6, 15	1
Foreign currency risk	268–277, 286–289, 291–305, 308	14
Gearing	177–182, 212–213	12
Interest rate risk	278–285, 290, 306–307, 309–310	15
Inventory management	46–48, 53, 62–63, 66–67, 71, 76–77, 83, 86	3
IRR	104–107, 109, 140, 150, 155, 163, 164	5
Leasing	108, 127–128, 132, 156, 158, 164	8
Market efficiency	223, 233–237, 241, 246	13
NPV	94–96, 100–103, 110–120, 148, 151–154, 157, 161–163, 165–166	5, 6, 7
Objectives	5, 7, 9, 10–13, 19–20, 161	1
Overtrading	70, 84, 85	3

Syllabus topic	Question numbers	Workbook chapter
Payables management	54, 87	3
Payback	92, 97, 98, 149, 163, 165	5
Ratio analysis	1, 3, 4, 8, 14, 16–18, 72	3, 9, 12
Receivables management	49–52, 64–65, 68, 72–73, 78, 82–83, 85, 87, 90	3
ROCE	91, 93, 98–99, 146–147, 163	5
Risk and uncertainty	121–125, 136–139, 145, 160–162	7
Sources of finance	167–177, 183–186, 210–213, 214, 216, 218–220, 222	9
Working capital financing	55, 59–60, 75, 80–81, 86, 88	4
Working capital management	42–45, 61, 69, 74 79, 81, 83	3

The exam

Computer-based exams

Applied Skills exams are all computer-based exams.

Approach to examining the syllabus

The technical articles section on ACCA's website include one called 'Financial Management Examiners approach'. This article outlines the key features of the syllabus, and the qualities candidates should demonstrate when answering FM questions. We reproduce some of the main points here.

Candidates who successfully pass the Financial Management exam will be able to:

- Discuss the role and purpose of the financial management function
- Assess and discuss the impact of the economic environment on financial management
- Discuss and apply working capital management techniques
- Carry out effective investment appraisal
- Identify and evaluate alternative sources of business finance
- Discuss and apply principles of business and asset valuations
- Explain and apply risk management techniques in business.

Summarising the advice ACCA's examining team gives for FM:

In order to pass Financial Management, candidates should:

- Clearly understand the objectives of Financial Management, as explained above, and in the Syllabus and in the accompanying Study Guide
- Read and study thoroughly a suitable financial management textbook
- Read relevant articles flagged by Student Accountant
- Practise exam-standard and exam-style questions on a regular basis
- Be able to communicate their understanding clearly in an examination context

Format of the exam

The exam will have a duration of 3 hours, and will comprise three exam sections:

Section	Style of question type	Description	Proportion of exam, %
A	Objective test (OT)	15 questions × 2 marks	30
B	Objective test (OT) case	3 questions × 10 marks Each question will contain 5 subparts each worth 2 marks	30
C	Constructed Response (Long questions)	2 questions × 20 marks	40
Total			100

Section A and B questions will be selected from the entire syllabus. The responses to each question or subpart in OT cases are marked automatically as either correct or incorrect by computer. In Sections A and B, it is important that candidates do not spend too much time on any one question that they may be struggling with. It is important to remember that each question is only worth two marks.

Sections A and B are designed to test your broad understanding of the whole of the FM syllabus.

Section C questions will **mainly** focus on the following syllabus areas but may include material from other areas of the syllabus:

- Working capital management (syllabus area C)
- Investment appraisal (syllabus area D)
- Business finance (syllabus area E)

The responses to these questions are human marked, so it continues to be absolutely vital that all workings are shown and assumptions are stated.

The balance of the marks in the exam will be approximately evenly split between marks for discussion and marks for calculations.

Syllabus and Study Guide

The complete FM syllabus and study guide can be found by visiting the exam resource finder on the ACCA website.

Helping you with your revision

BPP Learning Media – ACCA Approved Content Provider

As an ACCA **Approved Content Provider**, BPP Learning Media gives you the **opportunity** to use revision materials reviewed by the ACCA examining team. By incorporating the ACCA examining team's comments and suggestions regarding the depth and breadth of syllabus coverage, the BPP Learning Media Practice & Revision Kit provides excellent, **ACCA-approved** support for your revision.

These materials are reviewed by the ACCA examining team. The objective of the review is to ensure that the material properly covers the syllabus and study guide outcomes, used by the examining team in setting the exams, in the appropriate breadth and depth. The review does not ensure that every eventuality, combination or application of examinable topics is addressed by the ACCA Approved Content. Nor does the review comprise a detailed technical check of the content as the Approved Content Provider has its own quality assurance processes in place in this respect.

BPP Learning Media do everything possible to ensure the material is accurate and up to date when sending to print. In the event that any errors are found after the print date, they are uploaded to the following website: www.bpp.com/learningmedia/Errata.

The structure of this Practice & Revision Kit

FM exam questions mainly focus exclusively or mainly on one single syllabus area. Therefore questions in this Kit have been grouped according to the section of the syllabus to which they mainly relate.

There are also four mock exams which provide you the opportunity to refine your knowledge and skills as part of your final exam preparations.

Question practice

This is the most important thing to do if you want to get through. Many of the most up-to-date exam questions are in this Kit. Practice doing them under timed conditions, then go through the answers and go back to the Workbook for any topic you are really having trouble with. Come back to a question a week later and try it again – you will be surprised at how much better you are getting. Be very ruthless with yourself at this stage – you have to do the question in the time, without looking at the answer. This will really sharpen your wits and make the exam experience less worrying. Just keep doing this and you will get better at doing questions and you will really find out what you know and what you don't know.

Question practice under timed conditions is absolutely vital. We strongly advise you to create a revision study plan which focuses on question practice. This is so that you can get used to the pressures of answering exam questions in limited time, develop proficiency in the Specific FM skills and the Exam success skills. Ideally, you should aim to cover all questions in this Kit, and very importantly, all four mock exams.

Selecting questions

To help you plan your revision, we have provided a full **topic index** which maps the questions to topics in the syllabus (see page viii).

We provide signposts to help you plan your revision.

- A full **question index**
- A **topic index** listing all the questions that cover key topics, so that you can locate the questions that provide practice on these topics, and see the different ways in which they might be examined

Making the most of question practice

At BPP Learning Media we realise that you need more than just questions and model answers to get the most from your question practice.

- Our **top tips** included for certain questions provide essential advice on tackling questions, presenting answers and the key points that answers need to include.
- We include **marking guides** to show you what the examining team rewards.
- We include **comments from the examining team** to show you where students struggled or performed well in the actual exam.

Attempting mock exams

There are four mock exams that provide practice at coping with the pressures of the exam day. We strongly recommend that you attempt them under exam conditions. We strongly recommend that you attempt them under exam conditions. All the mock exams reflect the question styles and syllabus coverage of the exam.

Topics to revise

The structure of the exam is designed to test your understanding of the whole syllabus.

However, it is especially important to have a comprehensive understanding of all aspects of syllabus sections C (working capital), D (investment appraisal) and E (Business Finance) because these are commonly examined as the major component of the twenty marks Section C exam questions.

The aim of the Financial Management exam is to develop the knowledge and skills expected of a finance manager in relation to investment, financing and dividend decisions.

You need to be able to communicate your understanding clearly in an exam context. Calculations and discussions are equally important so do not concentrate on the numbers and ignore the written parts.

Gaining the easy marks

Some OTQs are easier than others. Answer those that you feel fairly confident about as quickly as you can. Come back later to those you find more difficult. This could be a way of making use of the time in the examination most efficiently and effectively.

Many OTQs will not involve calculations. Make sure that you understand the wording of 'written' OTQs before selecting your answer.

The calculations within a section C question will get progressively harder and easy marks will be available in the early stages. Set out your calculations clearly and show all your workings in a clear format. Use a proforma, for example in complex NPV questions and slot the simpler figures into the proforma straight away before you concentrate on the figures that need a lot of adjustment.

A Section C question may separate discussion requirements from calculations, so that you do not need to do the calculations first in order to answer the discussion part. This means that you should be able to gain marks from making sensible, practical comments without having to complete the calculations.

Discussions that are focused on the specific organisation in the question will gain more marks than regurgitation of knowledge. Read the question carefully and more than once, to ensure you are actually answering the specific requirements.

Pick out key words such as 'describe', 'evaluate' and 'discuss'. These all mean something specific.

- 'Describe' means to communicate the key features of
- 'Evaluate' means to assess the value of
- 'Discuss' means to examine in detail by argument

Clearly label the points you make in discussions so that the marker can identify them all rather than getting lost in the detail.

Remote invigilated exams

In certain geographical areas it may be possible for you to take your exam remotely. This option, which is subject to strict conditions, can offer increased flexibility and convenience under certain circumstances. Further guidance, including the detailed requirements and conditions for taking the exam by this method, is contained on ACCA's website at https://www.accaglobal.com/an/en/student/exam-entry-and-administration/about-our-exams/remote-exams/remote-session-exams.html.

Essential skills areas to be successful in Financial Management

We think there are three areas you should develop in order to achieve exam success in Financial Management (FM):

(a) Knowledge application

(b) Specific FM Skills

(c) Exam Success Skills

These are shown in the diagram below. At the revision and exam preparation phases these **should be developed together as part of a comprehensive study plan of focussed question practice.**

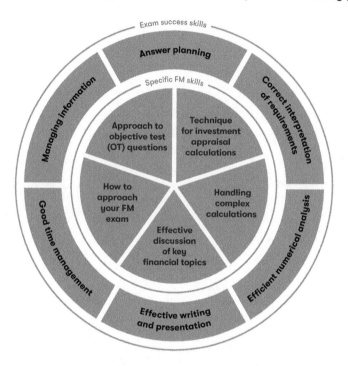

Specific FM skills

These are the skills specific to FM that we think you need to develop in order to pass the exam.

In the BPP Workbook, there are five **Skills Checkpoints** which define each skill and show how it is applied in answering a question. A brief summary of each skill is given below.

Skill 1: Approach to objective test (OT) questions

Section A of the exam will include 15 OT questions worth two marks each. Section B of the exam will include three OT cases, worth 10 marks each. Each OT case contains a group of five OT questions based around a single scenario. 60% of your FM exam is therefore made up of OT questions. It is essential that you have a good approach to answering these questions. OT questions are auto-marked, your workings will therefore not be considered, you have to answer the whole question correctly to earn their two marks.

A step-by-step technique for tackling OT questions is outlined below:

Step 1   **General guidance for approaching OT questions**

Answer the questions you know first.

If you're having difficulty answering a question, move on and come back to tackle it once you've answered all the questions you know. It is often quicker to answer discursive style OT questions first, leaving more time for calculations.

Step 2   Answer all questions.

There is no penalty for an incorrect answer in ACCA exams, there is nothing to be gained by leaving an OT question unanswered. If you are stuck on a question, as a last resort, it is worth selecting the option you consider most likely to be correct and moving on. Flag the question, so if you have time after you have answered the rest of the questions, you can revisit it.

Step 3   Guidance for answering specific OT questions

Read the requirement first!

The requirement will be stated in bold text in the exam. Identify what you are being asked to do, any technical knowledge required and **what type of OT question** you are dealing with. Look for key words in the requirement such as "which TWO of the following," " which of the following is NOT".

Step 4   Apply your technical knowledge to the data presented in the question.

Take your time working through calculations, making sure to read through each answer option with care. OT questions are designed so that each answer option is plausible. Work through each response option and eliminate those you know are incorrect

Skills Checkpoint 1 in the BPP Workbook for FM covers this technique in detail through application to an exam-standard OT case question. Consider revisiting Skills Checkpoint 1 to improve this skill.

Skill 2: Technique for investment appraisal calculations

Section C of the FM exam often includes a question on investment appraisal. You may be asked to calculate the net present value (NPV) of a project and advise whether the investment is financially acceptable. Section C is human marked and therefore it is important that your calculations are laid out clearly.

Key steps in preparing an NPV calculation are outlined below:

Step 1   Use a standard NPV proforma. This will help the marker to understand your workings and allocate the marks easily. It will also help you to work through the figures in a methodical and time-efficient way.

Step 2   Input easy numbers from the question directly onto your proforma. This will make sure that you pick up as many easy marks as possible before dealing with more detailed calculations.

Step 3   Always use formulae to perform basic calculations. Don't write out your working in a single cell; this wastes time and you may make a mistake. Use the spreadsheet functions instead!

Step 4   Show clear workings for any complex calculations. More complex calculations such as the tax relief on capital allowances will require a separate working. Keep your workings as clear and simple as possible and ensure they are cross-referenced to your NPV proforma.

Skills Checkpoint 2 in the BPP Workbook for FM covers this technique in detail through application to an exam-standard question. Consider revisiting Skills Checkpoint 2 to improve this skill.

Skill 3: Handling complex calculations

The business finance section of the syllabus often involves complex calculations such as the weighted average cost of capital (WACC) or ungearing and re-gearing beta factors.

A step-by-step technique for handling complex calculations is outlined below.

Step 1   Understanding the data in the question.

Where a question includes a significant amount of data, read the requirements carefully to make sure that you understand clearly what the question is asking you to do. You can use the highlighting function to pull out important data from the question. Use the data provided to think about what formula you will need to use. For example, if you are given a beta factor you will use CAPM to calculate the cost of equity, if you are given a dividend growth rate it will be the dividend growth model. If the question states that the debt is redeemable you will need to use the IRR formula to calculate the cost of debt.

Step 2   Use a standard proforma working.

For example, if you are asked to calculate the WACC use your standard proforma for calculating WACC and separately work through the individual parts of the calculation (Ke, Kd, Ve, Vd).

Step 3   Use spreadsheet formulae to perform basic calculations

Do not write out your workings, this wastes time and you may make a mistake. Use the spreadsheet formulae instead!

Skills Checkpoint 3 in the BPP Workbook for FM covers this technique in detail through application to an exam-standard question. Consider revisiting Skills Checkpoint 3 to improve this skill.

Skill 4: Effective discussion of key financial topics

The balance of the FM exam will be approximately 50:50 in terms of the number of marks available for discussion and the number of marks available for numerical calculations. It is very tempting to only practise numerical questions, as they are easy to mark because the answer is right or wrong, whereas written questions are more subjective, and a range of different answers will be given credit. Even when attempting written questions, it is tempting to write a brief answer plan and then look at the answer rather than writing a full answer to plan. Unless you practise written questions in full to time, you will never acquire the necessary skills to tackle discussion questions.

A step-by-step technique for effective discussion of key financial topics is outlined below.

Step 1   Read and analyse the requirement

The active verb used often dictates the approach that written answers should take. For example, discuss means examine in detail by using arguments in favour or against. Work out how many minutes you have to answer each sub requirement.

Step 2   Read and analyse the scenario.

Identify the type of company you are dealing with and how the financial topics in the requirement relate to that type of company. As you go through the scenario you should be highlighting key information which you think will play a key role in answering the specific requirements.

Step 3   Plan your answer

Ensure your answer is balanced in terms of identifying the potential benefits **and** limitations of topics that are being discussed or recommended

Step 4   Write your answer

As you write your answer, try wherever possible to apply your analysis to the scenario, instead of simply writing about the financial topic in generic, technical terms. As you write your answer, explain what you mean – in one (or two) sentence(s) – and then explain why this matter in the given scenario. This should result in a series of short paragraphs that address the specific context of the scenario.

Skills Checkpoint 4 in the BPP Workbook for FM covers this technique in detail through application to an exam-standard question. Consider revisiting Skills Checkpoint 4 to improve this skill.

Skill 5: How to approach your FM exam

You can answer your FM exam in whatever order you prefer. It is important that you adopt a strategy that works best for you. We would suggest that you decide on your preferred approach and practice it by doing a timed mock exam before your real exam.

A suggested approach to tackling your FM exam is outlined below.

Step 1   Complete section A first – allocated time 54 minutes

Tackle any easier OT questions first. Often discursive style questions can be answered quickly, saving more time for calculations. Do not leave any questions unanswered. Even if you are unsure make a reasoned guess.

Step 2   Complete section B next – allocated time 54 minutes

You will have 18 mins of exam time to allocate to each of the three OT case questions in section B. Use the same approach to OT questions as discussed for section A.

There will normally be three discursive and two numerical questions within each case. Again, it is better to tackle the discursive type questions first and make a reasoned guess for any questions you are unsure on.

Step 3   Finally, complete section C – allocated time 72 minutes

Start with the question you feel most confident with. The first sub requirement will normally involve some detailed calculations, these tend to be very time pressured. If possible, answer the discursive sub requirements first. This will ensure that you don't spend too much time on the calculations and then lose out on the easier discursive marks. Make it clear to your marker which sub requirement you are answering.

Skills Checkpoint 5 in the BPP Workbook for FM covers this technique in detail. Consider revisiting Skills Checkpoint 5 to improve this skill.

Exam success skills

Passing the FM exam requires more than applying syllabus knowledge and demonstrating the specific FM skills; it also requires the development of excellent exam technique through question practice. We consider the following six skills to be vital for exam success. These skills were introduced in the BPP Workbook for FM and you can revisit the five Skills Checkpoints in the Workbook for tutorial guidance on how to apply each of the six Exam success skills in your question practice and in the exam.

Try to consider your performance in all six Exam success skills during your revision stage question practice, and reflect on your particular strengths, and your weaker areas, which you can then work on.

Exam success skills 1

Managing information

Advice on developing managing information

Questions in the exam will present you with a lot of information. The skill is how you handle this information to make the best use of your time. The key is determining how you will approach the exam and then actively reading the questions.

You must take an active approach to reading each question. Focus on the requirement first, underlining key verbs such as 'evaluate', 'analyse', 'explain', 'discuss', to ensure you answer the question properly. Then read the rest of the question, underlining (using the Word processing functionality) and annotating important and relevant information, and making notes of any relevant technical information you think you will need (using the scratch pad provided).

Exam success skill 2

Correct interpretation of the requirements

The active verb used often dictates the approach that written answers should take (eg 'explain', 'discuss', 'evaluate'). It is important you identify and use the verb to define your approach. The **correct interpretation of the requirements** skill means correctly producing only what is being asked for by a requirement. Anything not required will not earn marks.

Advice on developing the correct interpretation of the requirements

This skill can be developed by analysing question requirements and applying this process:

Step 1 **Read the requirement**

Firstly, read the requirement a couple of times slowly and carefully and highlight the active verbs. Use the active verbs to define what you plan to do. Make sure you identify any sub-requirements.

In FM, it is important that you do this not only for section C questions but also for OT questions in sections A and B.

Step 2 **Read the rest of the question**

By reading the requirement first, you will have an idea of what you are looking out for as you read through the case overview and exhibits. This is a great time saver and means you don't end up having to read the whole question in full twice. You should do this in an active way – see Exam success skill 1: Managing Information.

Step 3 **Read the requirement again**

Read the requirement again to remind yourself of the exact wording before starting your written answer. This will capture any misinterpretation of the requirements or any missed requirements entirely. This should become a habit in your approach and, with repeated practice, you will find the focus, relevance and depth of your answer plan will improve

Exam success skill 3

Answer planning: Priorities, structure and logic

This skill requires the planning of the key aspects of an answer which accurately and completely responds to the requirement.

Advice on developing answer planning: priorities, structure and logic

Everyone will have a preferred style for an answer plan. For example, it may be a mind map or bullet-pointed lists. Choose the approach that you feel most comfortable with, or, if you are not sure, try out different approaches for different questions until you have found your preferred style.

For a discussion question, annotating the question paper is likely to be insufficient. It would be better to draw up a separate answer plan in the format of your choosing (eg a mind map or bullet-pointed lists).

Exam success skill 4

Efficient numerical analysis

This skill aims to maximise the marks awarded by making clear to the marker the process of arriving at your answer. This is achieved by laying out an answer such that, even if you make a few errors, you can still score subsequent marks for follow-on calculations. It is vital that you do not lose marks purely because the marker cannot follow what you have done.

Advice on developing efficient numerical analysis

This skill can be developed by applying the following process:

Step 1   Use a standard proforma working where relevant

If answers can be laid out in a standard proforma then always plan to do so. This will help the marker to understand your working and allocate the marks easily. It will also help you to work through the figures in a methodical and time-efficient way.

Step 2   Show your workings

Keep your workings as clear and simple as possible and ensure they are cross-referenced to the main part of your answer. Where it helps, provide brief narrative explanations to help the marker understand the steps in the calculation. This means that if a mistake is made you do not lose any subsequent marks for follow-on calculations

Step 3   Keep moving!

It is important to remember that, in an exam situation, it can sometimes be difficult to get every number 100% correct. The key is therefore ensuring you do not spend too long on any single calculation. If you are struggling with a solution then make a sensible assumption, state it and move on.

Exam success skill 5

Effective writing and presentation

Written answers should be presented so that the marker can clearly see the points you are making, presented in the format specified in the question. The skill is to provide efficient written answers with sufficient breadth of points that answer the question, in the right depth, in the time available.

Advice on developing effective writing and presentation

Step 1   Use headings

Using the headings and sub-headings from your answer plan will give your answer structure, order and logic. This will ensure your answer links back to the requirement and is clearly signposted, making it easier for the marker to understand the different points you are making. Underlining your headings will also help the marker.

Step 2   Write your answer in short, but full, sentences

Use short, clear sentences with the aim that every sentence should say something different and generate marks. Write in full sentences, ensuring your style is professional.

Step 3   Do your calculations first and explanation second

Questions often ask for an explanation with suitable calculations. The best approach is to prepare the calculation first but present it on the bottom half of the page of your answer, or on the next page. Then add the explanation before the calculation. Performing the calculation first should enable you to explain what you have done.

Exam success skill 6

Good time management

This skill means planning your time across all the requirements so that all tasks have been attempted at the end of the time available and actively checking on time during your exam. This is so that you can flex your approach and prioritise requirements which, in your judgement, will generate the maximum marks in the available time remaining.

Advice on developing good time management

The exam is 3 hours long, which translates to 1.8 minutes per mark. Each OT question in section A should be allocated 3.6 mins. Some OT questions involving calculations may take slightly longer than this however this will be balanced out with other discursive type OT questions that can be answered more quickly. Each OT case in section B should be allocated 18 minutes to answer the five questions totalling ten marks. Each section C question is worth 20 marks and therefore should be allocated 36 minutes. It is also important to allocate time between each sub requirement.

Keep an eye on the clock

Aim to attempt all requirements, but be ready to be ruthless and move on if your answer is not going as planned. The challenge for many is sticking to planned timings. Be aware this is difficult to achieve in the early stages of your studies and be ready to let this skill develop over time.

If you find yourself running short on time and know that a full answer is not possible in the time you have, consider recreating your plan in overview form and then add key terms and details as time allows. Remember, some marks may be available, for example, simply stating a conclusion which you don't have time to justify in full.

Exam formulae

Set out below are the formulae which you will be given in the exam, and formulae which you should learn. If you are not sure what the symbols mean, or how the formulae are used, you should refer to the appropriate chapter in the BPP FM workbook.

Exam formulae	*
Economic Order Quantity $$= \sqrt{\frac{2C_0 D}{C_h}}$$	3
Miller-Orr Model Return point = Lower limit + (1/3 × spread) $$\text{Spread} = 3\left[\frac{\frac{3}{4} \times \text{transaction cost} \times \text{variance of cash flows}}{\text{interest rate}}\right]^{\frac{1}{3}}$$	4
The Capital Asset Pricing Model $E(r_i) = R_f + \beta_i (E(r_m) - R_f)$	11
The Asset Beta Formula $$\beta a = \left[\frac{Ve}{(Ve + Vd(1-T))}\beta e\right] + \left[\frac{Vd(1-T)}{(Ve + Vd(1-T))}\beta d\right]$$	12
The Growth Model $$P_0 = \frac{D_0(1+g)}{(r_e - g)} \qquad\qquad r_e = \frac{D_0(1+g)}{P_0} + g$$	13
Gordon's Growth Approximation $g = br_e$	11, 13
The weighted average cost of capital $$WACC = \left[\frac{Ve}{Ve + Vd}\right]Ke + \left[\frac{Vd}{Ve + Vd}\right]Kd(1-T)$$	11
The Fisher formula $(1 + i) = (1 + r)(1 + h)$	5
Purchasing Power Parity $$S_1 = S_0 \times \frac{(1 + hc)}{(1 + hd)}$$	14
Interest Rate Parity $$F_0 = S_0 \times \frac{(1 + ic)}{(1 + id)}$$	14

*Found in which Workbook chapter

Formulae to learn

Profitability ratios include:

$$\text{ROCE} = \frac{\text{Profit before interest and tax (PBIT)}}{\text{Capital employed}}$$

$$\text{ROCE} = \frac{\text{PBIT}}{\text{Revenue}} \times \frac{\text{Revenue}}{\text{Capital employed}}$$

Debt ratios include:

$$\text{Gearing} = \frac{\text{Debt}}{\text{Equity}} \text{ or } \frac{\text{Debt}}{\text{Debt + Equity}} \text{ (and either book values or market values can be used)}$$

$$\text{Interest coverage} = \frac{\text{PBIT}}{\text{Interest}}$$

Liquidity ratios include:

Current ratio = Current assets: Current liabilities

Acid Test ratio = Current assets less inventory: Current liabilities

Shareholder investor ratios include:

$$\text{Dividend yield} = \frac{\text{Dividend per share}}{\text{Market price per share}} \times 100$$

$$\text{Earnings per share} = \frac{\text{Price distributable to ordinary shareholders}}{\text{Number of ordinary shares issued}}$$

$$\text{Price earning (P/E) ratio} = \frac{\text{Market price per share}}{\text{EPS}}$$

$$\text{Accounts collection period} = \frac{\text{Receivables}}{\text{(credit) sales}} \times 365 \text{ days}$$

Inventory holding period

(a) $\text{Finished goods} = \dfrac{\text{Finished goods}}{\text{Cost of sales}} \times 365 \text{ days}$

(b) $\text{WIP} = \dfrac{\text{Average WIP}}{\text{Cost of sales}} \times 365 \text{ days}$

(c) $\text{Raw material:} \dfrac{\text{Average raw material inventory}}{\text{Annual raw material purchases}} \times 365 \text{ days}$

Accounts payable payment period

$$= \frac{\text{Payables}}{\text{Credit purchases (or cost sales if purchases unavailable)}} \times 365 \text{ days}$$

$$IRR = a + \frac{NPVa}{NPVa - NPVb}(b - a)$$

$$\text{Equivalent annual cost} = \frac{\text{PV of cost over one replacement cycle}}{\text{Annuity factor for the number of years in the cycle}}$$

$$\text{Cost of debt} = Kd = \frac{i(1-T)}{P0}$$

$$\text{Cost of preference shares} = Kpref = \frac{\text{Preference Dividend}}{\text{Market Value(exdiv)}} = \frac{d}{P0}$$

$$\text{Profitability index} = \frac{\text{PV of cash flows (or NPV of project)}}{\text{Capital investment}}$$

Questions

PART A: FINANCIAL MANAGEMENT FUNCTION

The questions in this Part cover Financial management function, the subject of Chapter 1 of the BPP Financial Management Workbook.

OTQ bank 1 – Financial management and financial objectives (18 mins)

1   Last year ABC Co made profits before tax of $2,628,000. Tax amounted to $788,000.

ABC Co's share capital was $2,000,000 (2,000,000 shares of $1) and $4,000,000 6% preference shares.

What was the earnings per share (EPS) for the year (insert your answer to two decimal places)?

$ [   ]   (2 marks)

___

2   Which of the following statements describes the main objective of financial management?
                                                                         (September/December 2015)

O   Efficient acquisition and deployment of financial resources to ensure achievement of objectives

O   Providing information to management for day to day functions of control and decision making

O   Providing information to external users about the historical results of the organisation

O   Maximisation of shareholder wealth   **(2 marks)**

___

3   A company has recently declared a dividend of 12c per share. The share price is $3.72 cum div and earnings for the most recent year were 60c per share.

What is the P/E ratio?

[   ]   **(2 marks)**

___

4   The following information relates to a company:

Year	0	1	2	3
Earnings per share (cents)	30.0	31.8	33.9	35.7
Dividends per share (cents)	13.0	13.2	13.3	15.0
Share price at start of year ($)	1.95	1.98	2.01	2.25

Which of the following statements is correct?   **(June 2015)**

O   The dividend payout ratio is greater than 40% in every year in the period

O   Mean growth in dividends per share over the period is 4%

O   Total shareholder return for the third year is 26%

O   Mean growth in earnings per share over the period is 6% per year   **(2 marks)**

___

 BPP

5 Which of the following is LEAST likely to fall within financial management? *(December 2014)*

○ The dividend payment to shareholders is increased

○ Funds are raised to finance an investment project

○ Surplus assets are sold off

○ Non-executive directors are appointed to the remuneration committee **(2 marks)**

(Total = 10 marks)

OTQ bank 2 – Financial management and financial objectives (36 mins)

6 PT Co has just paid a dividend of 15 cents per share and its share price one year ago was $3.00 per share. The total shareholder return for the year was 25%.

What is the current share price (to two decimal places)? *(December 2014)*

$ [   ] **(2 marks)**

7 Which of the following does NOT form part of the objectives of a corporate governance best practice framework?

○ Separation of chairperson and CEO roles

○ Establishment of audit, nomination and remuneration committees

○ Minimisation of risk

○ Employment of non-executive directors **(2 marks)**

8 Are the following statements true or false? *(December 2014)*

	True	False
Maximising market share is an example of a financial objective	○	○
Shareholder wealth maximisation is the primary financial objective for a company listed on a stock exchange	○	○
Financial objectives should be quantitative so that their achievement can be measured	○	○

(2 marks)

9 ARP is a charity providing transport for people visiting hospitals.

Which of the following performance measures would BEST fit with efficiency in a value for money review? *(December 2018)*

○ Percentage of members who re-use the service

○ Cost per journey to hospital

○ A comparison of actual operating expenses against the budget

○ Number of communities served **(2 marks)**

10   H Co's share price is $3.50 at the end of 20X1 and this includes a capital gain of $0.75 since the beginning of the period. A dividend of $0.25 has been paid for 20X1.

What is the shareholder return (to 1 decimal place)?

[   ] %   **(2 marks)**

---

11   Are the following statements true or false?   **(December 2014)**

	True	False
Accounting profit is not the same as economic profit	○	○
Profit takes account of risk	○	○
Accounting profit can be manipulated by managers	○	○

                                                                 (2 marks)

---

12   A government body uses measures based upon the 'three Es' to measure value for money generated by a publicly funded hospital.

Which of the following relates to efficiency?

○   Cost per successfully treated patient

○   Cost per operation

○   Proportion of patients readmitted after unsuccessful treatment

○   Percentage change in doctors' salaries compared with previous year   **(2 marks)**

---

13   Which of the following statements is NOT correct?   **(June 2015)**

○   Return on capital employed can be defined as profit before interest and tax divided by the sum of shareholders' funds and prior charge capital

○   Return on capital employed is the product of net profit margin and net asset turnover

○   Dividend yield can be defined as dividend per share divided by the ex dividend share price

○   Return on equity can be defined as profit before interest and tax divided by shareholders' funds   **(2 marks)**

---

14   Geeh Co paid an interim dividend of $0.06 per ordinary share on 31 October 20X6 and declared a final dividend of $0.08 on 31 December 20X6. The ordinary shares in Geeh Co are trading at a cum-div price of $1.83.

What is the dividend yield (to one decimal place)?   **(September 2017)**

[   ] %   **(2 marks)**

15 Increasing which TWO of the following would be associated with the financial objective of shareholder wealth maximisation? *(June 2019)*

☐ Share price

☐ Dividend payment

☐ Reported profit

☐ Earnings per share

☐ Weighted average cost of capital

(2 marks)

(Total = 20 marks)

ABC Co   (18 mins)

This scenario relates to the following five questions.

Summary financial information for ABC Co is given below, covering the last two years.

STATEMENT OF PROFIT OR LOSS (EXTRACT)

	20X8	20X7
	$'000	$'000
Revenue	74,521	68,000
Cost of sales	28,256	25,772
Salaries and wages	20,027	19,562
Other costs	11,489	9,160
Profit before interest and tax	14,749	13,506
Interest	1,553	1,863
Tax	4,347	3,726
Profit after interest and tax	8,849	7,917
Dividends payable	4,800	3,100

STATEMENT OF FINANCIAL POSITION (EXTRACT)

	20X8	20X7
	$'000	$'000
Shareholders' funds	39,900	35,087
Long-term debt	14,000	17,500
	53,900	52,587

Other information

	20X8	20X7
Number of shares in issue ('000)	14,000	14,000
P/E ratio (average for year)		
ABC Co	14.0	13.0
Industry	15.2	15.0
Shareholders' investment		
EPS	$0.63	$0.57
Share price	$8.82	$7.41
Dividend per share	$0.34	$0.22

16 What is the percentage increase in return on capital (ROCE) for ABC Co between 20X7 and 20X8 (to one decimal place)?

☐ %   **(2 marks)**

17 What is the operating profit margin for 20X8 (to one decimal place)?

☐ %   **(2 marks)**

18 What is the total shareholder return?
   ○ 14.4%
   ○ 19.0%
   ○ 19.8%
   ○ 23.6%   **(2 marks)**

19   As well as the information above, the following extra data is available:

	20X8	20X7
Gearing (debt/equity)	35.1%	49.9%
Interest cover (PBIT/interest)	9.5	7.2
Inflation	3%	3%

Based on all of the information available, are the following statements true or false?

(1)   Employees may be unhappy with their wages in 20X8.

(2)   Financial risk for shareholders appears to be a problem area.

○   Statement 1 is true and statement 2 is false

○   Both statements are true

○   Statement 1 is false and statement 2 is true

○   Both statements are false   **(2 marks)**

_____

20   Accounting profits may not be the best measure of a company's performance.

Which of the following statements support this theory?

(1)   Profits are affected by accounting policies.

(2)   Profits take no account of risk.

(3)   Profits take no account of the level of investment made during the year.

(4)   Profits are measures of short-term historic performance.

○   2 and 4 only

○   1, 2, 3 and 4

○   2 and 3 only

○   1 only   **(2 marks)**

_____

                                                              (Total = 10 marks)

PART B: FINANCIAL MANAGEMENT ENVIRONMENT

The questions in this Part cover Financial management environment, the subject of Chapter 2 of the BPP Financial Management Workbook.

OTQ bank 1 – Financial management environment   (18 mins)

21   A government has adopted a contractionary fiscal policy.

How would this typically affect businesses?

○   Higher interest rates and higher inflation

○   Lower taxes and higher government subsidies

○   Higher taxes and lower government subsidies

○   Lower inflation and lower interest rates   **(2 marks)**

---

22   A government follows an expansionary monetary policy.

How would this typically affect businesses?

○   Higher demand from customers, lower interest rates on loans and increased availability of credit

○   A contraction in demand from customers, higher interest rates and less available credit

○   Lower taxes, higher demand from customers but less government subsidies/available contracts

○   Lower interest rates, lower exchange rates and higher tax rates   **(2 marks)**

---

23   Which FOUR of the following descriptions relate to the main macroeconomic policy objectives?   *(March / June 2022)*

☐   Ensuring minimum amounts of price increases

☐   Increasing national income and living standards

☐   Ensuring a balanced ratio of imports to exports

☐   Maintaining interest rates at minimum levels

☐   Balancing government spending with tax receipts

☐   Ensuring a stable and fully employed labour force   **(2 marks)**

---

24   Are the following statements true or false?   *(June 2015)*

	True	False
Monetary policy seeks to influence aggregate demand by increasing or decreasing the money raised through taxation	○	○
When governments adopt a floating exchange rate system, the exchange rate is an equilibrium between demand and supply in the foreign exchange market	○	○
Fiscal policy seeks to influence the economy and economic growth by increasing or decreasing interest rates	○	○

(2 marks)

 BPP

25   Which of the following organisations is most likely to benefit from a period of high price inflation?

    ○ An organisation which has a large number of long-term payables

    ○ An exporter of goods to a country with relatively low inflation

    ○ A supplier of goods in a market where consumers are highly price sensitive and substitute imported goods are available

    ○ A large retailer with a high level of inventory on display and low rate of inventory turnover
                                       (2 marks)

(Total = 10 marks)

OTQ bank 2 – Financial management environment   **(18 mins)**

26   A large, listed company is to issue 90-day commercial paper with a nominal value of $10m. Each paper will have a nominal value of $100,000. The annual required rate of return is 4% assuming a 365-day year.

    What will be the issue price of each paper?   **(September / December 2021)**

    ○ $99,023

    ○ $96,154

    ○ $99,014

    ○ $96,000   **(2 marks)**

27   A listed company is to enter into a sale and repurchase agreement on the money market.

    The company has agreed to sell $10 million of treasury bills for $9.6 million and will buy them back in 50 days' time for $9.65 million.

    Assume a 365-day year.

    What is the implicit annual interest rate in this transaction (to the nearest 0.01%)?
                                                        (June 2019)

    [   ] %   **(2 marks)**

28   What role would the money market have in a letter of credit arrangement?

                                                       (September 2017)

    ○ Initial arrangement of the letter of credit

    ○ Acceptance of the letter of credit

    ○ Issuing of a banker's acceptance

    ○ Discounting the banker's acceptance   **(2 marks)**

 BPP

29   Which of the following statements relating to money market instruments is/are correct?

(1)   Discounted instruments do not pay coupon interest

(2)   Commercial paper is secured on assets of the issuing company

(March/June 2021)

○   1 only

○   2 only

○   Both 1 and 2

○   Neither 1 nor 2   **(2 marks)**

---

30   Rank the following from highest risk to lowest risk from the investor's perspective.

(1)   Preference share

(2)   Treasury bill

(3)   Corporate bond

(4)   Ordinary share

○   1, 4, 3, 2

○   1, 4, 2, 3

○   4, 2, 1, 3

○   4, 1, 3, 2   **(2 marks)**

(Total = 10 marks)

OTQ bank 3 – Financial management environment   **(18 mins)**

31   Are the following statements true or false?   *(December 2014)*

	True	False
Securitisation is the conversion of illiquid assets into marketable securities	○	○
The reverse yield gap refers to equity yields being higher than debt yields	○	○
Disintermediation arises where borrowers deal directly with lending individuals	○	○

(2 marks)

 BPP

32   Governments have a number of economic targets as part of their fiscal policy.

Which of the following government actions relate predominantly to fiscal policy?

(1)   Decreasing interest rates in order to stimulate consumer spending.

(2)   Reducing taxation while maintaining public spending.

(3)   Using official foreign currency reserves to buy the domestic currency.

(4)   Borrowing money from the capital markets and spending it on public works.

(December 2014)

○ 1 only

○ 1 and 3

○ 2 and 4 only

○ 2, 3 and 4   **(2 marks)**

---

33   Which of the following statements are correct?

(1)   A certificate of deposit is an example of a money market instrument.

(2)   Money market deposits are short-term loans between organisations such as banks.

(3)   Treasury bills are bought and sold on a discount basis.

(June 2015)

○ 1 and 2 only

○ 1 and 3 only

○ 2 and 3 only

○ 1, 2 and 3   **(2 marks)**

---

34   Are the following statements true or false?   *(June 2015)*

	True	False
Capital market securities are assets for the seller but liabilities for the buyer	○	○
Financial markets can be classified into exchange and over-the-counter markets	○	○
A secondary market is where securities are bought and sold by investors	○	○

(2 marks)

---

35   Which of the following statements relating to money markets is/are true?

(1)   Lending is for periods greater than one year.

(2)   Lending is securitised.

(3)   Borrowers are mainly small companies.

(June 2017)

○ 1 and 2

○ 2 and 3

○ 1 and 3

○ 2 only   **(2 marks)**

(Total = 10 marks)

🛡 BPP

OTQ bank 4 – Financial management environment (18 mins)

36 The following statements relate to fiscal policy and demand management.
    Are the statements true or false?

	True	False
If a government spends more by borrowing more, it will raise demand in the economy	O	O
If demand in the economy is high then government borrowing will fall	O	O

(2 marks)

37 If the US dollar weakens against the pound sterling, will UK exporters and importers suffer or benefit?

	Benefit	Suffer
UK exporters to US	O	O
UK importers from US	O	O

(2 marks)

38 Which of the following represent forms of market failure where regulation may be a solution?

(1) Imperfect competition
(2) Social costs or externalities
(3) Imperfect information

O 1 only
O 1 and 2 only
O 2 and 3 only
O 1, 2 and 3

(2 marks)

39 Which TWO of the following are among the main goals of macroeconomic policy?

☐ Encouraging waste recycling
☐ Low and stable inflation
☐ Achievement of a balance between exports and imports
☐ Encouraging an equitable distribution of income

(2 marks)

 BPP

40   If a government has a macroeconomic policy objective of expanding the overall level of economic activity, which TWO of the following measures would be consistent with such an objective?

☐ Increasing public expenditure

☐ Increasing interest rates

☐ Increasing the exchange rate

☐ Decreasing taxation   (2 marks)

(Total = 10 marks)

PART C: WORKING CAPITAL MANAGEMENT

The questions in this Part cover Working capital management, the subject of Chapters 3–4 of the BPP Financial Management Workbook.

OTQ bank – Working capital   (18 mins)

41   A company's typical inventory holding period at any time is:

Raw materials:	15 days
Work in progress:	35 days
Finished goods:	40 days

Annual cost of goods sold as per the financial statements is $100 million of which the raw materials purchases account for 50% of the total.

The company has implemented plans to reduce the level of inventory held, the effects of which are expected to be as follows:

(1)   Raw material holding time to be reduced by 5 days

(2)   Production time to be reduced by 4 days

(3)   Finished goods holding time to be reduced by 5 days

Assuming a 365-day year, what will be the reduction in inventory held?   *(March 2017)*

O $2.603m

O $3.836m

O $1.918m

O $3.151m   **(2 marks)**

---

42   Which TWO of the following are correct descriptions of net working capital?

(March 2019)

☐   Current assets – current liabilities

☐   Inventory days + accounts receivable days – accounts payable days

☐   Current assets / current liabilities

☐   The long-term capital invested in net current assets   **(2 marks)**

---

43   For the coming year, a company has budgeted sales of $2 million per month, 80% of which will be on credit. It expects its accounts receivable payment period to be three months.

Forecast average inventory and average accounts payable for the coming year are $10 million and $4 million respectively.

What is the company's working capital requirement for the coming year (to one decimal place)?   *(March 2017)*

$ [   ] million   **(2 marks)**

 BPP

44   Which TWO of the following statements about overcapitalisation and overtrading are
        correct?   *(June 2018)*

        ☐ Overtrading often arises from a rapid increase in sales revenue

        ☐ Overcapitalisation results in a relatively low current ratio

        ☐ Overtrading may result in a relatively high accounts payable turnover period

        ☐ Overcapitalisation is the result of too much short-term capital   **(2 marks)**

---

45   A company has annual credit sales of $27 million and related cost of sales of $15 million.
        The company has the following targets for the next year:

Trade receivables collection period:	50 days
Inventory holding period:	60 days
Trade payables payment period:	45 days

        Assume there are 360 days in the year.

        What is the net investment in working capital required for the next year?   *(December 2014)*

        ○ $8,125,000

        ○ $4,375,000

        ○ $2,875,000

        ○ $6,375,000   **(2 marks)**

                                                                              (Total = 10 marks)

OTQ bank – Managing working capital   **(32 mins)**

46   TS Co has daily demand for ball bearings of 40 a day for each of the 250 working days
        (50 weeks) of the year. The ball bearings are purchased from a local supplier for $2 each.
        The cost of placing an order is $64 per order, regardless of the size of the order. The
        inventory holding costs, expressed as a percentage of inventory purchase price, is 25% per
        year.

        What is the economic order quantity (EOQ)?

        | | ball bearings   **(2 marks)**

---

47   EE Co has calculated the following in relation to its inventories.

Buffer inventory level	50 units
Reorder size	250 items
Fixed order costs	$50 per order
Cost of holding onto one item pa	$1.25 per year
Annual demand	10,000 items
Purchase price	$2 per item

What are the total inventory related costs for a year (to the nearest whole $)?

$ [   ]   (2 marks)

___

48   Which of the following statements concerning working capital management are correct?

(1)   Working capital should increase as sales increase.

(2)   An increase in the cash operating cycle will decrease profitability.

(3)   Overtrading is also known as undercapitalisation.

(December 2014)

O   1 and 2 only

O   1 and 3 only

O   2 and 3 only

O   1, 2 and 3   (2 marks)

___

49   Wallace Co has annual credit sales of $4,500,000 and on average customers take 60 days to pay, assuming a 360-day year. As a result, Wallace Co has a trade receivables balance of $750,000. The company relies on an overdraft to finance this at an annual interest rate of 10%.

Wallace Co is considering offering an early settlement discount of 1% for payment in 30 days. It expected that 25% of its customers (representing 35% of the annual credit sales figure) will pay in 30 days in order to obtain the discount.

If Wallace Co introduces the proposed discount, what will be the NET impact?

(September 2015)

O $1,875 saving

O $1,875 cost

O $2,625 saving

O $2,625 cost   (2 marks)

___

 BPP

50   Which of the following statements is/are correct?

(1)   Factoring with recourse provides insurance against bad debts.

(2)   The expertise of a factor can increase the efficiency of trade receivables management for a company.

(June 2015)

○ 2 only

○ 1 only

○ Neither 1 nor 2

○ 1 and 2   **(2 marks)**

---

51   Which of the following is LEAST likely to be used in the management of foreign accounts receivable?

○ Letters of credit

○ Bills of exchange

○ Invoice discounting

○ Commercial paper   **(2 marks)**

---

52   L Co is considering whether to factor its sales invoices. A factor has offered L Co a non-recourse package at a cost of 1.5% of sales and an admin fee of $6,000 per year. Bad debts are currently 2% of sales per year and sales are $1.5 million per year.

What is the cost of the package of L Co?

$ [   ]   **(2 marks)**

---

53   The inventory ordering policy of ZAR is to order 100,000 units when the inventory level falls to 20,000 units. The cost of placing and processing an order is $200, while the cost of holding inventory is $0.50 per unit per year. Orders are received one week after being placed with the supplier. The production requirement for the next year (50 weeks) is 600,000 units.

What is the cost of ZAR Co's inventory ordering policy?   *(March 2020)*

$ [   ]   **(2 marks)**

---

54   Which of the following is NOT a potential hidden cost of increasing credit taken from suppliers?

○ Damage to goodwill

○ Early settlement discounts lost

○ Business disruption

○ Increased risk of bad debts   **(2 marks)**

(Total = 18 marks)

OTQ bank – Working capital finance
(22 mins)

55   Match the characteristic below with the appropriate working capital strategy.
(September/December 2021)

Characteristic		Working capital strategy
Relatively high level of current assets		Conservative investment strategy
Relatively low level of current assets		Aggressive investment strategy
Relatively large amounts of short-term finance		Conservative financing strategy
Relatively small amounts of short-term finance		Aggressive financing strategy

(2 marks)

56   JP Co has budgeted that sales will be $300,100 in January 20X2, $501,500 in February, $150,000 in March and $320,500 in April. Half of sales will be credit sales. 80% of receivables are expected to pay in the month after sale, 15% in the second month after sale, while the remaining 5% are expected to be bad debts. Receivables who pay in the month after sale can claim a 4% early settlement discount.

What level of sales receipts should be shown in the cash budget for March 20X2 (to the nearest $)?

$ _____   (2 marks)

57   A company needs $150,000 each year for regular payments. Converting the company's short-term investments into cash to meet these regular payments incurs a fixed cost of $400 per transaction. These short-term investments pay interest of 5% per year, while the company earns interest of only 1% per year on cash deposits.

According to the Baumol Model, what is the optimum amount of short-term investments to convert into cash in each transaction (to the nearest $'000)?   *(June 2015)*

$ _____   (2 marks)

58   The treasury department in TB Co has calculated, using the Miller-Orr model, that the lowest cash balance they should have is $1 million, and the highest is $10 million. If the cash balance goes above $10 million they transfer the cash into money market securities.

Are the following true or false?

	True	False
When the balance reaches $10 million they would buy $6 million of securities	O	O
When the cash balance falls to $1 million they will sell $3 million of securities	O	O
If the variance of daily cash flows increases the spread between upper and lower limit will be increased	O	O

(2 marks)

---

59   Two companies, Acacia and Birch, have the following average levels of working capital:

Working capital level ($m)	Acacia	Birch
Maximum	10	12
Minimum	6	9

Acacia's working capital is financed with $4 million of long-term debt and Birch's working capital is financed with $9 million of long-term debt.

The balance of finance is from short-term sources.

Identify, by clicking on the relevant boxes in the table, which type of working capital funding strategy each company is employing.   *(March/June 2021)*

Acacia's working capital funding strategy	**AGGRESSIVE**	**MATCHING**
Birch's working capital funding strategy	**AGGRESSIVE**	**MATCHING**

(2 marks)

---

60   Which of the following is/are true?

(1) A conservative working capital investment policy implies a higher proportion of permanent current assets to fluctuating current assets

(2) Long-term finance is generally cheaper than short-term finance
                                                                (September/December 2020)

O   1 only is correct

O   2 only is correct

O   1 and 2 are correct

O   1 and 2 are incorrect

(2 marks)

(Total = 12 marks)

Section B questions

PKA Co (amended) (December 2007)　　　　　(18 mins)

This scenario relates to the following five questions

PKA Co is a European company that sells goods solely within Europe. The recently appointed financial manager of PKA Co has been investigating working capital management objectives and the working capital management of the company, and has gathered the following information about the inventory policy and accounts receivable.

Inventory management

The current policy is to order 100,000 units when the inventory level falls to 35,000 units. Forecast demand to meet production requirements during the next year is 625,000 units. The cost of placing and processing an order is $250, while the cost of holding a unit in stores is $0.50 per unit per year. Both costs are expected to be constant during the next year. Orders are received two weeks after being placed with the supplier. You should assume a 50-week year and that demand is constant throughout the year.

Accounts receivable management

Customers are allowed 30 days' credit, but the financial statements of PKA Co show that the average accounts receivable period in the last financial year was 75 days. This is in line with the industry average. The financial manager also noted that bad debts as a percentage of sales, which are all on credit, increased in the last financial year from 5% to 8%. The accounts receivables department is currently short staffed.

61　What are the main objectives of working capital management at PKA?

(1)　To ensure that PKA Co has sufficient liquid resources

(2)　To increase PKA Co's profitability

(3)　To ensure that PKA Co's assets give the highest possible returns

○　1 only

○　1 and 2 only

○　2 and 3 only

○　1, 2 and 3　　　　　　　　　　　　　　　　　　　**(2 marks)**

62　What is the current minimum inventory level at PKA Co?

○　10,000

○　12,500

○　22,500

○　35,000　　　　　　　　　　　　　　　　　　　**(2 marks)**

63　What is the economic order quantity?

○　250

○　3,536

○　17,678

○　25,000　　　　　　　　　　　　　　　　　　　**(2 marks)**

---

64   What are the best ways for PKA Co to improve the management of accounts receivable?

(1)   Assess the creditworthiness of new customers

(2)   Introduce early settlement discounts

(3)   Take legal action against the slow payers and non-payers

O   1 and 2 only

O   2 only

O   1 and 3 only

O   1, 2 and 3   (2 marks)

_____

65   In order to improve the management of receivables, PKA Co is considering using a debt factor on a 'with-recourse' basis.

Which of the following are benefits of 'with-recourse' factoring for PKA Co?

(1)   A fall in bad debts

(2)   A reduction in accounts receivable staffing costs

(3)   An improvement in short-term liquidity

O   2 only

O   1, 2 and 3

O   2 and 3 only

O   1 and 3 only   (2 marks)

_____

(Total = 10 marks)

Plot Co   **(18 mins)**

This scenario relates to the following five questions

Plot Co sells Product P with sales occurring evenly throughout the year.

Product P

The annual demand for Product P is 300,000 units and an order for new inventory is placed each month. Each order costs $267 to place. The cost of holding Product P in inventory is 10 cents per unit per year. Buffer inventory equal to 40% of one month's sales is maintained.

Other information

Plot Co finances working capital with short-term finance costing 5% per year. Assume that there are 365 days in each year.

66   What is the total annual cost of the current purchasing policy (to the nearest whole number)?

$ [   ]   (2 marks)

_____

67   What is the total annual cost of a policy based on using the economic order quantity (EOQ) (to the nearest $100)?

$ [   ]   (2 marks)

_____

68   Plot Co is considering offering a 2% early settlement discount to its customers. Currently sales are $10 million and customers take 60 days to pay. Plot Co estimates half the customers will take up the discount and pay cash. Plot is currently financing working capital using an overdraft on which it pays a 10% charge. Assume 365 days in a year.

What will be the effect of implementing the policy?

○   Benefit of $17,808

○   Cost of $17,808

○   Benefit of $82,192

○   Benefit of $182,192   (2 marks)

69   Plot Co managers are considering the cost of working capital management.

Are the following statements about working capital management true or false?

	True	False
A conservative working capital finance approach is low risk but expensive	○	○
Good working capital management adds to the wealth of shareholders	○	○

(2 marks)

70   If Plot Co were overtrading, which TWO of the following could be symptoms?

☐   Decreasing levels of trade receivables

☐   Increasing levels of inventory

☐   Increasing levels of long-term borrowings

☐   Increasing levels of current liabilities   (2 marks)

(Total = 10 marks)

Amax Co (March/June 2022)   (18 mins)

This scenario relates to the following five questions

Amax Co is a multinational company which has been reviewing its working capital management.

Inventory	Unit price
Component X	$25

Trade payables	$'000
Bard Co	1,000
Colix Co	3,200

Amax Co has received an offer of a discount for bulk purchase from Bard Co, one of its major suppliers. Bard Co has offered a 0.5% discount on orders of 60,000 units or more of Component X. Amax Co currently consumes 240,000 units of Component X each year and places orders of 20,000 units at the end of each month. Holding cost for Component X is $1 per unit per year and ordering costs are $250 per order. Amax Co does not maintain any buffer inventory of Component X.

Colix Co, a major supplier of Component M to Amax Co, has offered a 1% early settlement discount for payment within 30 days.

Amax Co currently takes 72 days to settle outstanding invoices with Colix Co. Amax Co has a cost of short-term finance of 6% through an overdraft and no surplus cash. Assume that there are 360 days in each year.

Amax Co currently has decentralised treasury operations, but is considering implementing a centralised treasury department

71   Using months as a basis, what is the financial consequence of accepting the bulk purchase discount?

   O   Benefit of $8,000 per year

   O   Benefit of $12,000 per year

   O   Cost of $13,000 per year

   O   Cost of $8,000 per year   **(2 marks)**

_____

72   Using days as a basis, what is the financial consequence of accepting the early settlement discount?

   O   Benefit of $48,000 per year

   O   Cost of $32,000 per year

   O   Cost of $80,000 per year

   O   Benefit of $80,000 per year   **(2 marks)**

_____

73   In relation to managing foreign accounts receivable, which of the following statements is correct?

   O   Companies expecting to receive foreign currency from foreign accounts receivable will be concerned about the risk of the foreign currency appreciating against the domestic currency

   O   The safest way to conduct business with foreign accounts receivable is by making a sale where goods are shipped and delivered before payment is due (open account)

   O   There is no need to assess the creditworthiness of foreign customers if a company has export credit insurance for foreign accounts receivable

   O   Discounting bills of exchange can reduce foreign accounts receivable default risk

                                                                                               (2 marks)

_____

74   In relation to Amax Co's proposed change to treasury management operations, which of the following statements is correct?

   O   Local management will be incentivised to maximise profitability

   O   Amax Co will be more responsive to localised needs for currency hedging

   O   Amax Co will suffer a loss of autonomy at a local level

   O   The change should increase the cost of hedging foreign currency risk for Amax Co

                                                                                               (2 marks)

_____

75   In relation to working capital funding strategy, which of the following statements is correct?

○   An aggressive strategy seeks to maximise liquidity at the expense of profitability

○   Short-term finance has a higher cost than long-term finance

○   Fluctuating current assets should be financed from a short-term source

○   A moderate or matching strategy finances current assets from a short-term source

(2 marks)

(Total = 10 marks)

Cat Co   (18 mins)

This scenario relates to the following five questions

Cat Co places monthly orders with a supplier for 10,000 components which are used in its manufacturing processes. Annual demand is 120,000 components. The current terms are payment in full within 90 days, which Cat Co meets, and the cost per component is $7.50. The cost of ordering is $200 per order, while the cost of holding components in inventory is $1.00 per component per year.

The supplier has offered a discount of 3.6% on orders of 30,000 or more components. If the bulk purchase discount is taken, the cost of holding components in inventory would increase to $2.20 per component per year due to the need for a larger storage facility.

76   What is the current total annual cost of inventory?

$ [   ]   **(2 marks)**

77   What is the total annual inventory cost if Cat Co orders 30,000 components at a time?

$ [   ]   **(2 marks)**

78   Cat Co has annual credit sales of $25 million and accounts receivable of $5 million. Working capital is financed by an overdraft at 10% interest per year. Assume 365 days in a year.

What is the annual finance cost saving if Cat Co reduces the collection period to 60 n (to the nearest whole number)?

$ [   ]   **(2 marks)**

79   Cat Co is reviewing its working capital management.

Which TWO of the following statements concerning working capital management are correct?

☐   The twin objectives of working capital management are profitability and liquidity

☐   A conservative approach to working capital investment will increase profitability

☐   Working capital management is a key factor in a company's long-term success

☐   Liquid assets give the highest returns leading to conflicts of objectives   **(2 marks)**

80   Management at Cat Co are considering an aggressive approach to financing working capital.

Which of the following statements relate to an aggressive approach to financing working capital management?

(1)   All non-current assets, permanent current assets and part of fluctuating current assets are financed by long-term funding.

(2)   There is an increased risk of liquidity and cash flow problems.

○   Both statements

○   Neither statement

○   Statement 1 only

○   Statement 2 only   (2 marks)

(Total = 10 marks)

Section C questions

81 Pumice Co (March/June 2020) (36 mins)

This scenario relates to four requirements.

Pumice Co plans to expand its business operations by opening several new outlets at a cost of $8 million, financed by an issue of loan notes. The company generates credit sales of $80.768 million before cost of sales of $27.700 million. All sales are on credit. The current statement of financial position of Pumice Co is as follows:

	$'000
Assets	
Non-current assets	54,070
Current assets	
Inventory	4,000
Trade receivables	12,320
Cash	800
	17,120
Total assets	**71,190**
Equity and liabilities	
Equity	6,000
Reserves	34,000
Total equity	40,000
Non-current liabilities	18,000
Current liabilities	
Trade payables	9,690
Overdraft	3,500
	13,190
Total equity and liabilities	**71,190**

Pumice Co expects that the expansion will increase credit sales by 18.7%, with cost of sales being 33% of credit sales and profit after tax being $6.818 million. Non-current assets will increase by 11%.

The bank has demanded that Pumice Co's overdraft be reduced to $3 million and the company expects its cash balance to be $700,000 after the expansion.

Pumice Co has been receiving complaints from its suppliers about late payment and the company plans to improve its working capital management as part of its expansion; it expects that the following working capital ratios will result:

Inventory holding period	50 days
Trade receivables payment period	60 days
Trade payables payment period	60 days

The finance director of Pumice Co wishes to investigate how the expansion will change the following ratios:

(1) trade payables payment period

(2) current ratio; and

(3) revenue/net working capital ratio (defining net working capital as inventory plus trade receivables less trade payables).

Assume there are 360 days in a year.

Required

(a) (i)   Prepare a forecast statement of financial position for Pumice Co; and   **(6 marks)**

     (ii) Calculate the effect of the proposed expansion on the working capital ratios listed by the finance director.   **(4 marks)**

(b) Discuss the ways in which implementing the proposed changes in working capital represent:

     (i)   Changes in working capital investment policy for Pumice Co; and   **(5 marks)**

     (ii) Changes in working capital funding policy for Pumice Co.   **(5 marks)**

(Total = 20 marks)

82 Pangli Co (March/June 2017)   (36 mins)

It is the middle of December 20X6 and Pangli Co is looking at working capital management for January 20X7.

Forecast financial information at the start of January 20X7 is as follows:

Inventory	$455,000
Trade receivables	$408,350
Trade payables	$186,700
Overdraft	$240,250

All sales are on credit and they are expected to be $3.5 million for 20X6. Monthly sales are as follows:

November 20X6 (actual)	$270,875
December 20X6 (forecast)	$300,000
January 20X7 (forecast)	$350,000

Pangli Co has a gross profit margin of 40%. Although Pangli Co offers 30 days credit, only 60% of customers pay in the month following purchase, while remaining customers take an additional month of credit.

Inventory is expected to increase by $52,250 during January 20X7.

Pangli Co plans to pay 70% of trade payables in January 20X7 and defer paying the remaining 30% until the end of February 20X7. All suppliers of the company require payment within 30 days. Credit purchases from suppliers during January 20X7 are expected to be $250,000.

Interest of $70,000 is due to be paid in January 20X7 on fixed rate bank debt. Operating cash outflows are expected to be $146,500 in January 20X7. Pangli Co has no cash and relies on its overdraft to finance daily operations. The company has no plans to raise long-term finance during January 20X7.

Assume that each year has 360 days.

Required

(a) (i)   Calculate the cash operating cycle of Pangli Co at the start of January 20X7.   **(2 marks)**

(ii)   Calculate the overdraft expected at the end of January 20X7.   **(4 marks)**

(iii) Calculate the current ratios at the start and end of January 20X7.   **(4 marks)**

(b) Discuss FIVE techniques that Pangli Co could use in managing trade receivables.   **(10 marks)**

(Total = 20 marks)

83 Kandy Co (September/December 2021)   (36 mins)

This scenario relates to five requirements.

Kandy Co purchases a number of different products from various manufacturers which it then sells on credit to a number of large retailers. Kandy Co is currently reviewing its working capital investment and two independent options are currently under consideration.

(1)   A bulk purchase discount from one of its biggest suppliers; and

(2)   Offering an early settlement discount to its customers.

Bulk purchase discount

One of Kandy Co's biggest selling items is the gimble. Kandy Co pays $30 for a gimble and annual sales demand is 18,000 units. At present Kandy Co's order size is 1,000 gimbles and each order costs $75 to place, excluding the purchase price. Annual holding costs are equivalent to 9% of the purchase price of a gimble. Due to the high level of demand for gimbles Kandy Co always holds a buffer inventory sufficient to cover two days' demand.

Kandy Co has been offered a bulk purchase discount of 1.5% off the purchase price if the company increase is its order size to 1,500 gimbles. Although this is 50% more than the size of the current order quantity Kandy Co feels that it has sufficient storage capacity to accommodate this, but annual holding costs for the gimble would increase to 10% of the purchase price. Also, the increased size of the order would result in higher delivery costs, increasing the cost of placing an order by $25 per order. If accepted, Kandy Co would still maintain a buffer inventory sufficient to cover two days' demand.

Early settlement discount

Kandy Co has total credit sales of $45 million per year and all of Kandy Co's customers are equal in terms of sales value. Although Kandy Co's credit terms require payment on 30 days, only 60% of its credit customers pay on time. The remaining 40% of customers pay on average on 40 days.

Kandy Co is considering the introduction of an early settlement discount of 0.5% for payment within 10 days. It expects that 50% of its customers will take advantage of the offer and pay in 10 days, 20% will still pay to terms and there will be 30% who will continue to pay on average on 40 days. Kandy Co finances in the short term at a cost of 7% per year.

Note. Assume a 360-day year for all calculations.

Required

(a) (i)   Calculate the financial effect on Kandy Co of accepting the bulk purchase discount.
(6 marks)

(ii)   Calculate the financial effect on Kandy Co of offering the early settlement discount.
(4 marks)

(iii) Using your results from (i) and (ii) above, comment on the financial acceptability of Kandy Co of each option.   **(2 marks)**

(b) Discuss the working capital objectives of liquidity and profitability and the conflict between these objectives.   **(4 marks)**

(c) Explain the cash operating cycle and discuss its relationship with the level of investment in working capital.

(4 marks)

(Total = 20 marks)

84 Wobnig Co (amended) (June 2012) (36 mins)

The following financial information relates to Wobnig Co.

	20X1	20X0
	$'000	$'000
Revenue	14,525	10,375
Cost of sales	10,458	6,640
Profit before interest and tax	4,067	3,735
Interest	355	292
Profit before tax	3,712	3,443
Taxation	1,485	1,278
Distributable profit	2,227	2,165

	20X1		20X0	
	$'000	$'000	$'000	$'000
Non-current assets		15,284		14,602
Current assets				
Inventory	2,149		1,092	
Trade receivables	3,200		1,734	
		5,349		2,826
Total assets		20,633		17,428
Equity				
Ordinary shares	8,000		8,000	
Reserves	4,268		3,541	
		12,268		11,541
Non-current liabilities				
7% bonds		4,000		4,000
Current liabilities				
Trade payables	2,865		1,637	
Overdraft	1,500		250	
		4,365		1,887
Total equity and liabilities		20,633		17,428

 BPP

Average ratios for the last two years for companies with similar business operations to Wobnig Co are as follows:

Current ratio	1.7 times
Quick ratio	1.1 times
Inventory holding period	55 days
Trade receivables collection period	60 days
Trade payables payment period	85 days
Sales revenue/net working capital	10 times

Required

(a) Using suitable working capital ratios and analysis of the financial information provided, evaluate whether Wobnig Co can be described as overtrading (undercapitalised). **(12 marks)**

(b) Critically discuss the similarities and differences between working capital policies in the following areas:

   (1) Working capital investment

   (2) Working capital financing

(8 marks)

(Total = 20 marks)

85 Oscar Co (September/December 2018)   (36 mins)

Oscar Co designs and produces tracking devices. The company is managed by its four founders, who lack business administration skills.

The company has revenue of $28 million, and all sales are on 30 days' credit. Its major customers are large multinational car manufacturing companies and are often late in paying their invoices. Oscar Co is a rapidly growing company and revenue has doubled in the last four years. Oscar Co has focused in this time on product development and customer service, and managing trade receivables has been neglected.

Oscar Co's average trade receivables are currently $5.37 million, and bad debts are 2% of credit sales revenue. Partly as a result of poor credit control, the company has suffered a shortage of cash and has recently reached its overdraft limit. The four founders have spent large amounts of time chasing customers for payment. In an attempt to improve trade receivables management, Oscar Co has approached a factoring company.

The factoring company has offered two possible options:

Option 1

Administration by the factor of Oscar Co's invoicing, sales accounting and receivables collection, on a full recourse basis. The factor would charge a service fee of 0.5% of credit sales revenue per year. Oscar Co estimates that this would result in savings of $30,000 per year in administration costs. Under this arrangement, the average trade receivables collection period would be 30 days.

Option 2

Administration by the factor of Oscar Co's invoicing, sales accounting and receivables collection on a non-recourse basis. The factor would charge a service fee of 1.5% of credit sales revenue per year. Administration cost savings and average trade receivables collection period would be as Option 1. Oscar Co would be required to accept an advance of 80% of credit sales when invoices are raised at an interest rate of 9% per year.

Oscar Co pays interest on its overdraft at a rate of 7% per year and the company operates for 365 days per year.

 BPP

Required

(a) Calculate the costs and benefits of each of Option 1 and Option 2 and comment on your findings. **(8 marks)**

(b) Discuss reasons (other than costs and benefits already calculated) why Oscar Co may benefit from the services offered by the factoring company. **(6 marks)**

(c) Discuss THREE factors which determine the level of a company's investment in working capital. **(6 marks)**

(Total = 20 marks)

86 Dusty Co (September/December 2019)   (36 mins)

Dusty Co wishes to improve its working capital management as part of an overall cost-cutting strategy to increase profitability. Two areas the company has been considering are working capital funding strategy and inventory management. Dusty Co currently follows a policy of financing working capital needs as much as possible from long-term sources of finance, such as equity. The company has been considering its inventory management and has been looking specifically at component K.

Current position

Dusty Co purchase 1,500,000 units of component K each year and consumes the component at a constant rate. The purchase price of component K is $14 per unit. The company places 12 orders each year. Inventory of component K in the financial statements of Dusty Co is equal to average inventory of component K.

The holding cost of component K, excluding finance costs, is $0.21 per unit per year. The ordering cost of component K is $252 per order.

Economic order quantity

Dusty Co wishes to investigate whether basing ordering of component K on the economic order quantity will reduce costs.

Bulk order discount

The supplier of component K has offered Dusty Co a discount of 0.5% on the purchase price of component K, providing the company orders 250,000 units per order.

Other information

Dusty Co has no cash but has access to short-term finance via an overdraft facility at an interest rate of 3% per year. This overdraft currently stands at $250,000.

Required

(a) (i) Calculate the annual holding and ordering costs of Dusty Co's current inventory management system. **(1 mark)**

(ii) Calculate the financial effect of adopting the Economic Order Quantity as the basis for ordering inventory. **(4 marks)**

(iii) Calculate the financial effect of accepting the bulk purchase discount. **(4 marks)**

(iv) Recommend, with justification, which option should be selected. **(1 mark)**

(b) Discuss the key factors in determining working capital funding strategies. **(10 marks)**

(Total = 20 marks)

 BPP

87 KXP Co (amended) (December 2012)   (36 mins)

KXP Co is an e-business which trades solely over the internet. In the last year the company had sales of $15 million. All sales were on 30 days' credit to commercial customers.

Extracts from the company's most recent statement of financial position relating to working capital are as follows:

	$'000
Trade receivables	2,466
Trade payables	2,220
Overdraft	3,000

In order to encourage customers to pay on time, KXP Co proposes introducing an early settlement discount of 1% for payment within 30 days, while increasing its normal credit period to 45 days. It is expected that, on average, 50% of customers will take the discount and pay within 30 days, 30% of customers will pay after 45 days, and 20% of customers will not change their current paying behaviour.

KXP Co currently orders 15,000 units per month of Product Z, demand for which is constant. There is only one supplier of Product Z and the cost of Product Z purchases over the last year was $540,000. The supplier has offered a 2% discount for orders of Product Z of 30,000 units or more. Each order costs KXP Co $150 to place and the holding cost is 24 cents per unit per year. KXP Co has an overdraft facility charging interest of 6% per year.

Required

(a) Calculate the net benefit or cost of the proposed changes in trade receivables policy and comment on your findings.   **(5 marks)**

(b) Calculate whether the bulk purchase discount offered by the supplier is financially acceptable and comment on the assumptions made by your calculation.   **(5 marks)**

(c) Identify and discuss the factors to be considered in determining the optimum level of cash to be held by a company.   **(5 marks)**

(d) Discuss the factors to be considered in formulating a trade receivables management policy.
                    (5 marks)

                    (Total = 20 marks)

88 CSZ Co (amended) (June 2014)   (36 mins)

The current assets and liabilities of CSZ Co at the end of March 20X4 are as follows:

	$'000	$'000
Inventory	5,700	
Trade receivables	6,575	12,275
Trade payables	2,137	
Overdraft	4,682	6,819
Net current assets		5,456

For the year to end of March 20X4, CSZ Co had sales of $40 million, all on credit, while cost of sales was $26 million.

For the year to end of March 20X5, CSZ Co has forecast that credit sales will remain at $40 million while cost of sales will fall to 60% of sales. The company expects current assets to consist of inventory and trade receivables, and current liabilities to consist of trade payables and the company's overdraft.

CSZ Co also plans to achieve the following target working capital ratio values for the year to the end of March 20X5:

Inventory holding period	60 days
Trade receivables collection period	75 days
Trade payables payment period	55 days
Current ratio	1.4 times

Required

(a) Calculate the working capital cycle (cash collection cycle) of CSZ Co at the end of March 20X4 and discuss whether a working capital cycle should be positive or negative. **(6 marks)**

(b) Calculate the target quick ratio (acid test ratio) and the target ratio of sales to net working capital of CSZ Co at the end of March 20X5. **(5 marks)**

(c) Analyse and compare the current asset and current liability positions for March 20X4 and March 20X5, and discuss how the working capital financing policy of CSZ Co would have changed. **(9 marks)**

(Total = 20 marks)

89 Flit Co (amended) (December 2014) (36 mins)

Flit Co is preparing a cash flow forecast for the three-month period from January to the end of March. The following sales volumes have been forecast:

	December	January	February	March	April
Sales (units)	1,200	1,250	1,300	1,400	1,500

Notes.

1 The selling price per unit is $800 and a selling price increase of 5% will occur in February. Sales are all on one month's credit.

2 Production of goods for sale takes place one month before sales.

3 Each unit produced requires two units of raw materials, costing $200 per unit. No raw materials inventory is held. Raw material purchases are on one month's credit.

4 Variable overheads and wages equal to $100 per unit are incurred during production, and paid in the month of production.

5 The opening cash balance at 1 January is expected to be $40,000.

6 A long-term loan of $300,000 will be received at the beginning of March.

7 A machine costing $400,000 will be purchased for cash in March.

Required

(a) Calculate the cash balance at the end of each month in the three-month period. **(5 marks)**

(b) Calculate the forecast current ratio at the end of the three-month period. **(2 marks)**

(c) Assuming that Flit Co expects to have a short-term cash surplus during the three-month period, discuss whether this should be invested in shares listed on a large stock market. **(3 marks)**

(d) Explain how the Baumol model can be employed to reduce the costs of cash management.

(5 marks)

(e) Renpec Co, a subsidiary of Flit Co, has set a minimum cash account balance of $7,500. The average cost to the company of making deposits or selling investments is $18 per transaction and the standard deviation of its cash flows was $1,000 per day during the last year. The average interest rate on investments is 5.11%.

Determine the spread, the upper limit and the return point for the cash account of Renpec Co using the Miller-Orr model and explain the relevance of these values for the cash management of the company.

(5 marks)

(Total = 20 marks)

90 Widnor Co (amended) (June 2015)   (36 mins)

The finance director of Widnor Co has been looking to improve the company's working capital management. Widnor Co has revenue from credit sales of $26,750,000 per year and, although its terms of trade require all credit customers to settle outstanding invoices within 40 days, on average customers have been taking longer. Approximately 1% of credit sales turn into bad debts which are not recovered.

Trade receivables currently stand at $4,458,000 and Widnor Co has a cost of short-term finance of 5% per year.

The finance director is considering a proposal from a factoring company, Nokfe Co, which was invited to tender to manage the sales ledger of Widnor Co on a with-recourse basis. Nokfe Co believes that it can use its expertise to reduce average trade receivables days (ie collection period) to 35 days, while cutting bad debts by 70% and reducing administration costs by $50,000 per year. A condition of the factoring agreement is that the company would also advance Widnor Co 80% of the value of invoices raised at an interest rate of 7% per year. Nokfe Co would charge an annual fee of 0.75% of credit sales.

Required

(a) Advise whether the factor's offer is financially acceptable to Widnor Co.   **(7 marks)**

(b) Briefly discuss how the creditworthiness of potential customers can be assessed.   **(3 marks)**

(c) Discuss how risks arising from granting credit to foreign customers can be managed and reduced.   **(10 marks)**

(Total = 20 marks)

 BPP

The questions in this Part cover Investment appraisal, the subject of Chapters 5–8 of the BPP Financial Management Workbook.

OTQ bank – Investment decisions   (36 mins)

91   NW Co is considering investing $46,000 in a new delivery lorry that will last for 4 years, after which time it will be sold for $7,000. Depreciation is charged on a straight-line basis. Forecast operating profits/(losses) to be generated by the machine are as follows.

Year	$
1	16,500
2	23,500
3	13,500
4	(1,500)

What is the return on capital employed (ROCE) for the lorry (using the average investment method, to the nearest %)?

[   ] %   (2 marks)

---

92   NW Co is considering investing $46,000 in a new delivery lorry that will last for 4 years, after which time it will be sold for $7,000. Depreciation is charged on a straight-line basis. Forecast operating profits/(losses) to be generated by the machine are as follows.

Year	$
1	16,500
2	23,500
3	13,500
4	(1,500)

Assuming operational cash flows arise evenly over the year, what is the payback period for this investment (to the nearest month)?

O   1 year 7 months

O   2 years 7 months

O   1 year 5 months

O   3 years 2 months   (2 marks)

---

93 In relation to the return on capital employed (ROCE) investment appraisal method, which of the following statements is correct? **(September/December 2021)**

O ROCE leads to better investment decisions since it uses accounting profit rather than estimated cash flows

O Investment projects with a ROCE greater than the weighted average cost of capital should be accepted

O Investment projects with a ROCE less than the current ROCE of an organisation should be rejected

O ROCE takes into account all years of operation of an investment project **(2 marks)**

---

94 SW Co has a barrel of chemicals in its warehouse that it purchased for a project a while ago at a cost of $1,000. It would cost $400 for a professional disposal company to collect the barrel and dispose of it safely. However, the chemicals could be used in a potential project which is currently being assessed.

What is the relevant cost of using the chemicals in a new project proposal?

O $1,000 cost

O $400 benefit

O $400 cost

O $Nil **(2 marks)**

---

95 A new project being considered by BLW Co would require 1,000 hours of skilled labour. The current workforce is already fully employed but more workers can be hired in at a cost of $20 per hour. The current workers are paid $15 per hour on a project that earns a contribution of $10 per hour.

What is the relevant cost of labour to be included in the project appraisal?

O $10,000

O $15,000

O $20,000

O $25,000 **(2 marks)**

---

96 LW Co has a half empty factory on which it pays $5,000 pa rent. If it takes on a new project, it will have to move to a new bigger factory costing $17,000 pa and it could rent the old factory out for $3,000 pa until the end of the current lease.

What is the rental cost to be included in the project appraisal?

O $14,000

O $17,000

O $9,000

O $19,000 **(2 marks)**

 BPP

97   Which of the following is a drawback of the payback period method of investment appraisal?

 ○ It is cash flow based

 ○ It considers the time value of money

 ○ It doesn't measure the potential impact on shareholder wealth

 ○ It is profit based   (2 marks)

---

98   A project has average estimated cash flows of $3,000 per year with an initial investment of $9,000.

 Depreciation is straight-line with no residual value and the project has a five-year life span. The company has a target return on capital employed (ROCE) of 15% and a target payback period of 2.5 years. ROCE is based on initial investment.

 Under which investment appraisal method(s), using the company's targets, will the project be accepted?

 (1) ROCE

 (2) Payback basis

 (March 2019)

 ○ 1 only

 ○ 2 only

 ○ Both 1 and 2

 ○ Neither 1 nor 2   (2 marks)

---

99   EE Co is considering investing in a new 40-year project which will require an initial investment of $50,000 (with zero scrap value) and has a payback period of 20 years. The 40-year project has consistent cash flows each year.

 What is the ROCE (using the average investment method, to one decimal place)?

 [   ] %.   (2 marks)

---

100   An accountant is paid $30,000 per year and spends 2 weeks working on appraising project Alpha.

 Why should the accountant NOT charge half of her month's salary to the project?

 ○ Because her salary cannot be apportioned

 ○ Because her salary is not incremental

 ○ Because her salary is not a cash flow

 ○ Because her salary is an opportunity cost   (2 marks)

(Total = 20 marks)

 BPP

OTQ bank – Investment appraisal using DCF (36 mins)

101 An investor has a cost of capital of 10%. She is due to receive a 5-year annuity starting in 3 years' time of $7,000 per year.

What lump sum amount would you need to offer today to make her indifferent between the annuity and your offer (to the nearest $)?

$ [   ]   **(2 marks)**

---

102 A newspaper reader has won first prize in a national competition and they have a choice as to how they take the prize:

- Option 1: Take $90,000 per year indefinitely starting in 3 years' time (and bequeath this right to their children and so on); or

- Option 2: Take a lump sum of $910,000 in 1 year's time.

Assuming a cost of capital of 10%, which would you advise and why?

O Option 1 because $90,000 p.a. indefinitely is an infinite amount of money compared to a one-off payment

O Option 1 because it is worth more in present value terms

O Option 2 because it is worth more in present value terms

O Option 2 because the lump sum has the flexibility to be invested and earn a larger return than $90,000 p.a.   **(2 marks)**

---

103 JCW Co is appraising an opportunity to invest in some new machinery that has the following cash flows.

Initial investment	$40,000
Net cash inflows for 5 years in advance	$12,000 per year
Decommissioning costs after 5 years	$15,000

At a cost of capital of 10% what is the net present value of this project (to the nearest $100)?

$ [   ]   **(2 marks)**

---

104 CWE Co is appraising an opportunity to invest in some new machinery that has the following cash flows.

Initial investment	$70,000
Net cash inflows for 5 years	$20,000 per year

What is the internal rate of return of the project, calculated using discount factors for 10% and 15% (to one decimal place)?

[   ] %   **(2 marks)**

---

105   Four mutually exclusive projects have been appraised using net present value (NPV),
      internal rate of return (IRR), return on capital employed (ROCE) and payback period (PP).
      The company objective is to maximise shareholder wealth.

      Which should be chosen?

	NPV	IRR	ROCE	PP
○ Project A	$1m	40%	34%	4 years
○ Project B	$1.1m	24%	35%	2.5 years
○ Project C	$0.9m	18%	25%	3 years
○ Project D	$1.5m	12%	18%	7 years

                                                                        (2 marks)

106   Which of the following are correct advantages of the IRR approach to investment
      appraisal, and which are not?

	Correct	Incorrect
Clear decision rule	○	○
Takes into account the time value of money	○	○
Assumes funds are reinvested at the IRR	○	○
Considers the whole project	○	○

                                                                        (2 marks)

107   A project has an initial outflow followed by years of inflows.

      What would be the effect on NPV and the IRR of an increase in the cost of capital?

      Match the technique described to the expected impact from this increase.

Item		Impact
NPV		Increase
IRR		No change
		Decrease

                                                                        (2 marks)

108 A lease agreement has an NPV of ($26,496) at a rate of 8%. The lease involves an immediate down payment of $10,000 followed by 4 equal annual payments.

What is the amount of the annual payment?

O $11,020

O $4,981

O $11,513

O $14,039   (2 marks)

---

109 Which of the following statements about NPV and IRR is accurate?

O Two NPV calculations are needed to estimate the IRR using linear interpolation

O The graphical approach to IRR is only an estimate; linear interpolation using the formula is required for a precise answer

O The IRR is unique

O An IRR graph with NPV on the 'Y' axis and discount rate on the 'X' axis will have a negative slope   (2 marks)

---

110 Paulo plans to buy a holiday villa in five years' time for cash. He estimates the cost will be $1.5m. He plans to set aside the same amount of funds each year for five years, starting immediately and earning a rate of 10% interest per year compound.

To the nearest $100, how much does he need to set aside each year?

$ [   ]   (2 marks)

(Total = 20 marks)

OTQ bank – Allowing for tax and inflation   (36 mins)

111 SW Co has a 31 December year end and pays corporation tax at a rate of 30%, 12 months after the end of the year to which the cash flows relate. It can claim tax-allowable depreciation at a rate of 25% reducing balance. It pays $1m for a machine on 31 December 20X4. SW Co's cost of capital is 10%.

What is the present value on 31 December 20X4 of the benefit of the first portion of tax-allowable depreciation?

O $250,000

O $227,250

O $68,175

O $75,000   (2 marks)

 BPP

112   A company receives a perpetuity of $20,000 per year in arrears, and pays 30% corporation tax 12 months after the end of the year to which the cash flows relate.

At a cost of capital of 10%, what is the after-tax present value of the perpetuity?

○ $140,000

○ $145,454

○ $144,000

○ $127,274

                                                           (2 marks)

---

113   A project has the following projected cash inflows.

Year 1	$100,000
Year 2	$125,000
Year 3	$105,000

Working capital is required to be in place at the start of each year equal to 10% of the cash inflow for that year. The cost of capital is 10%.

What is the present value of the working capital?

○ $Nil

○ $(30,036)

○ $(2,735)

○ $33,000

                                                            (2 marks)

---

114   AW Co needs to have $100,000 working capital in place immediately for the start of a 2-year project. The amount will stay constant in real terms. Inflation is running at 10% per year, and AW Co's money cost of capital is 12%.

What is the present value of the cash flows relating to working capital?

○ $(21,260)

○ $(20,300)

○ $(108,730)

○ $(4,090)

                                                            (2 marks)

---

115   NCW Co is considering investing $10,000 immediately in a 1-year project with the following cash flows.

Income	$100,000
Expenses	$35,000

The cash flows will arise at the end of the year. The above are stated in current terms. Income is subject to 10% inflation; expenses will not vary. The real cost of capital is 8% and general inflation is 2%.

Using the money cost of capital to the nearest whole percentage, what is the NET present value of the project?

○ $68,175

○ $60,190

○ $58,175

○ $78,175

                                                            (2 marks)

---

116 AM Co will receive a perpetuity starting in 2 years' time of $10,000 per year, increasing by the rate of inflation (which is 2%).

What is the present value of this perpetuity assuming a money cost of capital of 10.2%?

O $90,910

O $125,000

O $115,740

O $74,403 **(2 marks)**

---

117 FW Co is expecting a receipt of $10,000 (in real terms) in 1 year's time.

If FW Co expects inflation to increase, and receipts are expected to rise in line with the general rate of inflation, what impact will this have on the present value of that receipt?

O Nil

O Reduce

O Increase

O Cannot say **(2 marks)**

---

118 Shadowline Co has a money cost of capital of 10%.

If inflation is 4%, what is Shadowline Co's real cost of capital (to one decimal place)?

[ ] % **(2 marks)**

---

119 A company is appraising a three-year project which requires an initial outlay on 1 January 20X4 of $30,000. The project is expected to give the following cash inflows on 31 December of each year:

20X4	$10,000
20X5	$20,000
20X6	$25,000

All of the above cash flows are before taking account of specific annual inflation of 5% per year. The real cost of capital is 4% and the nominal cost of capital is 14%.

Using a nominal approach and the discount tables provided, what is the NPV of the project on 1 January 20X4 (to the nearest dollar)? **(September/December 2020)**

$ [ ] **(2 marks)**

---

120 Which of the following is true about the 'inflation' figure that is included in the money cost of capital?

O It is historic and specific to the business

O It is historic general inflation suffered by the investors

O It is expected and specific to the business

O It is expected general inflation suffered by the investors **(2 marks)**

(Total = 20 marks)

 BPP

OTQ bank – Project appraisal and risk

(18 mins)

121   Are the following statements true or false?   *(June 2015)*

	True	False
The sensitivity of a project variable can be calculated by dividing the project net present value by the present value of the cash flows relating to that project variable	O	O
The expected net present value is the value expected to occur if an investment project with several possible outcomes is undertaken once	O	O
The discounted payback period is the time taken for the cumulative net present value to change from negative to positive	O	O

(2 marks)

---

122   An investment project has a cost of $12,000, payable at the start of the first year of operation. The possible future cash flows arising from the investment project have the following present values and associated probabilities:

PV of Year 1 cash flow	Probability	PV of Year 2 cash flow	Probability
$		$	
16,000	0.15	20,000	0.75
12,000	0.60	(2,000)	0.25
(4,000)	0.25		

What is the expected value of the net present value of the investment project (to the nearest $100)?   *(June 2015)*

$ [   ]   **(2 marks)**

---

123   SAC Co has a cost of capital of 8% and is appraising project Gamma. It has the following cash flows.

T0	Investment	100,000
T1–5	Net cash inflow	40,000

What is the adjusted payback period for this project?

O   2.5 years

O   Just under 3 years

O   2 years

O   Just over 4 years

(2 marks)

 BPP

124 A project has the following cash flows.

| T0 | Investment | 110,000 |
| T1–4 | Net cash inflow | 40,000 |

At the company's cost of capital of 10% the NPV of the project is $16,800.

Applying sensitivity analysis to the cost of capital, what percentage change in the cost of capital would cause the project NPV to fall to zero?

O 70%

O 17%

O 5%

O 41%   **(2 marks)**

125 A company has calculated the NPV of a new project as follows:

	Present value
	$'000
Sales revenue	4,000
Variable costs	(2,000)
Fixed costs	(500)
Corporation tax at 20%	(300)
Initial outlay	(1,000)
NPV	200

What is the sensitivity of the project decision to a change in sales volume?

(September 2018)

O 12.5%

O 6.3%

O 10.0%

O 5.0%   **(2 marks)**

(Total = 10 marks)

OTQ bank – Specific investment decisions   **(36 mins)**

126 Which of the following statements is correct?   *(December 2014)*

O Tax-allowable depreciation is a relevant cash flow when evaluating borrowing to buy compared to leasing as a financing choice

O Asset replacement decisions require relevant cash flows to be discounted by the after-tax cost of debt

O If capital is rationed, divisible investment projects can be ranked by the profitability index when determining the optimum investment schedule

O Government restrictions on bank lending are associated with soft capital rationing

(2 marks)

127 PD Co is deciding whether to replace its delivery vans every year or every other year. The initial cost of a van is $20,000. Maintenance costs would be nil in the first year, and $5,000 at the end of the second year. Secondhand value would fall from $10,000 to $8,000 if it held onto the van for 2 years instead of just 1. PD Co's cost of capital is 10%.

How often should PD Co replace its vans, and what is the equivalent annual cost (EAC) of that option?

Replace every year	EAC
	$
◯ 1	10,910
◯ 1	12,002
◯ 2	10,093
◯ 2	8,761

(2 marks)

128 A lease versus buy evaluation has been performed. The management accountant performed the calculation by taking the saved initial outlay and deducting the tax-adjusted lease payments and the lost capital allowances. The accountant discounted the net cash flows at the post-tax cost of borrowing. The resultant net present value (NPV) was positive.

Assuming the calculation is free from arithmetical errors, what would the conclusion for this decision be?

◯ Lease is better than buy

◯ Buy is better than lease

◯ A further calculation is needed

◯ The discount rate was wrong so a conclusion cannot be drawn   (2 marks)

129 AB Co is considering either leasing an asset or borrowing to buy it, and is attempting to analyse the options by calculating the NPV of each. When comparing the two, AB Co is uncertain whether it should include interest payments in its option to 'borrow and buy' as it is a future, incremental cash flow associated with that option. AB Co is also uncertain which discount rate to use in the NPV calculation for the lease option.

How should AB Co treat the interest payments and what discount rate should it use?

Discount rate	Yes	No
After tax cost of the loan if they borrow and buy	◯	◯
AB Co's weighted average cost of capital	◯	◯
After-tax cost of the loan if they borrow and buy	◯	◯
AB Co's weighted after cost of capital	◯	◯

(2 marks)

130   Which of the following is always true about capital rationing?

	True	False
The profitability index is suitable for handling multiple-period capital rationing problems if projects are divisible	○	○
Projects being divisible is an unrealistic assumption	○	○

(2 marks)

---

131   NB Co is faced with an immediate capital constraint of $100m available to invest.

It is considering investing in four divisible projects:

	Initial cost $m	NPV $m
Project 1	40	4
Project 2	30	5
Project 3	50	6
Project 4	60	5

What is the NPV generated from the optimum investment programme?

$ [   ] m   (2 marks)

---

132   NB Co is faced with an immediate capital constraint of $100m available to invest.

It is considering investing in four divisible projects:

	Initial cost $m	NPV $m
Project 1	40	4
Project 2	30	5
Project 3	50	6
Project 4	60	5

What is the NPV generated from the optimum investment programme if the projects were indivisible?

$ [   ] m   (2 marks)

---

133   Which of the following is potentially a benefit to the lessee if they lease as opposed to buy?

O Avoiding tax exhaustion

O Attracting lease customers that may not have been otherwise possible

O Exploiting a low cost of capital

O Potential future scrap proceeds   (2 marks)

 BPP

134   A professional kitchen is attempting to choose between gas and electricity for its main heat source. Once a choice is made, the kitchen intends to keep to that source indefinitely. Each gas oven has an NPV of $50,000 over its useful life of 5 years. Each electric oven has an NPV of $68,000 over its useful life of 7 years. The cost of capital is 8%.

Which should the kitchen choose and why?

○ Gas because its average NPV per year is higher than electric

○ Electric because its NPV is higher than gas

○ Electric because its equivalent annual benefit is higher

○ Electric because it lasts longer than gas   (2 marks)

135   Which TWO of the following are typically benefits of a shorter replacement cycle?

☐ Higher scrap value

☐ Better company image and efficiency

☐ Lower annual depreciation

☐ Less time to benefit from owning the asset   (2 marks)

(Total = 20 marks)

Section B questions

Sensitivity analysis (18 mins)

This scenario relates to the following five questions

A company is considering a project with the following cash flows.

Year	Initial investment	Variable costs	Cash inflows	Net cash flows
	$'000	$'000	$'000	$'000
0	(11,000)			(11,000)
1		(3,200)	10,300	7,100
2		(3,200)	10,300	7,100

Cash flows arise from selling 1,030,000 units at $10 per unit. The company has a cost of capital of 9%.

The net present value (NPV) of the project is $1,490.

136   What is the sensitivity of the project to changes in sales volume (to one decimal place)?

    O   8.2%
    O   8.4%
    O   11.9%
    O   26.5%   (2 marks)

_____

137   What is the discounted payback of the project?

    O   1.18 years
    O   1.25 years
    O   1.55 years
    O   1.75 years   (2 marks)

_____

138   What is the internal rate of return (IRR) of the project (using discount rates of 15% and 20%)?

    O   18.9%
    O   21.2%
    O   24.2%
    O   44.3%   (2 marks)

_____

139   Which of the following statements is true?   (December 2015)

    O   The sensitivity of NPV to a change in sales volume can be calculated as NPV divided by the present value of future sales income

    O   The certainty equivalent approach converts risky cash flows into riskless equivalent amounts which are discounted by a capital asset pricing model (CAPM) derived project-specific cost of capital

    O   Using random numbers to generate possible values of project variables, a simulation model can generate a standard deviation of expected project outcomes

    O   The problem with risk and uncertainty in investment appraisal is that neither can be quantified or measured   (2 marks)

_____

 BPP

140 Which TWO of the following statements are true of the IRR and the NPV methods of appraisal?

☐ IRR ignores the relative sizes of investments

☐ IRR is easy to use where there are non-conventional cash flows (eg cash flow changes from negative to positive and then back to negative over time)

☐ NPV is widely used in practice

☐ IRR is technically superior to NPV

(2 marks)

(Total = 10 marks)

Guilder Co

(18 mins)

This scenario relates to the following five questions

Guilder Co is appraising four different projects but is experiencing capital rationing in Year 0. No capital rationing is expected in future periods but none of the four projects that Guilder Co is considering can be postponed, so a decision must be made now. Guilder Co's cost of capital is 12%.

The following information is available.

Project	Outlay in Year 0 $	PV $	NPV $
Amster	100,000	111,400	11,400
Eind	56,000	62,580	6,580
Utrec	60,000	68,760	8,760
Tilbur	90,000	102,400	12,400

141 Arrange the projects in order of their preference to Guilder using the profitability index, with the most attractive first.

Projects		Order of preference
Amster		1
Eind		2
Utrec		3
Tilbur		4

(2 marks)

 BPP

142 Which of the following statements about Guilder Co's decision to use PI is true?

    ○ The PI takes account of the absolute size of the individual projects

    ○ PI highlights the projects which are slowest in generating returns

    ○ PI can only be used if projects are divisible

    ○ PI allows for uncertainty about the outcome of each project   **(2 marks)**

---

143 Several years later, there is no capital rationing and Guilder Co decides to replace an existing machine. Guilder Co has the choice of either a Super machine (lasting four years) or a Great machine (lasting three years).

The following present value table includes the figures for a Super machine.

	0	1	2	3	4
Maintenance costs		(20,000)	(29,000)	(32,000)	(35,000)
Investment and scrap	(250,000)				25,000
Net cash flow	(250,000)	(20,000)	(29,000)	(32,000)	(10,000)
Discount at 12%	1.000	0.893	0.797	0.712	0.636
Present values	(250,000)	(17,860)	(23,113)	(22,784)	(6,360)

What is the equivalent annual cost (EAC) of the Super machine (to the nearest whole number)?

$ [   ]   **(2 marks)**

---

144 Which of the following statements concerning Guilder Co's use of the EAC are true?

(1) The use of equivalent annual cost is appropriate in periods of high inflation.

(2) The EAC method assumes that the machine can be replaced by exactly the same machine in perpetuity.

    ○ Both statements are true

    ○ Both statements are false

    ○ Statement 1 is true and statement 2 is false

    ○ Statement 1 is false and statement 2 is true   **(2 marks)**

---

145 The following potential cash flows are predicted for maintenance costs for the Great machine:

Year	Cash flow $	Probability
2	19,000	0.55
2	26,000	0.45
3	21,000	0.3
3	25,000	0.25
3	31,000	0.45

What is the expected present value of the maintenance costs for Year 2 (to the nearest whole number)?

$ [blank]   (2 marks)

___

(Total = 10 marks)

Trecor Co (amended) (Specimen exam 2007)   (18 mins)

This scenario relates to the following five questions

Trecor Co plans to buy a machine costing $250,000 which will last for 4 years and then be sold for $5,000.

Net cash flows before tax are expected to be as follows.

	T_1	T_2	T_3	T_4
Net cash flow $	122,000	143,000	187,000	78,000

Depreciation is charged on a straight-line basis over the life of an asset.

146 Calculate the before-tax return on capital employed (accounting rate of return) based on the average investment (to the nearest whole percentage).

[blank] %   (2 marks)

___

147 Are the following statements on return on capital employed (ROCE) true or false?

	True	False
If ROCE is less than the target ROCE then the purchase of the machine can be recommended	O	O
ROCE can be used to compare two mutually exclusive projects	O	O

(2 marks)

___

148 Trecor Co can claim tax-allowable depreciation on a 25% reducing balance basis. It pays tax at an annual rate of 30% one year in arrears.

What amount of tax relief would be received by Trecor in time 4 of a net present value (NPV) calculation?

$ [＿＿＿＿＿＿] (2 marks)

149 What is the payback period for the machine (to the nearest whole month)?

[＿＿＿＿] year(s) [＿＿＿＿] month(s) (2 marks)

150 Which TWO of the following statements about the internal rate of return (IRR) are TRUE?

☐ IRR ignores the relative sizes of investments.

☐ IRR measures the increase in company value.

☐ IRR can incorporate discount rate changes during the life of the project.

☐ IRR and NPV sometimes give conflicting rankings over which project should be prioritised. (2 marks)

(Total = 10 marks)

BRT Co (amended) (June 2011) (18 mins)

This scenario relates to the following five questions

BRT Co has developed a new confectionery line that can be sold for $5.00 per box and that is expected to have continuing popularity for many years. The finance director has proposed that investment in the new product should be evaluated over a four-year time-horizon, even though sales would continue after the fourth year, on the grounds that cash flows after four years are too uncertain to be included.

The variable cost (in current price terms) will depend on sales volume, as follows.

Sales volume (boxes)	Less than 1 million	1–1.9 million	2–2.9 million	3–3.9 million
Variable cost ($ per box)	2.80	3.00	3.00	3.05

Forecast sales volumes are as follows.

Year	1	2	3	4
Demand (boxes)	0.7 million	1.6 million	2.1 million	3.0 million

Tax

Tax-allowable depreciation on a 25% reducing balance basis could be claimed on the cost of equipment. Profit tax of 30% per year will be payable one year in arrears. A balancing allowance would be claimed in the fourth year of operation.

Inflation

The average general level of inflation is expected to be 3% per year for the selling price and variable costs. BRT Co uses a nominal after-tax cost of capital of 12% to appraise new investment projects.

A trainee accountant at BRT Co has started a spreadsheet to calculate the net present value (NPV) of a proposed new project:

	A	B	C	D	E	F	G
1	Year	0	1	2	3	4	5
2		$'000	$'000	$'000	$'000	$'000	$'000
3	Inflated sales						
4	Inflated variable costs						
5	Fixed costs		(1,030)	(1,910)	(3,060)	(4,277)	
6	Net cash flow		556	1,485	1,530	2,308	
7	Taxation						
8	Tax benefits						
9	Working capital	(750)	(23)	(23)	(24)	750	
10	Investment	(2,000)					
11	Project cash flows						
12	Discount factor 12%	1.000	0.893	0.797	0.712	0.636	0.567
13	Present value						

151   What is the sales figure for Year 2 (cell D3 in the spreadsheet), to the nearest $'000?

$ _____   **(2 marks)**

_____

152   What are the variable costs for Year 3 (cell E4 in the spreadsheet), to the nearest $'000?

$ _____   **(2 marks)**

_____

153   What are the tax benefits generated by the tax-allowable depreciation on the equipment in Year 4 (cell F8), to the nearest $'000?

$ _____   **(2 marks)**

_____

154   Which of the following statements about the project appraisal are true/false?

	True	False
The trainee accountant has used the wrong percentage for the cost of capital	O	O
Ignoring sales after four years underestimates the value of the project	O	O
The working capital figure in Year 4 is wrong	O	O

(2 marks)

_____

155 The trainee accountant at BRT Co has calculated the internal rate of return (IRR) for the project.

Are the following statements true or false?

(1) When cash flow patterns are conventional, the NPV and IRR methods will give the same accept or reject decision.

(2) The project is financially viable under IRR if it exceeds the cost of capital.

○ Both statements are true

○ Both statements are false

○ Statement 1 is true and statement 2 is false

○ Statement 2 is true and statement 1 is false

(2 marks)

(Total = 10 marks)

Section C questions

156 Melanie Co (September/December 2018) (36 mins)

Melanie Co is considering the acquisition of a new machine with an operating life of three years. The new machine could be leased for three payments of $55,000, payable annually in advance.

Alternatively, the machine could be purchased for $160,000 using a bank loan at a cost of 8% per year. If the machine is purchased, Melanie Co will incur maintenance costs of $8,000 per year, payable at the end of each year of operation. The machine would have a residual value of $40,000 at the end of its three-year life.

Melanie Co's production manager estimates that if maintenance routines were upgraded, the new machine could be operated for a period of four years with maintenance costs increasing to $12,000 per year, payable at the end of each year of operation. If operated for four years, the machine's residual value would fall to $11,000.

Taxation should be ignored.

Required

(a) (i) Assuming that the new machine is operated for a three-year period, evaluate whether Melanie Co should use leasing or borrowing as a source of finance. **(6 marks)**

(ii) Using a discount rate of 10%, calculate the equivalent annual cost of purchasing and operating the machine for both three years and four years, and recommend which replacement interval should be adopted. **(6 marks)**

(b) Critically discuss FOUR reasons why NPV is regarded as superior to IRR as an investment appraisal technique. **(8 marks)**

(Total = 20 marks)

157 Cabreras (March/June 2021) (36 mins)

Cabreras Co is a construction company. It uses a large earth moving vehicle called the Beast to prepare foundations for buildings. It needs to decide whether the cheapest replacement interval for the Beast is three or four years.

The following details are available:

Cabreras purchases the Beast from a manufacturer for $800,000 payable one year after delivery. Its resale value will fall by 40% of the purchase price at the end of its first year of operation. The resale value will then reduce by 25% of its previous year's resale value for each further year of operation.

Yearly maintenance costs are $20,000 at the end of its first year of operations rising by 5% per year. Maintenance must be provided in the year of sale.

Yearly fuel costs are $28,000 in the first year rising by $5,000 for each extra year it is operated.

If the Beast is operated beyond three years' it is subject to a government safety and carbon emissions test. The test would be paid for and would take place at the beginning of the fourth year of operation. Correction of any faults discovered by this test is mandatory. There is an 80% chance that the test and remedial work will cost Cabreras Co $50,000, and a 20% chance it will cost $120,000.

Cabreras Co's cost of capital is 8%.

Ignore taxation.

Required

(a) Calculate the equivalent annual cost of the three-year and four-year replacement intervals for the Beast and advise Cabreras Co which replacement interval to adopt. **(11 marks)**

(b) Discuss why replacement interval decisions should be based upon equivalent annual cost (EAC). **(4 marks)**

(c) Discuss why discounted cash flow methods of investment appraisal are considered superior to non-discounted cash flow methods. **(5 marks)**

(Total = 20 marks)

158 Dink Co (September/December 2019)   **(36 mins)**

Dink Co is a small company that is finding it difficult to raise funds to acquire a new machine costing $750,000. Dink Co would ideally like a four-year loan for the full purchase price at a before interest tax rate of 8.6% per year.

The machine would have an expected life of four years. At the end of this period the machine would have a residual value of $50,000. Tax-allowable servicing costs for the machine would be $23,000 per year. Tax-allowable depreciation on the full purchase price would be available on a 25% reducing balance basis.

A leasing company has offered a contract whereby Dink Co could have use of the new machine for four years in exchange for an annual lease rental payment of $200,000 payable at the start of each year. The contract states that the leasing company would undertake maintenance of the machine at no additional cost to Dink Co. At the end of four years the leasing company would remove the machine from the manufacturing facility of Dink Co.

Dink Co pays corporation tax of 30% one year in arrears.

Required

(a) For the new machine:

   (i) Calculate the present value of the cost of borrowing to buy. **(6 marks)**

   (ii) Calculate the present value of the cost of leasing. **(3 marks)**

   (iii) Recommend which option is more attractive in financial terms to Dink Co. **(1 mark)**

(b) (i) Discuss general reasons why investment capital may be rationed. **(6 marks)**

   (ii) Discuss ways in which the external capital rationing experienced by Dink Co might be overcome.

(4 marks)

(Total = 20 marks)

 BPP

159 Crocket Co (September/December 2020)   (36 mins)

Crocket Co is a manufacturing company that has three investment decisions for the coming year.

Investment decision 1

Six investment projects are being considered with the following details:

Project	Initial outlay $'000	Net Present Value $'000
A	1,000	390
B	1,500	Not yet known
C	750	325
D	1,125	590
E	1,850	840
F	1,300	635

Project B is expected to generate the following annual cash flows:

Year	1 $'000	2 $'000	3 $'000	4 $'000
Sales income	725	765	885	612
Costs	145	168	202	94

Project B cash flows are before allowing for inflation of 4% per year for sales income and 5% per year for costs. Crocket Co has a nominal cost of capital of 10%.

Due to management reluctance to raise new finance, capital for investment in the above projects is currently restricted to $5m. Projects A, B, D and F are all independent, but projects C and E are mutually exclusive. All of the above projects are divisible and none can be delayed or repeated.

Investment decision 2

A number of Crocket Co's employees have a company car. The entire company car fleet is now due for renewal and in the past, it has been replaced every four years. Management are not sure if this is the optimum length of time and feel that other fleet replacement cycles, such as every three or five years, should also be considered.

Investment decision 3

The management of Crocket Co are considering the financial viability of another project but as yet, no detailed financial information is available to perform an NPV appraisal. One of the reasons for this is that the various cash flows will be subject to a number of different rates of inflation that are very uncertain at present. For example, the selling price inflation may be no more than 2% per year whereas material cost inflation could be anything from 4% to 6% per year. The general rate of inflation is expected to differ from both of these. Management is not sure whether the appraisal could be performed by simply ignoring the inflation altogether.

Note. The $5m capital constraint outlined with investment decision 1 applies to that investment decision only and not to investment decisions 2 and 3.

Required

(a) For investment decision 1:

    (i) Calculate the net present value of project B; and   **(4 marks)**

    (ii) Given the capital constraint, calculate the optimum investment combination and the resulting net present value.   **(6 marks)**

(b) For investment decision 2, explain the approach Crocket Co should use to determine the optimum replacement cycle for the company car fleet.   **(4 marks)**

(c) In relation to investment decision 3, describe the two approaches for dealing with inflation AND provide a reasoned recommendation as to which approach Crocket Co's management should follow.   **(6 marks)**

          (Total = 20 marks)

160 Degnis Co (March/June 2016, amended)   **(36 mins)**

Degnis Co is a company which installs kitchens and bathrooms to customer specifications. It is planning to invest $4,000,000 in a new facility to convert vans and trucks into motorhomes. Each motorhome will be designed and built according to customer requirements.

Degnis Co expects motorhome production and sales in the first four years of operation to be as follows.

Year	1	2	3	4
Motorhomes produced and sold	250	300	450	450

The selling price for a motorhome depends on the van or truck which is converted, the quality of the units installed and the extent of conversion work required.

Degnis Co has undertaken research into likely sales and costs of different kinds of motorhomes which could be selected by customers, as follows:

Motorhome type:	Basic	Standard	Deluxe
Probability of selection	20%	45%	35%
Selling price ($/unit)	30,000	42,000	72,000
Conversion cost ($/unit)	23,000	29,000	40,000

Fixed costs of the production facility are expected to depend on the volume of motorhome production as follows:

Production volume (units/year)	200–299	300–399	400–499
Fixed costs ($'000/year)	4,000	5,000	5,500

Degnis Co pays corporation tax of 28% per year, with the tax liability being settled in the year in which it arises. The company can claim tax-allowable depreciation on the cost of the investment on a straight-line basis over ten years.

Degnis Co evaluates investment projects using an after-tax discount rate of 11%.

Required

(a) Calculate the expected net present value of the planned investment for the first four years of operation. **(7 marks)**

(b) After the fourth year of operation, Degnis Co expects to continue to produce and sell 450 motorhomes per year for the foreseeable future.

Calculate the effect on the expected net present value of the planned investment of continuing to produce and sell motorhomes beyond the first four years and comment on the financial acceptability of the planned investment. **(3 marks)**

(c) Critically discuss the use of probability analysis in incorporating risk into investment appraisal. **(5 marks)**

(d) Discuss the reasons why investment finance may be limited, even when a company has attractive investment opportunities available to it. **(5 marks)**

(Total = 20 marks)

161 Pinks Co (March/June 2019) (36 mins)

Pinks Co is a large company listed on a major stock exchange. In recent years, the board of Pinks Co has been criticised for weak corporate governance and two of the company's non-executive directors have just resigned. A recent story in the financial media has criticised the performance of Pinks Co and claims that the company is failing to satisfy the objectives of its key stakeholders.

Pinks Co is appraising an investment project which it hopes will boost its performance. The project will cost $20 million, payable in full at the start of the first year of operation. The project life is expected to be four years. Forecast sales volumes, selling price, variable cost and fixed costs are as follows:

Year	1	2	3	4
Sales (units/year)	300,000	410,000	525,000	220,000
Selling price ($/unit)	125	130	140	120
Variable cost ($/unit)	71	71	71	71
Fixed costs ($'000/year)	3,000	3,100	3,200	3,000

Selling price and cost information are in current price terms, before applying selling price inflation of 5% per year, variable cost inflation of 3.5% per year and fixed cost inflation of 6% per year.

Pinks Co pays corporation tax of 26%, with the tax liability being settled in the year in which it arises. The company can claim tax-allowable depreciation on the full initial investment of $20 million on a 25% reducing balance basis. The investment project is expected to have zero residual value at the end of four years.

Pinks Co has a nominal after-tax cost of capital of 12% and a real after-tax cost of capital of 8%. The general rate of inflation is expected to be 3.7% per year for the foreseeable future.

Required

(a) (i) Calculate the nominal net present value of Pinks Co's investment project. **(8 marks)**

(ii) Calculate the real net present value of Pinks Co's investment project and comment on your findings. **(4 marks)**

(b) Discuss **FOUR** ways to encourage managers to achieve stakeholder objectives. **(8 marks)**

(Total = 20 marks)

162 Copper Co (March/June 2018) **(36 mins)**

Copper Co is concerned about the risk associated with a proposed investment and is looking for ways to incorporate risk into its investment appraisal process.

The company has heard that probability analysis may be useful in this respect and so the following information relating to the proposed investment has been prepared:

Year 1		Year 2	
Cash flow ($)	Probability	Cash flow ($)	Probability
1,000,000	0.1	2,000,000	0.3
2,000,000	0.5	3,000,000	0.6
3,000,000	0.4	5,000,000	0.1

However, the company is not sure how to interpret the results of an investment appraisal based on probability analysis.

The proposed investment will cost $3.5m, payable in full at the start of the first year of operation. Copper Co uses a discount rate of 12% in investment appraisal.

Required

(a) Using a joint probability table:

(i) Calculate the mean (expected) NPV of the proposed investment. **(8 marks)**

(ii) Calculate the probability of the investment having a negative NPV. **(1 mark)**

(iii) Calculate the NPV of the most likely outcome. **(1 mark)**

(iv) Comment on the financial acceptability of the proposed investment. **(2 marks)**

(b) Discuss **TWO** of the following methods of adjusting for risk and uncertainty in investment appraisal:

(1) Simulation

(2) Adjusted payback

(3) Risk-adjusted discount rates

(8 marks)

(Total = 20 marks)

163 Melplash Co (March/June 2022) (36 mins)

Melplash Co manufactures motorcycles and is considering an investment in a new, high-performance model. The market for high-performance motorcycles is very competitive and Melplash Co's directors want to recover the costs of investment in the model quickly, before it is made obsolete by more advanced models at the end of four years. The directors also wish to show shareholders that the investment will be profitable.

The directors have therefore set a target payback period of two years and a target return on capital employed of 20% for the investment.

The directors have also asked the finance director to provide net present value (NPV) and internal rate of return (IRR) calculations for the investment. They plan to consider the results of these calculations if the investment fulfils the targets for payback and return on capital employed.

Melplash Co has prepared the following forecast of production and sales of the new model:

Year	1	2	3	4
Motorcycles	25,000	45,000	40,000	20,000

Melplash Co's finance director has prepared the following information relating to the investment proposal:

Initial Investment	$220m
Residual value at the end of four years	$30m
Selling price (year 1 price terms)	$20,000 per motorcycle
Expected selling price inflation	6% per year
Variable costs (year 1 price terms)	$14,000 per motorcycle
Expected variable cost inflation	6% per year
Incremental fixed costs (year 1 price terms)	$120m per year
Expected fixed cost inflation	10% per year
Nominal (money) discount rate	14%

Ignore taxation.

Required

(a) For the proposed investment in the new motorcycle, calculate the following:

  (i) Net present value; (5 marks)

  (ii) Internal rate of return; (2 marks)

  (iii) Payback period; and (1 mark)

  (iv) Return on capital employed (accounting rate of return) based on average investment. (3 marks)

(b) Discuss the suitability of the techniques used in (a) for determining whether to undertake an investment and advise whether Melplash Co's proposed investment is financially acceptable.

(9 marks)

(Total = 20 marks)

164 Hawker Co (September/December 2021) (36 mins)

Hawker Co is about to replace its existing delivery vehicle with a new design of vehicle that offers greater fuel economy. It estimates that replacing the existing vehicle will save running costs of $2,000 per year.

There are two financing options.

Option 1

The vehicle could be purchased for $34,000 using a bank loan with an after-tax cost of borrowing of 4% per year. The vehicle would have a useful life of four years and would have a residual value of $14,000 at the end of that period. Straight-line tax allowable depreciation is available on the vehicle. The vehicle would be subject to a government CO_2 emissions tax of $600 at the end of each year of operation. Emissions tax expenses are corporation tax deductible.

Option 2

The vehicle could be leased for a period of four years for a payment of $6,000 per year, payable at the start of each year. The lessor will pay the CO_2 emissions tax. Lease payments are a corporation tax deductible expense. Hawker Co's after-tax weighted average cost of capital is 8%. It pays corporation tax at a rate of 20% one year in arrears.

Required

(a) Evaluate whether Hawker Co should use leasing or borrowing as a source of finance for the new vehicle. **(10 marks)**

(b) Discuss TWO reasons (other than possible after-tax cost advantages) why Hawker Co may choose to lease rather than buy the new delivery vehicle. **(4 marks)**

(c) Discuss THREE advantages of using NPV rather than IRR in investment appraisal.

(Total = 20 marks)

165 Vyxyn Co (March/June 2017) (36 mins)

Vyxyn Co is evaluating a planned investment in a new product costing $20m, payable at the start of the first year of operation. The product will be produced for four years, at the end of which production will cease. The investment project will have a terminal value of zero. Financial information relating to the investment project is as follows:

Year	1	2	3	4
Sales volume (units/year)	440,000	550,000	720,000	400,000
Selling price ($/unit)	26.50	28.50	30.00	26.00
Fixed cost ($/year)	1,100,000	1,121,000	1,155,000	1,200,00

These selling prices have not yet been adjusted for selling price inflation, which is expected to be 3.5% per year. The annual fixed costs are given above in nominal terms.

Variable cost per unit depends on whether competition is maintained between suppliers of key components. The purchasing department has made the following forecast:

Competition	Strong	Moderate	Weak
Probability	45%	35%	20%
Variable cost ($/unit)	10.80	12.00	14.70

The variable costs in this forecast are before taking account of variable cost inflation of 4.0% per year.

Vyxyn Co can claim tax-allowable depreciation on a 25% per year reducing balance basis on the full investment cost of $20m and pays corporation tax of 28% per year one year in arrears.

It is planned to finance the investment project with an issue of 8% loan notes, redeemable in ten years' time. Vyxyn Co has a nominal after-tax weighted average cost of capital of 10%, a real after-tax weighted average cost of capital of 7% and a cost of equity of 11%.

Required

(a) Discuss the difference between risk and uncertainty in relation to investment appraisal.

(3 marks)

(b) Calculate the expected net present value of the investment project and comment on its financial acceptability and on the risk relating to variable cost. (9 marks)

(c) Critically discuss how risk can be considered in the investment appraisal process. (8 marks)

(Total = 20 marks)

166 Pelta Co (September/December 2017)   (36 mins)

The directors of Pelta Co are considering a planned investment project costing $25m, payable at the start of the first year of operation. The following information relates to the investment project:

	Year 1	Year 2	Year 3	Year 4
Sales volume (units/year)	520,000	624,000	717,000	788,000
Selling price ($/unit)	30.00	30.00	30.00	30.00
Variable costs ($/unit)	10.00	10.20	10.61	10.93
Fixed costs ($/year)	700,000	735,000	779,000	841,000

This information needs adjusting to take account of selling price inflation of 4% per year and variable cost inflation of 3% per year. The fixed costs, which are incremental and related to the investment project, are in nominal terms. The year 4 sales volume is expected to continue for the foreseeable future.

Pelta Co pays corporation tax of 30% one year in arrears. The company can claim tax-allowable depreciation on a 25% reducing balance basis.

The views of the directors of Pella Co are that all investment projects must be evaluated over four years of operations, with an assumed terminal value at the end of the fourth year of 5% of the initial investment cost. Both net present value and discounted payback must be used, with a maximum discounted payback period of two years. The real after-tax cost of capital of Pelta Co is 7% and its nominal after-tax cost of capital is 12%.

Required

(a) (i) Calculate the net present value of the planned investment project. (9 marks)

(ii) Calculate the discounted payback period of the planned investment project. (2 marks)

(b) Discuss the financial acceptability of the investment project. (3 marks)

(c) Critically discuss the views of the directors on Pelta Co's investment appraisal. (6 marks)

(Total = 20 marks)

PART E: BUSINESS FINANCE

The questions in this Part cover Business finance, the subject of Chapters 9–12 of the BPP Financial Management Workbook.

OTQ bank – Sources of finance   (18 mins)

167   Are the following statements about bonds are true or false?

	True	False
Unsecured bonds are likely to require a higher yield to maturity than equivalent secured bonds	O	O
Convertible bonds give the borrower the right but not the obligation to turn the bond into a predetermined number of ordinary shares	O	O
A Eurobond is a bond that is denominated in a currency which is not native to where the bond itself is issued	O	O

(2 marks)

168   According to the creditor hierarchy, list the following from high risk to low risk:

		Order of risk
Preference share capital		1
Trade payables		2
Bank loan with fixed and floating charges		3
Ordinary share capital		4

(2 marks)

169 Simon Co is planning a 1 for 4 rights issue. The value of rights has been calculated as $0.40 per existing share. Simon Co's market price is currently $7.00 per share.

What is the theoretical ex rights price (TERP) per share and the rights issue price per share?

$ price per share
5.00
5.40
6.20
6.60
5.00
7.00
7.40
8.60

TERP [   ]

Rights issue price [   ]   (2 marks)

---

170 Which of the following best describes the term 'coupon rate' as it applies to bonds?

O Return received taking into account capital repayment as well as interest payments

O Annual interest received as a percentage of the nominal value of the bond

O Annual interest received as a percentage of the ex interest market price of the bond

O Annual interest received as a percentage of the cum-interest market price of the bond

(2 marks)

---

171 Which of the following describes a *sukuk*?

O A bond in Islamic finance where the lender owns the underlying asset and shares in the risks and rewards of ownership

O Equity in Islamic finance where profits are shared according to a pre-agreed contract – dividends are not paid as such

O Trade credit in Islamic finance where a pre-agreed mark-up is agreed in advance for the convenience of paying later

O A lease in Islamic finance where the lessor retains ownership and the risk and rewards of ownership of the underlying asset   (2 marks)

(Total = 10 marks)

 BPP

OTQ bank – Dividend policy   (18 mins)

172   Which TWO of the following are assumptions for Modigliani and Miller's dividend irrelevance theory?

☐ Imperfect capital markets

☐ No taxes or tax preferences

☐ No transaction costs

☐ No inflation   (2 marks)

173   In which of the following situations is a residual dividend most likely to be appropriate?

○ A large publicly listed company

○ A small family-owned private company where the majority of the shareholders use dividend income to pay their living costs

○ A small listed company owned by investors seeking maximum capital growth on their investment

○ In a tax regime where individuals pay less tax on dividend income than on capital gains
                                                   (2 marks)

174   In Modigliani and Miller's dividend irrelevance theory, the process of 'manufacturing dividends' refers to which of the following?

○ Dividends from manufacturing businesses

○ Investors selling some shares to realise some capital gain

○ Creative accounting to allow dividends to be paid

○ Investing plans designed to create regular returns to shareholders   (2 marks)

175   Which of the following statements is correct?   **(December 2014)**

○ A bonus issue can be used to raise new equity finance

○ A share repurchase scheme can increase both earnings per share and gearing

○ Miller and Modigliani argued that the financing decision is more important than the dividend decision

○ Shareholders usually have the power to increase dividends at annual general meetings of a company   (2 marks)

BPP

176 Three companies (Sun Co, Moon Co and Nite Co) have the following dividend payments history:

Company	20X1	20X2	20X3
Sun Co – Dividend	100	110	121
Sun Co – Earnings	200	200	201
Moon Co – Dividend	50	150	25
Moon Co – Earnings	100	300	50
Nite Co – Dividend	nil	300	nil
Nite Co – Earnings	400	350	500

Which best describes their apparent dividend policies?

	Sun Co	Moon Co	Nite Co
O	Constant growth	Constant payout	Residual
O	Constant payout	Constant growth	Residual
O	High payout	Residual	Constant payout
O	Constant growth	Residual	Constant payout

(2 marks)

_____

(Total = 10 marks)

OTQ bank – Practical capital structure issues (36 mins)

177 A summary of HM Co's recent statement of profit or loss is given below:

	$'000
Revenue	10,123
Cost of sales	(7,222)
Gross profit	2,901
Expenses	(999)
Profit before interest and tax	1,902
Interest	(1,000)
Tax	(271)
Profit after interest and tax	631

70% of cost of sales and 10% of expenses are variable costs.

What is HM Co's operational gearing (as a number to two decimal places)?

[   ]

(2 marks)

_____

178   The following is an extract of ELW's statement of financial position.

	$m	$m
Total assets		1,000
$1 ordinary share capital	100	
Retained earnings	400	
Total equity	500	
Loan notes	500	
		1,000

The ordinary shares are currently quoted at $5.50, and loan notes are trading at $125 per $100 nominal.

What is ELW's financial gearing ratio (debt/debt + equity) using market values (to the nearest %)?

| | %

(2 marks)

---

179   The following are extracts from the statement of financial position of a company:

	$'000	$'000
Equity		
Ordinary shares	8,000	
Reserves	20,000	
		28,000
Non-current liabilities		
Bonds	4,000	
Bank loans	6,200	
Preference shares	2,000	
		12,200
Current liabilities		
Overdraft	1,000	
Trade payables	1,500	
		2,500
Total equity and liabilities		42,700

The ordinary shares have a nominal value of 50 cents per share and are trading at $5.00 per share. The preference shares have a nominal value of $1.00 per share and are trading at 80 cents per share. The bonds have a nominal value of $100 and are trading at $105 per bond.

 BPP

What is the market value-based gearing of the company, defined as prior charge capital/equity? *(December 2014)*

O 15.0%

O 13.0%

O 11.8%

O 7.3% **(2 marks)**

---

180 Beaver Co has 100 million equity shares in issue and has just reported a profit, after tax, of $55m.

A new issue of 50 million equity shares at an issue price of $1.50 is being considered. All proceeds would be used to redeem a bank loan with an annual cost of 8%.

Beaver Co pays corporation tax at a rate of 20%.

Assume that operating profit (profit before interest and tax) remains constant.

If the equity issue goes ahead and the bank loan is redeemed, what will be the new earnings per share figure? *(March/June 2022)*

O $0.399

O $0.367

O $0.598

O $0.388 **(2 marks)**

---

181 Which of the following statements is/are correct?

(1) Fintech has created a large market for private individuals to trade small amounts of currency on the currency futures market

(2) Companies are increasingly looking to raise equity finance using peer to peer lending due to the growth of FinTech

O 1 only

O 2 only

O Both 1 and 2

O Neither 1 nor 2 **(2 marks)**

---

182 Which of the following statements is/are correct?

(1) A drawback of crowdfunding as a means of raising equity finance is that it takes a long time to arrange

(2) Peer to peer lending has developed to allow start-up companies to raise debt finance

O 1 only

O 2 only

O Both 1 and 2

O Neither 1 nor 2 **(2 marks)**

---

183 Small and medium sized entities (SMEs) often face a funding gap problem.

Are the following statements about SMEs true or false?   *(September 2020)*

	True	False
SMEs will often experience a funding gap, due to them being seen as a higher risk investment than a larger company	O	O
Founding shareholders of an SME will often have to sacrifice limited liability in order to obtain bank finance	O	O
A lack of suitable, sufficient, non-current assets increases the funding gap problem for an SME	O	O

(2 marks)

184 Indicate whether the following statements, relating to small and medium-sized enterprises (SMEs), are true or false.

	True	False
Medium-term loans are harder to obtain than longer-term loans for SMEs	O	O
SMEs are prone to funding gaps	O	O

(2 marks)

185 Private individuals or groups of individuals can invest directly into a small business.

What is this known as?

O Reverse factoring

O Supply chain finance

O Venture capital

O Business angel financing   **(2 marks)**

186 Indicate whether the following statements, relating to supply chain finance (SCF), are true or false.

	True	False
SCF is considered to be financial debt	O	O
SCF allows an SME to raise finance at a lower interest rate than would normally be available to it	O	O

(2 marks)

(Total = 20 marks)

BPP

OTQ bank – The cost of capital

187 GG Co has a cost of equity of 25%. It has 4 million shares in issue, and has done for many years.

Its dividend payments in the years 20X9 to 20Y3 were as follows.

End of year	Dividends $'000
20X9	220
20Y0	257
20Y1	310
20Y2	356
20Y3	423

Dividends are expected to continue to grow at the same average rate into the future.

According to the dividend valuation model, what should be the share price at the start of 20Y4 (to two decimal places)?

$ [ ]   (2 marks)

___

188 IPA Co is about to pay a $0.50 dividend on each ordinary share. Its earnings per share was $1.50.

Net assets per share is $6. Current share price is $4.50 per share.

What is the cost of equity (to the nearest whole percentage)?

[ ] %   (2 marks)

___

189 Which of the following best describes systematic risk?

○ The chance that automated processes may fail

○ The risk associated with investing in equity

○ The diversifiable risk associated with investing in equity

○ The residual risk associated with investing in a well-diversified portfolio   (2 marks)

___

190 A share in MS Co has an equity beta of 1.3. MS Co's debt beta is 0.1. It has a gearing ratio of 20% (debt:equity). The market premium is 8% and the risk-free rate is 3%. MS Co pays 30% corporation tax.

What is the cost of equity for MS Co?

[ ] %   (2 marks)

___

191 Are the following statements true or false? **(December 2014)**

	True	False
An increase in the cost of equity leads to a fall in share price	O	O
Investors faced with increased risk will expect increased return as compensation	O	O
The cost of debt is usually lower than the cost of preference shares	O	O

(2 marks)

---

192 The following information is available for a listed company:

Dividend recently paid	$0.10 per share
Dividend cover	4 times
Price to earnings ratio	5 times
Estimated future growth in dividends	8%

Using the dividend growth model, what is the cost of equity for this company (to one decimal place)? **(September 2019)**

[_____] % **(2 marks)**

---

193 A company has announced that it will pay an annual dividend equal to 55% of earnings. Its earnings per share is $0.80 and it has ten million shares in issue. The return on equity is 20% and the current cum div share price is $4.60.

What is the cost of equity? **(September/December 2021)**

O 19.4%

O 20.5%

O 28.0%

O 22.7% **(2 marks)**

---

194 Which of the following are assumed if a company's current WACC is to be used to appraise a potential project?

	True	False
Capital structure will remain unchanged for the duration of the project	O	O
The business risk of the project is the same as the current business operations	O	O
The project is relatively small in size	O	O

(2 marks)

 BPP

195 On a market value basis, GFV Co is financed 70% by equity and 30% by debt. The company has an after-tax cost of debt of 6% and an equity beta of 1.2. The risk-free rate of return is 4% and the equity risk premium is 5%.

What is the after-tax weighted average cost of capital of GFV Co (to one decimal place)?

(June 2015)

[_____] %

(2 marks)

---

196 An 8% irredeemable $0.50 preference share is being traded for $0.30 cum-div currently in a company that pays corporation tax at a rate of 30%.

What is the cost of capital for these preference shares (to one decimal place)?

[_____] %

(2 marks)

(Total = 20 marks)

OTQ bank – Capital structure theories   **(18 mins)**

197 Why do Modigliani and Miller (with tax) assume increased gearing will reduce the weighted average cost of capital (WACC)?

○ Debt is cheaper than equity

○ Interest payments are tax deductible

○ Reduced levels of expensive equity capital will reduce the WACC

○ Financial risk is not pronounced at moderate borrowing levels   **(2 marks)**

---

198 Are the following statements true or false?   *(June 2015)*

	True	False
The asset beta reflects both business risk and financial risk	○	○
Total risk is the sum of systematic risk and unsystematic risk	○	○
Assuming that the beta of debt is zero will understate financial risk when ungearing an equity beta	○	○

(2 marks)

---

199 Shyma Co is a company that manufactures ships. It has an equity beta of 1.6 and a debt:equity ratio of 1:3. It is considering a new project to manufacture farm vehicles. Trant Co is a manufacturer of farm vehicles and has an asset beta of 1.1 and a debt:equity ratio of 2:3. The risk free rate of return is 5%, the market risk premium is 3% and the corporation tax rate is 40%.

Using CAPM, what would be the suitable cost of equity for Shyma to use in its appraisal of the farm machinery project (to one decimal place)?   *(December 2017)*

[_____] %

(2 marks)

---

200 Leah Co is an all equity financed company which wishes to appraise a project in a new area of activity. Its existing equity beta is 1.2. The industry average equity beta for the new business area is 2.0, with an average debt/debt + equity ratio of 25%. The risk-free rate of return is 5% and the market risk premium is 4%.

Ignoring tax and using the capital asset pricing model, calculate a suitable risk-adjusted cost of equity for the new project (to one decimal place).   *(March 2018)*

┌─────────────────┐
│   │ %   **(2 marks)**
└─────────────────┘

---

201 Are the following statements true or false, as explanations of why an asset beta is generally lower than an equity beta?

	True	False
An equity beta also includes an element of financial risk	O	O
Asset betas contain less business risk	O	O
This is only due to tax relief on debt finance	O	O

(2 marks)

(Total = 10 marks)

Section B questions

Nolciln (March/June 2021)   (18 mins)

This scenario relates to the following five questions

Nolciln Co needs to raise more capital and wants to identify the most appropriate capital structure to maximise its shareholders' wealth. The company has approached you for advice on aspects of its financial and operational gearing.

The following has been extracted from Nolciln Co's 20X9 financial statements:

	$'000
Revenue	9,540
Profit before interest and tax (PBIT)	1,590
Profit after tax	1,072
Dividends paid	500
Ordinary shares (nominal value $1)	7,800
8% loan notes	3,125

Detailed analysis has shown that variable costs are equal to 60% of Nolciln Co's revenue. You have been informed that it is company policy to calculate operational gearing as:

Operational gearing = contribution / PBIT

The directors of Nolciln Co are also seeking advice on the optimal capital structure. They are aware of the Modigliani and Miller models but seek further information, in particular in respect of what is meant by market imperfections.

202   What was Nolciln Co's operational gearing in 20X9 (to one decimal place)?

     [   ] times   **(2 marks)**

203   What was Nolciln Co's interest cover in 20X9 (to one decimal place)?

     [   ] times   **(2 marks)**

204   Which TWO of the following are consistent with traditional capital structure theory?

     ☐   There is no optimal capital structure

     ☐   The value of the company remains unchanged with increased gearing

     ☐   The cost of equity is higher when there is a high proportion of debt capital

     ☐   There is a point at which the weighted average cost of capital is minimised   **(2 marks)**

205   Responding to the directors' request for advice, which of the following is consistent with Modigliani and Miller's with-tax model?

     ○   The value of Nolciln Co decreases with increased gearing

     ○   The weighted average cost of capital remains constant with increased gearing

     ○   The optimal capital structure is made up almost entirely of debt

     ○   The cost of equity remains constant with increased gearing   **(2 marks)**

206 In relation to capital structure, which TWO of the following are valid statements about market imperfections?

☐ Tax exhaustion occurs when there is a very high proportion of equity capital

☐ Debt-holders may impose restrictive covenants in loan agreements

☐ Agency costs, tax exhaustion and bankruptcy risk encourage very high gearing levels

☐ When a company's gearing creates a high risk of bankruptcy the weighted average cost of capital will be higher   (2 marks)

_____

(Total = 10 marks)

Tulip Co (March/June 2019)   (18 mins)

This scenario relates to the following five questions

Tulip Co is a large company with an equity beta of 1.05. The company plans to expand existing business by acquiring a new factory at a cost of $20 million. The finance for the expansion will be raised from an issue of 3% loan notes, issued at nominal value of $100 per loan note. These loan notes will be redeemable after five years at nominal value or convertible at that time into ordinary shares in Tulip Co with a value expected to be $115 per loan note.

The risk-free rate of return is 2.5% and the equity risk premium is 7.8%.

Tulip Co is seeking additional finance and is considering using Islamic finance and, in particular, would require a form which would be similar to equity financing.

207 What is the cost of equity of Tulip Co using the capital asset pricing model?

○ 13.3%

○ 10.7%

○ 8.1%

○ 10.3%   (2 marks)

_____

208 Using estimates of 5% and 6%, what is the cost of debt of the convertible loan notes?

○ 3.0%

○ 5.2%

○ 6.9%

○ 5.7%   (2 marks)

_____

209 In relation to using the dividend growth model to value Tulip Co, which of the following statements is correct?

○ The model assumes that all shareholders of Tulip Co have the same required rate of return

○ The model assumes a constant share price and a constant dividend growth for Tulip Co

○ The model assumes that capital markets are semi-strong form efficient

○ The model assumes that Tulip Co's interim dividend is equal to the final dividend
                                                                            (2 marks)

_____

210 Which of the following statements about equity finance is correct?

○ Equity finance reserves represent cash which is available to a company to invest

○ Additional equity finance can be raised by rights issues and bonus issues

○ Retained earnings are a source of equity finance

○ Equity finance includes both ordinary shares and preference shares **(2 marks)**

---

211 Regarding Tulip Co's interest in Islamic finance, which of the following statements is/are correct?

(1) Murabaha could be used to meet Tulip Co's financing needs

(2) Mudaraba involves an investing partner and a managing or working partner

○ 1 only

○ 2 only

○ Both 1 and 2

○ Neither 1 nor 2 **(2 marks)**

(Total = 10 marks)

Section C questions

212 Spine Co (September/December 2020) (36 mins)

Spine Co is looking to spend $15m to expand its existing business. This expansion is expected to increase profit before interest and tax by 20%. Recent financial information relating to Spine Co can be summarised as follows:

	$'000
Profit before interest and taxation	13,040
Finance charges (interest)	240
Profit before taxation	**12,800**
Taxation	3,840
Profit for the year (earnings)	**8,960**

Spine Co is not sure whether to finance the expansion with debt or with equity. If debt is chosen, the company will issue $15m of 8% loan notes at their nominal value of $100 per loan note. If equity is chosen, the company will have a 1 for 4 rights issue at a 20% discount to the current market price of $6.25 per share. Spine Co has 12 million shares in issue. The company pays corporation tax at 30%.

Required

(a) Evaluate whether, on financial grounds, Spine Co should finance the expansion with debt or equity. **(10 marks)**

(b) Explain and discuss the relationship between systematic risk and unsystematic risk. **(5 marks)**

(c) Discuss the assumptions made by the capital asset pricing model. **(5 marks)**

(Total = 20 marks)

213 LaForge Co (March/June 2020) (36 mins)

LaForge Co is a listed company which designs and manufactures air-conditioning units, which are then sold through third party retailers and distributors. Economic growth in a number of Asian countries has increased the demand for its products and LaForge Co wishes to target these markets in order to generate sales and profit growth.

To target these markets, LaForge Co needs new machinery which will require investment of $25.48m.

Two options for raising the finance are being considered:

(1) A rights issue, at a discount of 30% on the current share price of $2.60 per share.

(2) An issue of 6% loan notes, redeemable at nominal value of $100, in ten years' time.

LaForge Co's P/E ratio is 11 times and this is expected to remain unchanged, whichever financing option is chosen.

Extracts from LaForge Co's most recent financial statements are as follows:

	$m
Profit from operations	25.50
Profit after tax	16.56
Share capital ($0.50 per share nominal)	35.00

Without the new investment, the forecast profit from operations for the coming year is expected to be the same as the previous year's actual result. If the investment is undertaken, the forecast profit from operations for the coming year is expected to increase by $4.5m.

LaForge Co pays tax at 20%.

Required

(a) For the rights issue, calculate the following:

    (i)   The theoretical ex-rights price; and   **(3 marks)**

    (ii)   The value of a right per existing share.   **(1 mark)**

(b) Assuming the investment goes ahead, calculate LaForge Co's forecast earnings per share, for the coming year AND the resulting share price, if it finances the investment using each of these alternatives:

    (i)   The rights issue; and   **(2 marks)**

    (ii)   The loan notes.   **(3 marks)**

(c) Discuss the ways in which a company can issue new equity shares.   **(5 marks)**

(d) At a recent board meeting to discuss the financing options, one of the directors suggested reducing the forthcoming dividend. In the past few years, LaForge Co has consistently paid an annual dividend of $0.08 per share. Its shareholders include both financial institutions and individuals.

    Discuss and recommend whether LaForge Co should raise the finance it requires by reducing its annual dividend.   **(6 marks)**

(Total = 20 marks)

214 Corfe Co (March/June 2019)   **(36 mins)**

The following information has been taken from the statement of financial position of Corfe Co, a listed company:

	$m	$m
Non-current assets		50
Current assets		
Cash and cash equivalents	4	
Other current assets	16	20
Total assets		70
Equity and reserves		
Ordinary shares	15	
Reserves	29	44
Non-current liabilities		
6% preference shares	6	
8% loan notes	8	
Bank loan	5	19
Current liabilities		7
Total equity and liabilities		70

The ordinary shares of Corfe Co have a nominal value of $1 per share and a current ex-dividend market price of $6.10 per share. A dividend of $0.90 per share has just been paid.

The 6% preference shares of Corfe Co have a nominal value of $0.75 per share and an ex-dividend market price of $0.64 per share.

The 8% loan notes of Corfe Co have a nominal value of $100 per loan note and a market price of $103.50 per loan note. Annual interest has just been paid and the loan notes are redeemable in five years' time at a 10% premium to nominal value.

The bank loan has a variable interest rate.

The risk-free rate of return is 3.5% per year and the equity risk premium is 6.8% per year. Corfe Co has an equity beta of 1.25.

Corfe Co pays corporation tax at a rate of 20%.

Investment in facilities

Corfe Co's board is looking to finance investments in facilities over the next three years, forecast to cost up to $25 million. The board does not wish to obtain further long-term debt finance and is also unwilling to make an equity issue. This means that investments have to be financed from cash which can be made available internally. Board members have made a number of suggestions about how this can be done:

Director A has suggested that the company does not have a problem with funding new investments, as it has cash available in the reserves of $29 million. If extra cash is required soon, Corfe Co could reduce its investment in working capital.

Director B has suggested selling the building which contains the company's headquarters in the capital city for $20 million. This will raise a large one-off sum and also save on ongoing property management costs. Head office support functions would be moved to a number of different locations rented outside the capital city.

Director C has commented that although a high dividend has just been paid, dividends could be reduced over the next three years, allowing spare cash for investment.

Required

(a) Calculate the after-tax weighted average cost of capital of Corfe Co on a market value basis.

(11 marks)

(b) Discuss the views expressed by the three directors on how the investment should be financed.

(9 marks)

(Total = 20 marks)

215 Zeddemore Co (March/June 2021) (36 mins)

Zeddemore Co is a listed company in the house construction industry. Over the past five years results have been disappointing and as a result the share price has fallen from a high of $3.50 per share five years ago to only $1.05 per share today. This deterioration in the performance and share price has been accompanied by an increase in financial gearing to a high level.

Zeddemore Co's capital structure is as follows:

	$m
Equity:	
Share capital ($0.50 per share nominal value)	40
Retained earnings	35

Long-term liabilities:

6.5% irredeemable loan notes ($100 per loan note nominal value)	250
7% bank loan	20

Zeddemore Co's loan notes are quoted at $65 per loan note and both the loan notes and the bank loan are secured. Zeddemore Co's equity beta is 2.3.

New venture

To improve performance Zeddemore Co is considering the construction of commercial properties such as office blocks and industrial complexes. This is a new activity for Zeddemore Co and it is expected that the risks involved will be different from its current activity. The financial director has proposed that a project specific discount rate should be used to appraise the new venture but the commercial director does not believe this is necessary.

Winston Commercial Properties Co (WCP) undertakes commercial construction projects similar to those being considered by Zeddemore Co. WCP has an equity beta of 1.25. WCP has $100 million of ordinary shares in issue currently quoted at $2.6 per $1 nominal value ordinary share. The company also has $110m of loan notes in issue currently quoted at $96 per $100 nominal value.

Both companies pay tax at 20%, the risk-free rate is 4% and the expected return on the market portfolio is 10%.

Required

(a) (i) Using the Capital Asset Pricing Model calculate Zeddemore Co's current cost of equity and a project specific cost of equity suitable for the new venture. **(6 marks)**

(ii) Refering to your calculations above, comment briefly on the view of the commercial director. **(2 marks)**

(b) Discuss THREE problems Zeddemore Co may be facing as a result of its current high level of gearing. **(6 marks)**

(c) In respect of both equity and debt, discussed the risk-return relationship and how it affects Zeddemore Co's financing costs. **(6 marks)**

(Total = 20 marks)

216 BKB Co (amended) (December 2012) (36 mins)

The statement of financial position of BKB Co provides the following information:

	$m	$m
Equity finance		
Ordinary shares ($1 nominal value)	25	
Reserves	15	40
Non-current liabilities		
7% convertible bonds ($100 nominal value)	20	
5% preference shares ($1 nominal value)	10	30

	$m	$m
Current liabilities		
Trade payables	10	
Overdraft	<u>15</u>	<u>25</u>
Total liabilities		<u>95</u>

BKB Co has an equity beta of 1.2 and the ex dividend market value of the company's equity is $125m. The ex interest market value of the convertible bonds is $21m and the ex dividend market value of the preference shares is $6.25m.

The convertible bonds of BKB Co have a conversion ratio of 19 ordinary shares per bond. The conversion date and redemption date are both on the same date in five years' time. The current ordinary share price of BKB Co is expected to increase by 4% per year for the foreseeable future.

The overdraft has a variable interest rate which is currently 6% per year and BKB Co expects this to increase in the near future. The overdraft has not changed in size over the last financial year, although one year ago the overdraft interest rate was 4% per year. The company's bank will not allow the overdraft to increase from its current level.

The equity risk premium is 5% per year and the risk-free rate of return is 4% per year. BKB Co pays profit tax at an annual rate of 30% per year.

Required

(a) Calculate the market value after-tax weighted average cost of capital of BKB Co, explaining clearly any assumptions you make. **(12 marks)**

(b) Discuss why market value weighted average cost of capital is preferred to book value weighted average cost of capital when making investment decisions. **(4 marks)**

(c) Discuss the attractions to a company of convertible debt compared to a bank loan of a similar maturity as a source of finance. **(4 marks)**

(Total = 20 marks)

217 Fence Co (amended) (June 2014)   (36 mins)

The equity beta of Fence Co is 0.9 and the company has issued 10 million ordinary shares. The market value of each ordinary share is $7.50. The company is also financed by 7% bonds with a nominal value of $100 per bond, which will be redeemed in 7 years' time at nominal value. The bonds have a total nominal value of $14m. Interest on the bonds has just been paid and the current market value of each bond is $107.14.

Fence Co plans to invest in a project which is different to its existing business operations and has identified a company in the same business area as the project, Hex Co. The equity beta of Hex Co is 1.2 and the company has an equity market value of $54m. The market value of the debt of Hex Co is $12m.

The risk-free rate of return is 4% per year and the average return on the stock market is 11% per year. Both companies pay corporation tax at a rate of 20% per year.

Required

(a) Calculate the current weighted average cost of capital of Fence Co. **(7 marks)**

(b) Calculate a cost of equity which could be used in appraising the new project. **(4 marks)**

(c) Explain the difference between systematic and unsystematic risk in relation to portfolio theory and the capital asset pricing model. **(4 marks)**

 BPP

(d) Explain the limitations of the capital asset pricing model. **(5 marks)**

(Total = 20 marks)

218 Tanza Co (March/June 2022)   **(36 mins)**

Tanza Co currently has the following sources of finance at 31 December 20X6. The capital structure and its nominal values have not changed for many years:

	Nominal value $m
Ordinary shares	50
6% convertible notes	150
4% bank loan	120

The ordinary shares are currently trading at $5.55 per share and have a nominal value of $0.50 per share. An ordinary dividend of $0.85 per share has recently been paid. The directors have indicated that a dividend of $0.90 will be paid on 31 December 20X7. Tanza Co's dividends and share price have grown steadily at 6% per year for several years and are expected to continue to do so.

Each loan note has a nominal value of $100 and is currently trading at $108.51. On 31 December 20X9, the investors holding the convertible loan notes may convert the loan notes into 20 ordinary shares. If they choose not to do so, the loan notes will be redeemed at nominal value on 31 December 20X9.

Tanza Co pays corporation tax at a rate of 15%.

Tanza Co needs to raise a further $200m of long-term finance and the directors have been discussing whether this should be borrowed (debt) or raised by issuing new share capital (equity). The finance is needed quickly for a new project.

During the discussion, Director A proposed the use of debt. She had heard that at high levels of gearing the company can make cost savings which improve the weighted average cost of capital.

Director B has pointed out that Tanza Co's capital gearing is amongst the lowest in the industry. 'Our competitors generally have higher gearing than we do and also have lower weighted average costs of capital (WACCs) than us. Although I do think when gearing gets high the WACC goes up again.'

Required

(a) Calculate the after-tax weighted average cost of capital for Tanza Co, at 31 December 20X6, on a market value basis. **(10 marks)**

(b) (i) Critically discuss, with reference to the relevant theory, the views of Director A and Director B on raising new finance. **(6 marks)**

    (ii) Discuss TWO other factors for Tanza Co to consider in making the decision to raise debt finance or equity finance. **(4 marks)**

(Total = 20 marks)

219 Grenarp Co (amended) (June 2015)   **(36 mins)**

Grenarp Co is planning to raise $11,200,000 through a rights issue. The new shares will be offered at a 20% discount to the current share price of Grenarp Co, which is $3.50 per share. The rights issue will be on a 1 for 5 basis and issue costs of $280,000 will be paid out of the cash raised.

The capital structure of Grenarp Co is as follows:

	$m	$m
Equity		
Ordinary shares (par value $0.50)	10	
Reserves	75	
		85
Non-current liabilities		
8% loan notes		30
		115

The net cash raised by the rights issue will be used to redeem part of the loan note issue. Each loan note has a nominal value of $100 and an ex interest market value of $104. A clause in the bond issue contract allows Grenarp Co to redeem the loan notes at a 5% premium to market price at any time prior to their redemption date. The price/earnings ratio of Grenarp Co is not expected to be affected by the redemption of the loan notes.

The earnings per share of Grenarp Co is currently $0.42 per share and total earnings are $8,400,000 per year. The company pays corporation tax of 30% per year.

Required

(a) Evaluate the effect on the wealth of the shareholders of Grenarp Co of using the net rights issue funds to redeem the loan notes. **(8 marks)**

(b) Discuss whether Grenarp Co might achieve its optimal capital structure following the rights issue. **(7 marks)**

(c) Discuss **TWO** ways in which FinTech has increased the availability of long-term finance. **(5 marks)**

(Total = 20 marks)

220 Dinla Co (March/June 2016)   (36 mins)

Dinla Co has the following capital structure

	$'000	$'000
Equity and reserves		
Ordinary shares	23,000	
Reserves	247,000	
		270,000
Non-current liabilities		
5% preference shares	5,000	
6% loan notes	11,000	
Bank loan	3,000	
		19,000
		289,000

 BPP

The ordinary shares of Dinla Co are currently trading at $4.26 per share on an ex dividend basis and have a nominal value of $0.25 per share. Ordinary dividends are expected to grow in the future by 4% per year and a dividend of $0.25 per share has just been paid.

The 5% preference shares have an ex dividend market value of $0.56 per share and a nominal value of $1.00 per share. These shares are irredeemable.

The 6% loan notes of Dinla Co are currently trading at $95.45 per loan note on an ex interest basis and will be redeemed at their nominal value of $100 per loan note in 5 years' time.

The bank loan has a fixed interest rate of 7% per year.

Dinla Co pays corporation tax at a rate of 25%.

Required

(a) Calculate the after-tax weighted average cost of capital of Dinla Co on a market value basis.
(8 marks)

(b) Discuss the connection between the relative costs of sources of finance and the creditor hierarchy.
(3 marks)

(c) Discuss the circumstances under which the current weighted average cost of capital of a company could be used in investment appraisal and indicate briefly how its limitations as a discount rate could be overcome.
(5 marks)

(d) Explain the differences between Islamic finance and other conventional finance.
(4 marks)

(Total = 20 marks)

221 Tufa Co (September/December 2017) (36 mins)

The following statement of financial position information relates to Tufa Co, a company listed on a large stock market which pays corporation tax at a rate of 30%.

	$m	$m
Equity and liabilities		
Share capital	17	
Retained earnings	15	
Total equity		32
Non-current liabilities		
Long-term borrowings	13	
Current liabilities	21	
Total liabilities		34
Total equity and liabilities		66

The share capital of Tufa Co consists of $12m of ordinary shares and $5m of irredeemable preference shares.

The ordinary shares of Tufa Co have a nominal value of $0.50 per share, an ex dividend market price of $7.07 per share and a cum dividend market price of $7.52 per share. The dividend for 20X7 will be paid in the near future. Dividends paid in recent years have been as follows:

Year	20X6	20X5	20X4	20X3
Dividend ($/share)	0.43	0.41	0.39	0.37

The 5% preference shares of Tufa Co have a nominal value of $0.50 per share and an ex dividend market price of $0.31 per share.

The long-term borrowings of Tufa Co consists of $10m of loan notes and a $3m bank loan. The bank loan has a variable interest rate.

The 7% loan notes have a nominal value of $100 per loan note and a market price of $102.34 per loan note. Annual interest has just been paid and the loan notes are redeemable in four years' time at a 5% premium to nominal value.

Required

(a) Calculate the after-tax weighted average cost of capital of Tufa Co on a market value basis.

(11 marks)

(b) Discuss the circumstances under which it is appropriate to use the current WACC of Tufa Co in appraising an investment project.

(3 marks)

(c) Discuss THREE advantages to Tufa Co of using convertible loan notes as a source of long-term finance.

(6 marks)

(Total = 20 marks)

222 Tin Co (March/June 2018)   (36 mins)

Tin Co is planning an expansion of its business operations which will increase profit before interest and tax by 20%. The company is considering whether to use equity or debt finance to raise the $2m needed by the business expansion.

If equity finance is used, a 1 for 5 rights issue will be offered to existing shareholders at a 20% discount to the current ex dividend share price of $5.00 per share. The nominal value of the ordinary shares is $1.00 per share.

If debt finance is used, Tin Co will issue 20,000 8% loan notes with a nominal value of $100 per loan note.

Financial statement information prior to raising new finance:

	$'000
Profit before interest and tax	1,597
Finance costs (interest)	(315)
Taxation	(282)
Profit after tax	1,000
	$'000
Equity	
Ordinary shares	2,500
Retained earnings	5,488
Long-term liabilities:	
7% loan notes	4,500
Total equity and long-term liabilities	12,488

The current price/earnings ratio of Tin Co is 12.5 times. Corporation tax is payable at a rate of 22%.

Companies undertaking the same business as Tin Co have an average debt/equity ratio (book value of debt divided by book value of equity) of 60.5% and an average interest cover of 9 times.

Required

(a) (i)   Calculate the theoretical ex rights price per share.   **(2 marks)**

   (ii)   Assuming equity finance is used, calculate the revised earnings per share after the
          business expansion.   **(4 marks)**

   (iii) Assuming debt finance is used, calculate the revised earnings per share after the
          business expansion.   **(3 marks)**

   (iv)   Calculate the revised share prices under both financing methods after the business
          expansion.   **(1 mark)**

   (v)   Use calculations to evaluate whether equity finance or debt finance should be used for
          the planned business expansion.   **(4 marks)**

(b) Discuss **TWO** Islamic finance sources which Tin Co could consider as alternatives to a rights
     issue or a loan note issue.   **(6 marks)**

                                                                     (Total = 20 marks)

PART F: BUSINESS VALUATIONS

The questions in this Part cover Business valuations, the subject of Chapter 13 of the BPP Financial Management Workbook.

OTQ bank – Business valuations   (36 mins)

223   ML Ltd is an unlisted accountancy firm owned by three shareholders. One of the shareholders has asked for an independent valuation of the company to be performed.

Which of the following is a valid reason for an independent valuation to be required?

O   The stock market is thought to be weak form efficient

O   The realisable value of inventory is felt to be underestimated in the latest financial statements

O   To evaluate a takeover bid by Company X which is offering to buy ML Ltd in exchange for shares in Company X

O   The latest published statement of financial position was 11 months ago   **(2 marks)**

224   The following financial information relates to QK Co, whose ordinary shares have a nominal value of $0.50 per share:

	$m	$m
Non-current assets		120
Current assets		
Inventory	8	
Trade receivables	12	20
Total assets		140
Equity		
Ordinary shares	25	
Reserves	80	105
Non-current liabilities		20
Current liabilities		15
Total equity and liabilities		140

Required

On an historic basis, what is the net asset value per share of QK Co?   *(June 2015)*

O $2.10 per share

O $2.50 per share

O $2.80 per share

O $4.20 per share   **(2 marks)**

225   ELW Co recently paid a dividend of $0.50 a share. This is $0.10 more than three years ago. Shareholders have a required rate of return of 10%.

Using the dividend valuation model and assuming recent dividend growth is expected to continue, what is the current value of a share (to two decimal places)?

$ _____

(2 marks)

---

226   Cant Co has a cost of equity of 10% and has forecast its future dividends as follows:

Current year: No dividend

Year 1: No dividend

Year 2: $0.25 per share

Year 3: $0.50 per share and increasing by 3% per year in subsequent years

What is the current share price of Cant Co using the dividend valuation model?

(March 2016)

O $7.35

O $5.57

O $6.11

O $6.28

(2 marks)

---

227   Jo Co is a company which is financed by equity only. It has just paid a dividend of $60m and earnings retained and invested were 60%. Return on investments is 20% and the cost of equity is 22%.

What is the market value of the company (in millions, to the nearest whole million)?

$ _____ million

(2 marks)

---

228   Alpha Co and Beta Co are two companies in different industries who are both evaluating the acquisition of the same target company called Gamma Co. Gamma Co is in the same industry as Alpha Co.

Alpha Co has valued Gamma Co at $100m but Beta Co has only valued Gamma Co at $90m.

Which of following statements would explain why Alpha Co's value of Gamma Co is higher?

(March 2018)

O Alpha Co has used more prudent growth estimates

O Beta Co could achieve more synergy

O Beta Co is a better negotiator than Alpha Co

O Gamma Co is a direct competitor of Alpha Co

(2 marks)

 BPP

229 Black Co has in issue 5% irredeemable loan notes, nominal value of $100 per loan note, on which interest is shortly to be paid. Black Co has a before-tax cost of debt of 10% and corporation tax is 30%.

What is the current market value of one loan note? *(December 2018)*

○ $55

○ $50

○ $76

○ $40 **(2 marks)**

---

230 A company has 7% loan notes in issue which are redeemable in 7 years' time at a 5% premium to their nominal value of $100 per loan note. The before-tax cost of debt of the company is 9%and the after-tax cost of debt of the company is 6%.

What is the current market value of each loan note? *(December 2014)*

○ $92.67

○ $108.90

○ $89.93

○ $103.14 **(2 marks)**

---

231 A company has in issue loan notes with a nominal value of $100 each. Interest on the loan notes is 6% per year, payable annually. The loan notes will be redeemed in eight years' time at a 5% premium to nominal value. The before-tax cost of debt of the company is 7% per year.

What is the ex interest market value of each loan note? *(June 2014)*

○ $94.03

○ $96.94

○ $102.91

○ $103.10 **(2 marks)**

---

232 Bilbo Co is an unlisted company with 800,000 issued shares. Seema is one of the founders and owns 20% of the issued shares.

Bilbo Co has just paid its annual dividend of $0.30 per share. It is expected that next year's dividend will be $0.32 per share. After that it is expected that dividends will grow indefinitely at 2% per year.

Shareholders expect a 12% return from their investment.

Using the dividend valuation model, calculate the value of Seema's shareholding.

(March/June 2021)

○ $512,000

○ $522,240

○ $489,600

○ $480,000 **(2 marks)**

(Total = 20 marks)

233 WC Co announces that it decided yesterday to invest in a new project with a huge positive net present value. The share price doubled yesterday.

What does this appear to be evidence of?

○ A semi-strong form efficient market

○ A strong form efficient market

○ Technical analysis

○ A weak form efficient market (2 marks)

---

234 The efficient markets hypothesis refers to the way in which the prices of traded financial securities reflect relevant information.

Which TWO of the following are true for a weak-form efficient market? **(December 2019)**

☐ Share prices fully and fairly represent past information

☐ Share prices fully and fairly represent private information

☐ Share prices appear to follow a random walk

☐ The market does not provide enough information to make good buying and selling decisions (2 marks)

---

235 Tryde Co is a listed company which has 800 million ordinary shares in issue.

Yesterday the ordinary share price closed at $6.00. Two days earlier, the board of directors approved the launch of two new innovative products, but this has not been publicly announced.

Product A has an NPV of $40m. The decision to launch product A will be announced publicly tomorrow.

Product B has an NPV of $160m. The decision to launch product B will be announced publicly this morning.

Assume all other things are equal and that the capital markets believe the projected NPVs. Both products will be financed using internally generated funds.

What will the ordinary share price be at the end of today if the capital market is (1) semi-strong form efficient and (2) strong form efficient? **(March/June 2022)**

Share prices		Level of capital market efficiency
$6.00		Semi-strong form
$6.05		Strong form
$6.20		
$6.25		

(2 marks)

---

236 Which of the following is evidence that stock markets are semi-strong form efficient?

- ○ Repeating patterns appear to exist
- ○ Attempting to trade on consistently repeating patterns is unlikely to work
- ○ The majority of share price reaction to news occurs when it is announced
- ○ Share price reaction occurs before announcements are made public **(2 marks)**

237 Which TWO of the following would be evidence of strong form market efficiency?

(September 2018)

- ☐ The lack of regulation on use of private information (insider dealing)
- ☐ Inability to consistently outperform the market and make abnormal gains
- ☐ Immediate share price reaction to company announcements to the market
- ☐ Regulation to ensure quick and timely public announcement of information **(2 marks)**

(Total = 10 marks)

Section B questions

Bluebell Co (March/June 2019)   **(18 mins)**

This scenario relates to the following five questions

Extracts from the financial statements of Bluebell Co, a listed company, are as follows:

	$m
Profit before interest and tax	238
Finance costs	(24)
Profit before tax	214
Corporation tax	(64)
Profit after tax	150
Assets	
Non-current assets	
Property, plant and equipment	768
Goodwill (internally generated)	105
	873
Current assets	
Inventories	285
Trade receivables	192
	477
Total assets	1,350

	$m
Equity and liabilities	
Total equity	688
Non-current liabilities	
Long-term borrowings	250
Current liabilities	
Trade payables	312
Short-term borrowings	100
Total current liabilities	412
Total liabilities	662
Total equity and liabilities	1,350

A similar size competitor company has a price/earnings ratio of 12.5 times.

This competitor believes that if Bluebell Co were liquidated, property, plant and equipment would only realise $600 million, while 10% of trade receivables would be irrecoverable and inventory would be sold at $30 million less than its book value.

Separately, Bluebell Co is considering the acquisition of Dandelion Co, an unlisted company which is a supplier of Bluebell Co.

238   What is the value of Bluebell Co on a net realisable value basis?

   O $140.8m

   O $470.8m

   O $365.8m

   O $1,027.8m   **(2 marks)**

239   What is the value of Bluebell Co using the earnings yield method?

   O $2,675m

   O $1,200m

   O $1,875m

   O $2,975m   **(2 marks)**

240   When valuing Bluebell Co using asset-based valuations, which of the following statements is correct?

   O An asset-based valuation would be useful for an asset-stripping acquisition

   O Bluebell Co's workforce can be valued as an intangible asset

   O Asset-based valuations consider the present value of Bluebell Co's future income

   O Replacement cost basis provides a deprival value for Bluebell Co   **(2 marks)**

241 Which of the following is/are indicators of market imperfections?

(1) Low volume of trading in shares of smaller companies

(2) Overreaction to unexpected news

O 1 only

O 2 only

O Both 1 and 2

O Neither 1 nor 2 **(2 marks)**

242 Which of the following statements is correct?

O Dandelion Co is easier to value than Bluebell Co because a small number of shareholders own all the shares

O Bluebell Co will have to pay a higher price per share to take control of Dandelion Co than if it were buying a minority holding

O Scrip dividends decrease the liquidity of shares by retaining cash in a company

O Dandelion Co's shares will trade at a premium to similar listed shares because it will have a lower cost of equity **(2 marks)**

(Total = 10 marks)

GWW Co **(18 mins)**

This scenario relates to the following five questions

GWW Co is a listed company which is seen as a potential target for acquisition by financial analysts. The value of the company has therefore been a matter of public debate in recent weeks and the following financial information is available:

Year	20Y2	20Y1	20Y0	20X9
Profit after tax ($m)	10.1	9.7	8.9	8.5
Total dividends ($m)	6.0	5.6	5.2	5.0

STATEMENT OF FINANCIAL POSITION INFORMATION FOR 20Y2

	$m	$m
Non-current assets		91.0
Current assets		
Inventory	3.8	
Trade receivables	4.5	8.3
Total assets		99.3
Equity finance		
Ordinary shares	20.0	
Reserves	47.2	67.2
Non-current liabilities		
8% bonds		25.0
Current liabilities		7.1
Total liabilities		99.3

 BPP

The shares of GWW Co have a nominal (par) value of 50c per share and a market value of $4.00 per share. The business sector of GWW Co has an average price/earnings ratio of 17 times.

The expected net realisable values of the non-current assets and the inventory are $86.0m and $4.2m respectively. In the event of liquidation, only 80% of the trade receivables are expected to be collectible.

243 What is the value of GWW Co using market capitalisation (equity market value) (in $m to the nearest whole million)?

$ [   ] million   (2 marks)

244 What is the value of GWW Co using the net asset value (liquidation basis) (in $m to the nearest whole million)?

$ [   ] million   (2 marks)

245 What is the value of GWW Co using the price/earnings ratio method (business sector average price/earnings ratio)?

  O $1.7m

  O $61.7m

  O $160m

  O $171.7m   (2 marks)

246 An investor believes that they can make abnormal returns by studying past share price movements.

In terms of capital market efficiency, to which of the following does the investor's belief relate?

  O Fundamental analysis

  O Operational efficiency

  O Technical analysis

  O Semi-strong form efficiency   (2 marks)

247 Assume that GWW Co's P/E ratio is 15. Its competitor's earnings yield is 6.25%.

When comparing GWW Co to its competitor, which of the following is correct?

	Earnings yield of GWW	P/E ratio of GWW
O	Higher	Higher
O	Higher	Lower
O	Lower	Higher
O	Lower	Lower

(2 marks)

(Total = 10 marks)

Corhig Co (amended) (June 2012)   (18 mins)

This scenario relates to the following five questions

Corhig Co is a company that is listed on a major stock exchange. The company has struggled to maintain profitability in the last two years due to poor economic conditions in its home country and as a consequence it has decided not to pay a dividend in the current year. However, there are now clear signs of economic recovery and Corhig Co is optimistic that payment of dividends can be resumed in the future. Forecast financial information relating to the company is as follows:

Year	1	2	3
Earnings ($'000)	3,000	3,600	4,300
Dividends ($'000)	nil	500	1,000

The current average price/earnings ratio of listed companies similar to Corhig Co is five times.

The company is optimistic that earnings and dividends will increase after Year 3 at a constant annual rate of 3% per year.

248   Using Corhig Co's forecast earnings for Year 1 and the average P/E ratio of similar companies, what is the value of Corhig Co using the price/earnings ratio method?

$ [   ] million   **(2 marks)**

249   Are the following statements true or false?

	True	False
A P/E valuation using average earnings of $3.63m would be more realistic than the P/E ratio method calculated above	O	O
Using the average P/E ratio of similar companies is appropriate in this situation	O	O

       (2 marks)

250   Assuming that the cost of equity is 12%, what is the present value of Corhig Co's Year 2 dividend?

$ [   ]   **(2 marks)**

 BPP

251 Corhig Co plans to raise debt in order to modernise some of its non-current assets and to support the expected growth in earnings. This additional debt would mean that the capital structure of the company would change and it would be financed 60% by equity and 40% by debt on a market value basis. The before-tax cost of debt of Corhig Co would increase to 6% per year. In order to stimulate economic activity the Government has reduced the tax rate for all large companies to 20% per year.

Assuming that the revised cost of equity is 14%, what is the revised weighted average after-tax cost of capital of Corhig Co following the new debt issue (give your answer to 2 decimal places)?

	%

(2 marks)

252 Match the description of the risk to the type of risk.

	Business Systematic	Financial
Risk linked to the extent to which the company's profits depend on fixed, rather than variable, costs	O	O
Risk that shareholder cannot mitigate by holding a diversified investment portfolio	O	O
Risk that shareholder return fluctuates as a result of the level of debt the company undertakes	O	O

(2 marks)

(Total = 10 marks)

Close Co (amended) (December 2011) **(18 mins)**

This scenario relates to the following five questions

Recent financial information relating to Close Co, a stock market listed company, is as follows.

	$m
Profit after tax (earnings)	66.6
Dividends	40.0

STATEMENT OF FINANCIAL POSITION INFORMATION

	$m	$m
Non-current assets		595
Current assets		125
Total assets		720

	$m	$m
Equity		
Ordinary shares ($1 nominal)	80	
Retained earnings	410	
		490
Non-current liabilities		
6% bank loan	40	
8% bonds ($100 nominal)	120	
		160
Current liabilities		70
Total equity and liabilities		720

Financial analysts have forecast that the dividends of Close Co will grow in the future at a rate of 4% per year. This is slightly less than the forecast growth rate of the profit after tax (earnings) of the company, which is 5% per year. The finance director of Close Co thinks that, considering the risk associated with expected earnings growth, an earnings yield of 11% per year can be used for valuation purposes.

Close Co has a cost of equity of 10% per year.

253 Calculate the value of Close Co using the net asset value method.

$ [   ] million   **(2 marks)**

254 Calculate the value of Close Co using the dividend growth model (DGM).

$ [   ] million   **(2 marks)**

255 Calculate the value of Close Co using the earnings yield method (in millions to 1 decimal places).

$ [   ] million   **(2 marks)**

256 The DGM has been used by financial analysts to value Close Co.

Are the following statements about the DGM true or false?

	True	False
It is very sensitive to changes in the growth rate	O	O
It can only be used if dividends have been paid or are expected to be paid	O	O

(2 marks)

257 Close Co is considering raising finance via convertible bonds.

Which of the following statements is correct about the current market value of a convertible bond where conversion is expected?

O   The sum of the present values of the future interest payments + the present value of the bond's conversion value

O   The sum of the present values of the future interest payments – the present value of the bond's conversion value

O   The higher of the sum of the present values of the future interest payments and the present value of the bond's conversion value

O   The lower of the sum of the present values of the future interest payments and the present value of the bond's conversion value

(2 marks)

(Total = 10 marks)

WAW Co   (18 mins)

This scenario relates to the following five questions

WAW Co is an unlisted company that has performed well recently. It has been approached by a number of companies in the industry as a potential acquisition target.

The directors of WAW Co are looking to establish an approximate valuation of the company.

Recent information on the earnings per share and dividend per share of WAW Co is as follows:

Year to September	20X3	20X4	20X5	20X6
Earnings $m	6	6.5	7.0	7.5
Dividend $m	2.4	2.6	2.8	3.0

WAW Co has an estimated cost of equity of 12% and $5m ordinary shares in issue with a par value of $0.50.

There has been no change in the number of ordinary shares in issue over this period.

WAW Co pays corporation tax at a rate of 20%.

Listed companies similar to WAW Co have a price/earnings ratio of 15.

258 What is the value of a share in WAW Co using the dividend growth model?

O $5.07

O $4.79

O $7.55

O $15.10

(2 marks)

259 Which of the following statements are problems in using the dividend growth model to value a company?

(1) It is difficult to estimate future dividend growth.

(2) It cannot be used for unlisted companies as they do not have a cost of equity.

(3) It is inaccurate to assume that dividend growth will be constant.

(4) It does not adjust for the value of holding a controlling interest in a company.

○ 1 and 3

○ 2 and 3

○ 1, 3 and 4

○ 1, 2, 3 and 4 (2 marks)

___

260 What is the value of WAW Co using the price/earnings ratio method?

○ $56.25 per share

○ $11.25 per share

○ $22.50 per share

○ $45.00 per share (2 marks)

___

261 A high price/earnings ratio is usually seen as an indication that:

○ The company's earnings are expected to be risky

○ The dividend payout is excessive

○ The share price is overstated

○ The company is expected to grow (2 marks)

___

262 Which of the following statements are true about WAW Co's dividend policy?

(1) Shareholders achieve steady dividend growth.

(2) The dividend payout ratio is constant.

(3) The dividend cover is 2.5 each year.

(4) Shareholders are indifferent between reinvesting in the business and the payment of a dividend.

○ 1, 2 and 3

○ 1, 2 and 4

○ 1 and 3

○ 2, 3 and 4 (2 marks)

___

(Total = 10 marks)

Dazvin Co (September/December 2021) (18 mins)

This scenario relates to the following five questions

The following financial information relates to Dazvin Co, a company that is listed on a stock market.

	$m
Revenue	35.5
Cost of sales	(20.0)
Other expenses	(8.4)
Finance costs	(1.4)
Profits before taxation	**5.7**
Corporation tax (30%)	(1.7)
Profit for the year	**4.0**

	$m
Ordinary share capital	26.0
Preference share capital	10.0
Retained earnings	21.5
Total equity	**57.5**
Non-current liabilities	
Long-term borrowings	18.0
Current liabilities	
Trade payables	11.1
Total liabilities	**29.1**
Total equity and liabilities	**86.6**

The preference share capital consists of irredeemable 6% preference shares with a nominal value of $0.50 per share. The cost of capital of the preference shares is 8%.

The ordinary shares have a nominal value of $1.00 per share. Dazvin Co has a price / earnings ratio of 12 times. Future share price growth on the stock market is expected to be 6% per year.

The long-term borrowings consist of 7.5% convertible loan notes with a nominal value of $100 per loan note. These loan notes can be converted at the end of six years into 40 ordinary shares of Dazvin Co, or redeemed on the same date at their nominal value of $100 per loan note. Dazvin Co has a before-tax cost of debt of 6%.

263 What is the market value of the preference shares of Dazvin Co?

- ○ $7.50m
- ○ $5.25m
- ○ $3.75m
- ○ $10.71m **(2 marks)**

---

264   Using the price/earnings ratio method, what is the value of Dazvin Co?

    O $48.0m

    O $68.4m

    O $43.2m

    O $40.8m   **(2 marks)**

---

265   Based on a current ordinary share price of $2.00 per share, what is the market value of the convertible debt of Dazvin Co?

    O $19.0m

    O $19.3m

    O $21.0m

    O $20.1m   **(2 marks)**

---

266   In relation to information requirements for valuing shares, which of the following statements is correct?

    O Only information on the market values of tangible assets should be used in valuing shares.

    O Shares are likely to be mispriced where managers and investors have different levels of information (information asymmetry).

    O Details of key personnel are not relevant to the market capitalisation of a listed company.

    O Since companies do not release information that undermines their competitive advantage, most of the published information about a company is not relevant to placing a value on its shares.   **(2 marks)**

---

267   In relation to behavioural finance, which of the following statements is/are correct?

    (1) When investors believe that recent share price increases will continue, this can lead to irrational investment decisions by uninformed investors.

    (2) Informed investors can contribute to speculative stock market bubbles.

    O 1 only

    O 2 only

    O Both 1 and 2

    O Neither 1 nor 2   **(2 marks)**

                                              (Total = 10 marks)

The questions in this Part cover Risk management, the subject of Chapters 14–15 of the BPP Financial Management Workbook.

OTQ bank – Foreign currency risk   (36 mins)

268 Exporters Co is concerned that the cash received from overseas sales will not be as expected due to exchange rate movements.

What type of risk is this?

O   Translation risk

O   Economic risk

O   Credit risk

O   Transaction risk   **(2 marks)**

___

269 The current euro/US dollar exchange rate is €1:$2. ABC Co, a Eurozone company, makes a $1,000 sale to a US customer on credit. By the time the customer pays, the euro has strengthened by 20%.

What will the euro receipt be (to the nearest euro)?

€ [   ]   **(2 marks)**

___

270 The forward rate is 0.8500 – 0.8650 euros to the 1$.

What will a €2,000 receipt be converted to at the forward rate?

O $1,730

O $2,312

O $2,353

O $1,700   **(2 marks)**

___

271 Which of the following derivative instruments are characterised by a standard contract size?

(1)   Futures contract

(2)   Exchange-traded option

(3)   Forward rate agreement

(4)   Swap

(March 2016)

O   1 and 2

O   2 and 3

O   3 and 4

O   1 and 4   **(2 marks)**

___

272 A US company owes a European company €3.5m due to be paid in 3 months' time. The spot exchange rate is $1.96 – $2:€1 currently. Annual interest rates in the two locations are as follows:

	Borrowing	Deposit
US	8%	3%
Europe	5%	1%

Required

What will be the equivalent US$ value of the payment using a money market hedge?

○ $6,965,432

○ $6,979,750

○ $7,485,149

○ $7,122,195   **(2 marks)**

---

273 In comparison to forward contracts, which TWO of the following are true in relation to futures contracts?

☐ They are more expensive

☐ They are only available in a small amount of currencies

☐ They are less flexible

☐ They may be an imprecise match for the underlying transaction   **(2 marks)**

---

274 A company whose home currency is the dollar ($) expects to receive 500,000 pesos in 6 months' time from a customer in a foreign country. The following interest rates and exchange rates are available to the company:

Spot rate	15.00 peso per $
Six-month forward rate	15.30 peso per $

	Home country	Foreign country
Borrowing interest rate	4% per year	8% per year
Deposit interest rate	3% per year	6% per year

Required

Working to the nearest $100, what is the 6-month dollar value of the expected receipt using a money market hedge?   *(December 2014)*

○ $32,500

○ $33,700

○ $31,800

○ $31,900   **(2 marks)**

---

275 The expected future spot rate in one year is 1.4505 euro per $1. The predicted inflation rates for the year ahead are:

Eurozone	Dollar
2% per year	3.5% per year

Required

What is the current spot rate (to four decimal places)? *(March/June 2021)*

☐ euro per $1   *(2 marks)*

---

276 Handria is a country that has the peso for its currency and Wengry is a country that has the dollar ($) for its currency.

The current spot exchange rate is 1.5134 pesos = $1.

Using interest-rate differentials, the one year forward exchange rate is 1.5346 pesos = $1.

The currency market between the peso and the dollar is assumed perfect and the International Fisher Effect holds.

Which of the following statements is true?   *(March 2017)*

○ Wengry has a higher forecast rate of inflation than Handria

○ Handria has a higher nominal rate of interest than Wengry

○ Handria has a higher real rate of interest than Wengry

○ The forecast future spot rate of exchange will differ from the forward exchange rate
                                                                                   (2 marks)

---

277 An investor plans to exchange $1,000 into euros now, invest the resulting euros for 12 months, and then exchange the euros back into dollars at the end of the 12-month period. The spot exchange rate is €1.415 per $1 and the euro interest rate is 2% per year. The dollar interest rate is 1.8% per year.

Compared to making a dollar investment for 12 months, at what 12-month forward exchange rate will the investor make neither a loss nor a gain?   *(June 2015)*

○ €1.223 per $1

○ €1.412 per $1

○ €1.418 per $1

○ €1.439 per $1   *(2 marks)*

(Total = 20 marks)

OTQ bank – Interest rate risk (29 mins)

278 Act Co wishes to hedge interest rate movements on a borrowing it intends to make three months from now for a further period of six months.

Which TWO of the following will best help Act Co hedge its interest rate risk?

(December 2017)

☐ Enter into a 3 v 6 forward rate agreement

☐ Enter into a 3 v 9 forward rate agreement

☐ Sell interest rate futures expiring in three months' time

☐ Buy interest rate futures expiring in three months' time **(2 marks)**

279 Which TWO of the following statements concerning the interest rate risk management method of smoothing are true? *(September/December 2020)*

☐ The debt portfolio will consist of a mixture of fixed and floating rate debt

☐ Interest payments will still increase if the interest rate rises

☐ Investments with a fixed cash flow will be financed with fixed rate debt

☐ Full benefit will be obtained from a fall in interest rates

☐ The net effect will be an interest payment which is fixed overall **(2 marks)**

280 Which of the following statements concerning the causes of interest rate fluctuations is correct? *(June 2016)*

○ Liquidity preference theory suggests that investors want more compensation for short-term lending than for long-term lending

○ According to expectations theory, the shape of the yield curve gives information on how inflation rates are expected to influence interest rates in the future

○ An inverted yield curve can arise if government policy is to keep short-term interest rates high in order to bring down inflation

○ Market segmentation theory suggests long-term interest rates depend on how easily investors can switch between market segments of different maturity **(2 marks)**

281 A company that has a $10m loan with a variable rate of interest, has acquired a forward rate agreement (FRA) with a financial institution that offered a 3–6, 3.2% – 2.7% spread.

What would be the payment made to the financial institution under the terms of the FRA if the actual rate of interest was 3% (to the nearest dollar)? *(June 2018)*

$ [   ] **(2 marks)**

282 Which of the following statements about an over-the-counter interest rate option are correct?

(1) It is an agreement with a financial institution

(2) It can be traded

(3) An immediate premium is payable

(4) It must be exercised

(March/June 2022)

- ○ 1 and 2 only
- ○ 1 and 3 only
- ○ 3 and 4 only
- ○ 1, 2 and 4

(2 marks)

---

283 Which of the following is a description of gap exposure? *(September 2019)*

- ○ The difference between short-term and long-term interest rates
- ○ The difference between the amount of interest-sensitive assets and liabilities
- ○ The difference between spot interest rates and futures interest rates
- ○ The difference between fixed and floating interest rates

(2 marks)

---

284 Which TWO of the following derivative instruments are characterised by standard contract sizes? *(March 2020)*

- ☐ Forward contract
- ☐ Forward rate agreement
- ☐ Futures contract
- ☐ Swap
- ☐ Over-the-counter option
- ☐ Exchange tradable option

(2 marks)

---

285 A company that has a $14m loan with a variable rate of interest, has acquired a forward rate agreement (FRA) with a financial institution that offered a 4–11, 2.85% – 2.35% spread.

What would be the amount received from the financial institution under the terms of the FRA if the actual rate of interest was 3.75% (to the nearest dollar)? *(July 2020)*

$ [   ]

(2 marks)

(Total = 16 marks)

Section B questions

Rose Co (amended) (June 2015) (18 mins)

This scenario relates to the following five questions

Rose Co expects to receive €750,000 from a credit customer in the European Union in 6 months' time. The spot exchange rate is €2.349 per $1 and the 6-month forward rate is €2.412 per $1. The following commercial interest rates are available to Rose Co:

	Deposit rate	Borrow rate
Euros	4.0% per year	8.0% per year
Dollars	2.0% per year	3.5% per year

Rose Co does not have any surplus cash to use in hedging the future euro receipt. It also has no euro payments to make.

Rose Co is also considering using derivatives such as futures, options and swaps to manage currency risk.

In addition, Rose Co is concerned about the possibility of future interest rate changes and wants to understand how a yield curve can be interpreted.

286   What could Rose Co do to reduce the risk of the euro value dropping relative to the dollar before the €750,000 is received?

   ○ Deposit €750,000 immediately

   ○ Enter into an interest rate swap for 6 months

   ○ Enter into a forward contract to sell €750,000 in 6 months

   ○ Matching payments and receipts to the value of €750,000   **(2 marks)**

---

287   What is the dollar value of a forward market hedge in six months' time?

   ○ $310,945

   ○ $319,285

   ○ $1,761,750

   ○ $1,809,000   **(2 marks)**

---

288   If Rose Co used a money market hedge, what would be the percentage borrowing rate for the period?

   ○ 1.75%

   ○ 2.00%

   ○ 4.00%

   ○ 8.00%   **(2 marks)**

---

289 Which of the following statements is correct?

○ Once purchased, a currency futures contract has a range of settlement dates

○ Currency swaps can be used to hedge exchange rate risk over longer periods than the forward market

○ Banks will allow forward exchange contracts to lapse if they are not used by a company

○ Currency options are paid for when they are exercised   **(2 marks)**

---

290 Which of the following statements is correct?

○ Governments can keep interest rates low by selling short-dated government bills in the money market

○ The normal yield curve slopes upward to reflect increasing compensation to investors for being unable to use their cash now

○ The yield on long-term loan notes is lower than the yield on short-term loan notes because long-term debt is less risky for a company than short-term debt

○ Expectations theory states that future interest rates reflect expectations of future inflation rate movements   **(2 marks)**

(Total = 10 marks)

Edwen Co   **(18 mins)**

This scenario relates to the following five questions

Edwen Co is based in Country C, where the currency is the C$. Edwen is expecting the following transactions with suppliers and customers who are based in Europe.

One month: Expected receipt of 240,000 euros

One month: Expected payment of 140,000 euros

Three months: Expected receipts of 300,000 euros

A one-month forward rate of 1.7832 euros per $1 has been offered by the company's bank and the spot rate is 1.7822 euros per $1.

Other relevant financial information is as follows:

Three-month European borrowing rate: 1.35%

Three-month Country C deposit rate: 1.15%

Assume that it is now 1 April.

291 What are the expected dollar receipts in one month using a forward hedge (to the nearest whole number)?

○ $56,079

○ $56,110

○ $178,220

○ $178,330   **(2 marks)**

292 What are the expected dollar receipts in three months using a money market hedge (to the nearest whole number)?

O $167,999

O $296,004

O $166,089

O $164,201 **(2 marks)**

293 Edwen Co is expecting a fall in the value of the C$.

What is the impact of a fall in a country's exchange rate?

(1) Exports will be given a stimulus.

(2) The rate of domestic inflation will rise.

O 1 only

O 2 only

O Both 1 and 2

O Neither 1 nor 2 **(2 marks)**

294 Edwen Co is considering a currency futures contract.

Which of the following statements about currency futures contracts are true?

(1) The contracts can be tailored to the user's exact requirements.

(2) The exact date of receipt or payment of the currency does not have to be known.

(3) Transaction costs are generally higher than other hedging methods.

O 1 and 2 only

O 1 and 3 only

O 2 only

O 3 only **(2 marks)**

295 Do the following features apply to forward contracts or currency futures?

(1) Contract price is in any currency offered by the bank

(2) Traded over the counter

O Both features relate to forward contracts

O Both features relate to currency futures

O Feature 1 relates to forward contracts and feature 2 relates to currency futures

O Feature 2 relates to forward contracts and feature 1 relates to currency futures

(2 marks)

(Total = 10 marks)

Zigto Co (amended) (June 2012) (18 mins)

This scenario relates to the following five questions

Zigto Co is a medium-sized company whose ordinary shares are all owned by the members of one family. The domestic currency is the dollar. It has recently begun exporting to a European country and expects to receive €500,000 in 6 months' time. The company plans to take action to hedge the exchange rate risk arising from its European exports.

Zigto Co could put cash on deposit in the European country at an annual interest rate of 3% per year, and borrow at 5% per year. The company could put cash on deposit in its home country at an annual interest rate of 4% per year, and borrow at 6% per year. Inflation in the European country is 3% per year, while inflation in the home country of Zigto Co is 4.5% per year.

The following exchange rates are currently available to Zigto Co:

Current spot exchange rate	2.000 euro per $
Six-month forward exchange rate	1.990 euro per $
One-year forward exchange rate	1.981 euro per $

Zigto Co wants to hedge its future euro receipt.

Zigto Co is also trying to build an understanding of other types of currency risk and the potential impact of possible future interest rate and inflation rate changes.

296   What is the dollar value of a forward exchange contract in six months' time (to the nearest whole number)?

$ [   ]   (2 marks)

_____

297   What is the dollar value of a money market hedge in six months' time (to the nearest whole number)?

$ [   ]   (2 marks)

_____

298   What is the one-year expected (future) spot rate predicted by purchasing power parity theory (to three decimal places)?

[   ] euro per $ (2 marks)

_____

299   Are the following statements true or false?

	True	False
Purchasing power parity tends to hold true in the short term	O	O
Expected future spot rates are based on relative inflation rates between two countries	O	O
Current forward exchange rates are based on relative interest rates between two countries	O	O

(2 marks)

_____

300   Are the following statements true or false?

	True	False
Transaction risk affects cash flows	○	○
Translation risk directly affects shareholder wealth	○	○
Diversification of supplier and customer base across different countries reduces economic risk	○	○

(2 marks)

(Total = 10 marks)

Marigold Co (September/December 2020)   (18 mins)

This scenario relates to the following five questions

Marigold Co is based in a country which uses the dollar ($) as its home currency. Marigold Co has a wholly- owned subsidiary based in a country which uses the M shilling (MS) as its currency. The subsidiaries financial statements are prepared in MS.

Due to economic uncertainty in both countries, an exchange loss at $100,000 is expected to occur after consolidating the results of the subsidiary into Marigold Co's group accounts.

Marigold co is expecting a receipt of MS300,000 from the subsidiary in 3 months time which it wishes to protect againstexchange rate movement. The following information is available:

Exchange rates	MS per $1
Spot rate	1.0950-1.1250
Three-month forward rate	1.0850-1.1125

Money Market Rates	Annual deposit %	Annual Borrow %
MS	3.6	4.0
$	6.0	7.0

301   What type of exchange rate risk would Marigold Co experience with the $100,000 loss in its consolidated financial statements?

   ○ Economic

   ○ Translation

   ○ Transaction

   ○ Political   (2 marks)

302

   If Marigold Co uses the forward market to hedge the MS receipt, what amount will be received (to the nearest $)?

   $ [   ]   (2 marks)

303 Match the appropriate value to the relevant target in order to reflect what amount Marigold Co will borrow and deposit if it uses the money market to hedge the MS receipt.

Amount to borrow: (1) [▼]

Amount to deposit: (2) [▼]

Pull down list 1
- MS288,461
- MS289,575
- MS297,030
- MS297,324

Pull down list 2
- $256,410
- $263,435
- $264,027
- $271,260

(2 marks)

304 Marigold Co is now considering the use of an option to hedge the currency risk on the MS receipt. Its bank has offered an over-the-counter option with an exercise price of MS1.1250 per $.

Which TWO of the following statements concerning the option are TRUE?

☐ The option will be more expensive to set up compared with either the forward contract or money market hedge

☐ An imperfect hedge will result as the option will be for a standard amount of currency and only a whole number of contracts may be used

☐ If the $ was to strengthen against the MS, Marigold Co is likely to be worse off by using the option compared to either the forward contract or money market hedge

☐ Using an option hedge will mean that Marigold Co is obligated to exercise the option in three months irrespective of the spot rate on the day (2 marks)

305 Marigold Co is unsure whether to use a forward contract or a money market hedge and is comparing the relative advantages and disadvantages of the two.

Which of the following statements is TRUE?

O The forward contract has the advantage of being tailored precisely to Marigold Co's requirements but the money market hedge will be a standardised instrument resulting in an imperfect hedge

O The forward contract will result in Marigold Co receiving the dollar equivalent of the MS receipt in three months' time, whereas the money market hedge will provide Marigold Co with dollar receipts today

O The forward contract will result in the effective rate of exchange being fixed whereas the money market hedge will allow Marigold Co to benefit from favourable movement in the exchange rate

O Marigold Co will be obligated to fulfil the forward contract in three months' time whereas the money market hedge could be traded on an exchange to another party before settlement (2 marks)

(Total = 10 marks)

Peony Co (March/June 2019)　　(18 mins)

This scenario relates to the following five questions

Peony Co's finance director is concerned about the effect of future interest rates on the company and has been looking at the yield curve.

Peony Co, whose domestic currency is the dollar ($), plans to take out a $100m loan in three months' time for a period of nine months. The company is concerned that interest rates might rise before the loan is taken out and its bank has offered a 3 v 12 forward rate agreement at 7.10–6.85.

The loan will be converted into pesos and invested in a nine-month project which is expected to generate income of 580 million pesos, with 200 million pesos being paid in six months' time (from today) and 380 million pesos being paid in 12 months' time (from today). The current spot exchange rate is 5 pesos per $1.

The following information on current short-term interest rates is available:

Dollars	6.5% per year
Pesos	10.0% per year

As a result of the general uncertainty over interest rates, Peony Co is considering a variety of ways in which to manage its interest rate risk, including the use of derivatives.

306　In relation to the yield curve, which of the following statements is correct?

○　Expectations theory suggests that deferred consumption requires increased compensation as maturity increases

○　An inverted yield curve can be caused by government action to increase its long-term borrowing

○　A kink (discontinuity) in the normal yield curve can be due to differing yields in different market segments

○　Basis risk can cause the corporate yield curve to rise more steeply than the government yield curve　　**(2 marks)**

307　If the interest rate on the loan is 6.5% when it is taken out, what is the nature of the compensatory payment under the forward rate agreement?

○　Peony Co pays bank $600,000

○　Peony Co pays bank $250,000

○　Peony Co pays bank $450,000

○　Bank pays Peony Co $600,000　　**(2 marks)**

308　Using exchange rates based on interest rate parity, what is the dollar income received from the project?

○　$112.3m

○　$114.1m

○　$116.0m

○　$112.9m　　**(2 marks)**

309   In respect of Peony Co managing its interest rate risk, which of the following statements is/are correct?

(1)   Smoothing is an interest rate risk hedging technique which involves maintaining a balance between fixed-rate and floating-rate debt.

(2)   Asset and liability management can hedge interest rate risk by matching the maturity of assets and liabilities.

○   1 only

○   2 only

○   Both 1 and 2

○   Neither 1 nor 2   (2 marks)

310   In relation to the use of derivatives by Peony Co, which of the following statements is correct?

○   Interest rate options must be exercised on their expiry date, if they have not been exercised before then

○   Peony Co can hedge interest rate risk on borrowing by selling interest rate futures now and buying them back in the future

○   An interest rate swap is an agreement to exchange both principal and interest rate payments

○   Peony Co can hedge interest rate risk on borrowing by buying a floor and selling a cap   (2 marks)

(Total = 10 marks)

 BPP

Answers

OTQ bank 1 – Financial management and financial objectives

1    $ 0.80

	$
Profit before tax	2,628,000
Less tax	788,000
Profit after tax	1,840,000
Less preference dividend (6% × 4,000,000)	240,000
Earnings attributable to ordinary shareholders	1,600,000
Number of ordinary shares	2,000,000
EPS = $1,600,000/2,000,000 =	$0.80

Syllabus area A3 (d)(i)

2   The correct answer is: Efficient acquisition and deployment of financial resources to ensure achievement of objectives

Notes on incorrect answers:

The second statement is a definition of management accounting.

The third statement is a definition of financial accounting.

The fourth statement is true for a profit seeking organisation but would not be relevant to a not for profit organisation. However, financial management is also relevant to a not for profit organisation.

Syllabus area A1(b)

3   6

$$\text{P/E ratio} = \frac{\text{MV ex div}}{\text{EPS}} = \frac{\$3.60}{60c} = 6$$

MV ex div = 3.72 − 0.12 = 3.60. The ex div price is used because it reflects the underlying value of the share after the dividend has been paid.

Syllabus area A3(d)

4   The correct answer is: Mean growth in earnings per share over the period is 6% per year

Mean growth in earnings per share =

$$\sqrt[3]{\frac{35.7}{30.0}} - 1 = 0.06 \text{ or } 6\%$$

Notes on incorrect answers:

Dividend payout is dividend/earnings, this does not deliver the value of 40%.

Mean growth in dividends per share =

$$\sqrt[3]{\frac{15.0}{13.0}} - 1 = 0.05 \text{ or } 5\%$$

 BPP

Total shareholder return can be calculated as:

$(P_1 - P_0 + D_1)/P_0$

P_0 is the share price at the beginning of the year 3 = $2.25

P_1 is the share price at the end of period – this is unknown so TSR cannot be calculated.

Syllabus area A3(d)

5   The correct answer is: Non-executive directors are appointed to the remuneration committee

Financial management decisions typically cover dividend decisions (first statement), investment decisions and financing decisions (second and third statements).

Syllabus area A1(a)

OTQ bank 2 – Financial management and financial objectives

6    $ ‎3.60

Shareholder return =

$$\frac{P_1 - P_0 + D_1}{P_0}$$

$$\therefore 0.25 = \frac{P_1 - 3.00 + 0.15}{3.00}$$

$\therefore 0.75 = P_1 - 3.00 + 0.15$

$\therefore P_1 = 3.60$

Syllabus area A3(d)

7   The correct answer is: Minimisation of risk

Corporate governance best practice aims to **manage** risk to desired and controlled levels, not to minimise risk. Running a business implies taking calculated risks in anticipation of a commensurate return.

Syllabus area A3(e)(ii)

8   The correct answers are:

- Maximising market share is an example of a financial objective - **False**
- Shareholder wealth maximisation is the primary financial objective for a company listed on a stock exchange - **True**
- Financial objectives should be quantitative so that their achievement can be measured - **True**

Statement 1: Maximising market share is not a financial objective.

Statement 2: The primary financial objective of any profit-making company is to maximise shareholder wealth.

Statement 3: Financial objectives should be quantifiable. These include, for example, target values for earnings per share, dividend per share and gearing which are all quantifiable measures.

Syllabus area A2(b)

9   The correct answer is: Cost per journey to hospital

Cost per journey to hospital is a measure of efficiency.

Percentage of members who re-use the service is a measure of effectiveness.

A comparison of actual operating expenses against the budget is an economy measure.

Number of communities served is an effectiveness measure.

Syllabus area A4(c)

10    $\boxed{36.4}$ %

Shareholder return = $(P_1 - P_0 + D_1)/P_0$.

∴ shareholder return = (0.75 + 0.25)/(3.50 − 0.75)

= 36.4%

Syllabus area A3(d)(ii)

11   The correct answers are:

- Accounting profit is not the same as economic profit - **True**
- Profit takes account of risk - **False**
- Accounting profit can be manipulated by managers - **True**

Statement 1: The economist's concept of profits is broadly in terms of cash, whereas accounting profits may not equate to cash flows.

Statement 2: Profit does not take account of risk.

Statement 3: Accounting profit can be manipulated to some extent by choices of accounting policies.

Syllabus area A2(b)

12   The correct answer is: Cost per successfully treated patient

Efficiency measures relate the resources used to the output produced (getting as much as possible for what goes in).

'Proportion of patients readmitted after unsuccessful treatment' relates to effectiveness. Effectiveness means getting done, by means of economy and efficiency, what was supposed to be done.

'Cost per operation' relates to economy (spending money frugally), as does 'Percentage change in doctors' salaries compared with previous year'.

Syllabus area A4(c)

13   The correct answer is: Return on equity can be defined as profit before interest and tax divided by shareholders' funds

This is NOT true as return on equity can be defined as profit **AFTER** interest and tax divided by shareholders' funds

Syllabus area A3(d)

14    $\boxed{8.0}$ %

Dividend yield is compares dividend paid over a year to the current ex-div share price. Dividend for the year is $0.08 + $0.06= $0.14

Ex div share price (representing the amount of money being invested in the share) = $1.83 − $0.08 = $1.75.

0.14/1.75 × 100 = 8.0%

Syllabus area A3(d)

15   The correct answers are:

- Share price
- Dividend payment

The sources of shareholder wealth are share prices and dividend payments, so increasing both of these would be associated with the objective of shareholder wealth maximisation.

Profit and EPS are not directly linked to shareholder wealth maximisation.

Increasing the WACC would reduce shareholder wealth.

Syllabus area A2(b)

ANSWERS

ABC Co

16 $\boxed{6.6}$ %

	20X8	**20X7**
ROCE (PBIT/Long-term capital)	$14,749/($53,900) = 27.4%	$13,506/($52,587) = 25.7%

Percentage increase =

$$\frac{27.4 - 25.7}{25.7} = 6.6\%$$

Syllabus area A3(d)

17 $\boxed{19.8}$ %

Operating profit margin =

$$\frac{PBIT}{Sales} = \frac{14,749}{74,521} = 19.8\%$$

Syllabus area A3(d)

18   The correct answer is: 23.6%

The total shareholder return is $(P_1 - P_o + D_1)/P_o = (8.82 - 7.41 + 0.34)/7.41 = 23.6\%$.

Syllabus area A3(d)

19   The correct answer is: Statement 1 is true and statement 2 is false

The shareholders of ABC would probably be reasonably pleased with the performance over the two years. (For example, share price has increased by 19% ((8.82 − 7.41)/7.41 × 100%).) However, salaries and wages have only increased by 2.4% ((20,027 − 19,562)/19,562 × 100%), which is below the rate of inflation, so employees may be less pleased with the situation. So statement 1 is true.

Statement 2 is false. The financial risk that the shareholders are exposed to does not appear to be a problem area as gearing has decreased from 49.9% to 35.1% and interest cover is more than sufficient.

Syllabus area A3(d)

20   The correct answer is: 1, 2, 3 and 4

Accounting profits can be manipulated to some extent by choices of accounting policies.

Profit does not take account of risk. Shareholders will be very interested in the level of risk, and maximising profits may be achieved by increasing risk to unacceptable levels.

Profits on their own take no account of the volume of investment that it has taken to earn the profit. Profits must be related to the volume of investment to have any real meaning.

Profits are reported every year (with half-year interim results for quoted companies). They are measures of short-term historic performance, whereas a company's performance should ideally be judged over a longer term and future prospects considered as well as past profits.

Syllabus area A2(b)

OTQ bank 1 – Financial management environment

21 The correct answer is: Higher taxes and lower government subsidies

Fiscal policy is the balance of government taxation and spending. A contractionary fiscal policy implies a government budget surplus – the Government is reducing demand by withdrawing higher amounts from the economy by way of higher taxation and/or spending less. The second statement would be the result of an expansionary fiscal policy.

The first statement and fourth statements are connected with monetary policy.

Syllabus area B1(c)

22 The correct answer is: Higher demand from customers, lower interest rates on loans and increased availability of credit

Monetary policy manages demand by influencing the supply of money (including the availability of credit) and interest rates. An expansionary policy implies low interest rates to encourage borrowing and investment, and to discourage saving. It also implies an increased availability of credit to encourage spending and the stimulation of demand in an economy. Tax rates are a tool of fiscal policy, so the third and fourth statements are incorrect. Statement 2 would be the result of a contractionary monetary policy.

Syllabus area B1(c)

23 The correct answers are:

- Ensuring minimum amounts of price increases
- Increasing national income and living standards
- Ensuring a balanced ratio of imports to exports
- Ensuring a stable and fully employed labour force

Maintaining interest rates at minimum levels is a possible monetary policy but is not a general and constant macroeconomic policy objective. The same can be said for balancing government spending (a possible fiscal policy objective) in that it is a possible policy but is not a general and constant macroeconomic policy objective.

Syllabus area B1(a)

24 The correct answers are:

- Monetary policy seeks to influence aggregate demand by increasing or decreasing the money raised through taxation - **False**
- When governments adopt a floating exchange rate system, the exchange rate is an equilibrium between demand and supply in the foreign exchange market - **True**
- Fiscal policy seeks to influence the economy and economic growth by increasing or decreasing interest rates - **False**

Statement 1 is **incorrect:** it is fiscal policy that involves changing tax rates

Statement 2 is **correct:** in a floating rate system the exchange rate is determined by demand and supply.

Statement 3 is **incorrect:** it is monetary policy that seeks to influence the economy and economic growth by increasing or decreasing interest rates

Syllabus area B1(b)

25 The correct answer is: An organisation which has a large number of long-term payables

Rationale: Debts lose 'real' value with inflation: a company that owes a lot of money would effectively pay less (in real terms) over time.

The other organisations would suffer because inflation would make exports relatively expensive and imports relatively cheap; business might be lost due to price rises; and the cost of implementing price changes would be high.

Syllabus area B1(d)

 BPP

OTQ bank 2 – Financial management environment

26 The correct answer is: $99,023

The issue price of each paper can be calculated by the nominal value divided by 1 plus the required rate of return, pro-rated for the 90-day issue period.

Issue price = $100,000 / (1 + (0.04 x 90/365)) = $99,023

Many candidates instead deducted the prorated rate of return from 1 and multiplied this by the nominal value. $100,000 x (1 – (0.4 x 90/365)) = $99,014

Syllabus area B3(c)

27 3.80 %

The calculation is as follows:

Increase in value = $9.65m – $9.6m = $0.05m

As a percentage of the original value = $0.05m/$9.6m = 0.52%

Annualising this value = 0.52% × 365/50 = 3.80%

Syllabus area B3(c)

28 The correct answer is: Discounting the banker's acceptance

A letter of credit involves a selling company and a buying company (who use the letter of credit reduce the credit risk of the selling company). The first and third statements are incorrect as these would be done by the buying company's bank. The second statement would be done by the selling company's bank.

Syllabus area B2(a)

29 The correct answer is: 1 only

Discounted instruments are originally sold for a price below their face value and do not pay interest

Commercial paper is an unsecured money market instrument.

Syllabus area B2(a)

30 The correct answer is: 4, 1, 3, 2

Ordinary shares are riskiest as all other investors are preferential to ordinary shareholders. Preference shares are riskier than corporate bonds as preference shares are paid after corporate bonds – bonds imply a contractual right to receive a predefined level of return. Treasury bills are short-term government borrowing hence are the lowest risk of all.

Syllabus area B2(d)

OTQ bank 3 – Financial management environment

31 The correct answers are:

- Securitisation is the conversion of illiquid assets into marketable securities - **True**
- The reverse yield gap refers to equity yields being higher than debt yields - **False**
- Disintermediation arises where borrowers deal directly with lending individuals - **True**

The reverse yield gap refers to yields on shares being lower than on low-risk debt. A reverse yield gap can occur because shareholders may be willing to accept lower returns on their investments in the short term, in anticipation that they will make capital gains in the future.

Syllabus area B2(b)

 BPP

32 The correct answer is: 2 and 4 only

Fiscal policy is action by the Government to spend money, or to collect money in taxes with the purpose of influencing the condition of the national economy.

Incorrect answers:

Decreasing interest rates in order to stimulate consumer spending – Decreasing interest rates relates to monetary policy.

Using official foreign currency reserves to buy the domestic currency – This is government policy on intervention to influence the exchange rate.

Syllabus area B1(b/c)

33 The correct answer is: 1, 2 and 3

Syllabus area B3

34 The correct answers are:

- Capital market securities are assets for the seller but liabilities for the buyer - **False**
- Financial markets can be classified into exchange and over-the-counter markets - **True**
- A secondary market is where securities are bought and sold by investors - **True**

Statement 1 is **incorrect**: a capital market security is like a share, is an asset to a buyer.

Statements 2 and 3 are **correct**.

Syllabus area B2

35 The correct answer is: 2 only

Statement 2 is the only correct statement as lending is securitised.

Statement 1 is **incorrect** as money markets are markets for short-term capital, of less than a year.

Statement 3 is **incorrect**, the money markets are mainly used by large companies.

Syllabus area B3(c)

OTQ bank 4 – Financial management environment

36 The correct answers are:

- If a government spends more by borrowing more, it will raise demand in the economy - **True**
- If demand in the economy is high then government borrowing will fall - **True**

If a government spends more, for example, on public services such as hospitals, without raising more money in taxation, it will increase expenditure in the economy and raise demand. Although the second statement appears to contradict the first, it is also true. After the government has kick-started demand (as in statement 1) then it should be able to repay the borrowing it has taken on as tax receipts rise due to higher economic activity.

Syllabus area B1(c)

37 The correct answers are:

- UK exporters to US - **Suffer**
- UK importers from US - **Benefit**

A weakening dollar implies, for example, an exchange rate that moves from, say, $1:£1 to $2:£1. A UK exporter will therefore receive less £ sterling for their $ revenue. However, a UK company importing from the US will benefit by way of a lower £ cost for any given $ price they need to pay for their imports.

Syllabus area B1(b)

38 The correct answer is: 1, 2 and 3

Options 1, 2 and 3 are all situations which may require regulation, because they are all examples of where the free market has failed.

Syllabus area B1(d)

 BPP

39   The correct answers are:

- Low and stable inflation

- Achievement of a balance between exports and imports

The four main objectives of macroeconomic policy relate to economic growth, stable inflation, unemployment and the balance of payments (balance between exports and imports). Equitable income distribution is a social/political issue. Recycling is an environmental issue.

Syllabus area B1(a)

40   The correct answers are:

- Increasing public expenditure

- Decreasing taxation

Rationale: increasing public spending and cutting taxes should both increase the level of consumer spending which will stimulate economic activity.

Notes on incorrect answers:

Increasing the exchange rate will increase the price of exported goods and lower the price of imported goods; this is likely to lead to a fall in domestic economic activity. Increasing interest rates will cut investment (by companies) and consumer expenditure, even if only after a time lag.

Syllabus area B1(b)

OTQ bank – Working capital

41   The correct answer is: $3.151m

Current raw material inventory

= 15/365 × purchases of (0.5 × $100m) = **$2.055m**

Current WIP inventory

= 35/365 × cost of goods sold $100m = **$9.589m**

Current finished goods inventory

= 40/365 × cost of goods sold $100m = **$10.959m**

A reduction of 5 days in raw material inventory

= 5/15 × 2.055 = **$0.685m**

A reduction of 4 days in WIP inventory

= 4/35 × 9.589 = **$1.096m**

A reduction of 5 days in finished goods inventory

= 5/40 × 10.959 = **$1.370m**

Total reduction = 0.685 + 1.096 + 1.370 = **$3.151m**

Syllabus area C3(a)

42   The correct answers are:

- Current assets – current liabilities
- The long-term capital invested in net current assets

Notes on incorrect answers:

Inventory holding period (days) + accounts receivable collection period (days) – accounts payable payment period (days) is the cash operating cycle

Current assets/current liabilities is the current ratio.

Syllabus area C1(a)

43      $ 10.8 million

This question tests the use and understanding of the elements of working capital. The correct calculation is as follows:

Accounts receivable = ($2m × 12 × 80% × 3/12) = $4.8m

Working capital requirement = $4.8m + $10m - $4m = $10.8m.

Syllabus area C1(a)

44   The correct answers are:

- Overtrading often arises from a rapid increase in sales revenue
- Overtrading may result in a relatively high accounts payable turnover period

The second statement is **incorrect** as overcapitalisation results in a relatively high current ratio.

The fourth statement is **incorrect** as overcapitalisation is the result of an organisation having too much long-term capital.

Syllabus area C1(a)

45 The correct answer is: $4,375,000

Inventory = 15,000,000 × 60/360 = $2,500,000

Trade receivables = 27,000,000 × 50/360 = $3,750,000

Trade payables = 15,000,000 × 45/360 = $1,875,000

Net investment required = 2,500,000 + 3,750,000 − 1,875,000 = $4,375,000

Syllabus area C3(a)

OTQ bank – Managing working capital

46 $\boxed{1,600}$ ball bearings

Annual demand = 40 × 250 = 10,000 ball bearings = D

Order cost = $64 = C_o

Holding cost per year per unit = 25% of $2 = $0.50 = C_h

EOQ =

$$\sqrt{\frac{2C_o}{C_h}} = \sqrt{\frac{2 \times 64 \times 10,000}{0.5}}$$

= 1,600 ball bearings

Syllabus area C2(c)

47 $ $\boxed{22,219}$

Total cost = Annual purchase costs + annual ordering cost + annual holding cost.

Annual purchase cost = 10,000 units × $2 = $20,000

Annual ordering cost = number of orders × cost per order = (10,000/250) × $50 = $2,000

Annual holding cost = Average inventory level × cost to hold per unit per year

= [(250/2) + 50] × $1.25 = $218.75

Total cost = $20,000 + $2,000 + $218.75 = $22,218.75 = $22,219 (to nearest $).

Syllabus area C2(c)

48 The correct answer is: 1, 2 and 3

Statement 1 is **correct**. If a business is profitable then an increase in sales should translate to more working capital.

Statement 2 is **correct**. The greater the cash operating cycle, the greater the working capital investment need is. Greater working capital means more cash tied up and therefore not earning profit.

Statement 3 is **correct**. Overtrading (or undercapitalisation) is where a business is over reliant on short-term finance to support its operations. It is trying to do too much too quickly with little long-term capital.

Syllabus area C1(b/c)

49   The correct answer is: $2,625 cost

Reduction in receivables = $4,500,000 × 30/360 × 35% = $131,250

Alternatively: average receivables days will fall to (60 × 0.65) + (30 × 0.35) = 49.5 days which is a reduction of 10.5 days; $4,500,000 × 10.5/360 = $131,250.

Interest saved at 10% = $131,250 × 0.1 = $13,125

Cost of discount = $4,500,000 × 35% × 1% = $15,750

Net cost = $13,125 − $15,750 = $2,625

$1,875 is incorrectly arrived at by using 25% based on total customers instead of credit customers.

Syllabus area C2(d)

50   The correct answer is: 2 only

Statement 1 is incorrect because it is factoring with **no recourse** that provides insurance against bad debts

Syllabus area C2(d)

51   The correct answer is: Commercial paper

Commercial paper is a source of finance and not directly applicable to the management of foreign debts.

Syllabus area C2(d)

52    $ 28,500

The cost is (total sales × 1.5%) + $6,000 = ($1.5m × 1.5%) + $6,000 = $28,500

Non-recourse means that the factor carries the risk of the bad debts.

Syllabus area C2(d)

53    $ 30,200

Ordering cost = $200 × (600,000/100,000) = $1,200 per year

Average inventory = order quantity / 2 + buffer inventory

Order quantity / 2 = 100,000 / 2 = 50,000

Buffer inventory = re-order level less usage during lead time

= 20,000 − (600,000 / 50 weeks) = 8,000

Average inventory = 50,000 + 8,000 = 58,000 units

Holding cost = 58,000 × $0.50 = $29,000

Total cost = $1,200 + $29,000 = $30,200

Syllabus area C2(c)

54   The correct answer is: Increased risk of bad debts
This relates to receivables, not payables.

Syllabus area C2(e)

OTQ bank – Working capital finance

55   The correct answers are:

Characteristic	Working capital strategy
Relatively high level of current assets	Conservative investment strategy
Relatively low level of current assets	Aggressive investment strategy
Relatively large amounts of short-term finance	Conservative financing strategy
Relatively small amounts of short-term finance	Aggressive financing strategy

A conservative investment policy involves carrying higher amounts of current assets, a conservative financing policy involves using more long-term finance than short-term finance.

Syllabus area C3(b)

56    $ 290,084

Receipts for March:

	$
50% March sales for cash (50% × $150,000)	75,000
80% × February credit sales less 4% discount (50% × 80% × $501,500 × 96%)	192,576
15% × January credit sales (50% × 15% × $300,100)	22,508
	290,084

Syllabus area C2(b)

57    $ 55,000

Optimum cash conversion =

$$\sqrt{\frac{2 \times 400 \times 150,000}{(0.05-0.01))}} = 54,772$$

This is 55,000 to the nearest '000.

Syllabus area C2(f)

58   The correct answers are:

- When the balance reaches $10 million they would buy $6 million of securities - **True**
- When the cash balance falls to $1 million they will sell $3 million of securities - **True**
- If the variance of daily cash flows increases the spread between upper and lower limit will be increased - **True**

Miller Orr defines the difference between the upper limit and lower limit as the 'spread'.

TB Co's spread is $10m – $1m = $9m.

Miller Orr also defines the return point as the lower limit plus a third of the spread. In this case:

1 + [(1/3) × 9] = $4m

When the upper limit is reached, sufficient securities are purchased to reduce the cash balance back to the return point. In this case $10m – $4m = $6m. Therefore statement 1 is correct.

When the lower limit is reached, sufficient securities are sold to increase the cash balance back up to the return point. In this case $4m – $1 = $3m. Therefore statement 2 is correct.

The spread is calculated as:

$$3 \left[\frac{\frac{3}{4} \times \text{transaction cost} \times \text{variance of cash flows}}{\text{interest rate}} \right]^{\frac{1}{3}}$$

An increase in variance will therefore increase the spread. Therefore statement 3 is correct.

Syllabus area C2(f)

59   The correct answers are:

Acacia's working capital funding strategy	AGGRESSIVE	
Birch's working capital funding strategy		MATCHING

Acacia has $4 million of long-term working capital finance, but permanent working capital of $6 million. Therefore it is using short-term finance for both fluctuating and some of its permanent working capital. This means its working capital funding strategy is aggressive.

Birch has $9 million of long-term working capital finance and permanent working capital of $9 million too. This means it is using short-term finance for fluctuating working capital and long-term finance for permanent working capital. Therefore this is a matching strategy.

Neither company is using long-term finance for any of its fluctuating working capital, which would be a conservative approach.

Syllabus area C3(b)

60   The correct answer is: 1 and 2 are incorrect

A conservative working capital investment policy refers to a higher amount invested in working capital. It does not relate to the proportions of permanent to fluctuating current assets so statement 1 is incorrect.

Long-term finance is not generally less expensive than short-term finance; it is more expensive as it is riskier for the lender, so statement 2 is also incorrect.

Syllabus area C3(b)

Section B questions

PKA Co (amended)

61 The correct answer is: 1 and 2 only

The two main objectives of working capital management are to ensure the business has sufficient liquid resources to continue the business and to increase its profitability. These two objectives will often conflict because liquid assets give the lowest returns. Statement 3 is therefore not correct.

Syllabus area C1(b)

62 The correct answer is: 10,000

Minimum inventory level = reorder level − (average usage × average lead time)

Average usage per week = 625,000 units/50 weeks = 12,500 units

Average lead time = 2 weeks

Reorder level = 35,000 units

Minimum inventory level = 35,000 − (12,500 × 2) = 10,000 units

Syllabus area C2(c)

63 The correct answer is: 25,000

Economic order quantity

$$EOQ = \sqrt{\frac{2C_oD}{C_h}} = \sqrt{\frac{2 \times 250 \times 625,000}{0.5}} = 25,000 \text{ units}$$

Syllabus area C2(c)

64 The correct answer is: 1 and 2 only

The key to reducing the percentage of bad debts is to assess the creditworthiness of customers. Since the industry average accounts receivable period is 75 days, PKA needs to be careful not to lose business as a result of over-stringent credit control action (such as legal action). A good approach would be to encourage early payment, for example, through early settlement discounts.

Syllabus area C2(d)

65 The correct answer is: 2 and 3 only

A factor should be able to accelerate receipts so that they are in line with PKA's terms of trade, this will reduce accounts receivable staffing costs and improve liquidity.

Notes on incorrect answers:

With-recourse factoring does not remove the risk of bad debts.

Customer relationships are more likely to deteriorate rather than improve with the use of a factor as the factor will deal with the customer when chasing debts as opposed to the company.

Syllabus area C2(d)

Plot Co

66 $ 5,454

Cost of current ordering policy

Total cost = order costs + holding costs

Ordering cost = 12 × $267 = $3,204 per year

Note. One order per month

Monthly order = monthly demand = 300,000/12 = 25,000 units

Buffer inventory = 25,000 × 0.4 = 10,000 units

Average inventory excluding buffer inventory = 25,000/2 = 12,500 units

Average inventory including buffer inventory = 12,500 + 10,000 = 22,500 units

Holding cost = 22,500 × 0.1 = $2,250 per year

Total cost = $3,204 + $2,250 = $5,454 per year

Syllabus area C2(c)

67 $ 5,000

Cost of ordering policy using economic order quantity (EOQ)

EOQ = $\sqrt{(2 \times C_o \times D)/C_h}$

EOQ = $\sqrt{(2 \times 267 \times 300,000)/0.10}$ = 40,025 per order

Number of orders per year = 300,000/40,025 = 7.5 orders per year

Order cost = 7.5 × 267 = $2,003

Average inventory excluding buffer inventory = 40,025/2 = 20,013 units

Average inventory including buffer inventory = 20,013 + 10,000 = 30,013 units

Holding cost = 30,013 × 0.1 = $3,001 per year

Total cost = $2,003 + $3,001 = $5,004 per year, so $5,000 to the nearest $100

Syllabus area C2(c)

68   The correct answer is: Cost of $17,808

Current receivables = $10m × (60/365) = $1,643,835.

Overdraft interest charge per year relating to current receivables = $1,643,835 × 10% = $164,383.50 pa

Interest saved when half customers pay cash = 0.5 × $164,383.50 = $82,191.75 per year

Annual cost of the discount = 0.5 × $10m × 2% = $100,000

Net cost of offering the early settlement discount = $100,000 – $82,191.75 = $17,808.25 cost per year

Syllabus area C1(c)

69   The correct answers are:

- A conservative working capital finance approach is low risk but expensive - **True**
- Good working capital management adds to the wealth of shareholders - **True**

In terms of working capital finance, organisations can have a conservative (mainly long-term finance) or aggressive (mainly short-term finance) approach. The former is likely to be low risk but expensive, the latter more risky but cheaper (as short-term finance is low risk from an investor's perspective).

Poor financial management of working capital can lead to cash flow difficulties or even the failure of a business. Good working capital management can also create profits and minimise costs, and this ultimately adds to the wealth of shareholders – a key objective in the vast majority of businesses.

Syllabus area C1(b)

 BPP

ANSWERS

70   The correct answers are:

  • Increasing levels of inventory

  • Increasing levels of current liabilities

The two symptoms of overtrading are increasing levels of inventory and current liabilities. Trade receivables increase during overtrading, not decrease so the first statement is not a symptom. Most of the increase in assets is financed by credit rather than long-term borrowings so the third statement is not a symptom.

Syllabus area C1(c)

Amax Co

71   The correct answer is: Benefit of $12,000 per year

Saving in ordering cost = 250 × (12 – 4) = $2,000 per year.

Increase in holding cost = 1 × [(60,000/2) – (20,000/2)] = $20,000 per year.

Purchase price of Component X = $25.00 per unit.

Annual saving using discount = 240,000 × 25 × 0.005 = $30,000 per year.

Benefit of using discount = 2,000 – 20,000 + 30,000 = $12,000 per year.

The most common errors here were to take the saving in ordering cost as a cost instead of a benefit, and get a benefit of $8,000 per year, or to use the order size as the average inventory amount and get a cost of $8,000 per year.

Syllabus area C2(d)

72   The correct answer is: Benefit of $48,000 per year

Annual purchases of Component M = 3.2m × (360/72) = $16,000,000 per year.

Revised trade payables = 16m × 30/360 = $1,333,333.

Increase in financing cost = 0.06 × (3,200,000 – 1,333,333) = $112,000 per year.

Discount saving = 16m × 0.01 = $160,000 per year.

Benefit = 160,000 – 112,000 = $48,000 per year.

The most common error here was to use the financing cost of revised trade payables, rather than of the change in trade payables and get a benefit of $80,000 per year.

Syllabus area C2(d)

73   The correct answer is: Discounting bills of exchange can reduce foreign accounts receivable default risk

It is correct that discounting bills of exchange can reduce foreign accounts receivable (FAR) default risk since it reduces the level of investment in FAR. A significant number of candidates selected the option A that suggested that an appreciation in the value of the foreign currency would be a risk, which is incorrect because companies expecting to receive foreign currency from FAR will be concerned about the risk of the foreign currency depreciating, rather than appreciating, against the domestic currency.

Syllabus area C2(d)

74   The correct answer is: Amax Co will suffer a loss of autonomy at a local level

Incorrect answer failed to recognise that centralised treasury management would be less responsive, rather than more responsive, to the requirements of local business units.

Increasing the cost of hedging was also a popular choice for candidates, but a centralised treasury department would minimise the number of hedging transactions and therefore reduce the costs of hedging foreign currency risk.

Syllabus area C2(f)

75 The correct answer is: Fluctuating current assets should be financed from a short-term source

It is correct, under the matching principle, to say that fluctuating current assets should be financed from a short-term source.

It is not correct to say that a moderate or matching strategy finances current assets from a short-term source, since the matching principle would require that permanent current assets be financed from a long-term source.

Syllabus area C3(b)

Cat Co

76 $ 907,400

Current cost = purchase cost + order cost + holding cost

Purchase cost = 120,000 units × $7.50 = $900,000 per year

Order costs = number of orders × fixed order cost = (120,000/10,000) × $200 = $2,400 per year

Holding cost = average inventory level × cost per unit per year = (10,000/2) × $1 = $5,000

Total current cost = $900,000 + $2,400 + $5,000 = $907,400.

Syllabus area C2(c)

77 $ 901,400

The cost = purchase cost + order cost + holding cost

Purchase cost = 120,000 units × $7.50 × (1 – 3.6%) = $867,600 per year

Order costs = number of orders × fixed order cost = (120,000/30,000) × $200 = $800 per year

Holding cost = average inventory level ×cost per unit per year = (30,000/2) × $2.20 = $33,000

Total cost = $867,600 + $800 + $33,000 = $901,400

Syllabus area C2(c)

78 $ 89,041

If the credit period is reduced to 60 days, receivables will become (60/365) × $25 million = $4,109,589.

This is ($5 million – $4,109,589 =) $890,411 lower than before, saving interest of 10% × $890,411 = $89,041 per year.

This interest is saved as lower receivables implies more money (lower overdraft) in the bank.

Syllabus area C2(d)

79 The correct answers are:

- The twin objectives of working capital management are profitability and liquidity
- Working capital management is a key factor in a company's long-term success

Statement 1 is **correct**. Sufficient working capital should be maintained to ensure bills can be paid on time; however, working capital (receivables, inventory, payables) do not earn a return as such, so excessive working capital is undesirable – spare cash for example should be temporarily placed to earn a return (provided risk is low).

Statement 2 is **incorrect**. A conservative approach to working capital investment implies aiming to keep relatively high levels of working capital. The reason for this is generally to reduce risk (less risk of inventory shortages, give customers plenty of time to pay, pay

ANSWERS

supplier cash) but it is expensive – it is money tied up not directly earning a return – hence will decrease profitability, not increase it.

Statement 3 is **correct**. Too much or too little working capital leads to poor business performance. Too much reduces profitability, too little is risky. Hence managing it to an appropriate level is important for a business if it is to be successful.

Statement 4 is **incorrect**. The two objectives of working capital management are to ensure the business has sufficient liquid resources and increase profitability. These objectives will often conflict as liquid assets give the lowest returns.

Syllabus area C1(b)

80   The correct answer is: Statement 2 only

Statement 1 relates to a conservative approach to financing working capital. Statement 2 relates to an aggressive approach.

Syllabus area C3(b)

Section C questions

81 Pumice Co

Marking guide			Marks	
(a)	(i)	Non-current assets	0.5	
		Revenue	0.5	
		Cost of sales	0.5	
		Inventory	1	
		Trade receivables	1	
		Trade payables	1	
		Reserves	1	
		Non-current liabilities	0.5	
		Overdraft	0.5	
		Maximum		6
	(ii)	Trade payables period	1	
		Current ratio	1	
		Revenue/net working capital	1	
		Changes	1	
				4
(b)	(i)	Aggressive investment policy	1	
		Conservative investment policy	1	
		Revenue/current assets	1	
		Changes discussion	2	
				5
	(ii)	Aggressive financing policy	1	
		Conservative financing policy	1	
		Matching financing policy	1	
		Changes discussion	2	
				5
Total				20

(a) (i) **Forecast statement of financial position for Pumice Co**

	$,000	Notes
Assets		
Non-current assets	60,018	11% increase on current value of 54,070
Current assets		
Inventory	4,394	See working 1
Trade receivables	15,979	See working 1
Cash	700	**Given in the question**
	21,073	
Total assets	**81,091**	
Equity and liabilities	$,000	
Equity	6,000	No change
Reserves	40,818	Increase by 6,818; given in the question
Total equity	46,818	
Non-current liabilities	26,000	Increase by 8,000; given in the question
Current liabilities		
Trade payables	5,273	See working 2
Overdraft	3,000	**Given in the question**
	8,273	
Total equity and liabilities	**81,091**	

Workings

1   Revenue = 80,768 × 1.187 = $95,872

    Cost of sales = 95,872 × 0.33 = $31,638

    Trade receivables = 95,872 × 60/360 = $15,979

    Inventory = 31,638 × 50/360 = $4,394

2   Trade payables = 31,638 × 60/360 = $5,273

Tutorial note. You will be provided with a spreadsheet in the exam to answer this type of question, and the basis for your calculations will therefore be available to the marker by viewing the formulae you have used in the relevant cell of the spreadsheet.

This will often mean that you do not need to show your workings separately although if the calculations are more complex the use of a separate workings section may make it easier for you to produce an accurate analysis.

The following example solution is shown in spreadsheet format with the formulae showing to illustrate one way of laying out your answer in the exam. The markers can following your workings in the cell references by looking at these formulae.

Spreadsheet

Edit Format

	A	B	C	D
1				**Forecast**
2			$000s	$000s
3	**Assets**			
4	Non-current			=54070*1.11
5	**Current assets**			
6	Inventories		=50/360*E30	
7	Trade receivables		=60/360*E29	
8	Cash etc		700	
9				=D10+D11+D12
10	**Total assets**			**=E8+E13**
11				
12	**Equity & liabilities**		$000s	$000s
13	Equity		=6000	
14	Reserves		=34000+6818	
15	**Total equity**			=D17+D18
16	**Non-current liabilities**			=18000+8000
17	**Current liabilities**			
18	Trade payables		=60/360*E30	
19	Overdraft		=3000	
20				=D22+D23
21	**Total**			**=E24+E20+E19**
22				
23	Workings			
24				
25	Credit sales			=80768*1.187
26	C.O.S			=E29*0.33

BPP

ANSWERS

(ii) *Trade payables payment period*

Currently this is (9,690/27,700) × 360 = 126 days

The company is targeting 60 days, a reduction of (126 – 60) = 66 days

Current ratio

Currently this is 17,120/13,190 = 1.30 times

After the expansion this becomes 21,073/8,273 = 2.55 times

Revenue/net working capital (NWC)

NWC currently = 4,000 + 12,320 – 9,690 = $6,630,000

Revised NWC = 4,394 + 15,979 – 5,273 = $15,100,000

Revenue/NWC currently = 80,768/6,630 = 12.18 times

Revised revenue/NWC = 95,872/15,100 = 6.35 times

(b) (i) **Changes in working capital investment policy**

Working capital investment policy considers the level of current assets used to support revenue generation in relation to different companies.

A company adopts an aggressive working capital investment policy relative to another company if it uses a lower level of current assets to support a similar level of revenue generation. Conversely, the second company adopts a conservative working capital investment policy relative to the first company.

While there are no companies here with which to compare Pumice Co's working capital investment policy, the effect of implementing the proposed changes in working capital can be measured by the revenue/current assets ratio. This shows that no significant change has occurred as a result of implementing the proposed changes in working capital, as it has only changed from 4.72 times to 4.55 times. This reflects that inventory and receivables have increased broadly in line with the increase in sales.

However, revenue/net working capital has changed from 12.18 times to 6.35 times as a result of the decreased reliance on trade payables. This is a dramatic change in policy and may create cash flow issues in future years if the company continues to grow as it represents a substantial increase in the capital required to support revenue.

Working

Revenue/current assets now = 80,768/17,120 = 4.72 times

Revised revenue/current assets = 95,872/21,073 = 4.55 times

Net working capital currently = 4,000 + 12,320 – 9,690 = $6,630,000

Revised net working capital = 4,394 + 15,979 – 5,273 = $15,100,000

Revenue/NWC currently = 80,768/6,630 = 12.18 times

Revised revenue/NWC = 95,872/15,100 = 6.35 times

(ii) **Changes in working capital funding policy**

Working capital funding policy can be characterised as conservative, matching or aggressive, depending on the extent to which fluctuating current assets and permanent current assets are financed from short-term or long-term sources.

A conservative funding policy will use long-term funds to finance permanent current assets and a proportion of fluctuating current assets. This is a lower-risk policy as long-term funds are less risky than short-term funds from a company perspective, but as long-term funds are more expensive than short-term funds, this policy also decreases profitability.

An aggressive funding policy will use short-term funds to finance fluctuating current assets and a proportion of permanent current assets. This is a higher-risk policy as short-term funds are more risky than long-term funds from a company perspective, but as short-term funds are cheaper than long-term funds, this policy also increases profitability.

A matching funding policy would apply the matching principle in using short-term funds to finance fluctuating current assets and using long-term funds to finance permanent current assets.

While there is insufficient information to determine the relative levels of permanent and fluctuating current assets, implementing the proposed changes in working capital shows a substantial movement to using long-term funds rather than short-term funds. Before the expansion, 77% of current assets are financed from short-term funds (trade payables plus overdraft). After the expansion, only 39% of current assets would be financed for short-term funds and 61% would be financed from long-term funds. This change is also apparent from the increase in the current ratio from 1.30 times to 2.55 times.

The proposed changes in working capital therefore suggest a movement by Pumice Co from an aggressive working capital funding policy to a conservative working capital funding policy.

This view is also evidenced by the $4,917,000 decrease in short-term funds relative to the $3,953,000 increase in current assets and the $14,818,000 increase in long-term funds: the company's current reliance on short-term funds has been reversed.

Working

Current assets financed by short-term funds:

Before expansion = 100 × (13,190/17,120) = 77%

After expansion = 100 × (8,273/21,073) = 39%

Decrease in short-term funds = 13,190 – 8,273 = $4,917,000

Increase in current assets = 21,073 – 17,120 = $3,953,000

Increase in long-term funds = (46,818 + 26,000) – (40,000 + 18,000) = $14,818,000

82 Pangli Co

Workbook references

Cash flow forecasting is covered in Chapter 4, liquidity ratios in Chapter 3, and managing accounts receivables is covered in Chapter 3.

Top tips

In part (a)(i), 2 marks you will need to read the question carefully to identify that you are asked to use 360 days not 365.

Part (a)(ii), this looks to be a very challenging question for the marks available. In fact because the operating cash flows are given, the only calculations required here relate to working capital movements. Ultimately, if you get stuck here you could move on to achieve most of the marks (at least 3 of the 4 marks) in part (a)(iii) and all of the 10 marks in part (b) as well

Easy marks

The discussions on trade receivables management in part (b) are straightforward.

Marking guide			Marks
(a)	(i)	Cost of sales	0.5
		Inventory days	0.5
		Receivables days	0.5
		Cash operating cycle	0.5
			2

(ii)	Inventory 31 January	0.5
	Receivables 31 January	1
	Payables 31 January	1
	Overdraft 31 January	1.5
		4
(iii)	Current ratio 1 January	2
	Current ratio 31 January	2
		4
(b)	First technique	2
	Second technique	2
	Third technique	2
	Fourth technique	2
	Fifth technique	2
		10
Total		20

(a) (i) The cash operating cycle can be calculated by adding inventory days and receivables days, and subtracting payables days.

Cost of sales = 3,500,000 × (1 – 0.4) = $2,100,000

Inventory days = 360 × 455,000/2,100,000 = 78 days

Trade receivables days = 360 × 408,350/3,500,000 = 42 days

Trade payables days = 360 × 186,700/2,100,000 = 32 days

Cash operating cycle of Pangli Co = 78 + 42 – 32 = 88 days

(ii) Inventory at end of January 20X7 = 455,000 + 52,250 = $507,250

At the start of January 20X7, 100% of December 20X6 receivables will be outstanding ($300,000), together with 40% of November 20X6 receivables ($108,350 = 40% × 270,875), a total of $408,350 as given.

	$
Trade receivables at start of January 20X7	408,350
Outstanding November 20X6 receivables paid	(108,350)
December 20X6 receivables, 60% paid	(180,000)
January 20X7 credit sales	350,000
Trade receivables at end of January 20X7	470,000

	$
Trade payables at start of January 20X7	186,700
Payment of 70% of trade payables	(130,690)
January 20X7 credit purchases	250,000
Trade payables at end of January 20X7	306,010

	$
Overdraft at start of January 20X7	240,250
Cash received from customers	(288,350)
Cash paid to suppliers	130,690
Interest payment	70,000
Operating cash outflows	146,500
Overdraft expected at end of January 20X7	299,090

(iii) Current assets at start of January 20X7 = 455,000 + 408,350 = $863,350

Current liabilities at start of January 20X7 = 186,700 + 240,250 = $426,950

Current ratio at start of January 20X7 = 863,350/426,950 = 2.03 times

Current assets at end of January 20X7 = 507,250 + 470,000 = $977,250

Current liabilities at end of January 20X7 = 306,010 + 299,090 = $605,100

Current ratio at end of January 20X7 = 977,250/605,100 = 1.62 times

(b) Pangli Co could use the following techniques in managing trade receivables: assessing creditworthiness; managing accounts receivable; collecting amounts owing; offering early settlement discounts: using factoring and invoice discounting; and managing foreign accounts receivable.

Assessing creditworthiness

Pangli Co can seek to reduce its exposure to the risks of bad debt and late payment by assessing the creditworthiness of new customers. In order to do this, the company needs to review information from a range of sources. These sources include trade references, bank references, credit reference agencies and published accounts. To help it to review this information, Pangli Co might develop its own credit scoring process. After assessing the creditworthiness of new customers, Pangli Co can decide on how much credit to offer and on what terms.

Managing accounts receivable

Pangli Co needs to make sure that its credit customers abide by the terms of trade agreed when credit was granted following credit assessment. The company wants its customers to settle their outstanding accounts on time and also to keep to their agreed credit limits. Key information here will be the number of overdue accounts and the degree of lateness of amounts outstanding. An aged receivables analysis can provide this information.

Pangli Co also needs to make sure that its credit customers are aware of the outstanding invoices on their accounts. The company will therefore remind them when payment is due and regularly send out statements of account.

Collecting amounts owing

Ideally, credit customers will pay on time and there will be no need to chase late payers. There are many ways to make payment in the modern business world and Pangli Co must make sure that its credit customers are able to pay quickly and easily. If an account becomes overdue, Pangli Co must make sure it is followed up quickly. Credit control staff must assess whether payment is likely to be forthcoming and if not, a clear policy must be in place on further steps to take. These further steps might include legal action and using the services of a debt collection agency.

Offering early settlement discounts

Pangli Co can encourage its credit customers to settle outstanding amounts by offering an early settlement discount. This will offer a reduction in the outstanding amount (the discount) in exchange for settlement before the due date. For example, if the credit customer agreed to pay in full after 40 days, an early settlement discount might offer a 2% discount for settling after 25 days.

Pangli Co must weigh the benefit of offering such an early settlement discount against the benefit expected to arise from its use by credit customers. One possible benefit might be a reduction in the amount of interest the company pays on its overdraft. Another possible benefit might be matching or bettering the terms of trade of a competitor.

Using factoring and invoice discounting

Pangli Co might use a factor to help manage its accounts receivable, either on a recourse or non-recourse basis. The factor could offer assistance in credit assessment, managing accounts receivable and collecting amounts owing. For a fee, the factor could advance a percentage of the face value of outstanding invoices. The service offered by the factor would be tailored to the needs of the company.

Invoice discounting is a service whereby a third party, usually a factor, pays a percentage of the face value of a collection of high value invoices. When the invoices are settled, the outstanding balance is paid to the company, less the invoice discounter's fee.

Managing foreign accounts receivable

Foreign accounts receivable can engender increased risk of non-payment by customers and can increase the value of outstanding receivables due to the longer time over which foreign accounts receivable are outstanding. Pangli Co could reduce the risk of non-payment by assessing creditworthiness, employing an export factor, taking out export credit insurance, using documentary credits and entering into countertrade agreements. The company could reduce the amount of investment in foreign accounts receivable through using techniques such as advances against collections and negotiating or discounting bills of exchange

---

ACCA Examining Team's Comments

Only five techniques were required to be discussed.

---

83 Kandy Co

Workbook references

Working capital management is covered in Chapter 3

Top tips

The requirements to part (a) does not tell you exactly what approach to take. Before you start your calculations you need to use the clues in the question to establish how you will approach the calculations.

Easy marks

Discussion marks in parts (b) and (c) should be straightforward (in terms of scoring a pass mark).

			Marks
(a)	(i)	Order cost (current)	0.5
		Average inventory (current)	1
		Purchase cost (current)	0.5
		New purchase price	0.5
		New ordering cost / order	0.5
		Order cost (new)	0.5
		Average inventory (new)	1
		Holding cost (new)	0.5
		Purchase cost (new)	0.5
			6
	(ii)	Purchase cost (new)	1
		Finance cost (current)	0.5
		Trade receivable (new)	1
		Finance cost (new)	0.5
		Discount cost	1
			4
	(iii)	Bulk comment	1
		Settlement comment	1
			2
(b)		Liquidity	1
		Profitability	1
		Conflict between them	2
			4
(c)		Explanation of cycle	2
		Link to investment	2
			4
Total			**20**

(a) (i) **Bulk purchase discount**

Current policy:

Buffer inventory = 18,000 x 2/360 = 100 units

Average inventory holding = (1,000/2) + 100 = 600 units

Total inventory-related cost = holding cost + purchase cost + ordering cost

Annual ordering cost = 18,000/1,000 x $75 = $1,350 per year

Annual holding cost = 600 x $30 x 0.09 = $1,620 per year

Purchase cost = 18,000 x $30 = $540,000 per year

Total inventory-related cost = $1,350 + $1,620 + $540,000 = $542,970 per year

Bulk purchase discount:

Purchase price = $30 x (1 − 0.015) = $29.55 per unit

Order cost = $75 + $25 = $100 per order

Annual ordering cost = 18,000/1,500 x $100 = $1,200 per year

Average inventory holding = (1,500/2) + 100 = 850 units

Annual holding cost = 850 x $29.55 x 0.10 = $2,512 per year

Purchase cost = 18,000 x $29.55 = $531,900 per year

Total inventory-related cost = $1,200 + $2,512 + $531,900 = $535,612 per year

(ii) **Early settlement discount**

Current situation:

30-day receivables = $45m x 0·6 x 30/360 = $2,250,000

40-day receivables = $45m x 0·4 x 40/360 = $2,000,000

Total receivables = $4,250,000

Current finance cost = $4,250,000 x 0·07 = $297,500

After introduction of discount:

10-day trade receivables = $45m x 0·5 x 10/360 = $625,000

30-day trade receivables = $45m x 0·2 x 30/360 = $750,000

40-day trade receivables = $45m x 0·3 x 40/360 = $1,500,000

Total receivables = $2,875,000

Finance cost = $2,875,000 x 0·07 = $201,250 per year

Discount cost = $45m x 0·005 x 0·5 = $112,500 per year

Total cost after introduction of the discount = $201,250 + $112,500 = $313,750 per year

(iii) **Comment on financial acceptability**

The bulk purchase discount is financially acceptable as it will reduce gimble stocking costs by $7,358 per year ($542,970 − $535,612).

The early settlement discount is not financially acceptable as it will increase costs by $16,250 ($313,750 − $297,500) per year.

(b)

The two main objectives of working capital management are to ensure profitability (generating return for investors) while at the same time ensuring liquidity (meeting its obligations when they fall due). In other words, it is about getting the right balance between current assets and current liabilities.

Having high levels of current assets can help in meeting short-term liabilities, particularly if there is a high cash balance. Good liquidity is important as it is cash which settles the liabilities, not profit. Profitable companies can still fail due to poor liquidity in the short term.

However, the problem with high levels of current assets is that they are not profitable. Cash, for example, does not generate a high return, if indeed any return at all. Holding inventory is similarly not generating any return for the company, only the sale of inventory generates the profitability. Carrying lower levels of current assets with more cash invested in long-term, non-current assets could generate higher returns for the company but would impact its ability to settle its liabilities. Consequently, there is a conflict, or trade off, between profitability and liquidity.

The bulk purchase discount Kandy Co is being offered is a good example of this conflict. By accepting the discount and buying in larger quantities, the cost is reduced (as demonstrated in a(i)), increasing profitability. But this will mean less cash in the bank due to higher levels of inventory holding. This lower level of cash will affect Kandy Co's ability to pay its current liabilities, thus liquidity will be affected.

This conflict between the two objectives is inevitable and there is no correct answer as to the level of current assets and liabilities to hold. It is for every business to determine itself.

(c)

The cash operating cycle refers to the average length of time it takes for a business to generate cash having paid for an item of inventory. In other words, having paid for the inventory, the cash operating cycle is the length of time it remains in inventory before being sold and then how long until the customer pays for it and cash is returned to the bank account.

It is calculated by adding the average inventory holding period and the average trade receivables collection period and then subtracting the average trade payables payment period.

The cash operating cycle is effectively measuring the business' liquidity in terms of cash generation – a long cash operating cycle would indicate potential liquidity problems as the business is without cash for a long time.

The relationship of the cash operating cycle with the investment in working capital is that higher levels of investment will generally increase the cash operating cycle. High inventory levels will usually mean longer inventory holding periods, increasing the cash operating cycle. High trade receivables are usually due to longer collection periods for collecting in debt, again increasing the cycle.

Finally, paying suppliers very quickly will increase the investment in working capital due to low levels of trade payables, but this will again increase the cash cycle.

ANSWERS

84 Wobnig Co (amended)

Marking guide		Marks
(a) Rapid increase in revenue	2	
Increase in trade receivables collection period	2	
Decrease in profitability	2	
Rapid increase in current assets	2	
Increased dependence on short-term finance	3	
Decrease in liquidity	3	
Conclusion as regards overtrading	1	
Marks Available	15	
Maximum		12
(b) Working capital investment policy	4	
Working capital financing policy	6	
Marks Available	10	
Maximum		8
Total		**20**

(a) Signs of overtrading:

Rapid increase in sales revenue: Wobnig Co's sales revenue has increased by 40% from $10,375k in 20X0 to $14,525k in 20X1. This rapid growth in revenue is not supported by a similar increase in long-term financing, which has only increased by 4.7% ($16,268k in 20X1 compared to $15,541k in 20X0).

Rapid increase in current assets: Wobnig Co's current assets have also nearly doubled, increasing from $2,826k in 20X0 to $5,349k in 20X1 (89%). This is striking, given that long-term financing has only increased by 4.7%. Trade receivables have increased by 85% ($1,734k in 20X0 and $3,200k in 20X1), and inventory levels have increased by 97% ($2,149k from $1,092k in 20X0).

Increase in inventory holding period: Linked to the above, inventory turnover has slowed noticeably, from 60 days in 20X0 to 75 days in 20X1, well above the industry average of 55 days. This may indicate that Wobnig Co is expecting further increases in sales volumes in the future.

Increase in receivable collection period: Perhaps a matter of greater concern is the fact that trade receivables are being paid much more slowly. Receivable days have increased from 61 days in 20X0 to 80 days in 20X1, again significantly above the industry average. It could be that in order to encourage sales, Wobnig Co has offered more favourable credit terms to its customers. However, the increase in receivable days may also indicate that Wobnig Co is lacking sufficient resources to effectively manage its receivables, and/or that its customers may be unable to settle their debts on time, as they are struggling financially.

Reduction in profitability: Although Wobnig Co's sales revenue has increased by 40% over the past year, its profit before interest and tax (PBIT) has only increased by 8.9%. The net profit margin has actually decreased, from 36% in 20X0 to 28% in 20X1. This may be due partly to the company selling at lower margins to increase sales volumes, but most likely points to increased costs of sales and operating costs.

With the additional costs associated with holding larger inventories, and increasing financing costs from overdrafts (see below), the company's profitability is likely to suffer even more in the future.

Increase in current liabilities: Wobnig Co is increasingly financed through current liabilities, which has increased by 131% (from $1,887k in 20X0 to $4,365k in 20X1) while long-term financing has increased only marginally by 4.7%. The sales revenue/net working capital ratio has increased from 11 times to 15 times in 20X1. In particular, overdraft has increased by 500% from 20X0 to 20X1. The payables payment period has lengthened from 90 days to 100 days, indicating that Wobnig Co is finding it more difficult to settle trade debts.

All of this will put further strain on financing costs, eroding the distributable profits. The company's interest expense has increased from $292k to $355k.

Reduced liquidity: The cause of Wobnig Co's increasing dependence on overdrafts and lengthening payables payment period lies in its reduced liquidity. Wobnig Co's current ratio has reduced from 1.5 times to 1.2 times, compared to the industry average of 1.7 times. The more sensitive quick ratio has reduced from 0.9 times to 0.7 times, against the average of 1.1 times. Wobnig Co does not yet have a liquid deficit, though, as its current assets still exceed its current liabilities.

Conclusion

From the trends discussed above, we can conclude that Wobnig Co is overtrading.

Working

Ratio	Formula	20X1	20X0
Net profit margin	PBIT/Revenue × 100%	28%	36%
Current ratio	Current assets/current liabilities	1.2 times	1.5 times
Quick ratio	(Current assets – inventory)/current liabilities	0.7 times	0.9 times
Inventory holding period	Inventory/cost of sales × 365	75 days	60 days
Receivables collection period	Trade receivables/revenue × 365	80 days	61 days
Payables payment period	Trade payables/cost of sales × 365	100 days	90 days
Net working capital	Current assets – current liabilities	$984,000	$949,000
Revenue/net working capital	Revenue/net working capital	15 times	11 times

Note. The Revenue/net working capital ratio can also be calculated excluding cash balances or overdraft.

(b) Working capital investment policy dictates how much a company chooses to invest in current assets. Working capital financing policy, on the other hand, determines how a company funds its day to day operations: with short-term or long-term sources. The working capital investment policy is therefore an investment decision, while the working capital financing policy is a financing decision.

Both working capital investment policy and working capital financing policy are described in terms of conservative, moderate and aggressive. However, these terms mean different things in the contexts of investment and financing.

In the context of working capital investment, a conservative policy aims to reduce the risk of system breakdown by holding high levels of working capital: generous credit terms for customers, high levels of inventory and quick payment of suppliers. This approach can result in a high financing cost and may give rise to cash flow problems. By contrast, an aggressive approach reduces financing cost and increases profitability by cutting inventories, collecting debts early from customers and delaying payment to suppliers.

In the context of working capital financing, current assets are divided into permanent current assets (the level of current assets that supports a standard level of business activity) and fluctuating assets (the level of current assets that rise and fall due to unexpected business demands). A conservative policy is one that uses long-term funding to finance most of the assets of the company, calling upon short-term financing only when fluctuations in current assets push total assets above a certain level. An aggressive policy, by contrast, is one that finances all fluctuating current assets and some permanent current assets out of short-term sources. This approach presents a greater risk of liquidity issues, but allows for lower financing costs. This is because short-term finance is cheaper than long-term finance.

Working capital investment and working capital financing therefore describe two different aspects of working capital management. In fact, it is possible for a company to adopt an aggressive working capital investment policy and a conservative working capital financing policy, or vice versa.

85 Oscar Co

Marking guide	Marks
(a) Option 1	
Revised trade receivables	1
Finance cost reduction	1
Admin savings	1
Factor fee	1
Option 2	
Bad debt saving	1
Finance cost increase	1
Factor fee	1
Comment	1
	8

	Marks
(b) Benefits	3
Oscar link	3
	6
(c) 2 marks per factor	6
	6
Total	20

(a) **Option 1**

	$	$
Current trade receivables	5,370,000	
Revised trade receivables (28,000,000 × 30/365)	2,301,370	
Reduction in receivables	3,068,630	
Reduction in financing cost = 3,068,630 × 0.07	214,804	
Reduction in admin costs	30,000	
Benefits		244,804
Factor's fee = 28,000,000 × 0.005		(140,000)
Net benefit		104,804

Option 2

	$	$
Reduction in financing cost = 3,068,630 × 0.07	214,804	
Reduction in admin costs	30,000	
Bad debts saved = 28,000,000 × 0.02	560,000	
Benefits		804,804
Increase in finance cost = 2,301,370 × 0.80 × 0.02	36,822	
Factor's fee = 28,000,000 × 0.015	420,000	
Costs		(456,822)
Net benefit		347,982

Both options are financially acceptable to Oscar Co, with Option 2 offering the greatest benefit and therefore it should be accepted.

(b) Oscar Co may benefit from the services offered by the factoring company for a number of different reasons, as follows:

Economies of specialisation

Factors specialise in trade receivables management and therefore can offer 'economies of specialisation'. They are experts at getting customers to pay promptly and may be able to achieve payment periods and bad debt levels which clients could not achieve themselves. The factor may be able to persuade the large multinational companies which Oscar Co supplies to pay on time.

Scale economies

In addition, because of the scale of their operations, factors are often able to do this more cheaply than clients such as Oscar Co could do on their own. Factor fees, even after allowing for the factor's profit margin, can be less than the clients' own receivables administration cost.

Free up management time

Factoring can free up management time and allow them to focus on more important tasks. This could be a major benefit for Oscar Co, where directors are currently spending a large amount of time attempting to persuade customers to pay on time.

Bad debts insurance

The insurance against bad debts shields clients from non-payment by customers; although this comes at a cost, it can be particularly attractive to small companies who may not be able to stand the financial shock of a large bad debt. This could well be the case for Oscar Co. As a small company which supplies much larger car manufacturing companies, it is particularly exposed to default by customers. On the other hand, it could be argued that large multinational companies are financially secure and default is unlikely, rendering bad debt insurance unnecessary.

Accelerate cash inflow

Factor finance can be useful to companies who have exhausted other sources of finance. This could be useful to Oscar Co if it cannot negotiate an increase in its overdraft limit.

Finance through growth

Although factor finance is generally more expensive than a bank overdraft, the funding level is linked to the company's volume of sales. This can help to finance expansion and protects the company against overtrading. In a rapid growth company such as Oscar Co, this could be a major advantage of factor finance.

(c) A company's working capital investment is equal to the sum of its inventories and its accounts receivable, less its accounts payable.

The following factors will determine the level of a company's investment in working capital:

The nature of the industry and the length of the working capital cycle

Some businesses have long production processes which inevitably lead to long working capital cycles and large investments in working capital. Housebuilding, for example, requires the building company to acquire land, gain government permission to build, build houses and when complete, sell them to customers. This process can often take more than a year and require large investment in work-in-progress and therefore in working capital.

Other industries, such as supermarkets, buy goods on long credit terms, have rapid inventory turnover and sell to customers for cash. They often receive payment from customers before they need to pay suppliers and therefore have little (or negative) investment in working capital.

Working capital investment policy

Some companies take a conservative approach to working capital investment, offering long periods of credit to customers (to promote sales), carrying high levels of inventory (to protect against stock-outs), and paying suppliers promptly (to maintain good relationships). This approach offers many benefits, but it necessitates a large investment in working capital.

Others take a more aggressive approach offering minimal credit, carrying low levels of inventory and delaying payments to suppliers. This will result in a low level of working capital investment.

Efficiency of management and terms of trade

If management of the components of working capital is neglected, then investment in working capital can increase. For example, a failure to apply credit control procedures such as warning letters or stop lists can result in high levels of accounts receivable. Failure to control inventory by using the EOQ model, or JIT inventory management principles, can lead to high levels of inventory.

 BPP

86 Dusty Co

> **Workbook references**
>
> Working capital management and financing are covered in Chapters 3 and 4.
>
> **Top tips**
>
> Read the discussion parts of the question carefully to make sure that you are answering the question that has been set and that are your answer relates to the scenario. Part (b) asked for a discussion of the key factors in determining working capital funding strategies. The scenario mentions that this company mainly uses long-term finance which is a good reference point for discussion points.
>
> **Easy marks**
>
> Analysis of holding and ordering costs in part (a) should form a good springboard to score pass marks in this part of the question.

Marking guide		Marks	
(a) (i) Current holding cost	0.5		
Current ordering cost	0.5		
		1	
(ii) EOQ calculation	1		
EOQ holding cost	0.5		
EOQ ordering cost	0.5		
Finance cost	1		
EOQ saving	1		
		4	
(iii) Bulk discount holding cost	0.5		
Bulk discount ordering cost	0.5		
Finance costs	1		
Bulk order discount value	1		
Bulk order discount saving overall	1		
		4	
(iv) Advice	1		
		1	
(b) Current asset types	2		
Finance cost/risk	2		
Matching principle	2		
Funding policies	2		
Other points	2		
		10	
Total		20	

(a) (i) Annual holding and ordering costs of the current inventory management system

Each current order is 1,500,000/12 = 125,000 units per order

Average inventory = 125,000/2 = 62,500 units

Current holding cost = 62,500 × 0.21 = $13,125 per year

Current ordering cost = 12 × 252 = $3,024 per year

Current total inventory management cost = $13,125 + $3,024 = $16,149 per year

> **Tutorial note.** Solutions which factor the financing cost into ordering cost (ie as $14 × 0.03 = $0.42 per unit added this to the $0.21 = $0.63), would also be acceptable. This would lead to a holding cost of $0.63 × 62,500 = $39,375 and a total inventory management cost of $42,399.

(ii) Financial effect of adopting EOQ model

EOQ = $(2 \times 252 \times 1,500,000/0.21)^{0.5}$ = 60,000 units/order

Number of orders = 1,500,000/60,000 = 25 orders per year

Average inventory = 60,000/2 = 30,000 units

Holding cost = 30,000 × 0.21 = $6,300 per year

Ordering cost = 25 × 252 = $6,300 per year

EOQ total inventory management cost = $6,300 + $6,300 = $12,600 per year

Reduction in total inventory management cost = $16,149 − $12,600 = $3,549 per year

Reduction in average inventory = (62,500 − 30,000) × 14 = $455,000

The overdraft will decrease by the same amount.

Finance cost saving = 455,000 × 0.03 = $13,650 per year

Overall saving = $3,549 + $13,650 = $17,199

> **Tutorial note.** Solutions based on factoring the financing cost into the holding cost (ie as $14 × 0.03 = $0.42 per unit added this to the $0.21 = $0.63), would also be acceptable.

(iii) Financial effect of accepting the bulk order discount

Number of orders = 1,500,000/250,000 = 6 orders per year

Average inventory = 250,000/2 = 125,000 units

Holding cost = 125,000 × 0.21 = $26,250 per year

Ordering cost = 6 × 252 = $1,512 per year

Total inventory management cost = $26,250 + $1,512 = $27,762 per year

Increase in total inventory management cost = $27,762 − $16,149 = $11,613 per year

Increase in value of average inventory = (125,000 × 13.93) − (62,500 × 14) = $866,250

The overdraft will increase by the same amount.

Finance cost increase = 866,250 × 0.03 = $25,987.5 per year

Bulk order discount = 1,500,000 × 14 × 0.005 = $105,000 per year

Overall saving = $105,000 − $11,613 − $25,987.5 = $67,399.5

[Alternatively: financing costs after the discount can be expressed as $14 × 0.995 × 0.03 = $0.4179 / unit and this can be added to $0.21 so that total holding costs (including financing costs) = $0.6279. If so, total holding costs = 125,000 × 0.6279 = $78,487.5 per year including financing costs and total inventory management cost = $78,487.5 + $1,512 ordering cost + $21,000,000 purchasing cost − $105,000 discount = $20,974,999.5.

Compared to current inventory costs of $42,399 (see tutorial note from (a)(i)) + $21,000,000 purchasing costs = $21,042,399, this is a saving of $67,399.5.]

BPP

(iv) The bulk order discount saves $67,399.5 compared to the current position, while the EOQ approach saves $17,199.

The bulk order discount is recommended as it leads to the greater cost saving.

(b) **Key factors in determining working capital funding strategies**

Permanent and fluctuating current assets

One key factor when discussing working capital funding strategies is to distinguish between permanent and fluctuating current assets. Permanent current assets represent the core level of current assets needed to support normal levels of business activity, for example, the level of trade receivables associated with the normal level of credit sales and existing terms of trade. Business activity will be subject to unexpected variations, however, such as some customers being late in settling their accounts, leading to unexpected variations in current assets. These can be termed fluctuating current assets.

Relative cost and risk of short-term and long-term finance

A second key factor is the relative cost of short-term and long-term finance. The normal yield curve suggests that long-term debt finance is more expensive than short-term debt finance, for example, because of investor liquidity preference or default risk. Provided the terms of loan agreements are adhered to and interest is paid when due, however, long-term debt finance is a secure form of finance and hence low risk.

While short-term debt finance is lower cost than long-term debt finance, it is higher risk. For example, an overdraft is technically repayable on demand, while a short-term loan is subject to the risk that it may be renewed on less favourable terms than those currently enjoyed.

Matching principle

A third key factor is the matching principle, which states that the maturity of assets should be reflected in the maturity of the finance used to support them. Short-term finance should be used for fluctuating current assets, while long-term finance should be used for permanent current assets and non-current assets.

Relative costs and benefits of different funding policies

A fourth key factor is the relative costs and benefits of different funding policies.

A matching funding policy would use long-term finance for permanent current assets and non-current assets, and short-term finance for fluctuating current assets. A conservative funding policy would use long-term finance for permanent current assets, non-current assets and some of the fluctuating current assets, with short-term finance being used for the remaining fluctuating current assets. An aggressive funding policy would use long-term finance for the non-current assets and part of the permanent current assets, and short-term finance for fluctuating current assets and the balance of the permanent current assets.

A conservative funding policy, using relatively more long-term finance, would be lower in risk but lower in profitability. An aggressive funding policy, using relatively more short-term finance, would be higher in risk but higher in profitability. A matching funding policy would balance risk and profitability, avoiding the extremes of a conservative or an aggressive funding policy.

Other key factors

Other key factors in working capital funding strategies include managerial attitudes to risk, previous funding decisions and organisation size. Managerial attitudes to risk can lead to a company preferring one working capital funding policy over another.

For example, a risk-averse managerial team might prefer a conservative working capital funding policy.

Previous funding decisions dictate the current short-term/long-term financing mix of a company. Organisational size can be an important factor in relation to, for example, access to different forms of finance in support of a favoured working capital funding policy.

87 KXP Co (amended)

Marking guide	Marks
(a) Revised trade receivables	0.5
Reduction in trade receivables	0.5
Reduction in financing cost	1
Cost of early settlement discount	1
Net cost of change in receivables policy	1
Comment on findings	1
	5
(b) Current annual ordering cost	0.5
Current holding cost	0.5
Total cost of current inventory policy	0.5
Revised cost of materials	0.5
Revised number of orders	0.5
Revised ordering cost	0.5
Revised holding cost	0.5
Net benefit of bulk purchase discount	0.5
Comment on assumptions	1
	5
(c) Transactions need for cash	2
Precautionary need for cash	2
Speculative need for cash	2

Other relevant discussion	2
Marks Available	8
Maximum	5
(d) Credit analysis	2
Credit control	2
Receivables collection	2
Cost and benefits of trade receivables policy	2
Marks Available	8
Maximum	5
Total	**20**

(a) **Cost/benefit of changing trade receivables policy**

Receivables paying within 30 days = 50% × $15m × 30/365 = $616,438

Receivables paying after 45 days = 30% × $15m × 45/365 = $554,795

Total receivables changing their payment patterns = $616,438 + $554,795 = $1,171,233

Original value of these receivables = 80% × $2,466k = $1,972,800

Reduction in receivables = **$801,567**

Cost of early payment discount = 50% × $15m × 1% = $75,000

Reduction in financing cost = $801,567 × 6% = $48,094

Net cost of changing trade receivables policy = $75,000 − $48,094 = **$26,906**

Alternative calculation for the reduction in receivables

Current receivable collection period = $2,466k/$15,000k × 365 = 60 days

Receivable days under new trade receivables policy = 50% × 30 + 30% × 45 + 20% × 60 = 40.5 days

Decrease in receivable collection period = 60 − 40.5 = 19.5 days

Reduction in receivables = $15m × 19.5/365 = **$801,370** (difference due to rounding)

Conclusion

The benefit of the new trade receivables policy is outweighed by the associated costs. KXP Co should not adopt the proposed policy. However, the analysis currently excludes bad debts and assumes constant sales throughout the year – the company may need to take these into account. Given that receivables on average are failing to meet the credit period, KXP Co may still want to consider how the trade receivables policy may be changed in order to encourage earlier payment.

(b) Total annual cost of inventory policy = cost of materials + ordering cost + holding cost

Current policy

Annual ordering cost = 12 × $150 = $1,800

Annual holding cost = $0.24 × (15,000/2) = $1,800

Total annual cost = $540,000 + $1,800 + $1,800 = $543,600

Proposed policy

Annual cost of materials = $540,000 × 98% = $529,200

KXP Co currently requires 180,000 units of Product Z per year (12 × 15,000).

To benefit from the bulk discount, KXP Co needs to order 30,000 units each time. This means KXP Co will make 6 orders per year (180,000/30,000).

Revised annual ordering cost = 6 × $150 = $900

Revised annual holding cost = $0.24 × (30,000/2) = $3,600

Total annual cost = $529,200 + $900 + $3,600 = $533,700

Net benefit

Net benefit of taking bulk purchase discount = $543,600 – $533,700 = $9,900

Conclusion

The analysis shows that the bulk discount should be accepted. However, KXP Co may wish to evaluate the appropriateness of a number of key assumptions first:

- Demand for Product Z is constant throughout the year, and does not change from year to year.
- Ordering costs and holding costs are both constant throughout the year.

(c) The optimum level of cash to be held by a company depends on the following factors:

The level of cash required for the company's operations

This includes holding enough cash to:

- Pay for the transactions expected to occur during the period (including the payment of suppliers, and finance costs). This can be achieved by drawing up a cash budget.
- Cover unexpected expenditure and account for uncertainty in the cash budget. In addition to the cash needs forecasted in the cash budget, the company needs to have a precautionary 'buffer' for unexpected events. This can be estimated based on previous experience.

The availability of finance

Not all sources of finance may be available to a company. A small or medium-sized company, for example, may not be able to obtain or extend bank loans as easily. An unlisted company will find it very difficult, and expensive, to raise funds through issuing securities. Where it is difficult and/or expensive to raise new finance, a company will need to hold more cash.

The availability and attractiveness of other uses for the cash

The amount of cash that a company holds will also depend on whether there are other, more attractive ways to use the cash. Instead of holding cash for no return, a company usually has the option of putting the cash in a deposit account with a bank, investing it in short- or long-term debt instruments, or investing in equity shares of listed companies. The extent to which the company will consider these alternative uses depends on the amount of investment required, the expected level of return (interest, dividends or capital growth), the term to maturity and the ease of realising the investment.

A company may also wish to hold cash in order to be able to take advantage of an unexpected speculative opportunity when it arises.

(d) Factors to consider in formulating a trade receivables management policy

The total credit

Each company must determine the level of total credit it is willing to offer. This involves finding a balance between maximising revenue from customers, and minimising the finance costs associated with funding the period of credit and also minimising bad debts.

Allowing a long period of credit may attract more sales, but the company may suffer from high finance costs. A short period of credit will reduce the need for additional finance, but the company may lose out on sales opportunities.

The cost of the additional finance – be it bank overdraft interest, loans or equity – must be considered.

Credit control

Companies need to have a policy in place for assessing the creditworthiness of customers. Verifying that new customers are creditworthy before concluding the sale reduces the risk of customer default.

This may involve requiring references for new customers, checking credit ratings through a credit rating agency, and offering a lower level of credit for new customers. A credit rating system may be devised to determine the appropriate level of credit to offer to new customers based on their characteristics (such as age and occupation).

Collection

A credit policy can only be maintained if it is policed effectively and the amounts owing collected. The company will need to monitor customers' payment records to ensure that the credit limits are maintained. An aged receivables analysis should be performed on a regular basis. Any breaches of credit limits should be brought to the attention of the credit controller.

Factors which would influence how tightly a company polices its credit policy include the number of customers requiring more credit, and the extent to which the company is exposed to accounts receivable.

The associated costs of collection, either internal or external, also need to be considered. The costs of collection should not be greater than the amount collected.

Changes to the credit policy

The credit policy needs to be reviewed regularly and revised as economic conditions and customer payment patterns change. The company may wish to assess whether it is beneficial to offer an early payment discount to encourage customers to pay earlier, or extend the credit period to encourage custom.

The associated costs and impact on the company's working capital must be considered. Only when the financial benefit of the change in policy outweighs the additional costs should the change go ahead.

88 CSZ Co (amended)

Workbook references.

The working capital cycle and liquidity ratios are covered in Chapter 3.

Top tips.

There are two requirements in part (a) and two requirements in part (b). Make sure that you don't accidentally miss out some of the requirements. You may have been thrown by the mention of a negative working capital cycle but, if you think about what the cycle actually means, you should be able to see that a negative cycle is possible.

Easy marks.

There are easy marks for calculations in part (a) and part (b) if you know the liquidity ratios.

ACCA examining team's comments.

The examining team commented that in part (a), many students incorrectly stated that the working capital cycle should be positive. Many students gained good marks in part (b). For part (c) some students discussed at length possible reasons for the changes in inventory, trade payables, trade receivables and so on, often writing as though the changes had occurred rather than having been forecast. The only discussion that was specifically required was in the area of working capital financing. This emphasises the need to read the question requirement carefully and to respond directly to what is required.

	Marks
(a) Inventory holding period	0.5
Trade receivables collection period	0.5
Trade payables payment period	0.5
Working capital cycle	0.5
Discussion of working capital cycle	4
	6
(b) Cost of sales	0.5
Inventory	0.5
Trade receivables	0.5
Current assets	0.5
Current liabilities	0.5
Target quick ratio	1
Net working capital cycle	0.5
Target sales/net working capital ratio	1
	5
(c) Trade payables	1
Overdraft	1
Analysis of current asset and liability positions	3
Comparison of current asset and liability positions	3
Discussion of change in financing policy	3
Marks Available	11
Maximum	9
Total	**20**

(a) Workings:

					Days
Inventory holding period	=	(Average inventory/ cost of sales) × 365	(5,500/26,000) × 365	=	80
A/cs receivable collection period	=	(Trade receivables/ credit sales revenue) × 365	(6,575/40,000) × 365	=	60
A/cs payable payment period	=	(Trade payables/ cost of sales) × 365	(2,137/26,000) × 365	=	(30)
		Working capital cycle:			110

The working capital cycle is the **period of time** which elapses between the point at which **cash begins to be expended** on the production of a product and the **collection of cash from a customer**. Therefore CSZ Co starts spending 110 days (on average) before cash is collected from the customer.

A **negative** working capital cycle would mean that CSZ Co was **paid by customers before** it started to **spend cash** on the **production**. This can sometimes occur. For example, supermarkets often receive payment for goods before they have paid for them.

A business does **not normally have a choice** on whether its working capital cycle is positive or negative because it depends on the inventory, receivables and payables days and these usually **depend** on the **nature of the business**. The length of the working capital cycle is usually **similar between** businesses in the **same sector**.

(b) Quick ratio = (current assets – inventory)/current liabilities = 8,219 / (5,073 + 3,616) = 0.95 times

Inventory holding period = 60 = (inventory/cost of sales) × 365 so (60 × 24,000)/ 365 = inventory = $3,945

Receivables collection period = 75 = (receivables/sales) × 365 so (75 × 40,000)/ 365 = receivables = $8,219

Payables payment period = 55 = (payables/cost of sales) × 365 so (55 × 24,000)/ 365 = payables = $3,616

Current ratio = (3,919 + 8,219) / (3,616 + overdraft) = 1.4

so 3,616 + overdraft = (3,919 + 8,219) / 1.4, so overdraft = $5,073

Net current assets at the end of March 20X5 = $3,945k + $8,219k – $3,616k – $5,073k

= $3,475,000

Target sales = $40m

Target ratio of sales to net working capital = 40,000/3,475 = 11.5 times

Note. The sales/net working capital ratio can also be calculated excluding cash balances or overdraft.

(c) The current liabilities at the end of March 20X5, calculated in part (b), can be divided into trade payables and the forecast overdraft balance.

Trade payables using target trade payables payment period = 24,000,000 × 55/365 = $3,616,438.

The overdraft (balancing figure) = 8,688,846 – 3,616,438 = $5,072,408

Comparing current assets and current liabilities:

	March 20X4		March 20X5	
	$'000	$'000	$'000	$'000
Inventory	5,700		3,945	
Trade receivables	6,575	12,275	8,219	12,164
Overdraft	2,137		3,616	
	4,682	6,819	5,072	8,688
Net current assets		5,456		3,476

The overdraft as a percentage of current liabilities will fall from 69% (4,682/6,819) to 58% (5,702/8,688). Even though the overdraft is expected to increase by 8.3%, current liabilities are expected to increase by 27.4% (8,688/6,819). Most of this increase is expected to be carried by trade payables, which will rise by 69.2% (3,616/2,317), with the trade payables payment period increasing from 30 days to 55 days.

At the end of March 20X4, current liabilities were 56% of current assets (100 × 6,819/12,275), suggesting that 44% of current assets were financed from a long-term source. At the end of March 20X5, current liabilities are expected to be 71% of current assets (100 × 8,688/12,164), suggesting that 29% of current assets are finance from a long-term source. This increasing reliance on short-term finance implies an aggressive change in the working capital financing policy of CSZ Co.

 BPP

89 Flit Co (amended)

Marking guide	Marks	
(a) Monthly receivables	1	
Loan	0.5	
Raw materials	1	
Variable costs	1	
Machine	0.5	
Closing balances	1	
		5
(b) Closing finished goods inventory	0.5	
Closing trade receivables	0.5	
Closing trade payables	0.5	
Current ratio	0.5	
		2
(c) Temporary nature of short-term cash surplus	1	
Investment should have no risk of capital loss	1	
Shares are not suitable for investment	1	
		3
(d) Discussion of Baumol model 2–3 marks per valid point	5	
Maximum		5
(e) Calculation of spread	1	
Calculation of upper limit	1	
Calculation of return point	1	
Explanation of findings	2	
		5
Total		20

(a) Workings:

	Jan	Feb	Mar
	$'000	$'000	$'000
Sales revenue (W1)	960	1,000	1,092
Loan income			300
Total cash receipts	960	1,000	1,392
Production costs (W2)	500	520	560
Variable overheads (W3)	130	140	150
Machine purchase			400
Total cash payments	630	660	1,110
Net surplus	330	340	282
Opening balance	40	370	710
Closing balance	370	710	992

Workings

1 **Sales**

Month of sale				Cash received
Dec	1,200 units × $800	=	$960,000	Jan
Jan	1,250 units × $800	=	$1,000,000	Feb
Feb	1,300 units × $800 × 1.05	=	$1,092,000	Mar

2 **Production costs (W2)**

Month of production				Cash paid
Dec	1,250 units × 2 units × $200	=	$500,000	Jan
Jan	1,300 units × 2 units × $200	=	$520,000	Feb
Feb	1,400 units × 2 units × $200	=	$560,000	Mar

3   *Variable overheads*

Month of production			Cash paid	
Jan	1,300 units × $100	=	$130,000	Jan
Feb	1,400 units × $100	=	$140,000	Feb
Mar	1,500 units × $100	=	$150,000	Mar

(b) Current ratio = current assets / current liabilities

Current assets

Inventory = finished goods for April sales of 1,500 units

Cost of production = materials + variable costs = $400 + $100 = $500 per unit

1,500 units × $500 = $750,000

Cash = $992,000

Trade receivables = March 1,400 units × $800 × 1.05 = $1,176,000

Current liabilities

Trade payables = cash owed for March raw materials = 1,500 units × 2 units × $200 = $600,000

∴ Current ratio = (750,000 + 992,000 + 1,176,000) / 600,000 = 4.9 times

(c) When investing a cash flow surplus the company should consider the following.

Liquidity ie how quickly and easily an asset can be converted into cash.

Shares in a listed company on a large stock market should be liquid.

Profitability. The company should seek to obtain a good return for the risk incurred.

A good return on shares usually requires a long-term investment. However, the cash flow surplus is only temporary ie short-term.

Safety ie the risk of the asset reducing in value.

Share values can go down as well as up which could lead to capital losses and this may cause significant problems in meeting future cash outflows if the cash is needed in the short-term, as is the case here.

The question states that the surplus is a short-term surplus. Investing in shares is therefore inappropriate. Placing funds in a deposit account with a bank would be more appropriate.

(d) **The Baumol model and cash management**

A number of different cash management models indicate the optimum amount of cash that a company should hold. One such model is based on the idea that deciding on optimum cash balances is like deciding on optimum inventory levels, and suggests the optimum amount to be transferred regularly from investments to current account.

We can distinguish two types of cost which are involved in obtaining cash:

(1)   The fixed cost represented, for example, by the issue cost of equity finance or the cost of negotiating an overdraft

(2)   The variable cost (opportunity cost) of keeping the money in the form of cash

The Baumol approach has the following drawbacks for companies such as Flit Co.

(1) In reality, it is unlikely to be possible to predict amounts required over future periods with much certainty.

(2) No buffer inventory of cash is allowed for. There may be costs associated with running out of cash.

(3) There may be other normal costs of holding cash, which increase with the average amount held.

(4) It assumes constant transaction costs and interest rates.

(e) **Determination of spread**

Daily interest rate = 5.11/365 = 0.014% per day

Variance = (standard deviation)^2 so variance of cash flows = 1,000 × 1,000 = $1,000,000 per day

Transaction cost = $18 per transaction

Spread = 3 × ((0.75 × transaction cost × variance)/interest rate)1/3

= 3 × ((0.75 × 18 × 1,000,000)/0.00014)1/3 = 3 × 4,585.7 = $13,757

Lower limit = $7,500

Upper limit = $(7,500 + 13,757) = $21,257

Return point = $7,500 + ($13,757/3) = $12,086

Relevance of the values

The Miller-Orr model takes account of **uncertainty** in relation to cash flows. The cash balance of Renpec Co is allowed to vary between the lower and upper **limits** calculated by the model.

If the cash balance reaches an **upper limit** the firm **buys sufficient securities** to return the cash balance to a normal level (called the 'return point'). When the cash balance reaches a lower limit, the firm sells securities to bring the balance back to the return point.

The Miller-Orr model therefore helps Renpec Co to decrease the risk of running out of cash, while avoiding the loss of profit caused by having unnecessarily high cash balances.

90 Widnor Co (amended)

Marking guide	Marks	
(a) Reduction in trade receivables	1	
Reduction in financing cost	1	
Reduction in administration costs	1	
Saving in bad debts	1	
Increase in financing cost	1	
Advice on acceptance of factor's offer	1	
Advice on acceptance of factor's offer	1	
		7
(b) Bank and other references	1	
Credit rating	1	
Other relevant discussion	1	
		3
(c) Relevant discussion 2–3 marks per valid point		
Maximum		10
Total		20

(a) The factor's offer will be financially acceptable to Widnor Co if it results in a net benefit rather than a net cost.

	$	$
Current trade receivables	4,458,000	
Revised trade receivables = 26,750,000 × 35/360 =	2,600,694	
Reduction in trade receivables	1,857,306	
Reduction in financing cost = 1,857,306 × 0.05 =	92,865	
Saving in bad debts = 26,750,000 × 0.01 × 0.7 =	187,250	
Reduction in administration costs	50,000	
Benefits		330,115
Increase in financing cost = 2,600,694 × 0.8 × 0.07 – 0.05 =	41,611	
Factor's annual fee = 26,750,000 × 0.0075 =	200,625	
Costs		(242,236)
Net benefit		87,879

The factor's offer is therefore financially acceptable.

(b) The creditworthiness of potential customers can be assessed from a range of different sources of information. References are useful in this respect, and potential customers should supply a bank reference and a trade or other reference when seeking credit on purchases. Another source of information is the credit rating of the potential customer, which can be checked by a credit rating agency or credit reference agency. For larger potential customers, a file can be opened where additional information can be located, evaluated and stored, such as the annual report and accounts of the potential customer, press releases and so on.

(c) **Risks arising from granting credit to foreign customers**

Foreign debts raise the following special problems. When goods are sold abroad, the customer might ask for credit. Exports take time to arrange, and there might be complex paperwork. Transporting the goods can be slow, if they are sent by sea. These **delays in foreign trade** mean that exporters often build up **large investments** in inventories and accounts receivable. These working capital investments have to be financed somehow.

The **risk of bad debts** can be greater with foreign trade than with domestic trade. If a foreign customer refuses to pay a debt, the exporter must pursue the debt in the customer's own country, where procedures will be subject to the laws of that country.

How risks can be managed and reduced

A company can reduce its investment in foreign accounts receivable by insisting on **earlier payment** for goods. Another approach is for an exporter to arrange for a **bank to give cash for a foreign debt**, sooner than the exporter would receive payment in the normal course of events. There are several ways in which this might be done.

Where the exporter asks their bank to handle the collection of payment (of a bill of exchange or a cheque) on their behalf, the bank may be prepared to make an **advance** to the exporter against the collection. The amount of the advance might be 80% to 90% of the value of the collection.

Negotiation of bills or cheques is similar to an advance against collection, but would be used where the bill or cheque is payable outside the exporter's country (for example in the foreign buyer's country).

Discounting bills of exchange is where a bank buys the bill before it is due and credits the value of the bill after a discount charge to the company's account.

Export factoring could be considered where the exporter pays for the specialist expertise of the factor in order to reduce bad debts and the amount of investment in foreign accounts receivable.

Documentary credits provide a method of payment in international trade, which gives the exporter a secure risk-free method of obtaining payment. The buyer (a foreign buyer, or a domestic importer) and the seller (a domestic exporter or a foreign supplier) first of all agree a contract for the sale of the goods, which provides for payment through a documentary credit. The buyer then requests a bank in their country to issue a letter of credit in favour of the exporter. The issuing bank, by issuing its letter of credit, guarantees payment to the beneficiary.

Countertrade is a means of financing trade in which goods are exchanged for other goods.

Export credit insurance is insurance against the risk of non-payment by foreign customers for export debts. If a credit customer defaults on payment, the task of pursuing the case through the courts will be lengthy, and it might be a long time before payment is eventually obtained.

Premiums for export credit insurance are, however, very high and the potential benefits might not justify the cost.

OTQ bank – Investment decisions

91 $\boxed{49}$ %

Return on capital employed = Average annual accounting profits/Average investment

Average annual accounting profits = (16,500 + 23,500 + 13,500 − 1,500)/4 = $13,000 p.a.

Note. accounting profits are **after** depreciation so no adjustment is required.

Average investment = (initial investment + scrap)/2 = ($46,000 + $7,000)/2 = $26,500

ROCE = 13,000/26,500 = 49%

Syllabus area D1(d)

92 The correct answer is: 1 year 7 months

Payback period is the amount of time taken to repay the initial investment.

Time		Profit	Depreciation*	Cash flow	Cumulative cash flow
		$	$	$	$
0	Investment			(46,000)	(46,000)
1	Cash inflow	16,500	9,750	26,250	(19,750)
2	Cash inflow	23,500	9,750	33,250	13,500

* Depreciation = ($46,000 − $7,000)/4

Payback period = 1 + (19,750/33,250) = 1.59 years or 1 year 7 months to the nearest month.

Syllabus area D1(b)

93 The correct answer is: ROCE takes into account all years of operation of an investment project

A common error was to elect the options linking ROCE to accepting or rejecting a project, not recognising that investment decisions should be made on the basis of discounted cash flows and that there is no relationship between ROCE and the weighted average cost of capital which would lead to good investment decisions.

Syllabus area D1(d)

94 The correct answer is: $400 benefit

The $1,000 is sunk. If the chemical is used in a new project it would save SW Co $400 that it would otherwise have to spend to dispose of the chemical. This equates to an effective net cash inflow (or, more precisely, the avoidance of an outflow) of $400. Thus the project appraisal should show an inflow of $400 in relation to using this chemical.

Syllabus area D1(a)

95 The correct answer is: $20,000

We assume BLW Co would choose the cheapest source of labour.

Cost to buy in = $20 × 1,000 hours = $20,000

Cost to divert existing labour = lost contribution + labour cost ie ($10 + $15) × 1,000 hours = $25,000

The cheapest alternative is therefore to buy in at a cost of $20,000.

To calculate how the existing BLW Co project would suffer as a result of diverting labour, the current labour cost is added back to the lost contribution to give the full impact of diverting labour away from its current role.

Syllabus area D1(a)

96   The correct answer is: $14,000

The current rental cost is $5,000. The net new rental cost, should the project proceed, would be ($17,000 + $5,000 − $3,000) = $19,000, so an increment of $19,000 − $5,000 = $14,000.

Syllabus area D1(a)

97   The correct answer is: It doesn't measure the potential impact on shareholder wealth

On the assumption that the basic reason for approving a project is that it will increase shareholder wealth, a major drawback of the payback period is that it does not attempt to measure the impact on shareholder wealth should the project go ahead.

Notes on incorrect answers:

The 1st statement is a benefit, not a drawback.

The 2nd statement is incorrect. The payback period does not take account of the time value of money.

The 4th statement is incorrect. The calculation is not based on profit.

Syllabus area D1(b)

98   The correct answer is: Neither 1 nor 2

The ROCE calculation is as follows

Depreciation per year = $9,000/5 years = $1,800

Profit per year = $3,000 − $1,800 = $1,200

ROCE = Profit/Initial investment = $1,200/$9,000 = 13.33%

The target ROCE is 15% therefore the project would be rejected.

Project payback calculation = $9,000/$3,000 = 3 years

Target payback is 2.5 years therefore the project would be rejected.

Therefore the correct answer is neither 1 nor 2.

Syllabus area D1(b,d)

99 | 5.0 | %.

A payback of 20 years suggests net annual inflow of 50,000/20 = $2,500 per year.

Return on capital employed (ROCE) = Average annual accounting profit/Average investment.

Average annual accounting profit = $2,500 cash inflows less depreciation.

Depreciation = 50,000/40 = $1,250 per year.

So average annual accounting profit = $2,500 − $1,250 = $1,250.

Average investment = ($50,000 + 0)/2 = $25,000.

Therefore ROCE = $1,250/$25,000 = 0.05 or 5% per year.

Syllabus area D1(d)

100   The correct answer is: Because her salary is not incremental

The cost should not feature in the project appraisal as the accountant is paid anyway, ie her salary is not incremental.

Syllabus area D1(a)

OTQ bank – Investment appraisal using DCF

101 $\boxed{21{,}924}$

The present value of the annuity = $\$7{,}000 \times AF_{3\text{-}7}$

where $AF_{3\text{-}7}$ is the 10% annuity factor from years 3–7 inclusive.

$AF_{3\text{-}7} = AF_{1\text{-}7} - AF_{1\text{-}2}$

$= 4.868 - 1.736$ (from tables)

$= 3.132$

Therefore the present value = $\$7{,}000 \times 3.132 = \$21{,}924$

Syllabus area D1(e)

102 The correct answer is: Option 2 because it is worth more in present value terms

Step 1 Calculate the future value of the perpetuity using the cost of capital

$\$90{,}000/0.1 = \$900{,}000$

Step 2 Discount it back to today using a discount factor of 10% at the end of year 2

$PV = \$900{,}000 \times 0.826 = \$743{,}400$

Alternatively, the PV can be calculated using a discount factor of $[1/r -$ annuity factor for time periods 1–2]. This gives $\$90{,}000 \times (1/0.1 - 1.736) = \$743{,}760$ which would be the same answer as the PV of $\$743{,}400$ if the discount factors (in both methods) were calculated to more than 3 decimal places. Either approach would be acceptable.

Option 2

The present value of the lump sum = $\$910{,}000 \times DF_1$

Where DF_1 is the 1 year 10% discount factor from tables = 0.909

So present value of lump sum = $\$910{,}000 \times 0.909 = \$827{,}190$

The lump sum should be chosen because it has a higher net present value.

Syllabus area D1(e)

103 $\boxed{700}$

Remember that a cash outlay or receipt which occurs at the beginning of a time period is taken to occur at the end of the previous year. Therefore an inflow of $\$12{,}000$ in advance for 5 years (ie starting now) is taken to occur in years 0, 1, 2, 3 and 4.

NPV at 10%:

Time		$	DF 10%	PV $
0	Investment	(40,000)	1	(40,000)
0–4	Net cash inflows	12,000	1 + 3.17 = 4.17	50,040
5	Decommissioning	(15,000)	0.621	(9,315)
	Net present value			725

= $\$700$ to the nearest $\$100

Syllabus area D1(e)

 BPP

104 | 13.3 | %

$$IRR = a + \left[\frac{NPV_a}{NPV_a - NPV_b} \times (b-a) \right]$$

Where:

a = lower % discount rate

b = higher % discount rate

NPV_a = NPV at a%

NPV_b = NPV at b%

NPV at 10% = $5,820

Time		$	DF 10%	PV $
0	Investment	(70,000)	1	(70,000)
1–5	Net cash inflows	20,000	3.791	75,820
	Net present value			5,820

NPV at 15%:

Time		$	DF 15%	PV $
0	Investment	(70,000)	1	(70,000)
1–5	Net cash inflows	20,000	3.352	67,040
	Net present value			(2,960)

Therefore IRR = 10% + [(5,820/(5,820 + 2,960)) × (15% – 10%)] = 13.3%(to one decimal place)

Note that cash flows are assumed to be in arrears unless a question states otherwise, this is why the cash inflows are assumed to arise in time periods 1 to 5.

Syllabus area D1(f)

105 The correct answer is:

	NPV	IRR	ROCE	PP
Project D	$1.5m	12%	18%	7 years

The project with the highest NPV will maximise shareholder wealth as NPV directly measures the impact on shareholder wealth.

Syllabus area D1(g)

106 The correct answers are:

- Clear decision rule - **Incorrect**
- Takes into account the time value of money - **Correct**
- Assumes funds are reinvested at the IRR - **Incorrect**
- Considers the whole project - **Correct**

Statement 1 is not an advantage. The decision rule depends on the shape of the IRR curve. There could be several IRRs and whether the IRR needs to be higher or lower than the cost of capital depends on the project cash flows.

Statement 2 is an advantage. IRR is a discounting technique hence takes into account the time value of money.

Statement 3 is a disadvantage. The 'reinvestment assumption' is a flaw in IRR. There is no reason to suppose that funds generated early on in a project will be reinvested at the IRR after that point. The funds may well be distributed elsewhere.

Statement 4 is an advantage. Unlike the payback period, the IRR considers **all** of the future incremental cash flows associated with a decision in its calculation.

Syllabus area D1(f)

107 The correct answers are:

Item	Impact
	Increase
IRR	No change
NPV	Decrease

A higher cost of capital will discount future inflows more heavily, reducing the NPV of the project.

The cost of capital does not feature in the calculation of the IRR, only in the decision rule that follows the calculation.

108 The correct answer is: $4,981

The net present value of the agreement is $26,496, hence:

$26,496	$= (\$a \times AF_{1-4}) + 10{,}000$	Where AF_{1-4} is the 4-year 8% annuity factor
$16,496	$= \$a \times 3.312$	(from tables)
$a	$= \$16{,}496/3.312$	
	$= \$4{,}981$	

Syllabus area D1(e)

109 The correct answer is: Two NPV calculations are needed to estimate the IRR using linear interpolation

The IRR formula requires two NPV calculations at different rates to estimate the IRR.

The 2nd statement is inaccurate. Linear interpolation is still an estimate. It is not 100% precise.

The 3rd statement is inaccurate. There may be more than one IRR. It depends on whether the cash flows are conventional or not.

The 4th statement is not necessarily true. For example, an unusual project with an initial large inflow followed by years of outflows will have a positive slope.

Syllabus area D1(h)

110    $ \boxed{223,400}

The present value of the holiday home = $1.5m × (DF for time 5 at 10%) = $1.5m × 0.621 = $931,500

Therefore the present value of the annuity = $931,500.

$931,500 = $a × AF_{0-4}

Where AF_{0-4} is the annuity factor from time 0 to time 4

AF_{0-4} = 1 + AF_{1-4} = 1 + 3.170 = 4.170

So $931,500 = $a × 4.170

$a = $931,500/4.170

    = $223,381 or $223,400 to the nearest $100

Syllabus area D1(e)

OTQ bank – Allowing for tax and inflation

111   The correct answer is: $68,175

The asset is purchased on 31 December 20X4 (T0) so the first portion of tax-allowable depreciation is accounted for on that date (as this is the end of the year). The amount of the depreciation would be $1m × 25% = $250,000.

Claiming this allowance will save ($250,000 × 30% =) $75,000 tax when it is paid at T1 (one-year delay) hence the present value = $75,000 × DF_1 = $75,000 × 0.909 = $68,175.

Syllabus area D2(b)

112   The correct answer is: $145,454

As tax is paid one year in arrears, the $20,000 and associated tax are treated separately:

PV of perpetuity: $20,000 × 1/0.1 = $200,000

Less PV of tax: ($20,000 × 30%) × (AF_{2-\infty})

AF_{2-\infty} = (1/0.1) − DF_1 = 10 − 0.909 = 9.091

PV of tax = $20,000 × 30% × 9.091 = $(54,546)

After tax = $145,454

Syllabus area D2(b)

113   The correct answer is: $(2,735)

	Working capital required (10% × sales)	Increments = cash flow	Discount factor 10%	Present value
	$	$		$
T0	10,000	(10,000)	1	(10,000.00)
T1	12,500	(2,500)	0.909	(2,272.50)
T2	10,500	2,000	0.826	1,652.00
T3	0	10,500	0.751	7,885.50
				(2,735.00)

Syllabus area Syllabus area D1(e)

 BPP

114　The correct answer is: $(21,260)

The working capital required will inflate year on year, then the inflated amount will be 'returned' at the end of the project:

	Working capital required (with 10% inflation)	Increments = cash flow	Discount factor 12%	Present value
	$	$		$
T0	100,000	(100,000)	1	(100,000)
T1	110,000	(10,000)	0.893	(8,930)
T2	0	110,000	0.797	87,670
				(21,260)

Syllabus area D2(a)

115　The correct answer is: $58,175

As not all cash flows will inflate at the same rate, cash flows will be inflated where necessary and discounted using the money rate.

(1 + money rate) = (1.08) × (1.02) = 1.1016 so m = 10% to the nearest whole percentage

Nominal income = $100,000 × (1 + income inflation) = $100,000 × 1.1 = $110,000

Nominal expenses = $35,000 (zero inflation)

Therefore NPV = [(110,000 – 35,000) × DF_1] – 10,000　　where DF_1 = the 1 year 10% discount factor (tables)

= (75,000 × 0.909) – 10,000 = $58,175

Syllabus area D2(a)

116　The correct answer is: $115,740

In order to use the perpetuity factor (1/r) the annual amount must be constant, so the calculation needs to be done in real terms.

The money cost of capital is given in the question, so the real rate needs to be calculated using:

(1 + r) × (1 + h) = (1 + i)

where r = real rate, h = inflation, i = money rate, so

(1 + r) × (1.02) = (1.102)

(1 + r) = 1.102/1.02 = 1.08 or 8%.

The perpetuity factor from T2-∞ = (1/r) – DF1 = (1/0.08) – 0.926 = 11.574

Therefore the present value = 10,000 × 11.574 = $115,740

Syllabus area D2(a)

117　The correct answer is: Nil

Increased expectation of inflation will have two effects.

(1)　Higher expected nominal cash flow

(2)　Higher nominal discount rate

These will cancel each other out exactly.

Syllabus area D2(a)

 BPP

118   5.8 %

$(1 + r) \times (1 + h) = (1 + i)$

where r = real rate, h = inflation, i = money rate, so

$(1 + r) \times (1.04) = (1.10)$

$(1 + r) = 1.10/1.04 = 1.058$ or 5.8%.

Syllabus area D2(a)

119    $ 15,701

Year 1 PV = $10,000 \times 1.05 \times 0.877 = \$9,209$

Year 2 PV = $20,000 \times 1.05^2 \times 0.769 = \$16,957$

Year 3 PV = $25,000 \times 1.05^3 \times 0.675 = \$19,535$

NPV = 9,209 + 16,957 + 19,535 - 30,000 = \$15,701

Note. Other answers which differ due to roundings applied, would also be marked as correct.

Syllabus area D2(a)

120   The correct answer is: It is expected general inflation suffered by the investors

The inflation included in the money cost of capital is required by the investors to compensate them for the loss of general purchasing power their money will suffer in the future as a result of investing in the business.

Syllabus area D2(a)

OTQ bank – Project appraisal and risk

121   The correct answers are:

- The sensitivity of a project variable can be calculated by dividing the project net present value by the present value of the cash flows relating to that project variable - **True**

- The expected net present value is the value expected to occur if an investment project with several possible outcomes is undertaken once - **False**

- The discounted payback period is the time taken for the cumulative net present value to change from negative to positive - **True**

Statement 2 is incorrect because the expected net present value is the value expected to occur if an investment project with several possible outcomes is undertaken **many times**.

Syllabus area D3(c)

122    $ 11,100

Total cash flow	Joint probability	EV of cash flow
$		$
36,000	0.1125	4,050
14,000	0.0375	525
32,000	0.4500	14,400
10,000	0.1500	1,500
16,000	0.1875	3,000
(6,000)	0.0625	(375)
		23,100
Less initial investment		(12,000)
EV of the NPV		11,100

Syllabus area D3(c)

123   The correct answer is: Just under 3 years

Adjusted payback period is payback period based on discounted cash flows:

Time	Cash flow	DF 8%	Discounted cash flow	Cumulative discounted cash flow
	$		$	
0	(100,000)		(100,000)	(100,000)
1	40,000	0.926	37,040	(62,960)
2	40,000	0.857	34,280	(28,680)
3	40,000	0.794	31,760	3,080

Syllabus area D3(d)

124   The correct answer is: 70%

To force an NPV = 0, the 4-year annuity factor, AF_{1-4} = 110,000/40,000 = 2.75

Proof: the NPV calculation would be (2.75 × 40,000) – 110,000 = 0

From tables, the 4-year annuity factor closest to 2.75 is 2.743, corresponding to a discount rate of 17%.

In terms of sensitivity: (17 – 10)/10 = 70% sensitivity

The cost of capital can therefore increase by 70% before the NPV becomes negative.

Note. Alternatively the IRR could be estimated to find the 17% instead of tables.

NPV when cost of capital is 18% = –110,000 + (40,000 × 2.69) = (2,400)

$$IRR = 10 + \left[\frac{16,800}{16,800 + 2,400} \times (18-10)\right] = 17\%$$

Syllabus area D3(b)

125   The correct answer is: 12.5%

Sensitivity = 200,000/((4,000,000 − 2,000,000) × 0.8) × 100 = **12.5%**

A change in sales volume affects sales revenue and variable costs, but not fixed costs. The sensitivity of the NPV to a change in contribution must therefore be calculated. However, a change in contribution will cause a change in the corporation tax liability, so it is essential that the after-tax contribution be considered.

Contribution = 4,000,000 − 2,000,000 = $2,000,000

After-tax contribution = 2,000,000 × 0.8 = $1,600,000

Sensitivity = NPV/PV of project variable = 200,000/1,600,000 × 100 = 12.5%

Syllabus area D3(d)

OTQ bank – Specific investment decisions

126   The correct answer is: If capital is rationed, divisible investment projects can be ranked by the profitability index when determining the optimum investment schedule

The first statement is **incorrect**. With buying an asset, the company receives tax allowances (tax-allowable depreciation) which results in cash savings on tax. It is the tax saving that is the relevant cash flow as opposed to the tax allowable depreciation. With leasing, the lessor does not receive these allowances. However, the lease rental is allowable for tax purposes which results in cash savings on tax.

The second statement is **incorrect**. They need to be discounted at the cost of capital, not just the cost of debt.

The third statement is **correct**. Ranking using the profitability index can be used if projects are divisible.

The final statement is **incorrect**. Soft capital rationing is brought about by internal factors and decisions by management, not external government decisions.

Syllabus area D4(c)

127   The correct answer is:

Replace every year	EAC
	$
2	10,093

Net present cost of 1-year cycle = 20,000 − (10,000 × 0.909) = $10,910 cost

Net present cost of 2-year cycle = 20,000 − [(8,000 − 5,000) × 0.826] = $17,522 cost

EAC 1-year cycle = $10,910/0.909 = 12,002

EAC 2-year cycle = $17,522/1.736 = 10,093

The 2-year cycle should be chosen with an equivalent annual cost of $10,093.

Syllabus area D4(b)

128   The correct answer is: Lease is better than buy

The saved outlay is a benefit of the lease so if it outweighs the present value of the costs relevant to the lease then the lease is financially worthwhile.

Syllabus area D4(a)

129   The correct answers are:

- After tax cost of the loan if they borrow and buy - **Yes**
- AB Co's weighted average cost of capital - **Yes**
- After-tax cost of the loan if they borrow and buy - **No**
- AB Co's weighted after cost of capital - **Yes**

Interest should not be included as a cash flow as it is part of the discount rate.

As a financing decision the alternatives should be assessed at the after-tax cost of borrowing – the risk associated with each is the risk of borrowing (or not), and not related to what is done with the asset.

Syllabus area D4(a)

130   The correct answers are:

- The profitability index is suitable for handling multiple-period capital rationing problems if projects are divisible - **False**
- Projects being divisible is an unrealistic assumption - **False**

The profitability index is only suitable for handling single-period capital rationing problems if projects are divisible.

Whether a project may be considered divisible or not depends on the project – for example investing in a machine is unlikely to be divisible (half a machine will not generate half the return); however, buying a chain of shops could be divisible; it might be possible to buy half the chain for half the cost and expect half the net present value.

Syllabus area D4(c)

131    $ [13] m

Project	Initial cost	NPV	Profitability index*	Ranking
	$m	$m		
1	40	4	1.10	3
2	30	5	1.167	1
3	50	6	1.12	2
4	60	5	1.08	4

*(NPV + initial cost)/initial cost

Investment plan:

	Investment	NPV
	$m	$m
100% of Project 2	30	5
100% of Project 3	50	6
50% of Project 1	20	2
	100	13

Syllabus area D4(c)

132 $ [11] m

Projects 2 and 3 give the highest NPV without breaking the $100m constraint.

Syllabus area D4(c)

133 The correct answer is: Avoiding tax exhaustion

'Avoiding tax exhaustion' is potentially a benefit. Tax exhaustion is when a business has negative taxable income so it cannot benefit from tax relief such as tax-allowable depreciation. In this case, it may be beneficial to lease the asset from a business that **can** benefit from the tax-allowable depreciation and share in that benefit via lower lease payments.

'Attracting lease customers that may not have been otherwise possible' is a potential benefit to a lessor, not a lessee.

'Exploiting a low cost of capital' is a potential benefit for the purchaser, not the lessee.

'Potential future scrap proceeds' is a potential benefit for the purchaser, not the lessee, as the lessee is not entitled to scrap proceeds.

Syllabus area D4(a)

134 The correct answer is: Electric because its equivalent annual benefit is higher

The NPVs cannot be directly compared as they relate to different time periods. Equivalent annual benefits (EAB) should be compared. This is similar in principle to equivalent annual cost.

EAB gas = $50,000/AF$_{1-5}$ = 50,000/3.993 = $12,522 pa

EAB electric = $68,000/AF$_{1-7}$ = 68,000/5.206 = $13,062 pa

Therefore electric should be chosen as its EAB is higher.

Syllabus area D4(b)

135 The correct answers are:

- Higher scrap value
- Better company image and efficiency

Statement 1 is a benefit. Scrapped assets will be newer hence worth more.

Statement 2 is a benefit. Newer assets look better, motivate employees and are more efficient.

Statement 3 is not true hence not a benefit. Typically depreciation is higher in earlier years, meaning annual depreciation charges will be higher with a shorter replacement cycle.

Statement 4 is inaccurate hence not a benefit. Although owned for a shorter period, the asset will be replaced so ownership of that type of asset will be indefinite.

Syllabus area D4(b)

Section B questions

Sensitivity analysis

136   The correct answer is: 11.9%

Year	Contribution	Discount factor 9%	PV
	$'000		$'000
1-2	7,100	1.759	12,489
	(10,300 - 3,200)		

Sensitivity of project to sales volume = 1,490 / 12,489 × 100% = 11.9%

Syllabus area D3(b)

137   The correct answer is: 1.75 years

Year	Net cash flow	Discount factor 9%	PV	Cumulative PV
	$'000		$'000	$'000
0	(11,000)	1	(11,000.00)	(11,000.00)
1	7,100	0.917	6,510.70	(4,489.30)
2	7,100	0.842	5,978.20	

4,489.30/5,978.20 = 0.75

Therefore the discounted payback = 1.75 years

Syllabus area D3(d)

138   The correct answer is: 18.9%

Using discount rates of 15% and 20% per the question we have:

Year	Net cash flow	Discount factor 15%	PV	Discount factor 20%	PV
	$'000		$'000		$'000
0	(11,000)	1	(11,000)	1	(11,000)
1	7,100	0.870	6,177	0.833	5,914
2	7,100	0.756	5,368	0.694	4,927
			NPV = 545		NPV = (159)

$$IRR = \left[15 + \frac{545}{545 + 159} \times (20-15)\right] = 18.9\%$$

Syllabus area D1(f)

139   The correct answer is: Using random numbers to generate possible values of project variables, a simulation model can generate a standard deviation of expected project outcomes

The statement concerning simulation models is true. They use probabilities to carry out a statistical analysis of possible project outcomes.

Notes on incorrect answers:

Sensitivity definition

Selecting this answer indicates a lack of understanding of sensitivity analysis. The sensitivity of NPV to a change in sales volume can be calculated as NPV divided by the present value of contribution. Comparing NPV to the present value of future sales income would be estimating the sensitivity of NPV to a change in selling price.

The certainty equivalent approach

This approach to investment appraisal requires that the riskless equivalent amounts are discounted by a riskless discount rate; that is, the risk-free rate of return. A CAPM-derived project-specific cost of capital is not the risk-free rate of return, but rather a rate of return that reflects the systematic risk of a particular investment project.

Risk and uncertainty

A common way to distinguish between risk and uncertainty is to say that risk can be quantified whereas uncertainty cannot be quantified, so stating that neither can be measured or quantified is not true.

Syllabus area D3

140   The correct answers are:

- IRR ignores the relative sizes of investments
- NPV is widely used in practice

The IRR ignores the relative sizes of investments. It therefore does not measure the absolute increase in company value, and therefore shareholder wealth, which can be created by an investment.

Where cash flows change from negative to positive more than once there may be as many IRRs as there are changes in the direction of cash flows. So IRR is not easy to use in this situation.

Syllabus area D1(h)

Guilder Co

141   The correct answers are:

Projects		Order of preference
Utrec		1
Tilbur		2
Eind		3
Amster		4

PI = PV of future cash flows/PV of capital investment

Project	Outlay in Year 0 $	PV $	NPV $	Ratio (PV/ outlay)	Ranking
Amster	100,000	111,400	11,400	1.114	4th
Eind	56,000	62,580	6,580	1.118	3rd
Utrec	60,000	68,760	8,760	1.146	1st
Tilbur	90,000	102,400	12,400	1.138	2nd

Syllabus area D4(c)

142 The correct answer is: PI can only be used if projects are divisible

The weaknesses of the PI method are:

It does not take into account the absolute size of the individual projects. A project with a high index might be very small and therefore only generate a small NPV.

It does not highlight the projects which are slowest in generating returns. It is possible that the project with the highest PI is the slowest in generating returns.

It does not allow for uncertainty about the outcome of each project. In fact it assumes that there is complete certainty about each outcome.

Syllabus area D4(c)

143 $ 105,406

Present value of cash flows = (250,000 + 17,860 + 23,113 + 22,784 + 6,360) = ($320,117)

Cumulative present value factor = 3.037

Equivalent annual cost = $320,117/3.037 = $105,406

Syllabus area D4(b)

144 The correct answer is: Statement 1 is false and statement 2 is true

The equivalent annual cost method is the most convenient method of analysis to use in a period of **no** inflation, because it is converting the NPV of the cost of buying and using the asset into an equivalent annual cost. In times of high inflation, this cost would keep increasing (so statement 1 is false).

The EAC method assumes that the machine can be replaced by exactly the same machine in perpetuity and this is one of the weaknesses of the EAC method. It is not usually possible to replace something with exactly the same thing as assets are constantly developing. Computers, in particular, are developing very quickly and so it can make sense to replace certain assets more often than the EAC method dictates.

Syllabus area D4(b)

145 $ 17,654

EV of Year 2 cash flow = (19,000 × 0.55) + (26,000 × 0.45) = 22,150

PV discounted at 12% = 22,150 × 0.797 = $17,654

Syllabus area D3(c)

Trecor Co (amended)

146 56 %

Depreciation = $250,000 – $5,000 – $245,000

Accounting profit = total cash inflows – depreciation = $530,000 – $245,000 = $285,000

Average profit per year = $285,000/4 = $71,250

Average investment = (250,000 + 5,000)/2 = $127,500

ROCE = 71,250/127,500 × 100 = 56%

Syllabus area D1(d)

147 The correct answers are:

- If ROCE is less than the target ROCE then the purchase of the machine can be recommended - **False**
- ROCE can be used to compare two mutually exclusive projects - **True**

ROCE needs to be higher than the target ROCE for the machine purchase to be recommended. The second statement is true. Two (or more) mutually exclusive projects can be compared using ROCE. The project with the highest ROCE should be selected.

Syllabus area D1(d)

148 $ 10,547

Tax-allowable depreciation			Tax benefits	
	$			$
1 250,000 × 0.25 =	62,500	2 62,500 × 0.3 =		18,750
2 62,500 × 0.75 =	46,875	3 46,875 × 0.3 =		14,063
3 46,875 × 0.75 =	35,156	4 35,156 × 0.3 =		10,547

Syllabus area D2(b)

149 1 year(s) 11 month(s)

Year 1 cumulative balance = −250,000 + 122,000 = −128,000

(128,000/143,000) × 12 months = 11 months ∴ payback is 1 year 11 months

Syllabus area D1(b)

150 The correct answers are:

- IRR ignores the relative sizes of investments.
- IRR and NPV sometimes give conflicting rankings over which project should be prioritised.

The IRR ignores the relative sizes of investments.

It therefore does not measure the absolute increase in company value, and therefore shareholder wealth, which can be created by an investment. Therefore statement 2 is false.

When discount rates are expected to differ over the life of the project, such variations can be incorporated easily into NPV calculations, but not into IRR calculations. Therefore statement 3 is also false.

Statement 4 is true. NPV and IRR methods can give conflicting rankings as to which project should be given priority.

Syllabus area D1(h)

BRT Co (amended)

151 $ 8,487 (or $8,488)

1,600,000 × $5 × 1.03² = $8,487,200 or

1,600,000 × 5.305 = $8,488,000 (if you have rounded the inflated price)

Syllabus area D2(a)

152 $ \boxed{6,884}$

2,100,000 × \$3 × 1.03^3 = \$6,884,180

Syllabus area D2(a)

153 $ \boxed{84}$

Year	Tax-allowable depreciation	Year	Tax benefits
1	2,000,000 × 0.25 = \$500,000	2	\$500,000 × 0.3 = \$150,000
2	500,000 × 0.75 = \$375,000	3	\$375,000 × 0.3 = \$112,500
3	\$375,000 × 0.75 = \$281,250	4	\$281,250 × 0.3 = \$84,375

Syllabus area D2(b)

154   The correct answers are:

- The trainee accountant has used the wrong percentage for the cost of capital - **False**
- Ignoring sales after four years underestimates the value of the project - **True**
- The working capital figure in Year 4 is wrong - **True**

Statement 1: As inflated sales and costs have been used, the cost of capital should be the nominal cost of capital (at 12%).

Statement 2: Cutting off cash flows after four years will underestimate the value of the project as future cash inflows will be ignored.

Statement 3: The final year should recover the total working capital and so should be: \$750k + \$23k + \$23k + \$24k = \$820k.

Syllabus area D1(a)

155   The correct answer is: Both statements are true

When there are **unconventional** cash flow patterns there may be multiple IRRs and so the NPV and IRR decisions may not be the same.

A project is financially viable under the IRR criteria if the IRR is greater than the cost of capital (12% in this case).

Syllabus area D1(h)

Section C questions

156 Melanie Co

Workbook references

Equivalent annual costs and leasing are both covered in Chapter 8, and the comparison of NPV to IRR is covered in Chapter 5.

Top Tips

In leasing questions, the timing of the cash flows is always important. Always check whether they are in advance or arrears. Also don't rush the calculations, read the requirement very carefully before beginning. It is easy in part (a)(ii) to miss that this discount rate has changed to 10%.

Easy marks

In part b, the discussion points should be easy however in the exam not enough attention is directed towards achieving these marks (see examiner comments below).

Examining team's comments

For part (b) most answers gained very few marks because they did not adopt a comparative approach to answering the question requirement, for example, by making a statement about NPV without referring to IRR and vice versa, and hence not discussing the superiority of NPV over IRR.

Furthermore, some responses:

- Could not gain full marks because they offered fewer than the number of reasons required by the question;

- Incorrectly stated that IRR is inferior to NPV because IRR ignores the time value of money;

Were expressed only too briefly and in terms that were too general such as quick, easy, simple to understand.

Marking guide			Marks
(a)	(i)	Lease timing	1
		PV leasing	1
		Maintenance cost	1
		Purchase cost	0.5
		Residual value	0.5
		PV buy	1
		Decision	1
			6
	(ii)	3-year PV cost	1
		3-year EAC	1
		Maintenance 4-year	0.5
		Residual value 4-year	0.5
		4-year PV cost	1
		4-year EAC	1
		Decision	1
			6

 BPP

(b) Each (of four) reasons worth 2 marks each	<u>8</u>
	8
Total	20

(a) (i)

Time	0	1	2	3
	$	$	$	$
Lease				
Lease payment	(55,000)	(55,000)	(55,000)	
PV factor at 8%	<u>1.000</u>	<u>0.926</u>	<u>0.857</u>	
Present value	(55,000)	(50,930)	(47,135)	
Present value cost	**(153,065)**			
Borrow and buy				
Initial cost	(160,000)			
Residual value				
Maintenance		(8,000)	(8,000)	(8,000)
Total	(160,000)	(8,000)	(8,000)	32,000
PV factor at 8%	1.000	0.926	0.857	0.794
Present value	(160,000)	(7,408)	(6,856)	25,408
Present value cost	(148,856)			

As borrow and buy offers the cheapest present value cost the machine should be financed by borrowing.

(ii)

	Year 0	Year 1	Year 2	Year 3	Year 4
	$	$	$	$	$
3-year replacement cycle					
Initial cost	(160,000)				
Residual value				40,000	
Maintenance		(8,000)	(8,000)	(8,000)	
Total	(160,000)	(8,000)	(8,000)	32,000	
PV factor at 10%	1.000	0.909	0.826	0.751	
Present value	(160,000)	(7,272)	(6,608)	24,032	
Present value cost	(149,848)				
EAC 3-year cycle = PV cost/Annuity factor 3 years at 10%					
EAC = −$149,848/2.487	(60,253)				

	Year 0	Year 1	Year 2	Year 3	Year 4
	$	$	$	$	$
4-year replacement cycle					
Initial cost	(160,000)				
Residual value					11,000
Maintenance		(12,000)	(12,000)	(12,000)	(12,000)
Total	(160,000)	(12,000)	(12,000)	(12,000)	(1,000)
PV factor at 10%	1.000	0.909	0.826	0.751	0.683
Present value	(160,000)	(10,908)	(9,912)	(9,012)	(683)
Present value cost	(190,515)				

EAC 4-year cycle = PV cost/Annuity factor 4 years at 10%

EAC = –$190,515/3.170 = (60,099)

Recommendation

The machine should be replaced every four years as the equivalent annual cost is lower.

(b) In most simple accept or reject decisions, IRR and NPV will select the same project.

However, NPV has certain advantages over IRR as an investment appraisal technique.

NPV and shareholder wealth

The NPV of a proposed project, if calculated at an appropriate cost of capital, is equal to the increase in shareholder wealth which the project offers. In this way NPV is directly linked to the assumed financial objective of the company, the maximisation of shareholder wealth. IRR calculates the rate of return on projects, and although this can show the attractiveness of the project to shareholders, it does not measure the absolute increase in wealth which the project offers.

Absolute measure

NPV looks at absolute increases in wealth and thus can be used to compare projects of different sizes. IRR looks at relative rates of return and in doing so ignores the relative size of the compared investment projects.

Non-conventional cash flows

In situations involving multiple reversals in project cash flows, it is possible that the IRR method may produce multiple IRRs (that is, there can be more than one interest rate which would produce an NPV of zero). If decision-makers are aware of the existence of multiple IRRs, it is still possible for them to make the correct decision using IRR, but if unaware they could make the wrong decision.

Mutually-exclusive projects

In situations of mutually-exclusive projects, it is possible that the IRR method will (incorrectly) rank projects in a different order to the NPV method. This is due to the inbuilt reinvestment assumption of the IRR method. The IRR method assumes that any net cash inflows generated during the life of the project will be reinvested at the project's IRR. NPV on the other hand assumes a reinvestment rate equal to the cost of capital. Generally NPV's assumed reinvestment rate is more realistic and hence it ranks projects correctly.

Changes in cost of capital

NPV can be used in situations where the cost of capital changes from year to year. Although IRR can be calculated in these circumstances, it can be difficult to make accept or reject decisions as it is difficult to know which cost of capital to compare it with.

Note. Only four reasons were required to be discussed.

157 Cabreras

Marking guide	Marks
(a) Purchase cost	0.5
3-year maintenance cost	1
3-year fuel cost	1
3-year resale value	1
3-year NPV	1
3-year EAC	0.5
4th year maintenance	0.5
4th year fuel	0.5
Safety test cost	1
4-year resale value	0.5
4-year NPV	1
4-year EAC	0.5
Recommendation	2
	11
(b) Discussion of EAC (to 2 marks per relevant point)	4
	4
(c) Discussion of methods (to 2 marks per relevant point)	5
	5
Total	20

(a) **Optimal replacement interval**

Three-year cycle

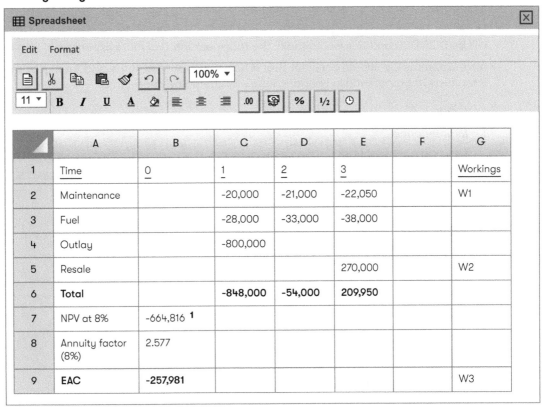

	A	B	C	D	E	F	G
1	Time	0	1	2	3		Workings
2	Maintenance		-20,000	-21,000	-22,050		W1
3	Fuel		-28,000	-33,000	-38,000		
4	Outlay		-800,000				
5	Resale				270,000		W2
6	**Total**		**-848,000**	**-54,000**	**209,950**		
7	NPV at 8%	-664,816 [1]					
8	Annuity factor (8%)	2.577					
9	**EAC**	**-257,981**					W3

[1] =NPV(0.08,C6:E6)

Four-year cycle

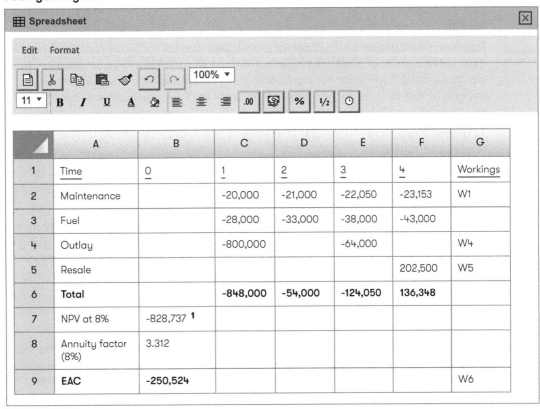

	A	B	C	D	E	F	G
1	Time	0	1	2	3	4	Workings
2	Maintenance		-20,000	-21,000	-22,050	-23,153	W1
3	Fuel		-28,000	-33,000	-38,000	-43,000	
4	Outlay		-800,000		-64,000		W4
5	Resale					202,500	W5
6	**Total**		**-848,000**	**-54,000**	**-124,050**	**136,348**	
7	NPV at 8%	-828,737 [1]					
8	Annuity factor (8%)	3.312					
9	**EAC**	**-250,524**					W6

[1] =NPV(0.08,C6:F6)

Recommendation

The four-year replacement interval has the lowest equivalent annual cost and on an expected cost basis, Cabreras Co should replace the Beast every four years.

However, it is a close decision and there is a 20% chance that the cost of the government test will be $120,000 and this would make the four-year interval more expensive.

Also, Cabreras Co should consider that it has only looked at three and four-year replacement intervals. Other, potentially cheaper, intervals should be considered.

Workings

1 **Maintenance**

$20,000 × 1.05 = 21,000

$20,000 × 1.05 × 1.05 = 22,050

2 **Resale (three-year cycle)**

$800,000 × 0.6 × 0.75 × 0.75 = $270,000

3 **EAC (three-year cycle)**

NPV/3-year annuity factor at 8% $664,816/2.577 = $257,981

4 **Outlay (four-year cycle)**

$50,000 × 0.8 + $120,000 × 0.2 = $64,000

5 **Resale (four-year cycle)**

$800,000 × 0.6 × 0.75 × 0.75 × 0.75 = $202,500

6 **EAC (four-year cycle)**

NPV/4-year annuity factor at 8% = $828,737/3.312 = $250,524

(b) In simple situations, choosing between one-off projects of different length lives is quite straight forward; the NPV technique is used to evaluate the costs and benefits of a project over its life and the project with the largest NPV is selected in order to maximise shareholder wealth.

However, when projects with different length lives can be endlessly repeated, and form part of an infinite chain of identical projects, then the situation is more complicated. In this situation, project NPVs cannot be meaningfully compared. Is a chain of three-year projects with an NPV of $20 per project better than a chain of five-year projects with an NPV of $30 per project?

To answer this, the NPV earned by the project needs to be related to the period of time required to earn it.

Deciding the optimal replacement interval for an asset which will be required for the foreseeable future is very similar to the problem of choosing between investment projects of different length lives which form part of an infinite chain of similar projects.

Each possible replacement interval is a project (for example, a three-year replacement interval project, a four-year replacement interval project, etc). If the asset is going to be required by the business for the foreseeable future, then each replacement interval forms part of an infinite chain of similar replacement intervals.

To choose the optimal replacement interval, the NPV of each possible replacement interval needs to be calculated to take into account the time value of money and the costs and benefits which are spread across the interval.

In order to allow for the different lengths of the replacement intervals, the NPVs are divided by the annuity factor appropriate to their lives (three-year factors for a three-year interval, etc). The resultant figure is the EAC. The EAC represents the cost payable at the end of each year of the replacement interval which is equivalent to the NPV of the replacement interval.

The calculation above allows for the present value cost of the replacement interval and the length of the interval. If it is assumed that continual replacement of like with like assets continues, EACs for different lengths of replacement interval can be compared meaningfully to find the optimal replacement interval.

(c) Discounted cash flow (DCF) based methods of investment appraisal include NPV, IRR and discounted payback.

They all share the same two advantages.

First, they allow for the time value of money and recognise that a $ received today is worth more than a $ received in one year's time.

The two commonly used non-discounted cash flow methods of investment appraisal, accounting rate of return and payback, do not consider the time value of money.

Second, DCF methods are cash flow (rather than accounting profit) based. Cash is the lifeblood of a business and is used to pay the claims of stakeholders. Profit is an accounting concept. The amount of profit earned in a period is sometimes quite a subjective matter and depends upon the accounting policies followed. The amount of cash received in a period is a far more objective measure.

Accounting rate of return is based upon accounting profit and ignores cash flow.

Both NPV and IRR have clear cut decision rules which should lead to the maximisation of shareholder wealth. Under NPV, any projects with positive NPVs should be adopted and the size of the NPV is directly related to the increase in shareholder wealth from adopting the project. Under IRR, projects with IRRs bigger than the company's cost of capital should be adopted, and if they are, shareholder wealth will increase.

Accounting rate of return and payback have arbitrarily set targets based upon internal corporate targets.

NPV and IRR both consider returns earned throughout a project's life. Payback only considers returns up to the payback point, and as a result ignores later returns.

158 Dink Co

> **Workbook references**
>
> Analysis of leasing and capital rationing are covered in Chapter 8.
>
> **Top tips**
>
> Neat workings will be important to avoid careless errors in part (a), for example over the timing of the lease payments and the tax relief on the lease payments.
>
> **Easy marks**
>
> Discussion marks in part (b) should be straightforward as long as answers do not stray into irrelevant areas such as how to manage capital rationing issues using techniques such as the profitability index etc. Ideally discussion points would recognise that the company is an SME so points such as crowdfunding, grants, business angels would also be relevant as well as points such as delaying projects and joint ventures.

Marking guide			Marks
(a) (i)	Kd after tax		1
	TAD		1
	TAD benefits		1
	Service tax benefit		1
	Tax timing		1
	PV buying		1
			6

(ii)	Lease tax benefits	1	
	Lease timing	1	
	PV leasing	1	
			3
(iii)	Recommendation	1	
			1
(b) (i)	Hard rationing reasons	3	
	Soft rationing reasons	3	
			6
(ii)	Ways to overcome	4	
			4
Total			20

(a) (i) After-tax cost of borrowing = 8.6 × (1 − 0.3) = 8.6 × 0.7 = 6%

Calculating PV of cost of borrowing to buy:

	Year 0	Year 1	Year 2	Year 3	Year 4	Year 5
	$	$	$	$	$	$
Purchase	(750,000)					
Residual value					50,000	
Service costs		(23,000)	(23,000)	(23,000)	(23,000)	
TAD benefit			56,250	42,188	31,641	79,922
Service cost tax benefits			6,900	6,900	6,900	6,900
Net cash flow	(750,000)	(23,000)	40,150	26,088	65,541	86,822
Discount at 6%	1.000	0.943	0.890	0.840	0.792	0.747
	(750,000)	(21,689)	35,734	21,914	51,908	64,856

PV of cost of borrowing to buy is $597,277.

Using the spreadsheet NPV function and spreadsheet-calculated discount factors, PV of cost of borrowing to buy is $597,268.

Working

TAD benefit

Year	0	1	2	3	4	5
	$	$	$	$	$	$
Purchase	750,000					
TAD		187,500	140,625	105,469	266,406*	
30% TAD benefit			56,250	42,188	31,641	79,922

*750,000 − 187,500 − 140,625 − 105,469 − 50,000 = $266,406

(ii) Calculating PV of cost of leasing:

	Year 0	Year 1	Year 2	Year 3	Year 4	Year 5
	$	$	$	$	$	$
Lease rentals	(200,000)	(200,000)	(200,000)	(200,000)		
Tax benefits			60,000	60,000	60,000	60,000
Net cash flow	(200,000)	(200,000)	(140,000)	(140,000)	60,000	60,000
Discount at 6%	1.000	0.943	0.890	0.840	0.792	0.747
	(200,000)	(188,600)	(124,600)	(117,600)	47,520	44,820

PV of cost of leasing is $538,460.

> **Tutorial note.** The spreadsheet NPV function helps to produce this analysis more quickly and you should consider using this is the exam. Here the calculation is slightly more accurate and gives a value of $538,464 for the cost of leasing.
>
> When using the NPV function in a spreadsheet you need to be aware that **the formula assumes that the first cash flow is in time 1 (not time 0) so time 0 has to be dealt with separately.**
>
> This is illustrated in the following tables, first showing the numbers and then showing the formulae used.

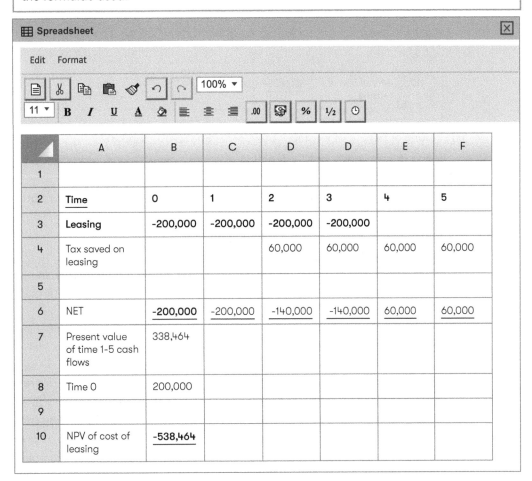

	A	B	C	D	D	E	F
1							
2	**Time**	0	1	2	3	4	5
3	**Leasing**	-200,000	-200,000	-200,000	-200,000		
4	Tax saved on leasing			60,000	60,000	60,000	60,000
5							
6	NET	**-200,000**	-200,000	-140,000	-140,000	60,000	60,000
7	Present value of time 1-5 cash flows	338,464					
8	Time 0	200,000					
9							
10	NPV of cost of leasing	**-538,464**					

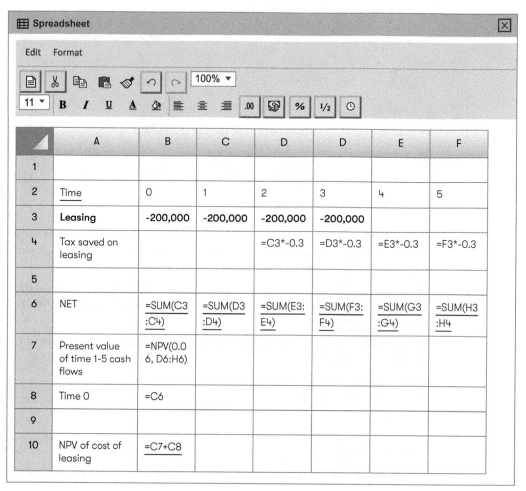

	A	B	C	D	D	E	F
1							
2	Time	0	1	2	3	4	5
3	**Leasing**	-200,000	-200,000	-200,000	-200,000		
4	Tax saved on leasing			=C3*-0.3	=D3*-0.3	=E3*-0.3	=F3*-0.3
5							
6	NET	=SUM(C3:C4)	=SUM(D3:D4)	=SUM(E3:E4)	=SUM(F3:F4)	=SUM(G3:G4)	=SUM(H3:H4
7	Present value of time 1-5 cash flows	=NPV(0.06, D6:H6)					
8	Time 0	=C6					
9							
10	NPV of cost of leasing	=C7+C8					

(iii) Financial benefit of leasing = $597,277 − $538,460 = $58,817

Using the spreadsheet NPV function and spreadsheet-calculated discount factors, financial benefit of leasing = $597,268 − $538,464 = $58,804.

Leasing the new machine is recommended as the option which is more attractive in financial terms to Dink Co.

(b) (i) **Reasons why investment capital may be rationed**

Theoretically, the objective of maximising shareholder wealth can be achieved in a perfect capital market by investing in all projects with a positive NPV. In practice, companies experience capital rationing and are limited in the amount of investment finance available, so shareholder wealth is not maximised.

Hard capital rationing is due to external factors, while soft capital rationing is due to internal factors or management decisions.

General reasons for hard capital rationing affect many companies, for example, the availability of new finance may be limited because share prices are depressed on the stock market or because of government-imposed restrictions on bank lending.

If a company only requires a small amount of finance, issue costs may be so high that using external sources of finance is not practical.

Reasons for hard capital rationing may be company-specific, for example, a company may not be able to raise new debt finance if banks or investors see the company as being too risky to lend to. The company may have high gearing or low interest cover, or a poor track record, or if recently incorporated, no track record at all. Companies in the service sector may not be able to offer assets as security for new loans.

Reasons for soft capital rationing include managerial aversion to issuing new equity, for example, a company may want to avoid potential dilution of its EPS or avoid the possibility of becoming a takeover target. Managers might alternatively be averse to issuing new debt and taking on a commitment to increased fixed interest payments, for example, if the economic outlook for its markets is poor.

Soft capital rationing might also arise because managers wish to finance new investment from retained earnings, for example, as part of a policy of controlled organisational growth, rather than a sudden increase in size which might result from undertaking all investments with a positive net present value.

One reason for soft capital rationing may be that managers want investment projects to compete for funds, in the belief that this will result in the acceptance of stronger, more robust investment projects.

(ii) **Ways in which Dink Co's external capital rationing might be overcome**

Dink Co is a small company and the hard capital rationing it is experiencing is a common problem for SMEs, referred to as the funding gap. A first step towards overcoming its capital rationing could be for Dink Co to obtain information about available sources of finance, since SMEs may lack understanding in this area.

One way of overcoming the company's capital rationing might be business angel financing. This informal source of finance is from wealthy individuals or groups of investors who invest directly in the company and who are prepared to take higher risks in the hope of higher returns. Information requirements for this form of finance may be less demanding than those associated with more common sources of finance.

Dink Co could consider crowdfunding, whereby many investors provide finance for a business venture, for example, via an internet-based platform, although this form of finance is usually associated with entrepreneurial ventures.

Dink Co might be entitled to grant aid from a government, national or regional source which could be linked to a specific business area or to economic regeneration in a specified geographical area.

On a more general basis, Dink Co could consider a joint venture as a way of decreasing the need for additional finance, depending on the nature of its business and its business plans, and whether the directors of Dink Co are prepared to sacrifice some control to the joint venture partner.

Rather than conventional sources of finance, Dink Co could evaluate whether Islamic finance, for example, an ijara contract, might be available, again depending on the nature of its business and its business plans.

159 Crocket Co

> **Workbook references**
>
> Analysis of NPV with inflation is covered in chapter 6. Capital rationing and capital replacement are covered in Chapter 8.
>
> **Top tips**
>
> Neat workings will be important to avoid careless errors in part (a)(i).
>
> **Easy marks**
>
> Discussion marks in parts (b) and (c) should be straightforward as long as answers do not stray into irrelevant areas.

Marking guide		Marks
(a) (i)	Inflated sales	1
	Inflated costs	1
	NPV	2
		4
(ii)	PI calculation	2
	PI ranking	1
	Choose project E over C	1
	Optimal NPV	2
		6
(b)	Determine cash flows	1
	PV for each cycle	1
	Calculate EAC	1
	Decision rule	1
		4
(c)	Specific inflation	1
	Cost of capital	1
	Nominal and real methods	2
	Other points	1
	Recommendation	1
		6
Total		20

(a) (i)   **Calculate the NPV of project B**

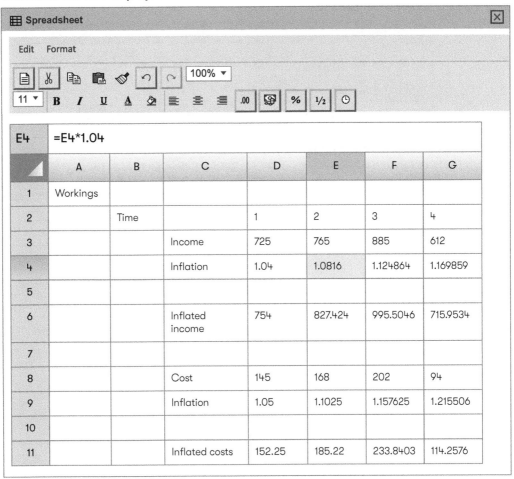

The income and costs are calculated by multiplying the given uninflated numbers by the inflation adjustment as shown.

The NPV calculation can use the spreadsheet shortcut as shown in the following spreadsheet extract:

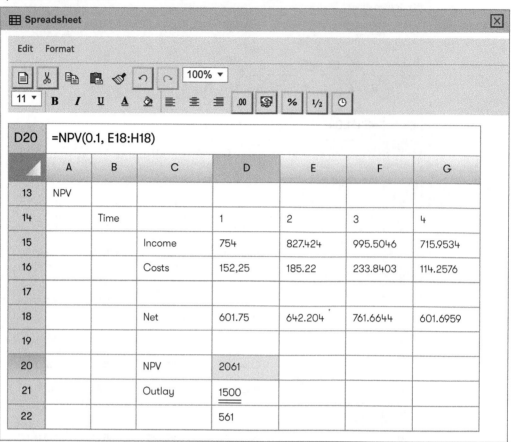

D20 | =NPV(0.1, E18:H18)

	A	B	C	D	E	F	G
13	NPV						
14		Time		1	2	3	4
15			Income	754	827.424	995.5046	715.9534
16			Costs	152,25	185.22	233.8403	114.2576
17							
18			Net	601.75	642.204	761.6644	601.6959
19							
20			NPV	2061			
21			Outlay	1500			
22				561			

(ii) Firstly, as the projects are divisible, calculate the profitability index for each project and rank. The calculation of the profitability index (PI) is shown in the spreadsheet.

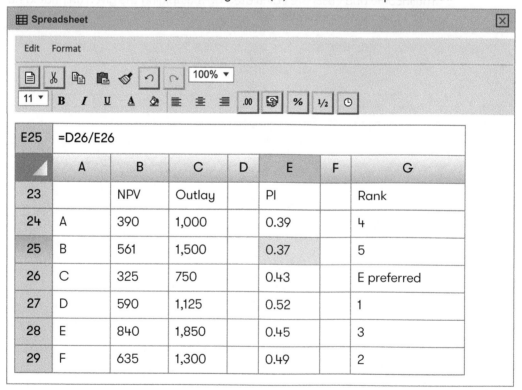

E25 | =D26/E26

	A	B	C	D	E	F	G
23		NPV	Outlay		PI		Rank
24	A	390	1,000		0.39		4
25	B	561	1,500		0.37		5
26	C	325	750		0.43		E preferred
27	D	590	1,125		0.52		1
28	E	840	1,850		0.45		3
29	F	635	1,300		0.49		2

Project C is rejected as its PI is below project E's.

The optimal combination is then:

Rank	Project	%	Capital	NPV
			$'000	$'000
1	D	100	1,125	590
2	F	100	1,300	635
3	E	100	1,850	840
4	A	72.5	725 (balance)	283 (0.725 × 390)
Total			**5,000**	**2,348**

After selection of project E, only $725,000 of capital remains. Consequently, only 72.5% (725/1,000=0.725) of project A can be undertaken. This will result in only 72.5% of the NPV (0.725 x $390,000 = $283,000).

The optimum investment plan is to invest fully in projects D, F and E and only 72.5% in project A. This will yield a maximum net present value of $2,348,000

(b) Firstly, the cash flows must be determined for each cycle under consideration (3, 4 and 5 years). These cash flows will include the initial outlay of the car fleet, maintenance and running costs and the residual value of the car fleet at the end of the cycle.

These cash flows will then require discounting at a suitable discount rate to determine the present value (PV) for each cycle. All of the PVs will be negative as they represent the cost of running the company car fleet with no relevant income attributable.

Given the continual replacement nature of the decision, a common timescale must then be incorporated. To put it simply, while the PV of the three year cycle will appear the cheapest, it will be incurred more times than the four or five year cycles going forward indefinitely.

To allow for the difference in timescales, the PV for each cycle will need converting to an equivalent annual cost (EAC). The EAC will represent the annuity cash flow which when discounted gives the same PV as the actual cash flows themselves. The EAC would be calculated by taking each cycle's PV and dividing by the annuity factor for the cycle length. For example, the three-year PV will need to be divided by a three-year annuity factor.

Once the EAC has been calculated for each cycle, the lowest figure, ie cheapest, will indicate the optimum replacement cycle for the fleet. By comparing the EAC for each cycle, a common timescale (one year) will be considered making the figures comparable.

(c) When appraising an investment, the treatment of inflation needs to be considered as it will affect both cash flows and the required rate of return used as the discount rate. Real-terms and nominal-terms approaches to investment appraisal differ in the way that the effects of inflation are incorporated into the appraisal calculation.

Nominal-terms approach

With the nominal-terms approach, both the cash flows and the discount rate incorporate the effects of inflation. The cost of capital would also need to include the effects of general inflation on the investors' required rate of return. This means Crocket Co will need to apply the specific rates of inflation to sales, material costs and other cash flows and ensure the cash flows in the appraisal incorporate these. The uncertainty surrounding the rates of inflation that Crocket Co faces with this project will certainly make an appraisal in nominal-terms more difficult to prepare with any accuracy and this should be considered when reviewing the results.

Real-terms approach

A real terms approach would exclude the effects of general inflation. Therefore, nominal cash flows incorporating the effects of specific inflation rates would be deflated by the general rate of inflation to give real-terms cash flows. The discount rate will also exclude the effects of inflation. Consequently, a real discount rate would be used which represents the investors' base level of return for risk before inflation is taken into account.

Choice of approach

A real-terms approach would result in a much easier appraisal exercise for Crocket Co as the uncertainty surrounding the estimation of inflation is removed, however, a number of conditions must be met in order for the real-terms approach to be suitable.

Firstly, there must be a single rate of inflation affecting all of the project's cash flows. Given that the estimated increase in material costs is different to the expected rise in sales prices this means that a real-terms approach is already deemed unsuitable. As Crocket Co expects the rate of inflation on sales to be less than the rate of inflation on its costs, particularly materials, then it would be expected that any real-terms NPV is likely to be overstated compared to a nominal-terms NPV as costs will be rising faster than income.

Secondly, the single rate of inflation affecting the cash flows must also be the same as the general rate of inflation suffered by investors. If the inflation rate affecting cash flows is the same as the inflation rate ignored by the real discount rate, this common rate of inflation can be ignored. Given that Crocket Co expects the general rate of inflation to differ from the rates affecting sales and material cost, this also means a real-terms approach ignoring specific inflation is not suitable.

Recommendation

As a result of the above conditions not being met, use of the real-terms approach will not be suitable for Crocket Co to appraise this project. A nominal-terms approach should be used.

160 Degnis Co

> **Workbook references**
>
> Investment appraisal and risk is covered in Chapter 7.
>
> **Top tips**
>
> Read the question carefully before starting the calculations. Some candidates incorrectly had tax cash flows payable one year in arrears and, although the question required candidates to use straight-line tax-allowable depreciation, some answers used 25% reducing balance instead. Part (c) illustrates the importance of having a clear understanding about the difference between risk and uncertainty in the context of investment appraisal.

Marking guide		Marks
(a) Sales income		1
Conversion cost		1
Before-tax cash flow		1
Tax paid		1
Tax-allowable depreciation benefits		1
After-tax cash flow		1
NPV calculations		1
		7
(b) PV of future cash flows ignoring tax-allowable depreciation		1
PV of tax-allowable depreciation benefits		1
Comment on financial acceptability		1
		3

Marking guide		Marks
(c) Risk and uncertainty		1
Explanation of probability analysis		3
Problems – repeatability assumption, difficulty in determining probabilities		$\frac{4}{}$
Marks Available		8
Maximum		5
(d) Reason for hard rationing		4
Reasons for soft rationing		$\frac{4}{}$
Marks Available		8
Maximum		$\frac{5}{}$
Total		$\frac{20}{}$

(a) **Calculation of NPV over four years**

Year	1	2	3	4
	$'000	$'000	$'000	$'000
Sales income	12,525	15,030	22,545	22,545
Conversion cost	(7,913)	(9,495)	(14,243)	(14,243)
Contribution	4,612	5,535	8,302	8,302
Fixed costs	(4,000)	(5,000)	(5,500)	(5,500)
Before-tax cash flow	612	535	2,802	2,802
Tax-allowable depreciation benefits	(171)	(150)	(785)	(785)
After-tax cash flow	112	112	112	112
Discount at 11%	553	497	2,129	2,129
Present values	0.901	0.812	0.731	0.659
	498	404	1,556	1,403

	$'000
Sum of present values	3,861
Initial investment	4,000
NPV	(139)

Working

Average selling price = (30,000 × 0.20) + (42,000 × 0.45) + (72,000 × 0.35) = $50,100 per unit

Average conversion cost = (23,000 × 0.20) + (29,000 × 0.45) + (40,000 × 0.35) = $31,650 per unit

BPP

ANSWERS

Year	1	2	3	4
Sales volume (units/year)	250	300	450	450
Average selling price ($/unit)	50,100	50,100	50,100	50,100
Sales income ($'000/year)	12,525	15,030	22,545	22,545

Year	1	2	3	4
Sales volume (units/year)	250	300	450	450
Average selling price ($/unit)	31,650	31,650	31,650	31,650
Sales income ($'000/year)	7,913	9,495	14,243	14,243

Contribution may be calculated directly, with small rounding differences. Average contribution = 50,100 – 31,650 = $18,450 per unit.

Year	1	2	3	4
Sales volume (units/year)	250	300	450	450
Average selling price ($/unit)	18,450	18,450	18,450	18,450
Sales income ($'000/year)	4,613	5,535	8,303	8,303

Tax-allowable depreciation = 4,000,000/10 = $400,000 per year

Benefit of tax-allowable depreciation = 400,000 × 0.28 = $112,000 per year

(b) Ignoring tax-allowable depreciation, after-tax cash flow from Year 5 onwards will be:

2,802,000 – 785,000 = $2,017,000 per year

Present value of this cash flow in perpetuity = (2,017,000/0.11) × 0.659 = $12,083,664

There would be a further six years of tax benefits from tax-allowable depreciation. The present value of these cash flows would be 112,000 × 4.231 × 0.659 = $312,282.

Increase in NPV of production and sales continuing beyond the first four years would be:

12,083,664 + 312,282 = $12,395,946 or approximately $12.4m.

If only the first four years of operation are considered, the NPV of the planned investment is negative and so it would not be financially acceptable. If production and sales beyond the first four years are considered, the NPV is strongly positive and so the planned investment is financially acceptable. In fact, the NPV of the planned investment becomes positive if only one further year of operation is considered:

NPV = (2,129,000 × 0.593) – 139,000 = 1,262,497 – 139,000 = $1,123,497

(c) Risk in investment appraisal refers to a range of outcomes whose probability of occurrence can be quantified. Risk can therefore be distinguished from uncertainty in investment appraisal, where the likelihood of particular outcomes occurring cannot be quantified.

As regards incorporating risk into investment appraisal, probability analysis can be used to calculate the values of possible outcomes and their probability distribution, the value of the worst possible outcome and its probability, the probability that an investment will generate a positive NPV, the standard deviation of the possible outcomes and the expected value (mean value) of the NPV. Standard deviation is a measure of risk in financial management.

One difficulty with probability analysis is its assumption that an investment can be repeated a large number of times. The expected value of the NPV, for example, is a mean or average value of a number of possible NPVs, while standard deviation is a measure of dispersal of possible NPVs about the expected (mean) NPV. In reality, many investment projects cannot be repeated and so only one of the possible outcomes will actually occur. The expected (mean) value will not actually occur, causing difficulties in applying and interpreting the NPV decision rule when using probability analysis.

Another difficulty with probability analysis is the question of how the probabilities of possible outcomes are assessed and calculated. One method of determining probabilities is by considering and analysing the outcomes of similar investment projects from the past. However, this approach relies on the weak assumption that the past is an acceptable guide to the future. Assessing probabilities this way is also likely to be a very subjective process.

(d) Theoretically, a company should invest in all projects with a positive net present value in order to maximise shareholder wealth. If a company has attractive investment opportunities available to it, with positive net present values, it will not be able to maximise shareholder wealth if it does not invest in them, for example, because investment finance is limited or rationed.

If investment finance is limited for reasons outside a company, it is called 'hard capital rationing'. This may arise because a company is seen as too risky by potential investors, for example, because its level of gearing is so high that it is believed it may struggle to deliver adequate returns on invested funds.

Hard capital rationing could also arise if a company wants to raise debt finance for investment purposes, but lacks sufficient assets to offer as security, leading again to a risk-related problem. During a time of financial crisis, investors may seek to reduce risk by limiting the amount of funds they are prepared to invest and by choosing to invest only in low-risk projects. It is also true to say that companies could struggle to secure investment when the capital markets are depressed, or when economic prospects are poor, for example, during a recession.

If investment funds are limited for reasons within a company, the term 'soft capital rationing' is used. Investing in all projects with a positive net present value could mean that a company increases in size quite dramatically, which incumbent managers and directors may wish to avoid in favour of a strategy of controlled growth, limiting the investment finance available as a consequence. Managers and directors may limit investment finance in order to avoid some consequences of external financing, such as an increased commitment to fixed interest payments if new debt finance were raised, or potential dilution of earnings per share if new equity finance were raised, whether from existing or new shareholders.

Investment finance may also be limited internally in order to require investment projects to compete with each other for funds. Only robust investment projects will gain access to funds, it is argued, while marginal projects with low net present values will be rejected. In this way, companies can increase the likelihood of taking on investment projects which will actually produce positive net present values when they are undertaken, reducing the uncertainty associated with making investment decisions based on financial forecasts.

161 Pinks Co

 BPP

			Marks
(a)	(i)	Sales nominal	1
		Variable costs nominal	1
		Fixed costs nominal	1
		Tax liabilities	1
		TAD	1
		TAD benefits	1
		Tax timing	1
		PVs and nominal NPV	1
			8
	(ii)	Real cash flow before tax	1
		Tax treatment	1
		Present values and real NPV	1
		Comment	1
			4
(b)		First way	2
		Second way	2
		Third way	2
		Fourth way	2
			8
Total			20

(a) (i) Nominal terms appraisal of the investment project

Year	1	2	3	4
	$'000	$'000	$'000	$'000
Sales revenue	39,375	58,765	85,087	32,089
Variable cost	(22,047)	(31,185)	(41,328)	(17,923)
Contribution	17,328	27,580	43,759	14,166
Fixed costs	(3,180)	(3,483)	(3,811)	(3,787)
Cash flows before tax	14,148	24,097	39,948	10,379
Tax at 26%	(3,679)	(6,265)	(10,387)	(2,699)
TAD benefits	1,300	975	731	2,194
Cash flows after tax	11,769	18,807	30,292	9,874
Discount at 12%	0.893	0.797	0.712	0.636
Present values	10,510	14,989	21,568	6,280

				$'000
Sum of PVs of future cash flows				53,347
Initial investment				20,000
NPV				33,347

Working

Year	1	2	3	4
Selling price ($/unit)	125	130	140	120
Inflated by 5%/year	131.25	143.33	162.07	145.86
Sales volume (units/year)	300,000	410,000	525,000	220,000
Sales revenue ($'000/year)	39,375	58,765	85,087	32,089
Variable cost ($/unit)	71	71	71	71
Inflated by 3.5%/year	73.49	76.06	78.72	81.47
Sales volume (units/year)	300,000	410,000	525,000	220,000
Variable cost ($'000/year)	22,047	31,185	41,328	17,923
Fixed costs ($'000/year)	3,000	3,100	3,200	3,000
Inflated by 6%/year	3,180	3,483	3,811	3,787
TAD ($'000)	5,000	3,750	2,813	8,437
TAD benefits ($'000)	1,300	975	731	2,194

Time	1	2	3	4
	$'000	$'000	$'000	$'000
Nominal cash flows after tax	11,769	18,807	30,292	9,874
Deflated at 3.7% pa	0.964	0.930	0.897	0.865
Real cash flows after tax	11,345	17,491	27,172	8,541
Discount at real rate 8%	0.926	0.857	0.794	0.735
Present value	10,505	14,990	21,575	6,278

				$'000
Sum of the PV of cash inflows				53,348
Investment outlay				(20,000)
NPV				33,348

(ii) **Comment**

The two approaches give the same outcome (there is a small rounding difference).

The first approach has higher cash flows due to inflation, and a higher cost of capital due to inflation. The second approach strips the general rate of inflation out of both the cash flows and the cost of capital and therefore has no impact on the NPV.

 BPP

Working

The deflation factors are calculated as $(1 + 0.0.37)-n$, where n is the time period.

> **Tutorial note.** The spreadsheet NPV function is quicker to use in the exam, rather than using discount tables, and you should consider using this is the exam.
>
> When using the NPV function in a spreadsheet you need to be aware that **the formula assumes that the first cash flow is in time 1 (not time 0) so time 0 has to be dealt with separately.**
>
> This is illustrated in the following calculations, first showing the numbers and then showing the formulae used.

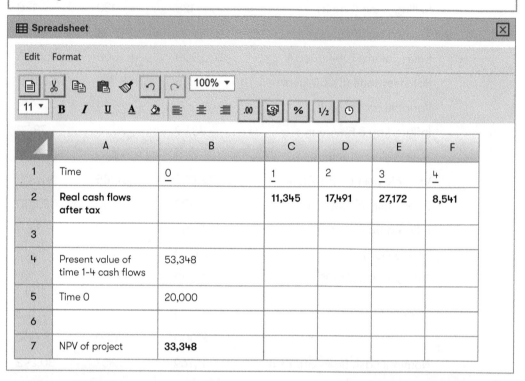

	A	B	C	D	E	F
1	Time	0	1	2	3	4
2	Real cash flows after tax		11,345	17,491	27,172	8,541
3						
4	Present value of time 1-4 cash flows	53,348				
5	Time 0	20,000				
6						
7	NPV of project	**33,348**				

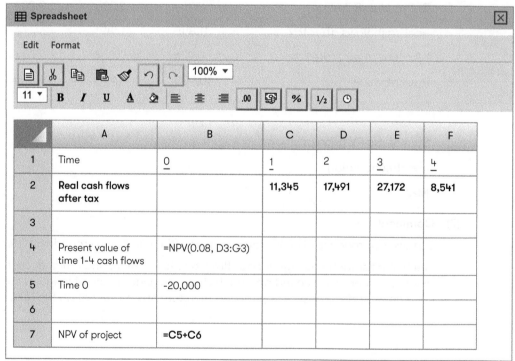

	A	B	C	D	E	F
1	Time	0	1	2	3	4
2	Real cash flows after tax		11,345	17,491	27,172	8,541
3						
4	Present value of time 1-4 cash flows	=NPV(0.08, D3:G3)				
5	Time 0	-20,000				
6						
7	NPV of project	=C5+C6				

 BPP

(b) The achievement of stakeholder objectives by managers can be encouraged by managerial reward schemes, for example, share option schemes and performance-related pay (PRP), and by regulatory requirements, such as corporate governance codes of best practice and stock exchange listing regulations.

Share option schemes

The agency problem arises due to the separation of ownership and control, and managers pursuing their own objectives, rather than the objectives of shareholders, specifically the objective of maximising shareholder wealth. Managers can be encouraged to achieve stakeholder objectives by bringing their own objectives more in line with the objectives of stakeholders such as shareholders. This increased goal congruence can be achieved by turning the managers into shareholders through share option schemes, although the criteria by which shares are awarded need very careful consideration.

Performance-related pay

Part of the remuneration of managers can be made conditional upon their achieving specified performance targets, so that achieving these performance targets assists in achieving stakeholder objectives. Achieving a specified increase in earnings per share, for example, could be consistent with the objective of maximising shareholder wealth. Achieving a specified improvement in the quality of emissions could be consistent with a government objective of meeting international environmental targets. However, PRP performance objectives need very careful consideration if they are to be effective in encouraging managers to achieve stakeholder targets. In recent times, long-term incentive plans (LTIPs) have been accepted as more effective than PRP, especially where a company's performance is benchmarked against that of its competitors.

Corporate governance codes of best practice

Codes of best practice have developed over time into recognised methods of encouraging managers to achieve stakeholder objectives, applying best practice to many key areas of corporate governance relating to executive remuneration, risk assessment and risk management, auditing, internal control, executive responsibility and board accountability. Codes of best practice have emphasised and supported the key role played by non-executive directors in supporting independent judgement and in following the spirit of corporate governance regulations.

Stock exchange listing regulations

These regulations seek to ensure a fair and efficient market for trading company securities such as shares and loan notes. They encourage disclosure of price-sensitive information in supporting pricing efficiency and help to decrease information asymmetry, one of the causes of the agency problem between shareholders and managers. Decreasing information asymmetry encourages managers to achieve stakeholder objectives as the quality and quantity of information available to stakeholders gives them a clearer picture of the extent to which managers are attending to their objectives.

Monitoring

One theoretical way of encouraging managers to achieve stakeholder objectives is to reduce information asymmetry by monitoring the decisions and performance of managers. One form of monitoring is auditing the financial statements of a company to confirm the quality and validity of the information provided to stakeholders.

Note. Only four ways to encourage the achievement of stakeholder objectives were required to be discussed.

162 Copper Co

Marking guide			Marks
(a) (i)	Initial present values	1	
	Total present values	2	
	Joint probability analysis (3 sets)	3	
	Expected NPV	2	
			8
(ii)	Negative NPV probability	1	
			1
(iii)	Most likely NPV	1	
			1
(iv)	Comment on expected NPV	1	
	Comment on risk	1	
			2
(b)	First method	4	
	Second method	4	
			8
Total			20

(a) (i) Expected NPV (ENPV) calculation

Year	PV of Y1 (W) $'000	Prob	PV of Y2 (W) $'000	Prob	Total PV $'000	Joint prob	PV × JP $'000	NPV $'000
PV scen. 1	893	0.1	1,594	0.3	2,487	0.03	74.6	(1,013)
			2,391	0.6	3,284	0.06	197.0	(216)
			3,985	0.1	4,878	0.01	48.8	1,378
PV scen. 2	1,786	0.5	1,594	0.3	3,380	0.15	507.0	(120)
			2,391	0.6	4,177	0.30	1,253	1,677
			3,985	0.1	5,771	0.05	288.6	2,271
PV scen. 3	2,679	0.4	1,594	0.3	4,273	0.12	512.8	773
			2,391	0.6	5,070	0.24	1,216.8	1,570
			3,985	0.1	6,664	0.04	266.6	3,164
						Sum of PV		4,365
						Investment		(3,500)
						ENPV =		865

Working

Discounting at 12%; discount factor time 1 = 0.893, time 2 = 0.797

Time	1	PV	2	PV
Low cash flow	1,000	893	2,000	1,594
Medium cash flow	2,000	1,786	3,000	2,391
High cash flow	3,000	2,679	5,000	3,985

Joint probabilities are calculated by multiplying the probabilities in year 1 and year 2 eg the first joint probability shown of 0.03 is calculated as 0.1 (year 1) × 0.3 (year 2).

(ii) Sum of joint probabilities with negative NPVs = 0.03 + 0.06 + 0.15 = 0.24 or 24%.

(iii) The outcome with the highest joint probability (0.30) has a present value of $4,177 – $3,500 = ($'000) 677.0.

(iv) The mean (expected) NPV is positive and so it might be thought that the proposed investment is financially acceptable. However, the mean (expected) NPV is not a value expected to occur because of undertaking the proposed investment, but a mean value from undertaking the proposed investment many times. There is no clear decision rule associated with the mean (expected) NPV.

A decision on financial acceptability must also consider the risk (probability) of a negative NPV being generated by the investment. At 24%, this might appear too high a risk to be acceptable. The risk preferences of the directors of Copper Co will inform the decision on financial acceptability; there is no clear decision rule to be followed here.

(b) Simulation

Simulation is a computer-based method of evaluating an investment project whereby the probability distributions associated with individual project variables and interdependencies between project variables are incorporated.

Random numbers are assigned to a range of different values of a project variable to reflect its probability distribution; inevitably this involves a degree of subjectivity. Each simulation run randomly selects values of project variables using random numbers and calculates a mean (expected) NPV.

A picture of the probability distribution of the mean (expected) NPV is built up from the results of repeated simulation runs. The project risk can be assessed from this probability distribution as the standard deviation of the expected returns, together with the most likely outcome and the probability of a negative NPV.

Adjusted (discounted) payback

Discounted payback adjusts for risk in investment appraisal in that risk is reflected by the discount rate employed. Discounted payback can therefore be seen as an adjusted payback method.

The (discounted) payback period can be shortened to increase the emphasis on cash flows which are nearer to the present time and hence less uncertain. A weakness of this approach is that it does not consider cash flows that lie outside the payback period.

Risk-adjusted discount rates

The risk associated with an investment project can be incorporated into the discount rate as a risk premium over the risk-free rate of return. The risk premium can be determined on a subjective basis, for example, by recognising that launching a new product is intrinsically riskier than replacing an existing machine or a small expansion of existing operations.

The risk premium can be determined theoretically by using the capital asset pricing model in an investment appraisal context. A proxy company equity beta can be ungeared and the resulting asset can be regeared to reflect the financial risk of the investing company, giving a project-specific equity beta which can be used to find a project-specific cost of equity or a project-specific discount rate.

ACCA Examining Team's Comments

Only two methods were required to be discussed.

---

163 Melplash Co

Workbook reference

Investment appraisal with tax and inflation is covered in Chapter 6

Top Tips

Make sure that you show your workings for this type of question (in part (a)) to minimise the risk of making careless mistakes. Then move quickly move on to parts (b) and (c) which are worth more than half of the total marks for this question.

Easy marks

Part (a), for eleven marks, asked for a NPV, IRR and ROCE. This featured the normal elements of a basic NPV calculation including inflation but no tax. This question should have been an area of strength for any well-prepared candidate.

ACCA examining team comments

Part (a)

The requirement necessitates the production of a cash flow forecast over the four-year life of the project, with net cash flow from each year discounted at the stated nominal (money) discount rate in order to get the net present value of the project. A well-prepared candidate should have few difficulties in executing this task and many candidates scored full marks here.

As stated above, the selling price and variable costs per motorcycle, together with the incremental fixed costs, are all stated in year 1 price terms and therefore it is incorrect to apply the expected inflation to the year 1 figures. This was the most common error on this question.

Other errors, although far less frequent than the above, included:

- Failure to compound the inflation eg, the year 3 selling price needs to be the year 1 selling price inflated by two years' worth of 6% per year inflation, $20,000 * 1.06^2 = $20,000 * 1.1236 = $22,472. Sometimes errors occur because of careless useof spreadsheet functionality in that the 6% per year inflation figure is applied to theyear 1 figure in both year 3 and year 4, instead of applying the inflation figure to the prior year eg, the year 3 selling price should be 6% higher than the year 2selling price;

- Inclusion of the initial investment in year 1;

- Omission of the residual value;

- Careless use of the sum formula such that the whole column of figures for a year were added, which caused the contribution to be double counted;

- Errors of magnitude such as income and variable costs being shown in $ or $000 but fixed costs shown incorrectly as $m.

In more general terms, candidates always need to show all workings, which can be shown in a separate workings' area or within cells or a combination of both. It is not acceptable for a cell to simply contain a typed-in number with no supporting workings. If the figure is incorrect, then it is impossible to award method marks in cases like this.

Finally, work should be presented as it would in the professional work environment. Rows and columns should be labelled correctly, with the magnitude of the figures clearly stated. The suggested solution uses $m, but $000 is perfectly acceptable providing that the magnitude is used consistently.

In (a) (ii) IRR can be calculated using spreadsheet functionality. This is the quickest and most efficient way of performing this task. Typing "=IRR" and then selecting the row of net cash flow figures, placed inside brackets, returns the IRR for that series of cash flows.

Care must be taken, however, to select the correct figures. Some candidates incorrectly used the PVs instead of the net cash flow figures and hence scored zero marks here. If candidates plan on using this method in future, it is advisable to practice the technique in advance of the actual examination.

In (a) (iv) Understanding the difference between cash flow and accounting profit is fundamental knowledge, which was lacking in many responses which made no attempt to deduct deprecation. The second most common error was to include the $30m of residual value as part of the project profit.

Part (b)

In general, this part-question was answered very well by candidates, with many scoring high marks.

Where candidates did not score high marks, the following was observed:

- Too much focus on a discussion of the results calculated in part (a) rather than the

suitability of the techniques

- A scattergun, short bullet point approach trying to cover too much too quickly. This approach rarely scores many, if any, marks and is to be avoided as the part (b) requirement states "Discuss….", meaning that a discussion is required

- The advice was not clear. Instead of being based solely on NPV, some hedging of the advice took place where all four investment techniques were discussed, with no clear conclusion.

The key messages from this question overall are:

- Read the requirements carefully

- Look at the marks available for each requirement

- "Discuss" type questions require more than brief points

- Practice published questions and other questions in the materials published by ACCA's Approved Content Providers.

 BPP

Marking guide			Marks	
(a)	(i)	Income	1	
		Variable costs	1	
		Fixed costs	1	
		Initial investment	0.5	
		Residual value	0.5	
		PVs and NPV	1	
				5
	(ii)	IRR setup	1	
		IRR calculation	1	
				2
	(iii)	Playback	1	
				1
	(iv)	Average accounting profit	1	
		Average investment	1	
		ROCE	1	
				3
(b)		NPV	2	
		IRR	2	
		Payback	2	
		ROCE	2	
		Advice	1	
				9
Total				20

(a) (i)   Calculation of net present value (NPV)

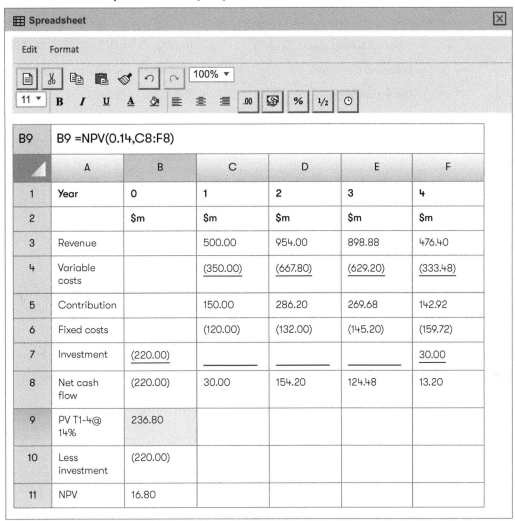

Workings

1 *Calculation of income*

Year	1	2	3	4
Inflated selling price ($/unit)	20,000	21,200	22,472	23,820
Demand (units/yr)	25,000	45,000	40,000	20,000
Revenue ($m/yr)	500.00	954.00	898.88	476.40

2 **Calculation of variable costs**

Year	1	2	3	4
Inflated selling price ($/unit)	14,000	14,840	15,730	16,674
Demand (units/yr)	25,000	45,000	40,000	20,000
Revenue ($m/yr)	350.00	667.80	629.20	333.48

(ii) Calculation of internal rate of return (IRR)

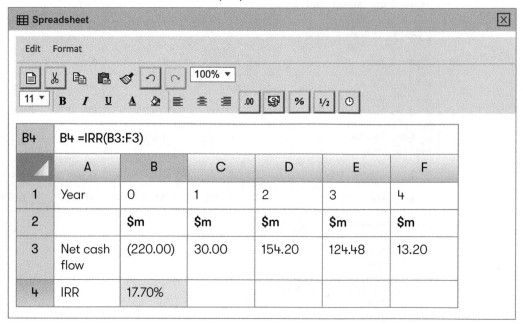

(iii) **Calculation of payback period**

Year	0	1	2	3
	$m	$m	$m	$m
Net cash flow	(220.00)	30.00	154.20	124.48
Cumulative cash flow		(190.00)	(35.80)	88.68

Payback period = 2 + (12 x (35.80/(35.80 + 88.68))) = 2 years 3 months

Or payback period = 2 + (35.80/(35.80 + 88.68)) = 2.3 years

(iv) **Calculation of return on capital employed (ROCE)**

Total cash inflow = $30.00m + $154.20m + $124.48m + $(13.20 − 30)m = $291.88m

Total depreciation = $220m − $30m = $190m

Total accounting profit = $291.88m − $190m = $101.88m

Average accounting profit = $101.88m/4 = $25.47m

Average investment = ($220m + $30m)/2) = $125m

ROCE = ($25.47m/$125m) x 100% = 20.4%

(b)

Net present value (NPV)

NPV uses cash flows rather than subjective profits. It takes into account the time value of money and the whole investment life. It is an absolute measure, enabling better business planning. The cost of capital it uses takes into account the risk of the investment and its financing. However, the results of the NPV calculation will depend on whether the cost of capital has been accurately estimated.

If the options which the board is considering are mutually exclusive, NPV can be used to rank them, as it indicates the effect on shareholder wealth. However, if shareholders have a short time horizon, they may not be prepared to wait for an investment to generate returns over its later life, even if it does have the best NPV.

Internal rate of return (IRR)

IRR takes into account the time value of money, cash flows and the whole life of the investment. However, whilst IRR can be calculated without knowing the company's cost of capital, a benchmark is needed to determine whether the IRR is acceptable or not.

If IRR is being used for comparison, it does not indicate which investment will generate more wealth for shareholders. It may give a different result to NPV because rather than being an indicator of wealth creation, it shows how sensitive the investment is to changes in the cost of capital. In some situations, there is more than one IRR.

Payback

Payback has the advantage of using cash flows. It indicates when the investment will break even and whether this is before projected cash flows become very uncertain. However, payback ignores the cash flows after the payback period, which for years 3–4 here are a significant proportion of total cash flows. It also ignores the total return on the investment. The simple payback figure ignores the time value of money, although a discounted payback figure can be calculated. The payback target is subjective.

Using payback to compare investments may result in choosing shorter-term investments giving immediate returns, rather than investments offering greater returns in the longer term. However, investments with a shorter period for recouping the amount invested may be preferred if Melplash Co has liquidity problems.

Return on capital employed (ROCE)

The ROCE method may reflect the wishes of shareholders that the company generates sufficient profits and does consider the entire life of the investment. However, the choice of an acceptable rate is subjective, here the justification for choosing the 20% figure is unclear. ROCE does not take into account the time value of money. It is possible that an investment which increases company value will be rejected if its ROCE is below the target ROCE. The acceptability of the ROCE may also depend on the assumptions about realisable value at the end of the project.

As ROCE is a percentage measure, it can be used to compare this investment with other options. However, the ROCE does not indicate the absolute change in shareholder wealth generated by different investments.

Advice

The investment is acceptable using three of the four methods, but fails the payback test which the directors have set. However, the directors should choose to go ahead with the investment if they can, on the basis that it has a positive NPV and therefore will increase

ANSWERS

long-term shareholder wealth. If the directors are concerned about the uncertainties of the income in later years, they should carry out sensitivity analysis.

164 Hawker Co

Workbook references

Lease versus buy is covered in Chapter 8 and a comparison of NPV and IRR is covered in Chapter 5.

Top tips

Neat workings will be important to avoid careless errors in part (a). Pay careful attention to the timing of cash flows.

Easy marks

Discussion marks in parts (b) and (c) should be straightforward as long as answers do not stray into irrelevant areas. However, to score 2 marks per point (in parts b and c) the point should be discussed in sufficient detail in that the reason should be developed and/or illustrated (best done by reference to the scenario, ie the circumstances of Hawker), or by developing the point. The ACCA Examiner's report stressed the importance of this issue.

Marking guide		Marks
(a) Disposal value	1	
TAD	1	
TAD benefits	1	
CO_2 tax	1	
CO_2 tax benefits	1	
PV of borrowing	1	
Lease payment	1	
Tax relief on lease payment	1	
PV of leasing	1	
Decision	1	
		10
(b) First reason	2	
Second reason	2	
		4
(c) First advantage	2	
Second advantage	2	
Third advantage	2	
		6
Total		20

(a) Option 1: Borrow and buy

The present value of the cost of interest, and capital, repayments on the loan is assumed to be equivalent of the present value of the loan.

The savings in running costs are disregarded as they are not affected by the financing decision.

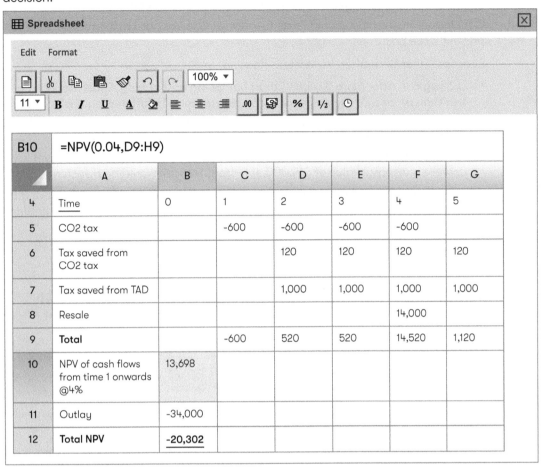

Spreadsheet

Edit   Format

100% ▼   11 ▼

B10	=NPV(0.04,D9:H9)						
	A	B	C	D	E	F	G
4	Time	0	1	2	3	4	5
5	CO2 tax		-600	-600	-600	-600	
6	Tax saved from CO2 tax			120	120	120	120
7	Tax saved from TAD			1,000	1,000	1,000	1,000
8	Resale					14,000	
9	**Total**		-600	520	520	14,520	1,120
10	NPV of cash flows from time 1 onwards @4%	13,698					
11	Outlay	-34,000					
12	**Total NPV**	**-20,302**					

Note. The NPV calculation can use the spreadsheet shortcut as shown or can be shown in full.

Option 2: Leasing

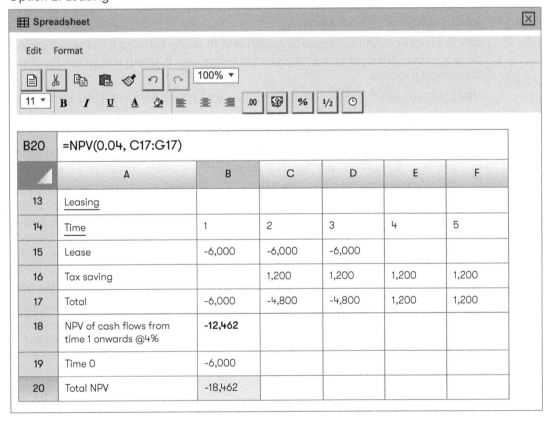

Spreadsheet

Edit   Format

100% ▼   11 ▼

B20	=NPV(0.04, C17:G17)					
	A	B	C	D	E	F
13	Leasing					
14	Time	1	2	3	4	5
15	Lease	-6,000	-6,000	-6,000		
16	Tax saving		1,200	1,200	1,200	1,200
17	Total	-6,000	-4,800	-4,800	1,200	1,200
18	NPV of cash flows from time 1 onwards @4%	**-12,462**				
19	Time 0	-6,000				
20	Total NPV	-18,462				

Note. Note: the tax payments start at time 2 because the first lease payment (at time 0) affects taxable profit in year 1 and tax relief is delayed by one year.

Conclusion: Hawker Co should lease the new vehicle because this option has the lower present value cost.

(b) Reasons, other than after-tax cost, for leasing

- Leasing can offer more flexibility than borrowing and buying. Lease periods can be for less than an asset's useful life, or break clauses may be offered by the lessor. If technology changes and the asset becomes out of date before the end of its expected life, the lessee does not have to keep on using it.

- Under the borrow and buy option, Hawker Co would carry the risk of the vehicle failing to achieve a disposal value of $14,000. If leased, this risk would be transferred to the lessor.

- The lessee may not have enough cash to pay for the vehicle and might have difficulty obtaining a bank loan. If this is the case, leasing may be the only way of getting use of the asset.

Note. Only two reasons were required

(c)

In most simple accept or reject decisions, IRR and NPV will select the same project. However, NPV has certain advantages over IRR.

The NPV of a proposed project, if calculated at an appropriate cost of capital, is equal to the increase in shareholder wealth which the project offers. In this way, NPV is directly linked to the assumed objective of the company, the maximisation of shareholder wealth. IRR calculates the rate of return on projects, and although this can show the attractiveness of the project to shareholders, it does not measure the absolute increase in wealth which the project offers.

NPV looks at absolute increases in wealth and thus can be used to compare projects of different sizes. IRR looks at relative rates of return and in doing so ignores the size of the investment projects.

NPV is not subject to the technical difficulties which limit the usefulness of the IRR method.

First, in situations involving multiple reversals in project cash flows, it is possible that the IRR method may produce multiple IRRs (that is, there can be more than one interest rate which would produce an NPV of zero). If decision makers are aware of the existence of multiple IRRs, it is still possible for them to make the correct accept or reject decision using IRR, but if unaware, they could make the wrong decision.

Second, in situations of mutually exclusive projects, it is possible that the IRR method will (incorrectly) rank projects in a different order to the NPV method. This is due to the inbuilt reinvestment assumption of the IRR method. The IRR method assumes that any net cash inflows generated during the life of the project will be reinvested at the project's IRR. NPV, on the other hand, assumes a reinvestment rate equal to the cost of capital. Generally NPV's assumed reinvestment rate is more realistic and hence it ranks projects correctly.

Finally, NPV can be used in situations where the cost of capital changes from year to year. Although IRR can be calculated in these circumstances, it can be difficult to make accept or reject decisions as it is difficult to know which cost of capital to compare it with.

165 Vyxyn Co

Marking guide		Marks
(a) Explain risk	1	
Explain uncertainty	1	
Discuss difference	1	
		3
(b) Inflated revenue	1	
Mean variable cost	1	
Inflated variable cost	1	
Tax liabilities	1	
TAD benefits	1	
Timing of tax flows	1	
Calculation of PVs	1	
Comment on variable cost	1	
Comment on NPV	1	
		9
(c) Sensitivity analysis	2	
Probability analysis	2	
Risk-adjusted rate	2	
Adjusted payback2	2	
		8
Total		20

(a) The terms risk and uncertainty are often used interchangeably in everyday discussion, however, there is a clear difference between them in relation to investment appraisal.

Risk refers to the situation where an investment project has several possible outcomes, all of which are known and to which probabilities can be attached, for example, on the basis of past experience. Risk can therefore be quantified and measured by the variability of returns of an investment project.

 BPP

Uncertainty refers to the situation where an investment project has several possible outcomes but it is not possible to assign probabilities to their occurrence. It is therefore not possible to say which outcomes are likely to occur.

The difference between risk and uncertainty, therefore, is that risk can be quantified whereas uncertainty cannot be quantified. Risk increases with the variability of returns, while uncertainty increases with project life.

(b) **NPV calculation**

Year	1	2	3	4	5
	$'000	$'000	$'000	$'000	$'000
Sales income	12,069	16,791	23,947	11,936	
Variable cost	(5,491)	(7,139)	(9,720)	(5,616)	
Contribution	6,578	9,652	14,227	6,320	
Fixed cost	(1,100)	(1,121)	(1,155)	(1,200)	
Taxable cash flow	5,478	8,531	13,072	5,120	
Taxation at 28%		(1,534)	(2,389)	(3,660)	(1,434)
TAD tax benefits		1,400	1,050	788	2,362
After-tax cash flow	5,478	8,397	11,733	2,248	928
Discount at 10%	0.909	0.826	0.751	0.683	0.621
Present values	4,980	6,936	8,812	1,535	576

	$'000
PV of future cash flows	22,839
Initial investment	(20,000)
NPV	2,839

Comment

The probability that variable cost per unit will be $12.00 per unit or less is 80% and so the probability of a positive NPV is therefore at least 80%. However, the effect on the NPV of the variable cost per unit increasing to $14.70 per unit must be investigated, as this may result in a negative NPV.

The expected NPV is positive and so the investment project is likely to be acceptable on financial grounds.

Workings

1 **Sales revenue**

Year	1	2	34	
Selling price ($/unit)	26.50	28.50	30.00	26.00
Inflated at 3.5% per year	27.43	30.53	33.26	29.84
Sales volume ('000 units/year)	440	550	720	400
Sales income ($'000/year)	12,069	16,791	23,947	11,936

2 **Variable cost**

Mean variable cost = (0.45 × 10.80) + (0.35 × 12.00) + (0.20 × 14.70) = $12.00/unit

Year	1	2	3	4
Variable cost ($/unit)	12.00	12.00	12.00	12.00
Inflated at 4% per year	12.48	12.98	13.50	14.04
Sales volume ('000 units/year)	440	550	720	400
Variable cost ($'000/year)	5,491	7,139	9,720	5,616
TAD ($'000)	5,000	3,750	2,813	8,437
Tax benefits at 28% ($'000)	1,400	1,050	788	2,362*

*(20,000 × 0.28) – 1,400 – 1,050 – 788 = $2,362,000

Alternative calculation of after-tax cash flow

Year	1	2	3	4	5
	$'000	$'000	$'000	$'000	$'000
Taxable cash flow	5,478	8,531	13,072	5,120	
TAD	(5,000)	(3,750)	(2,813)	(8,437)	
Taxable profit	478	4,781	10,259	(3,317)	
Taxation at 28%		(134)	(1,339)	(2,873)	929
After-tax profit	478	4,647	8,920	(6,190)	929
Add back TAD	5,000	3,750	2,813	8,437	
After-tax cash flow	5,478	8,397	11,733	2,247	929

(c) There are several ways of considering risk in the investment appraisal process.

Sensitivity analysis

This technique looks at the effect on the NPV of an investment project of changes in project variables, such as selling price per unit, variable cost per unit and sales volume. There are two approaches which are used. The first approach calculates the relative (percentage) change in a given project variable which is needed to make the NPV zero. The second approach calculates the relative (percentage) change in project NPV which results from a given change in the value of a project variable (for example, 5%).

Sensitivity analysis considers each project variable individually. Once the sensitivities for each project variable have been calculated, the next step is to identify the key or critical variables. These are the project variables where the smallest relative change makes the NPV zero, or where the biggest change in NPV results from a given change in the value of a project variable. The key or critical project variables indicate where underlying assumptions may need to be checked or where managers may need to focus their attention in order to make an investment project successful. However, as sensitivity analysis does not consider risk as measured by probabilities, it can be argued that it is not really a way of considering risk in investment appraisal at all, even though it is often described as such.

Probability analysis

This technique requires that probabilities for each project outcome be assessed and assigned. Alternatively, probabilities for different values of project variables can be assessed and assigned. A range of project NPVs can then be calculated, as well as the mean NPV (the expected NPV or ENPV) associated with repeating the investment project many times. The worst and best outcomes and their probabilities, the most likely outcome and its probability and the probability of a negative NPV can also be calculated. Investment decisions could then be based on the risk profile of the investment project, rather than simply on the NPV decision rule.

Risk-adjusted discount rate

It is often said that 'the higher the risk, the higher the return'. Investment projects with higher risk should therefore be discounted with a higher discount rate than lower risk investment projects. Better still, the discount rate should reflect the risk of the investment project.

Theoretically, the capital asset pricing model (CAPM) can be used to determine a project-specific discount rate which reflects an investment project's systematic risk. This means selecting a proxy company with similar business activities to a proposed investment project, ungearing the proxy company equity beta to give an asset beta which does not reflect the proxy company financial risk, regearing the asset beta to give an equity beta which reflects the financial risk of the investing company, and using the CAPM to calculate a project-specific cost of equity for the investment project.

Adjusted payback

If uncertainty and risk are seen as being the same, payback can consider risk by shortening the payback period. Because uncertainty (risk) increases with project life, shortening the payback period will require a risky project to pay back sooner, thereby focusing on cash flows which are nearer in time (less uncertain) and so less risky.

Discounted payback can also be seen as considering risk because future cash flows can be converted into present values using a risk-adjusted discount rate. The target payback period normally used by a company can then be applied to the discounted cash flows. Overall, the effect is likely to be similar to shortening the payback period with undiscounted cash flows.

166 Pelta Co

Workbook references

This question spans a number of investment appraisal topics, which are covered in chapters 5-8.

Top tips

Read the question carefully to ensure that you do not over-complicate it. For example even though the question clearly says that the project extends beyond four years, the question later says that the directors only want an evaluation over a four year period.

Easy marks

There are many easy marks available here, but as ever the discussion areas should (if related to the scenario) be a relatively easy source of marks.

Examining team's comments

In part (b), stand-alone comments such as 'accept' or 'positive NPV' should be explained.

In part (c), a critical discussion should look at a viewpoint or statement in more than one way.

Marking guide		Marks
(a) (i) Inflated sales		1
Inflated VC/unit		1
Inflated total VC		1
Tax liabilities		1
TAD benefits yrs 1–3		1

TAD benefits yr 4	1	
Timing of tax flows	1	
Terminal value	1	
Calculate PVs	1	
		9
(ii) Cumulative NPV	1	
Discounted payback	1	
		2
(b) Acceptability – NPV	1	
Acceptability – Payback	1	
Correct advice	1	
		3
(c) Evaluation period	2	
Terminal value	2	
Discounted payback	2	
		6
Total		20

(a) (i)

Year	1	2	3	4	5
	$'000	$'000	$'000	$'000	$'000
Sales income	16,224	20,248	24,196	27,655	
Variable costs	(5,356)	(6,752)	(8,313)	(9,694)	
Contribution	10,868	13,495	15,883	17,962	
Fixed costs	(700)	(735)	(779)	(841)	
Cash flows before tax	10,168	12,760	15,104	17,121	
Corporation tax		(3,050)	(3,828)	(4,531)	(5,136)
TAD tax benefits		1,875	1,406	1,055	2,789
After-tax cash flow	10,168	11,585	12,682	13,644	(2,347)
Terminal value				1,250	
Project cash flow	10,168	11,585	12,682	14,894	(2,347)
Discount at 12%	0.893	0.797	0.712	0.636	0.567
Present values	9,080	9,233	9,030	9,473	(1,331)

	$'000
PV of future cash flows	35,485
Initial investment	(25,000)
NPV	10,485

Working

Year	1	2	3	4
Sales volume (units/year)	520,000	624,000	717,000	788,000
Selling price ($/unit)	30.00	30.00	30.00	30.00
Inflated by 4% per year	31.20	32.45	33.75	35.10
Income ($'000/year)	16,224	20,248	24,196	27,655
Sales volume (units/year)	520,000	624,000	717,000	788,000
Variable cost ($/unit)	10.00	10.20	10.61	10.93
Inflated by 3% per year	10.30	10.82	11.59	12.30
Total ($'000/year)	5,356	6,752	8,313	9,694
Fixed costs ($'000 per year)	700	735	779	841
TAD ($'000 per year)	6,250	4,688	3,516	9,297
TAD benefits ($'000/year)	1,875	1,406	1,055	2,789

(ii)

Year	1	2	3	4	5
	$'000	$'000	$'000	$'000	$'000
Present values	9,080	9,233	9,030	9,473	(1,331)
Cumulative net present value	(15,920)	(6,687)	2,343	11,815	10,485
Discounted payback (years)					

Discounted payback occurs approximately 74% (6,687/9,030) through the third year ie the discounted payback period is about 2.7 years.

(b) The investment project is financially acceptable under the NPV decision rule because it has a substantial positive NPV.

The discounted payback period of 2.7 years is greater than the maximum target discounted payback period of two years and so from this perspective the investment project Is not financially acceptable.

The correct advice is given by the NPV method, however, and so the investment project is financially acceptable.

(c) The views of the directors on investment appraisal can be discussed from several perspectives.

Evaluation period

Sales are expected to continue beyond year 4 and so the view of the directors that all investment projects must be evaluated over four years of operations does not seem sensible. The investment appraisal would be more accurate if the cash flows from further years of operation were considered.

Assumed terminal value

The view of the directors that a terminal value of 5% of the initial investment should be assumed has no factual or analytical basis to it. Terminal values for individual projects could be higher or lower than 5% of the initial investment and in fact may have no relationship to the initial investment at all.

A more accurate approach would be to calculate a year 4 terminal value based on the expected value of future sales.

Discounted payback method

The directors need to explain their view that an investment projects discounted payback must be no greater than two years. Perhaps they think that an earlier payback will indicate an investment project with a lower level of risk. Although the discounted payback method does overcome the failure of simple payback to take account of the time value of money, it still fails to consider cash flows outside the payback period. Theoretically, Pelta Co should rely on the NPV investment appraisal method.

OTQ bank – Sources of finance

167 The correct answers are:

- Unsecured bonds are likely to require a higher yield to maturity than equivalent secured bonds - **True**

- Convertible bonds give the borrower the right but not the obligation to turn the bond into a predetermined number of ordinary shares - **False**

- A Eurobond is a bond that is denominated in a currency which is not native to where the bond itself is issued - **True**

Convertible bonds give the **investor**, not the borrower, the right but not the obligation to turn the bond into a predetermined number of ordinary shares.

Syllabus area E1(a)

168 The correct answers are:

	Order of risk
Ordinary share capital	1
Preference share capital	2
Trade payables	3
Bank loan with fixed and floating charges	4

Ordinary shares are most risky from the debt holder's perspective – the company can decide whether and how much of a dividend to pay.

Preference shares are next most risky – dividends are only payable if profit is available to pay dividends from.

Trade payables are next because they have to be paid before shareholders but are typically unsecured.

Finally, **banks** with fixed and floating charges face least risk.

Syllabus area E1(b)

169 **TERP** $6.60

Rights issue price $5.00

TERP is the market price before the rights issue less the value of a right per existing share = $7.00 – $0.40 = $6.60.

The issue price can be calculated from the TERP by subtracting the value of a right.

The value of a right can be calculated by multiplying the value of a right per existing share by the number of shares needed for one right.

Value of a right = 4 x $0.40 = $1.60

So the rights issue price is $6.60 – $1.60 = $5.00

Syllabus area E1(c)

170 The correct answer is: Annual interest received as a percentage of the nominal value of the bond

First statement describes the redemption yield.

Third statement describes the interest yield.

Fourth statement is incorrect.

Syllabus area E1(b)

171 The correct answer is: A bond in Islamic finance where the lender owns the underlying asset and shares in the risks and rewards of ownership

A key principle is that charging interest and making money from money lending alone is forbidden under Sharia law, so providers of finance are more directly involved with the risks and rewards of the businesses they finance.

Statement 2 is *mudaraba*.

Statement 3 is *murabaha*.

Statement 4 is *ijara*.

Syllabus area E1(d)

OTQ bank – Dividend policy

172 The correct answers are:

- No taxes or tax preferences
- No transaction costs

Modigliani and Miller (M&M) assume **perfect** capital markets so there is no information content in dividend policy. They assume no taxes or tax preferences so investors will be indifferent between income and capital gains. They also assume no transaction costs so investors can switch between income and capital gains without cost – eg if a company withholds a dividend when the investor would prefer cash, the investor can sell some of their shares (known as 'manufacturing a dividend'). M&M's theory is not contingent upon the existence or otherwise of inflation.

Syllabus area E1(e)

173 The correct answer is: A small listed company owned by investors seeking maximum capital growth on their investment

A residual dividend will not give a reliable income stream, and is geared to financing investments that will give capital gains.

Syllabus area E1(e)

174 The correct answer is: Investors selling some shares to realise some capital gain

M&M stated that income preference is irrelevant in deciding dividend policy because, if you 'assume away' taxation and transaction costs, it is costless for investors to switch from capital gain to dividends by selling some shares.

Syllabus area E1(e)

175 The correct answer is: A share repurchase scheme can increase both earnings per share and gearing

By reducing the number of shares in issue, the company can increase the earnings per share. This allows debt to be substituted for equity so gearing is raised.

First statement is **false**. A bonus issue is when a company offers free additional shares to existing shareholders. Therefore, it does not raise new equity finance.

Third statement is **false**. In a zero tax world neither the dividend decision nor the financing decision matters (according to Modigliani & Miller theory). Where tax does exist, both decisions are important.

Fourth statement is **false**. Shareholders are entitled to receive a share of any agreed dividends but directors decide on the amount and frequency of dividend payments (if any).

Syllabus area E1(e)

176   The correct answer is:

Sun Co	Moon Co	Nite Co
Constant growth	*Constant payout*	*Residual*

Company Sun Co dividends are growing at 10% per year even though earnings are not.

Company Moon Co is paying 50% of its earnings out as a dividend consistently.

Company Nite Co's dividends are not obviously connected with reported earnings, so its policy is either residual (ie only paying dividends once investment plans are budgeted for) or random.

Syllabus area E1(e)

OTQ bank – Practical capital structure issues

177    $\boxed{2.61}$

Operational gearing = Contribution/Profit before interest and tax.

Contribution = Revenue – variable cost = 10,123 – (70% × 7,222) – (10% × 999) = 4,967.70

Operational gearing = 4,967.70/1,902 = 2.61

Syllabus area E3(d)

178    $\boxed{53}$ %

Market value of equity = $5.50 × $100m = $550m

Market value of long-term debt = $500m × (125/100) = $625m

Therefore financial gearing = 625/(625 + 550) = 53%

Syllabus area E3(d)

179   The correct answer is: 15.0%

Market value of preference shares = 2,000 shares × 80c = $1,600.

Prior charge capital = preference shares + bonds + loan.

∴ Prior charge capital = $1,600 + ($4,000 × ($105/$100)) + $6,200

= $12,000

Market value of equity:

Number of shares = $8,000 ÷ 50c = 16,000 shares

16,000 shares × $5 = $80,000

Gearing = $12,000 / $80,000 × 100% = 15.0%

Syllabus area E3(d)

180   The correct answer is: $0.399

New earnings (profit after tax) = $55m + ($50m x $1.50 x 0.08 x (1 – 0.2)) = $59.8m

New earnings per share = $59.8m / (100m + 50m) = $0.399

A common error was that candidates did not adjust the earnings figure and instead used $55m to get $0.367 or did not adjust the number of shares to get $0.598.

Another error was taking the equity proceeds to be $50m (rather than $50m x $1.50), which results in earnings per share of $0.388.

Syllabus area E3(d)

181   The correct answer is: Neither 1 nor 2

Statement 1: This is not true. Currency futures are traded in standard contract sizes and therefore are not suitable for trades in small amounts of currency. This statement would be true for currency forward contracts.

Statement 2: This is not true. This statement would be true for crowdfunding but is not true for peer-to-peer lending (which is a way of raising debt finance).

Syllabus area E5(d)

182   The correct answer is: Neither 1 nor 2

Statement 1: This is not true. Crowdfunding is a relatively quick way of raising equity finance, this is one of its advantages.

Statement 2: This is not true. Peer to peer lending is not normally available to start-up companies because investors require an established trading history. Platforms usually require borrowers to have a trading track record, to submit financial accounts, and will perform credit checks as part of the credit assessment.

Syllabus area E5(d)

183   The correct answers are:

- SMEs will often experience a funding gap, due to them being seen as a higher risk investment than a larger company - **True**
- Founding shareholders of an SME will often have to sacrifice limited liability in order to obtain bank finance - **True**
- A lack of suitable, sufficient, non-current assets increases the funding gap problem for an SME - **True**

SMEs are seen as higher risk due to a lack of trading history as well as fewer assets to provide security.

The lack of suitable assets for security will often make it difficult to obtain bank finance unless the founders provide personal guarantees on the debt. These guarantees mean the sacrificing of limited liability as the founders will now be personally liable for the debt.

Syllabus area E5(b)

184   The correct answers are:

- Medium-term loans are harder to obtain than longer-term loans for SMEs - **True**
- SMEs are prone to funding gaps - **True**

Statement 1: For long-term loans, security can be provided in the form of property (eg mortgages) but SMEs may not have suitable security for a medium-term loan due to mismatching of the maturity of assets and liabilities. This problem is known as the maturity gap.

Statement 2: A funding gap is a shortfall in capital needed to fund the ongoing operations and this is a common problem for SMEs.

Syllabus area E5

185   The correct answer is: Business angel financing

This is known as business angel financing. Business angels are prepared to take high risks in the hope of high returns.

Syllabus area E5

186   The correct answers are:

- SCF is considered to be financial debt - **False**
- SCF allows an SME to raise finance at a lower interest rate than would normally be available to it - **True**

Statement 1: SCF allows a buyer to extend the time in which it settles its accounts payable. For the supplier, it is a sale of their receivables.

Statement 2: The buyer is usually a large company with a good credit rating. This means that low interest rates are charged to the supplier by the intermediary fund provider, for providing the supplier with finance, ie in the form of purchasing its invoices.

Syllabus area E5

OTQ bank – The cost of capital

187    $ $\boxed{1.73}$

20X9 to 20Y3 covers four years of growth, so the average annual growth rate =

$$\sqrt[4]{(423/220)}-1 = 0.178 = 17.8\%$$

$$K_e = \frac{d_0(1 + g)}{P_0} + g$$

$$K_e - g = \frac{d_0(1 + g)}{P_0}$$

$$P_0 = \frac{d_0(1 + g)}{K_e - g}$$

= (423,000 × 1.178)/(0.25 – 0.178) = $6,920,750 for 4 million shares = $1.73 per share

Syllabus area F2(c)

188    $\boxed{31}$ %

Using Gordon's growth approximation, g = br

g = proportion of profits retained × rate of return on investment

Proportion of earnings retained = ($1.50 – $0.5)/$1.50 = 66.7%

Rate of return on investment = EPS/net assets per share = $1.5/$6 = 0.25 so 25%

g = 66.7% × 25% = 16.7%

$$K_e = \frac{d_0(1 + g)}{P_0} + g$$

$$= \frac{\$0.50 \times (1.167)}{(\$4.50 - \$0.50)} + 0.167$$

= 31%

Note. Share price given is cum div.

Syllabus area E2(a)

 BPP

189 The correct answer is: The residual risk associated with investing in a well-diversified portfolio

'The chance that automated processes may fail' is **incorrect**. Systematic risk refers to return volatility, not automated processes.

'The risk associated with investing in equity' is **incorrect**. This describes **total** risk, which has both systematic and unsystematic elements.

'The diversifiable risk associated with investing in equity' is **incorrect**. Systematic risk cannot be diversified away.

'The residual risk associated with investing in a well-diversified portfolio' is **correct**. It is the risk generated by undiversifiable systemic economic risk factors.

Syllabus area E2(a)

190 $\boxed{13.4}$ %

The equity beta relates to the cost of equity, hence gearing and the debt beta are not relevant.

$E(r_i) = R_f + \beta \, (E(R_m) - R_f) = 3\% + (1.3 \times 8\%) = 13.4\%$

Syllabus area E2(a)

191 The correct answers are:

- An increase in the cost of equity leads to a fall in share price - **True**
- Investors faced with increased risk will expect increased return as compensation - **True**
- The cost of debt is usually lower than the cost of preference shares - **True**

Statement 1: An increase in the cost of equity will lead to a fall in share price. Think about the dividend valuation model and how P0 will be affected if Ke increases.

Statement 2: This is known as the risk-return trade-off.

Statement 3: Preference shares are riskier than debt and therefore a more expensive form of finance.

Syllabus area E3(a/b)

192 $\boxed{13.4}$ %

This question tests the use and understanding of the dividend growth model and its inputs.

To use the dividend growth model we need the share price.

To calculate the share price we need to use the price to earnings ratio of 5.

Earnings are 4 times the dividend (using dividend cover) so this is $0.10 x 4 = $0.40

So the share price is $0.40 × 5 = $2.00

$$K_e = \frac{d_0(1 + g)}{P_0} + g$$

$$= \frac{(0.10 \times 1.08)}{2.00} + 0.08$$

= 0.134 or 13.4%

Syllabus area E2(a)

193   The correct answer is: 20.5%

Dividend to be paid = $0.44 ($0.80 × 55%)

Current Earnings = $8m (10m × $0.80)

Retention ratio = 45% (100% – 55%)

Dividend growth rate = 9% (45% × 20%)

ke = [($0.44 × 1.09 / ($4.60-$0.44) + 0.09] = 20.5%

A common error was to fail to adjust the cum dividend share price and instead used $4.60 or incorrectly used the given payout ratio as the retention ratio.

Syllabus area E2(a)

194   The correct answers are:

- Capital structure will remain unchanged for the duration of the project - **True**
- The business risk of the project is the same as the current business operations - **True**
- The project is relatively small in size - **True**

Changes in capital structure will affect the WACC so need to stay constant. The current WACC reflects a risk premium relating to current operations, hence the new project should be of a similar risk profile to current operations. The project should be small in size; large projects are both riskier (commanding a risk premium) and likely to affect the value of equity, in turn affecting the WACC.

Syllabus area E3(e)

195    $\boxed{8.8}$ %

Cost of equity = 4 + (1.2 × 5) = 4 + 6 = 10%

WACC = (10 × 0.7) + (6 × 0.3) = 7 + 1.8 = 8.8%

Syllabus area E2

196    $\boxed{15.4}$ %

Ex div share price = $0.30 – (8% × $0.50) = $0.26

K_p = $0.50 × 8%/$0.26 = 15.4%

Note. Dividends are not tax deductible hence no adjustment for corporation tax is required.

Syllabus area E2(b)

OTQ bank – Capital structure theories

197   The correct answer is: Interest payments are tax deductible

'Debt is cheaper than equity': Although true, higher gearing increases the cost of equity (financial risk) therefore this doesn't in itself explain a reducing WACC.

'Interest payments are tax deductible' is **correct**: The only difference between MM (no tax) and MM (with tax) is the tax deductibility of interest payments. MM demonstrated that when a business does not pay tax, returns are not affected by capital structure. However, as interest is tax deductible (and dividends are not), paying relatively more interest will reduce tax payable and increase total returns to investors.

'Reduced levels of expensive equity capital will reduce the WACC' is similar to Statement A.

'Financial risk is not pronounced at moderate borrowing levels' refers to the traditional view. MM assume financial risk is consistently proportionate to gearing across all levels.

Syllabus area E4(b)

198 The correct answers are:

- The asset beta reflects both business risk and financial risk - **False**
- Total risk is the sum of systematic risk and unsystematic risk - **True**
- Assuming that the beta of debt is zero will understate financial risk when ungearing an equity beta - **False**

Statement 1 is **incorrect** because the asset beta is an ungeared beta and therefore reflects **only** business risk.

Statement 3 is **incorrect** because an asset beta will be lower than an equity beta. The difference between an asset beta and an equity beta reflects the impact of financial risk. However, this difference (reflecting financial risk) will be **higher** if a debt beta is assumed to be zero.

Syllabus area E3(e)

199 $\boxed{9.0}$ %

To reflect the business risk of the new investment, Shyma Co's beta of 1.6 should be ignored and instead the proxy beta of 1.1 should be used. This proxy beta is already an asset beta so does not need to be **ungeared**.

The asset beta does need to be **regeared** for Shyma Co's debt:equity ratio.

Equity beta = 1.1 × (3 + 1(1 – 0.4))/3 = 1.32

Using CAPM, k_e = 5 + 1.32 × 3 = 8.96% = 9.0% to 1 decimal place.

Syllabus area E3(e)

200 $\boxed{11.0}$ %

In this case, candidates should ignore the existing equity beta of 1.2 and use the industry average equity beta of 2.0. This proxy beta needs to be ungeared.

β_a = 2 × (75/100) = 1.5

The asset beta does not need to be regeared.

Using CAPM, k_e = 5 + 1.5× 4 = 8.96% = 11.0%.

201 The correct answers are:

- An equity beta also includes an element of financial risk - **True**
- Asset betas contain less business risk - **False**
- This is only due to tax relief on debt finance - **False**

An equity beta reflects both business and financial risk, an asset beta only reflects business risk.

Notes on incorrect statements:

Asset and equity betas both contain (the same) business risk.

Even if tax is zero an asset beta is less than an equity beta.

Syllabus area E3(e)

Section B questions

Nolciln

202　$\boxed{2.4}$ times

Variable costs are 60% of revenue, so contribution is 40% of revenue.

Contribution = 0.40 x $9,540,000 = $3,816,000.

Operational gearing = Contribution / PBIT

$3,816,000/$1,590,000 = 2.4 times

The most common error here was to take the 60% variable costs figure and use this as the contribution percentage. This gave an answer of 3.6.

Syllabus area E2(a)

203　$\boxed{6.4}$ times

Interest cover is PBIT / interest.

Interest = 0.08 x 3,125,000 = $250,000

$1,590,000 / $250,000 = 6.4 times.

Syllabus area E3(d)

204　The correct answers are:

- The cost of equity is higher when there is a high proportion of debt capital
- There is a point at which the weighted average cost of capital is minimised

Traditional capital structure theory states that there will be a point at which the weighted average cost of capital is minimised and also that the cost of equity will be higher when there is a high proportion of debt capital.

Syllabus area E4(a)

205　The correct answer is: The optimal capital structure is made up almost entirely of debt

Modigliani and Miller's theory stated that the optimal capital structure is made up almost entirely of debt. Under this model companies should have high financial gearing.

Syllabus area E4(b)

206　The correct answers are:

- Debt-holders may impose restrictive covenants in loan agreements
- When a company's gearing creates a high risk of bankruptcy the weighted average cost of capital will be higher

Debt-holders may impose restrictive covenants in loan agreements and when a company's gearing creates a high risk of bankruptcy the weighted average cost of capital will be higher. This is because higher returns will be required as compensation for the higher risk of bankruptcy.

Agency costs, tax exhaustion and bankruptcy risk discourage very high gearing levels and tax exhaustion occurs when there is a very high proportion of debt capital.

Syllabus area E4(a-b)

Tulip Co

207　The correct answer is: 10.7%

k_e = 2.5 + (1.05 × 7.8) = 10.7%

Syllabus area E2(a)

208   The correct answer is: 5.7%

Year	$	5%DF	PV	6% DF	PV
0	(100.00)	1.000	(100.00)	1.000	(100.00)
1–5	3.00	4.329	12.99	4.212	12.64
5	115.00	0.784	90.16	0.747	85.91
			3.15		(1.45)

$k_d = 5 + (3.15/(3.15 + 1.45)) = 5.7\%$

Syllabus area E2(b)

209   The correct answer is: The model assumes that all shareholders of Tulip Co have the same required rate of return

Notes on incorrect answers:

A constant share price is not assumed.

An efficient market would already have an accurate valuation of Tulip.

Syllabus area E2(a)

210   The correct answer is: Retained earnings are a source of equity finance

Notes on incorrect answers:

Equity finance does not represent cash.

A bonus issue does not raise cash.

Preference shares are not a source of equity capital.

Syllabus area E1(e)

211   The correct answer is: 2 only

Murabaha is similar to trade credit and therefore would not meet Tulip Co's needs. It is correct to state that Mudaraba involves an investing partner and a managing or working partner.

Syllabus area E1(d)

Section C questions

212 Spine Co

Marking guide	Marks	
(a) Debt		
Increased PBIT	0.5	
Increased interest	1	
Increased PBT	0.5	
Increased PAT	0.5	
Revised EPS and capital gain	2	
Equity		
Increased PBT	0.5	
Revised EPS	1	
TERP and capital gain	2	
Recommendation	1	
Other discussion	1	
		10
(b) Portfolio diversification	2	
Systematic risk	1	
Unsystematic risk	1	
Other points	1	
		5
(c) Diverse portfolio	1	
Single-period	1	
Perfect capital market	1	
Risk-free rate	1	
Other points	1	
		5
Total		20

(a) Increased PBIT = 13.040m × 1.2 = $15,648,000

Financing by debt

Current interest payment = $240,000

Increase in interest = 15m × 0.08 = $1,200,000

Revised interest payment = 1,200,000 + 240,000 = $1,440,000

Revised PBT = 15,648,000 − 1,440,000 = $14,208,000

Revised PAT = 14,208,000 × 0.7 = $9,945,600

Current EPS = 8,960,000/ 12,000,000 = $0.747 per share

Revised EPS = 9,945,600/12,000,000 = $0.829 per share

Current PER = 6.25/ 0.747 = 8.37 times

Revised share price = 8.37 × 0.829 = $6.94 per share

Capital gain = 6.94 − 6.25 = $0.69 per share

Financing by equity

Revised PBT = 15,648,000 − 240,000 = $15,408,000

Revised PAT = 15,408,000 × 0.7 = $10,785,600

Revised number of shares = 12m x 1.25 = 15m shares

Revised EPS = 10,785,600/15,000,000 = $0.719

Current PER = 6.25/ 0.747 = 8.37 times

Revised share price = 8.37 × 0.719 = $6.02 per share

TERP = ((4 x 6.25) + 5.00)/ 5 = $6.00 per share

Capital gain = 6.02 − 6.00 = $0.02 per share

Comment on findings

Financing by debt is recommended as this leads to the larger capital gain for the shareholders. This recommendation could have been made on the basis of EPS values alone, as the price/earnings ratio multiplier is the same for both financing choices. However, it is important to compare the share price arising from the equity financing option with the theoretical ex rights share price, rather than with the cum rights share price.

(b) With any investment, there is a risk that the actual outcome may be different from the expected or predicted outcome. This risk can be reduced by holding several different investments, since different investments are affected to differing extents by changes in economic variables such as interest rates and inflation rates. The return from one investment may increase, for example, when the return from a different investment decreases. Holding a range of different investments is known as portfolio diversification.

Experience shows that there is a limit to the reduction in total risk that can be achieved as a result of portfolio diversification. The risk that cannot be removed by portfolio diversification is called systematic risk. It represents risk relating to the financial system as a whole that cannot be avoided by any company in which an investment is made.

The risk that can be removed through portfolio diversification is called unsystematic risk or specific risk, as it relates to specific companies in which investments are made.

Experience has shown that investing in the shares of between 20 and 30 companies is sufficient to eliminate almost all of the unsystematic risk from an investment portfolio.

Systematic risk contains both business risk and financial risk. A company with no debt finance faces business risk alone, while a company with both equity and debt finance faces both business risk and financial risk.

(c) The capital asset pricing model (CAPM) is based on several key assumptions.

Investors hold diversified portfolios

While portfolio theory considers total risk, the CAPM considers only systematic risk, as it makes the assumption that all investors hold diversified portfolios. Investors will therefore only require compensation for the systematic risk in their portfolios.

Single-period transaction horizon

In order to compare the returns on different assets such as shareholdings, the CAPM assumes that all returns are over a standard single-period transaction horizon, usually taken to be one year.

Perfect capital market

The CAPM assumes a perfect capital market, with no taxes, no transaction costs and perfect information freely available to all participants.

Borrowing and lending at the risk-free rate

The CAPM assumes that all investors can borrow and lend at the risk-free rate of return. This represents a minimum rate of return required by all investors and is one of the variables in the CAPM equation.

[Note other relevant points would also receive credit]

213 LaForge Co

Workbook references

This question mainly focuses on sources of finance which is covered in Chapter 9, and dividend policy which is covered in Chapter 10.

Top tips

Careful reading of the requirements will help you to identify when a topic can be discussed in general terms and when you have to discuss the particular company in the question's scenario. For example, in part (c) a general discussion was appropriate as the requirement refers to 'a company', but part (d) clearly requires more than a general discussion because it specifically refers to LaForge.

Marking guide			Marks
(a) (i)	Existing shares		0.5
	New shares		0.5
	Issue price		1
	TERP		1
			3
(ii)	Value of rights per new share		0.5
	Value of rights per existing share		0.5
			1
(b) (i)	New PAT		0.5
	EPS		0.5
	Share price		1
			2
(ii)	Interest		0.5
	New PAT		1
	EPS		0.5
	Share price		1
			3

(c)	Up to 2 marks per method		5	
			—	
				5
(d)	Signalling effect		2	
	Clientele effect		2	
	Other		1	
	Recommendation		1	
			—	
	Maximum			6
Total				20

(a) (i) **TERP**

Current number of shares = $35m / $0.50 = 70m

Issue price = $2.60 × (1 – 0.3) = $1.82 per share

Number of shares to be issued = $25.48m / $1.82 = 14 million shares

TERP =

Current value

70m × $2.60 = $182m

Rights issue

$25.48m

New value

$207.48m

New number of shares

70m + 14m = 84m

TERP

207.48/84 = $2.47 per share

Alternatively:

Ratio of issued shares = 14m:70m = 0.2, and therefore a 1 for 5 issue

TERP = ($1.82 + 5 × $2.60) / (1 + 5) = $2.47 per share

(ii) **Value of a right (VOR)**

VOR per new share = $2.47 - $1.82 = $0.65 per new share

VOR per existing share = $0.65 × 14m / 70m = $0.13 per existing share

Alternately using 1 for 5 ratio = $0.65 / 5 = $0.13 per existing share

(b) (i) **Rights issue**

Forecast increase in profit after tax = $4.5m × (1 - 0.2) = $3.6m

Forecast PAT = $16.56m + $3.6m = $20.16m

Forecast EPS = $20.16m / 84m = $0.24 per share

Forecast share price = $0.24 × P/E ratio 11 = $2.64 per share

(ii) **Loan notes**

Extra interest = $25.48m × 6% = $1.53m

Forecast increase in profit after tax = ($4.5m- $1.53m) × (1 – 0.2) = $2.38m

Forecast PAT = $16.56m + $2.38m = $18.94m

The number of shares is unchanged at 70m.

Forecast EPS = $18.94m / 70m = $0.2706 per share

Forecast share price = $0.2706 × P/E ratio of 11 = $2.98 per share

(c) **Methods of issuing new equity shares**

Rights issue

A rights issue involves issuing shares to the existing shareholders in proportion to their existing holding. Rights issues are often successful, easier to price and are cheaper to arrange than a public issue but the amount of finance raised is limited as there is a finite amount that shareholders will be willing to invest. A rights issue would be mandatory if shareholders have not elected to waive their pre-emptive rights.

Private placing

A private placing is when a company, usually with the assistance of an intermediary, seeks out new investors on a one-to-one basis. Shares are normally issued to financial institutions when performing a placing rather than to individuals. This can be a useful source of new equity for an unlisted company but control of the company will be diluted as a result. A placing is also cheaper to arrange than a public issue but only useful for relatively small issues.

Public offer

If the company is listed, it may undertake a public offer whereby shares are offered for sale to the public at large. This is an expensive way of issuing shares as there are significant regulatory costs involved and like the placing, control of the existing shareholders will be diluted. A public issue will, however, allow very large amounts of equity finance to be raised, and will also give a wide spread of ownership.

Initial public offering (IPO)

If the company is not listed, it can list through the process of an IPO which will raise equity at the same time. An IPO will be more expensive than a public offer as there are further regulations having to be complied with, increasing costs. Consequently, only a large company wishing to raise a significant amount of finance would consider this option.

(d) The director's suggestion of reducing the forthcoming dividend would raise at most, $5.6m (70m × $0.08) so in itself, would not be sufficient but would provide 22% ($5.6m / $25.48m) of the total required. This would reduce the amount of new external finance needing to be raised, potentially reducing financing cost, but there are further problems with this suggestion.

Signalling effect

The signalling argument suggests that in the absence of perfect information, for example in a semi-strong form efficient capital market, the dividend announcement will send a message or "signal" to the market. Generally, a reduction in dividend (such as proposed here) could be interpreted as bad news by investors and result in a fall in LaForge Co's share price.

Clientele effect

Different investors have different needs relating to income or capital growth. LaForge Co has consistently paid dividends in the past so switching to a lower/zero pay-out could alienate some shareholders, resulting in large volumes of share sales. Given the different shareholders that LaForge Co has, this could be a real issue for them.

Liquidity preference

Generally, it is thought that shareholders, even those who prefer low pay-outs/high reinvestment, still wish to receive some dividend now as this is a certain return compared with the more risky and uncertain future dividends or capital growth.

Recommendation

Given that LaForge Co is a listed company with different shareholders and has consistently paid dividends in the past, a reduction in dividend could damage shareholder relations and possibly result in reduced shareholder wealth. The reduction in dividend is not recommended.

214 Corfe Co

Workbook references

Cost of capital is covered in Chapter 11. Sources of finance and dividend policy are mainly covered in Chapters 9 and 10.

Top tips

In part (a) if you are using the IRR function to calculate the after-tax cost of debt of the 8% loan notes be careful to apply this to cash flows for each of six years separately.

Examining team's comments

Part (a) provided information which allowed the capital asset pricing model (CAPM) to be used to calculate the cost of equity and most candidates were able to calculate this correctly. Some candidates incorrectly used the equity risk premium as the return on the market, when the equity risk premium is the difference between the return on the market and the risk-free rate of return. Some candidates ignored the cost of debt of the bank loan, even though it was identified in the question as a non-current liability. Some candidates correctly identified the after-tax cost of debt of the loan notes as an appropriate proxy value, while other argued for the after-tax interest rate on the loan notes. Some candidates used a value without providing an explanation for their choice. Whatever approach was adopted, the bank loan could not be ignored. Surprisingly, some candidates used the cost of equity, calculated using the CAPM, as the cost of debt of the bank loan.

In part (b) many candidates incorrectly believed that the company's equity reserves were cash which could be invested... many candidates did not quantify the finance which might be available from a dividend cut, even though information which allowed such a calculation was given in the question.

Marking guide	Marks
(a) Cost of equity set-up	1
Cost of equity calculation	1
Cost of preference shares calculation	1
After-tax cost of interest of loan notes	1
Cost of debt set-up	1
Cost of debt calculation	1
Cost of bank loan	1
Market value of equity shares	0.5
Market value of preference shares	0.5
Market value of loan notes	0.5
Market value of bank loan	0.5
Weighted average cost of capital	2
	11
(b) Director A	3
Director B	3
Director C	3
	9
Total	20

(a) $k_e = 3.5\% + (1.25 \times 6.8\%) = 12.00\%$

$k_{pref} = (0.06 \times 0.75)/0.64 = 7.03\%$

Loan notes

After tax interest payment	$8\% \times (1 - 0.2) = 6.4\%$
Nominal value of loan notes	100.00
Market value of loan notes	103.50
Time to redemption (years)	5
Redemption premium (%)	10

Year		$	5%DF	PV ($)	10% DF	PV ($)
0	MV	(103.50)	1.000	(103.50)	1.000	(103.50)
1–5	Interest	6.40	4.329	27.71	3.791	24.26
5	Redeem	110.00	0.784	86.24	0.621	68.31
				10.45		(10.93)

$IRR = 5 + ((10 - 5) \times (10.45/(10.45 + 10.93))) = 7.44\%$

Alternatively IRR can be calculated using the =IRR spreadsheet function based on these cash flows:

Time	0	1	2	3	4	5
	(103.5)	6.4	6.4	6.4	6.4	116.4

This approach gives an IRR of 7.3%

This figure can also be used for the cost of debt of the bank loan.

Market values and WACC calculation

	BV	Nominal	MV	MV	Cost	MV × Cost
	($m)			($m)	(%)	(%)
Equity shares	15	1.00	6.10	91.50	12.00	1,098.00
Preference shares	6	0.75	0.64	5.12	7.03	35.99
Loan notes	8	100	103.50	8.28	7.44	61.60
Bank loan	5			5.00	7.44	37.20
				109.90		1,232.79

$WACC = 100\% \times 1{,}232.79/109.90 = 11.22\%$

(b) **Director A**

Director A is incorrect in saying that $29m of cash reserves are available. Reserves are $29m, but this figure represents backing for all Corfe Co's assets and not just cash.

Corfe Co has $4m of cash. Some of this could be used for investment, although the company will need a minimum balance of cash to maintain liquidity for its day-to-day operations.

Corfe Co's current ratio is (20/7) = 2.86. This may be a high figure (depending on the industry Corfe Co is in), so Corfe Co may have scope to generate some extra cash by reducing working capital. Inventory levels could be reduced by just-in-time policies, trade receivables reduced by tighter credit control and payments delayed to suppliers. All of these have possible drawbacks. Just-in-time policies may result in running out of inventory, and tighter policies for trade receivables and payables may worsen relations with customers and suppliers. Again also, Corfe Co would have to maintain minimum levels of each element of working capital, so it seems unlikely that it could raise the maximum $25m solely by doing what Director A suggests.

Director B

Selling the headquarters would raise most of the sum required for investment, assuming that Director B's assessment of sales price is accurate. However, Corfe Co would lose the benefit of the value of the site increasing in future, which may happen if the headquarters is in a prime location in the capital city. Being able to sell the headquarters would be subject to the agreement of lenders if the property had been used as security for a loan. Even if it has not been used as security, the sale could reduce the borrowing capacity of the company by reducing the availability of assets to offer as security.

An ongoing commitment to property management costs of an owned site would be replaced by a commitment to pay rent, which might also include some responsibility for property costs for the locations rented. It is possible that good deals for renting are available outside the capital city. However, in the longer term, the rent may become more expensive if there are frequent rent reviews.

There may also be visible and invisible costs attached to moving and splitting up the functions. There will be one-off costs of moving and disruption to work around the time of the move. Staff replacement costs may increase if staff are moved to a location which is not convenient for them and then leave. Senior managers may find it more difficult to manage functions which are in different locations rather than the same place. There may be a loss of synergies through staff in different functions not being able to communicate easily face-to-face anymore.

Director C

The dividend just paid of $13.5m seems a large amount compared with total reserves. If a similar level of funds is available for distribution over the next two years, not paying a dividend would fund the forecast expenditure.

However, shareholders may well expect a consistent or steadily growing dividend. A cut in dividend may represent a significant loss of income for them. If this is so, shareholders may be unhappy about seeing dividends cut or not paid, particularly if they have doubts about the directors' future investment plans. They may see this as a signal that the company has poor prospects, particularly if they are unsure about why the directors are not seeking finance from external sources.

The directors' dividend policy may also be questioned if the dividend just paid was a one-off, high payment. Such a payment is normally made if a company has surplus cash and does not have plans to use it. However, the directors are planning investments, and shareholders may wonder why a high dividend was paid when the directors need money for investments.

215 Zeddemore Co

Workbook references

Project-specific cost of equity is covered in Chapter 12. Capital structure theories are also explained in Chapter 12.

Top tips

In part (b) many problems could be discussed but, to obtain strong marks, the points chosen needed to link to financial gearing (not operational gearing) and to relate to the question scenario instead of being purely generic points.

Examining team's comments

In part (c) the ACCA examining team report suggested that 'ideally the discussion would have then expanded on the loan notes and the bank loan and whether they are irredeemable/redeemable; secured/unsecured on Zeddemore Co's assets. Using the figures from part (a)(i), the discussion should have further related to the financing costs with equity (17.8%) and comparing it to the cheaper loan notes (10%) and the bank loan (7%)'.

 BPP

(a)	(i)	Current cost of equity	0.5
		WCP Co equity MV	0.5
		WCP Co debt MV	0.5
		Asset beta	1
		Number of shares	0.5
		Zeddemore Co equity MV	0.5
		Zeddemore Co debt MV	0.5
		Total debt	0.5
		Equity beta	1
		Project cost of equity	0.5
			6
	(ii)	Higher risk/return	1
		Wrong decision	1
			2
(b)		Problem 1	2
		Problem 2	2
		Problem 3	2
			6
(c)		Risk-return principle	2
		Equity v debt	2
		Irredeemable debt	1
		Secured debt	1
			6
Total			**20**

(a) (i) **Current ke:**

Using Zeddemore's own equity beta:

ke = 4% + 2.3 (10% − 4%) = 17.8%

Project specific ke:

Need to use the proxy (WCP) to derive a suitable beta as Zeddemore Co's own beta is not suitable for the new venture due to different risk.

Degear the proxy beta first.

Asset beta = equity beta × {Ve/(Ve + Vd ×(1 − t))}

Ve = 100m × $2.60 = $260m

Vd = $110m × 0.96 = $105.6m

Asset beta = 1.25 × {$260m/($260m + $105.6m × (1 − 0.2))} = 0.94

Now regear using Zeddemore Co's gearing:

Ve = $40m/$0.50 × $1.05 = $84m

Vd (Loan notes) = $250m × 0.65 = $162.5m

Vd (Loan) = $20m

Total Vd = $162.5m + $20m = $182.5m

Equity beta = asset beta x {(Ve + Vd(1 − t))/Ve}

Equity beta = 0.94 × {($84m + $182.5m × (1 − 0.2))/$84m} = 2.57

ke = 4% + 2.57 × (10% − 4%) = 19.42%(aii)

(ii) Comment

The project-specific cost of equity is higher than the current cost of equity, indicating that a higher return would be needed by shareholders to compensate for the higher risk of the new venture. Appraising the venture using the existing cost of equity, as advised by the commercial director, would therefore result in an over-statement of the venture's net present value, potentially leading to an incorrect decision being made.

(b) Gearing problems

Increased earnings volatility

High gearing increases the volatility of Zeddemore Co's earnings as the interest payable is unaffected by any change in the activity level. If Zeddemore Co experiences a reduction in its activity level, the percentage reduction in earnings will be greater than the percentage reduction in activity level. This increased volatility in earnings represents the financial risk of the company.

Cost of equity finance

Increased volatility of earnings will increase the cost of equity, making equity finance more expensive. The financial risk premium can be seen by comparing the asset beta of 0.94 (ke = 9.64%) with the equity beta of 2.57 (ke = 19.42%).

Debt capacity

The gearing level will affect Zeddemore Co's ability to raise new debt finance and how much debt it can support (debt capacity). Given its high gearing level, Zeddemore Co may find that it cannot raise any more debt finance.

Bankruptcy risk

High gearing leads to a high interest obligation for Zeddemore Co and an increased risk of being unable to pay all of its interest following an unexpected reduction in profits/cash flow. This could result in default by Zeddemore Co on its interest payments and subsequent forced liquidation by its lenders.

Note. Only three problems were required.

(c) Risk-return relationship

The risk-return relationship explains why different sources of finance have different costs. An investor's required rate of return will be determined primarily by the level of risk the investment has. If an investment carries a high level of risk, the investor will require a high rate of return to compensate for that risk. Investing in a low-risk investment will mean a lower level of return will be required.

A rational investor would not invest in a high-risk investment offering a low return as they could obtain the same return from a lower-risk investment. A low-risk investment offering high returns would not exist as it would be undervalued and the high demand for that investment would increase the price and therefore reduce the return.

Zeddemore Co's finance costs

The risk-return relationship will result in Zeddemore Co's shareholders and lenders having different required rates of return.

The equity holders have no guaranteed return as Zeddemore Co is under no obligation to pay a dividend each year and capital growth is also not guaranteed (in fact, the share price has fallen). Also, if the company was liquidated, the equity holders would come last in the order of payment and possibly receive nothing.

By comparison, the lenders (loan note holders and the bank) face lower risk as their interest is a contractual obligation and must be paid. The fall in share price will not directly affect the lenders as they do not participate in any capital growth/decline. Zeddemore Co's lenders do face the risk of default in the event of Zeddemore Co being unable to pay the interest, but

BPP

ANSWERS

both the loan notes and the bank loan are secured on Zeddemore Co's assets so the risk of any loss on default is reduced, assuming the assets realise sufficient value to repay the debt.

The above effects can be seen in Zeddemore Co's finance costs with their cost of equity being higher than their cost of debt. For example, the current cost of equity is 17.8% which is higher than the cost of the bank loan which is only 7%. The loan notes are also cheaper, costing 10% ($6.50/$65.00). The loan notes are more expensive than the bank loan as they are irredeemable and thus have no guaranteed repayment date, increasing the risk compared with the bank loan which is repayable in the future.

216 BKB Co (amended)

Workbook references

Weighted average cost of capital (WACC) is covered in Chapter 11. The advantages of issuing convertible bonds are discussed in Chapter 9.

Top tips

If you know your formulas well, the calculations in part (a) should be straightforward. You should know that overdrafts should not be considered as part of the capital structure.

You will need to apply logic in answering part (b). In part (c), briefly plan your answer before you start to answer the question.

Easy marks

Marks are available for straightforward calculations in part (a).

Examining team's comments

In part (a) few answers were able to calculate correctly the cost of the preference shares and some answers chose to use the dividend percentage relative to nominal as the cost of capital, or to assume a value for the cost of capital. Some answers mistakenly calculated the after-tax cost of the preference shares. As preference shares pay a dividend, which is a distribution of after-tax profit, they are not tax efficient. A common error was to mix bond-related values (such as the $4.90 after-tax interest payment) with total debt-related values (such as the $21m market value of the bond issue), producing some very high values in the linear interpolation calculation. Some candidates were unable to calculate the future share price as part of the conversion value calculation. Most candidates were able to calculate a WACC value, although some omitted the cost of preference shares from the calculation. In part (b) many answers were not of a high standard and tried to make some general points about market efficiency or about the window-dressing of financial statements. The important point here is that the weightings used in the WACC calculation need to reflect the relative importance of the different sources of finance used by a company if the WACC is to be used in investment appraisal.

Marking guide	Marks
(a) Calculation of cost of equity using CAPM	2
Calculation of bond market price	0.5
Calculation of current share price	0.5
Calculation of future share price	1
Calculation of conversion value	1
After-tax interest payment	1
Setting up interpolation calculation	1
Calculation of after-tax cost of debt	1
Calculation of cost of preference shares	1

 BPP

	Marks
Calculation of after-tax WACC	2
Explanation of any assumptions made	$\underline{1}$
	12
(b) Market values reflect current market conditions	2
Market values and optimal investment decisions	2
Other relevant discussion or illustration	$\underline{2}$
Marks Available	6
Maximum	4
(c) Self-liquidating	1
Lower interest rate	1
Increase in debt capacity on conversion	1
Other relevant advantages of convertible debt	$\underline{3}$
Marks Available	6
Maximum	$\underline{4}$
Total	$\underline{\underline{20}}$

(a) **Equity**

The market value (MV) of equity is given as $125m.

CAPM: $E(r_j) = R_f + \beta_i(E(r_m) - R_f)$

R_f = Risk-free rate = 4%

β_i = Equity beta = 1.2

$(E(r_m) - R_f)$ = Equity risk premium = 5%

Therefore the cost of equity = 4% + 1.2 × 5% = 10%

Convertible bonds

Assume that bondholders will convert if the MV of 19 shares in 5 years' time is greater than $100.

MV per bond = $100 × $21m/$20m = $105

MV per share today = $125m/25m = $5

MV per share in 5 years' time = $5 × 1.04^5 = $6.08 per share

Conversion value = $6.08 × 19 = $115.52

The after-tax cost of the convertible bonds can be calculated by linear interpolation, assuming the bondholders will convert.

Time	Cash flow $	Discount factor 7%	Present value $	Discount factor 5%	Present value $
0	(105)	1	(105)	1	(105)
1–5	4.9*	4.100	20.09	4.329	21.21
5	115.52	0.713	$\underline{82.37}$	0.784	$\underline{90.57}$
			$\underline{(2.54)}$		$\underline{6.78}$

* After-tax interest payment = 7 × (1 − 0.3) = $4.90 per bond

Cost of convertible bonds = 5 + [(7 − 5) × 6.78/6.78 + 2.54)] = 5 + 1.45 = 6.45%

Preference shares

After-tax cost of preference shares = 5% × $10m/$6.25m = 8%

WACC

Total value = $125m + $21m + $6.25m = $152.25m

After-tax WACC = [($125m × 10%) + ($21m × 6.45%) + ($6.25m × 8%)/$152.25m]

After-tax WACC = 9.4% per year

Note. As overdraft represents a short-term source of finance, it has been assumed not to form part of the company's capital and has therefore been excluded from the WACC calculation. The overdraft is large, however, and seems to represent a fairly constant amount. The company should evaluate whether it should be taken into account.

(b) MVs are preferable to book values when calculating WACC, because they reflect the current value of the company's capital.

If book values are used instead of MVs, this will seriously understate the proportion that equity represents in the company's capital structure. This is because the MV of ordinary shares is usually significantly higher than its nominal book value.

Understating the impact of the cost of equity on the WACC will most likely cause the WACC to be understated since, as we can see in the answer above, the cost of equity is greater than the cost of debt. Underestimating the WACC will skew the company's investment appraisal process as a lower discount rate is used, and cause the company to make sub-optimal investment decisions.

Using book values instead of market values will also change the value of debt in the company's capital structure. The impact of understating or overstating the value of debt would be less significant than is the case for equity, because debt instruments are often traded at close to their nominal value.

(c) Convertible bonds are attractive for companies for the following reasons:

(1) **Lower rates of interest:** Investors are normally willing to accept a lower coupon rate of interest on convertible bonds, because of the additional value offered by the conversion rights. This helps to ease the burden on cash flows.

(2) **The possibility of not redeeming the debt at maturity:** Companies issue convertible bonds with the expectation that they will be converted. If the bonds are converted, this frees the company from a cash repayment at redemption. The cash advantage is further augmented by the greater flexibility that equity shares allow in terms of returns.

(3) **Availability of finance:** Issuing convertible bonds may allow greater access to finance, as lenders who would otherwise not provide ordinary loan finance may be attracted by the conversion rights.

(4) **Impact on gearing:** On conversion, the company's gearing will be reduced not only because of the removal of debt, but also because equity replaces the debt. This can send positive signals about the company's financial position.

(5) **Delayed equity:** The fact that convertible bonds allow the issue of shares at a predetermined point in the future permits the company to plan the impact on its earnings per share upon conversion.

217 Fence Co (amended)

Marking guide	Marks	
(a) Calculation of equity risk premium	1	
Calculation of cost of equity	1	
After-tax interest payment	1	
Setting up IRR calculation	1	
Calculating after-tax cost of debt	1	
Market value of equity	0.5	
Market value of debt	0.5	
Calculating WACC	1	
		7
(b) Ungearing proxy company equity beta	2	
Regearing equity beta	1	
Calculation of cost of equity	1	
		4
(c) Risk diversification	1	
Systematic risk	1	
Unsystematic risk	1	
Portfolio theory and the CAPM	1	
		4
(d) 1–2 marks per point made		
Maximum		5
Total		**20**

(a) After-tax cost of debt (K_d) can be calculated by linear interpolation.

Year		Cash flow	Discount factor 4%	PV	Discount factor 5%	PV
		$		$		$
0	Market value	(107.14)	1.000	(107.14)	1.000	(107.14)
1–7	Interest (7 × (1 – 0.2))	5.60	6.002	33.61	5.786	32.40
7	Redemption	100.00	0.760	76.00	0.711	71.10
				2.47		(3.64)

After-tax cost of debt =

$$4\% + \frac{2.47}{2.47 + 3.64}(5\%-4\%) = 4.4\%$$

Alternatively IRR can be calculated using the =IRR spreadsheet function based on these cash flows:

Time	0	1	2	3	4	5	6	7
	(107.14)	5.6	5.6	5.6	5.6	5.6	5.6	105.6

This approach also gives an IRR of 4.4%

Cost of equity (K_e) can be found using CAPM.

$E(r_j) = R_f + \beta_i(E(r_m) - R_f)$

$ = 4 + 0.9 (11 - 4)$

$ = 10.3\%$

Market value of equity (V_e) = $10m × $7.50 = $75m

Market value of debt (V_d) = $14m × 107.14/100= $15m

$$WACC = \left[\frac{V_e}{V_e + V_d}\right]K_e + \left[\frac{V_d}{V_e + V_d}\right]K_d$$

$$WACC = \left[\frac{75}{75 + 15}\right]10.3 + \left[\frac{15}{75 + 15}\right]4.4$$

= 9.3%

(b) Ungear to remove the financial risk

$$\beta_a = \beta_e \times \frac{V_e}{V_e + V_d(1-t)}$$

$$\beta_a = 1.2 \times \frac{54}{54 + 12(1-0.2)}$$

= 1.019

Convert back to a geared beta

$$\beta_e = \beta_a \times \frac{V_e + V_d(1-t)}{V_e}$$

$$\beta_e = 1.019 \times \frac{75 + 15(1-0.2)}{75}$$

= 1.182

Use CAPM to estimate cost of equity.

Equity or market risk premium = 11 − 4 = 7%

Cost of equity = 4 + (1.182 × 7) = 4 + 8.3 = 12.3%

(c) **Unsystematic** risk can be **diversified away** but even well-diversified portfolios will be exposed to **systematic risk**. This is the risk **inherent in the market as a whole**, which the shareholder cannot mitigate by holding a diversified investment portfolio.

Portfolio theory is concerned with **total risk** (systematic and unsystematic). The **CAPM** assumes that investors will hold a fully diversified portfolio and therefore ignores unsystematic risk.

(d) **Diversification**

Under the CAPM, the return required from a security is **related** to its **systematic risk** rather than its total risk. Only the risks that **cannot** be **eliminated** by diversification are **relevant**. The assumption is that investors will hold a **fully diversified portfolio** and therefore deal with the unsystematic risk themselves. However, in practice, markets are **not totally efficient** and investors do not all hold fully diversified portfolios. This means that total risk is relevant to investment decisions, and that therefore the relevance of the CAPM may be limited.

Excess return

In practice, it is difficult to determine the excess return ($R_m − R_f$). **Expected rather than historical returns** should be used, although historical returns are used in practice.

Risk-free rate

It is similarly difficult to **determine the risk-free rate**. A risk-free investment might be a government security; however, interest rates vary with the term of the debt.

Risk aversion

Shareholders are risk averse, and therefore **demand higher returns** in compensation for increased levels of risk.

Beta factors

Beta factors based on historical data may be a **poor basis** for future **decision making**, since evidence suggests that beta values fluctuate over time.

Unusual circumstances

The CAPM is unable to forecast accurately returns for companies with low price/earnings ratios, and to take account of seasonal 'month of the year' and 'day of the week' effects that appear to influence returns on shares.

 BPP

218 Tanza Co

Marking guide	**Marks**
(a) **Cost of equity**	1
Future share price	0.5
Conversion value	0.5
Conversion decision	1
Cost of convertible loan notes	3
Cost of bank loan	1
Market value of equity	0.5
Market value of convertible debt	0.5
WACC	2
	10

(b)	(i)	Director A	3
		Director B	3
			6
	(ii)	Factor 1	2
		Factor 2	2
			4
Total			20

(a) Cost of equity (k_e)

$k_e = d_1/p_0 + g = 90/555 + 0.06 = 22.2\%$

Cost of convertible loan notes (k_{conv})

k_{conv} = internal rate of return of relevant cash flows

Conversion value = anticipated share value on conversion/redemption date

Each share = $5.55 \times 1.06^3 = \$6.61$

20 shares = $6.61 × 20 = $132.20 (greater than redemption value of $100)

Time		$	DF 10%	$	DF 15%	$
0	Current market value	(108.51)	1.00	(108.51)	1.00	(108.51)
1-3	Interest × (1 – t)	5.10	2.49	12.68	2.28	11.65
3	Conversion value	132.20	0.75	99.28	0.66	86.99
				3.45		(9.87)

IRR = 10 + 3.45/(3.45 + 9.87) × (15 – 10) = 11.3%

Note. If IRR formula is used the answer is 11.2%

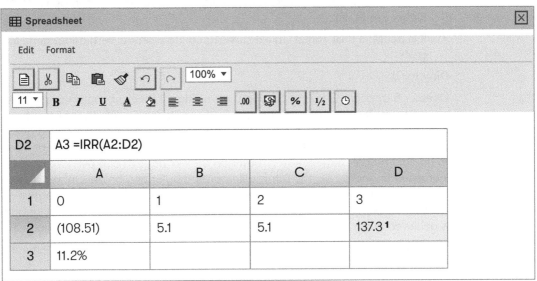

D2	A3 =IRR(A2:D2)			
	A	B	C	D
1	0	1	2	3
2	(108.51)	5.1	5.1	137.3 [1]
3	11.2%			

[1] (5.1 + 132.2)

Cost of bank loan

4% × (1 – 0.15) = 3.4%

BPP

ANSWERS

Market value of capital structure and WACC

	$ million	Cost	WACC
Equity			
(50m/0.5) = 100m x $5.55	555.0	22.2%	14.7%
Convertible loan notes			
108.51/100 x $150 million = $162.8m	162.8	11.3%	2.2%
Bank loan	120.0	3.4%	0.5%
Total	837.8		17.4%

(b) (i)

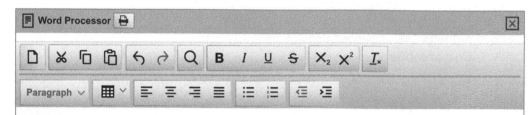

Director A

Director A is suggesting that Modigliani & Miller's (M&M) theory of capital structure is most relevant. M&M suggested that a company's weighted average cost of capital (WACC) is primarily determined by its business activities rather than its capital structure.

They also proposed that the only way a company's capital structure can affect the WACC and therefore the value of the company is by introducing more debt and thereby increasing the tax shield (the present value of the tax savings made because interest is tax-deductible whereas dividends are not).

It is based on this theory that Director A is suggesting a much more aggressive regearing of Tanza Co. The problems or risks that this would pose:

- Providers of debt finance (e.g. banks) are not likely to tolerate such high levels of capital gearing as it increases the risk of default. If the banks are willing to lend at all, they are likely to require a much higher interest rate to compensate them for higher credit risk.

- It is possible that Tanza Co exhausts its taxable profits with deductions for interest costs.

Director B

Director B appears to be supporting the traditional theory by suggesting that there is an optimum. Because the cost of debt is generally lower than that of equity, by increasing gearing, Tanza Co's WACC would fall. However, as borrowing gets larger, equity investors see their financial risk increasing as more and more debt interest has to be paid before they receive a return on their equity. To compensate for this increased financial risk, the returns demanded by equity holders increase. As gearing continues to increase, the benefit of cheap debt finance is eventually outweighed by the cost of more expensive equity and WACC starts to rise. The optimal gearing level is achieved when WACC has stopped falling but has not yet started rising.

The problem with this is that the optimum level of gearing can only be estimated by trial and error.

(ii)

Other factors to consider:

- The finance is needed quickly, this would favour the use of debt which is less time consuming to raise. Because of this and other administrative factors, it is also less expensive to raise.

- The cost of new debt may be lowered if Tanza Co has any non-current assets to offer as security. Using non-current assets as collateral will lower the risk for the lender.

- It is important to consider the clientele effect too. The current shareholder-base seems to be comfortable with a gearing level which is lower than average for the industry. By changing that policy, this may change the investors' perceived risk exposure, leading to the sale of their shares.

219 Grenarp Co (amended)

Workbook references

FinTech is covered in Chapter 2. Rights issues and sources of finance are covered in Chapter 9. Capital structure is covered in Chapter 12.

Top tips

For part (a), start by considering the planned rights issue and calculate the rights issue price, the number of new shares offered in the rights issue, the net cash raised after issue costs and the theoretical ex-rights price (TERP). For part (b), start by defining an optimal capital structure.

Easy marks

There are easy marks for calculations in part (a) and you should score well in parts (b) and (c) if you have learnt the material on capital structure and sources of finance.

Examining team's comments

For part (a) many students did not gain many marks. Some answers adopted a 5 for 1 basis for the rights instead of 1 for 5. Some students added the issue costs to the cash raised figure provided. Many answers to part (b) were unsatisfactory. Some answers incorrectly stated that an optimal capital structure was a 50/50 mix of equity and debt.

Marking guide	Marks
(a) Rights issue price	0.5
New shares issued	0.5
Net cash raised by rights issue	0.5
TERP per share	1
Buy-back price of loan notes	0.5
Nominal value of loan notes redeemed	1
Before-tax interest saving	0.5
After-tax interest saving	0.5

Revised earnings	0.5
Revised earnings per share	0.5
Revised share price using P/E ratio method	1
Comment on effect of redemption on shareholders' wealth	1
	8
(b) Traditional view of capital structure	3
M&M views of capital structure	3
Other relevant discussion	3
Marks Available	9
Maximum	7
(c) 1 mark for definition of FinTech, 1–2 marks per point (1 for description, 1 for discussion)	5
Maximum	5
Total	20

(a) Rights issue price = 3.50 × 0.8 = $2.80 per share

Grenarp Co currently has 20 million shares in issue ($10m/0.5)

The number of new shares issued = 20m/5 = 4 million shares

Cash raised by the rights issue before issue costs = 4m × 2.80 = $11,200,000

Net cash raised by the rights issue after issue costs = 11,200,000 − 280,000 = $10,920,000

Revised number of shares = 20m + 4m = 24 million shares

Market value of Grenarp Co before the rights issue = 20,000,000 × 3.50 = $70,000,000

Market value of Grenarp Co after the rights issue = 70,000,000 + 10,920,000 = $80,920,000

TERP = 80,920,000/24,000,000 = $3.37 per share

(Alternatively, issue costs are $0.07 per share (280,000/4m) and this is a 1 for 5 rights issue, so the TERP = (5 × 3.50 + (2.80 − 0.07))/6 = 20.23/6 = $3.37 per share.)

Redemption price of loan notes = 104 × 1.05 = $109.20 per loan note

Nominal value of loan notes redeemed = 10,920,000/(109.20/100) = $10,000,000

Before-tax interest saving = 10,000,000 × 0.08 = $800,000 per year

After-tax interest saving = 800,000 × (1 − 0.3) = $560,000 per year

Earnings after redeeming loan notes = 8,400,000 + 560,000 = $8,960,000 per year

Revised earnings per share (EPS) = 100 × (8,960,000/24,000,000) = $0.373 per share

Price/earnings ratio of Grenarp Co before the rights issue = 3.50/0.42 = 8.33 times

This price/earnings ratio is not expected to be affected by the redemption of loan notes.

Share price of Grenarp Co after redeeming loan notes = 8.33 × 0.373 = $3.11 per share (total market value = $3.11 × 24m shares = $74.64m).

The wealth of shareholders of Grenarp Co has decreased as they have experienced a capital loss of $0.26 per share ($3.37 − $3.11) compared to the TERP per share. This means that shareholder wealth has fallen by $0.26 × 24m shares = $6.24m (excluding issue costs, or $6.24 + $0.28m issue costs = $6.52m after issue costs).

Alternative solution

Revised shareholder wealth

After the rights issue and debt repayment shareholder wealth could be measured as:

(1)   The revised value of the company's shares **less**

(2)   The amount shareholders invest in the company via the rights issue

The revised value of the shares can be assessed by valuing Grenarp's revised earnings by multiplying them by the current P/E ratio.

Current earnings are $0.42 × 20m shares = $8.4m. The amount raised net of issue costs is $11.2m – $0.28m = $10.92m. This will be used to buy back debt, and the interest saved will boost earnings.

$10.92m of debt is bought back. The redemption price is 5% above the market price of debt of $104; this is: 1.05 × 104 = $109.2. So $10.92m buys back $10m (ie 10.92 × 100/109.4 in terms of book value of debt. This saves interest of $10m × 8% = $0.8m, which is a saving after tax of $0.56m (calculated as 0.8 × 0.7). So the revised earnings will be $8.4m + $0.56m = $8.96m.

The **current** EPS is $0.42, so the current P/E ratio is 3.5/0.42 = 8.333.

The new value of the shares can be estimated as $8.96m × 8.333 which is approximately $74.66m.

So, after subtracting the $11.2m invested in the rights issue, shareholders' wealth has become $74.66m – $11.2m = $63.46m.

This is a fall in shareholder wealth of $6.54m.

(b)   The capital structure is considered to be optimal when the weighted average cost of capital (WACC) is at a minimum and the market value of a company is at a maximum. The goal of maximising shareholder wealth might be achieved if the capital structure is optimal.

The question of whether Grenarp Co might achieve its optimal capital structure following the rights issue can be discussed from a theoretical perspective by looking at the traditional view of capital structure, the views of Miller and Modigliani on capital structure, and other views such as the market imperfections approach. It is assumed that a company pays out all of its earnings as dividends, and that these earnings and the business risk of the company are constant. It is further assumed that companies can change their capital structure by replacing equity with debt, and vice versa, so that the amount of finance invested remains constant, irrespective of capital structure. The term 'gearing up' therefore refers to replacing equity with debt in the context of theoretical discussions of capital structure.

Traditional view

The traditional view of capital structure, which ignores taxation, held that an optimal capital structure did exist. It reached this conclusion by assuming that shareholders of a company financed entirely by equity would not be very concerned about the company gearing up to a small extent. As expensive equity was replaced by cheaper debt, therefore, the WACC would initially decrease. As the company continued to gear up, shareholders would demand an increasing return as financial risk continued to increase, and the WACC would reach a minimum and start to increase. At higher levels of gearing still, the cost of debt would start to increase, for example, because of bankruptcy risk, further increasing the WACC.

Views of Miller and Modigliani

Miller and Modigliani assumed a perfect capital market, where bankruptcy risk does not exist and the cost of debt is constant. In a perfect capital market, there is a linear relationship between the cost of equity and financial risk, as measured by gearing. Ignoring taxation, the increase in the cost of equity as gearing increases exactly offsets the decrease in the WACC caused by the replacement of expensive equity by cheaper debt, so that the WACC is constant. The value of a company is therefore not affected by its capital structure.

When Miller and Modigliani included the effect of corporate taxation, so that the after-tax cost of debt was used instead of the before-tax cost of debt, the decrease in the WACC caused by the replacement of expensive equity by cheaper debt was greater than the increase in the cost of equity, so that the WACC decreased as a company geared up. The

 BPP

implication in terms of optimal capital structure was that a company should gear up as much as possible in order to decrease its WACC as much as it could.

Market imperfections view

When other market imperfections are considered in addition to the existence of corporate taxation, the view of Miller and Modigliani that a company should gear up as much as possible is no longer true. These other market imperfections relate to high levels of gearing, bankruptcy risk and the costs of financial distress, and they cause the cost of debt and the cost of equity to increase, so that the WACC increases at high levels of gearing.

Grenarp Co

The question of whether Grenarp Co might achieve its optimal capital structure following the rights issue can also be discussed from a practical perspective, by considering if increasing the gearing of the company would decrease its WACC. This would happen if the marginal cost of capital of the company were less than its WACC. Unfortunately, there is no information provided on the marginal cost of capital of Grenarp Co, although its gearing is not high. Before the rights issue, the debt/equity ratio of Grenarp Co was 35% on a book value basis and 45% on a market value basis, while after the redemption of loan notes the debt/equity ratio would fall to 21% on a book value basis and 28% on a market value basis.

(c) Fintech is an abbreviation of financial technology, and has had an important impact on financial markets and institutions. One impact of Fintech has been to increase the availability of long-term finance.

Crowdfunding

The use of crowdfunding by companies looking to raise **equity finance** is becoming increasingly common and is closely tied to growth of internet technology, which enables millions of potential investors to be accessed.

Crowdfunding allows a company to access finance by using an online crowdfunding platform to pitch for finance from a large number of investors who choose whether or not to invest based on the quality of the proposed business plan and the quality of the management team (i.e. their skills and experience).

Peer to peer lending

Peer-to-peer lending connects established businesses looking to borrow with investors who want to lend via an online platform.

Platforms usually require borrowers to have a trading track record, to submit financial accounts, and will perform credit checks as part of the credit assessment. Platforms offer either a fixed rate or, in some cases, lenders bid for loans by offering an interest rate at which they would lend.

P2P lending also allows customers and family / friends to share in the returns of the business. Investors can lend small parts of individual loans, for very small amounts, which encourages a wide range of lenders to participate in multiple loans. However, P2P loans can also be for large loans of several million pounds.

Security token offering

Blockchain technology has facilitated the use of security token offerings to raise long-term finance.

With a security token offering, an investor receives a token e.g. a share in exchange for payment made in a cryptocurrency such as bitcoin.

Historically there have been fewer regulations surrounding security token offerings which has increased their attraction to companies as a way of raising long-term equity finance.

Note that other relevant points would also receive credit, and that only two points were required.

220 Dinla Co

Marking guide		Marks
(a) Cost of equity	1	
Cost of preference shares	1	
Cost of loan notes	3	
Cost of bank loan	1	
Market values	1	
WACC	1	
		8
(b) Explanation of creditor hierarchy	1	
Relative risks and costs of sources of finance	2	
		3
(c) WACC and business risk	2	
WACC and financial risk	2	
CAPM and project-specific risk	1	
		5
(d) 1–2 marks for sharing of risk and reward and riba	4	
Other relevant discussion	2	
Marks Available	6	
Maximum		4
Total		20

(a) **Cost of equity**

The dividend growth model can be used to calculate the cost of equity.

$Ke = ((0.25 \times 1.04)/4.26) + 0.04 = 10.1\%$

Cost of preference shares

$Kp = (0.05 \times 1.00)/0.56 = 8.9\%$

Cost of debt of loan notes

After-tax annual interest payment = 6 × (1 – 0.25) = 6 × 0.75 = $4.50 per year

Time	Cash flow	5% discount	PV		$
	$		$		
0	(95.45)	1.000	(95.45)	1.000	(95.45)
1–5	4.50	4.329	19.48	4.212	18.95
5	100.00	0.784	78.40	0.747	74.70
			2.43		(1.80)

After-tax cost of debt of loan notes:

Kd = 5 + (1 × 2.43)/(2.43 + 1.0) = 5 + 0.57 = 5.6%

Alternatively IRR can be calculated using the =IRR spreadsheet function based on these cash flows:

Time	0	1	2	3	4	5
	(95.45)	4.5	4.5	4.5	4.5	104.5

This approach also gives an IRR of 5.6%

Cost of debt of bank loan

The after-tax fixed interest rate of the bank loan can be used as its cost of debt. This will be 5.25% (7 × 0.75). Alternatively, the after-tax cost of debt of the loan notes can be used as a substitute for the after-tax cost of debt of the bank loan.

Market values

	$'000
Equity: 4.26 × (23,000,000/0.25) =	391,920
Preference shares: 0.56 × (5,000,000/1.00) =	2,800
Loan notes: 95.45 × (11,000,000/100) =	10,500
Bank loan	3,000
	408,220

After-tax weighted average cost of capital (WACC)

Using the formula from the formula sheet:

$$WACC = \left[\frac{V_e}{V_e + V_d}\right]K_e + \left[\frac{V_d}{V_e + V_d}\right]K_d$$

WACC = (391,920/408,220) 10.1% + (2,800/408,220) 8.9% + (10,500/408,220) 5.6% + (3,000/408,220) 5.25% = **9.90%**

(b) The creditor hierarchy refers to the order in which financial claims against a company are settled when the company is liquidated.

The hierarchy, in order of decreasing priority, is secured creditors, unsecured creditors, preference shareholders and ordinary shareholders. The risk of not receiving any cash in a liquidation increases as priority decreases. Secured creditors (secured debt) therefore face the lowest risk as providers of finance and ordinary shareholders face the highest risk.

The return required by a provider of finance is related to the risk faced by that provider of finance. Secured creditors therefore have the lowest required rate of return and ordinary shareholders have the highest required rate of return. The cost of debt should be less than the cost of preference shares, which should be less than the cost of equity.

(c) The current WACC of a company reflects the required returns of existing providers of finance.

The cost of equity and the cost of debt depend on particular elements of the existing risk profile of the company, such as business risk and financial risk. Providing the business risk and financial risk of a company remain unchanged, the cost of equity and the cost of debt, and hence the WACC, should remain unchanged.

In investment appraisal, the discount rate used should reflect the risk of investment project cash flows. Therefore, using the WACC as the discount rate will only be appropriate if the investment project does not result in a change in the business risk and financial risk of the investing company.

One of the circumstances which is likely to leave business risk unchanged is if the investment project were an expansion of existing business activities. WACC could therefore be used as the discount rate in appraising an investment project which looked to expand existing business operations.

However, business risk depends on the size and scope of business operations as well as on their nature, and so an investment project which expands existing business operations should be small in relation to the size of the existing business.

Financial risk will remain unchanged if the investment project is financed in such a way that the relative weighting of existing sources of finance is unchanged, leaving the existing capital structure of the investing company unchanged. While this is unlikely in practice, a company may finance investment projects with a target capital structure in mind, about which small fluctuations are permitted.

If business risk changes as a result of an investment project, so that using the WACC of a company in investment appraisal is not appropriate, a project-specific discount rate should be calculated. The capital asset pricing model (CAPM) can be used to calculate a project-specific cost of equity and this can be used in calculating a project-specific WACC.

(d) Wealth creation in Islamic finance requires that risk and reward, in terms of economic benefit, are shared between the provider of finance and the user of finance. Economic benefit includes wider economic goals such as increasing employment and social welfare.

Conventional finance, which refers to finance which is not based on Islamic principles and which has historically been used in the financial system, does not require the sharing of risks and rewards between the provider of finance (the investor) and the user of finance. Interest (riba) is absolutely forbidden in Islamic finance and is seen as immoral. This can be contrasted with debt in conventional finance, where interest is seen as the main form of return to the debt holder, and with the attention paid to interest rates in the conventional financial system, where interest is the reward for depositing funds and the cost of borrowing funds.

Islamic finance can only support business activities which are acceptable under Sharia law. Murubaha and sukuk are forms of Islamic finance which can be compared to conventional debt finance. Unlike conventional debt finance, however, murubaha and sukuk must have a direct link with underlying tangible assets.

BPP

221 Tufa Co

Marking guide	Marks
(a) Dividend for 20X7	1
Dividend growth rate	1
Cost of equity	1
Cost of pref shares	1
After-tax interest	1
Kd calculation setup	1
Calculating Kd	1
Cost of bank loan	0.5
MV ordinary shares	0.5
MV preference shares	0.5
MV loan notes	0.5
WACC calculations	2
	11
(b) Business risk	1
Financial risk	1
Size on investment	1
	3
(c) First advantage	2
Second advantage	2
Third advantage	2
	6
Total	20

(a)

Interest rate of loan notes (%)	7
Nominal value of loan notes ($)	100.00
Market price of loan notes ($)	102.34
Time to redemption (year)	4
Redemption premium (%)	5
Tax rate (%)	30

Year	Item	$	5% DF	PV ($)	6% DF	PV ($)
0	MV	(102.34)	1.000	(102.34)	1.000	(102.34)
1–4	Interest	4.90	3.546	17.38	3.465	16.98
4	Redeem	105.00	0.823	86.42	0.792	83.16
				1.45		(2.20)

IRR (%)

5 + (1.45/(1.45 + 2.20)) = 5.40

Alternatively IRR can be calculated using the =IRR spreadsheet function based on these cash flows:

Time	0	1	2	3	4
	(102.34)	4.9	4.9	4.9	109.9

This approach also gives an IRR of 5.4%

Cost of bank loan (%) = 5.40 (assumed)

The total market value of the loan notes = $10m × 102.34/100 = $10.234m

Cost of preference shares = dividend/market price = (0.05 × $0.50)/$0.31 = 8.06%

The total market value of the preference shares = $5m/$0.5 nominal value × $0.31 market value = $3.1m.

Cost of ordinary shares using

$$r_e = \frac{d_0(1 + g))}{P_0} + g$$

The current dividend can be calculated as the difference between the ex div and the cum div share price: $7.52 – $7.07 = $0.45.

Annual growth over 4 time periods between 20X3 and 20X7 is

$$\left(\frac{0.45}{0.37}\right)^{1/4} - 1 = 5\%$$

Po = the ex div share price of $7.07

So cost of equity =

$$\frac{0.45 \times 1.05}{7.07} + 0.05 = 0.117 \text{ or } 11.7\%$$

There are 24m ordinary shares ($12m/$0.5 nominal value), so Ve = 24m shares × $7.07 = $169.68m

Total capital employed using market values = $10.234 loan notes + $3m bank loan + $3.1m preference shares + $169.68m ordinary shares = $186.014m

Overall WACC = (11.7 × 169.68/186.014) + (8.1 × 3.1/186.014) + (5.40 × 10.234/186.014) + (5.4 × 3/186.014) = **11.19%**

(b) The current WACC of Tufa Co represents the mean return required by the company's investors, given the current levels of business risk and financial risk faced by the company.

The current WACC can be used as the discount rate in appraising an investment project of the company provided that undertaking the investment project does not change the current levels of business risk and financial risk faced by the company.

The current WACC can therefore be used as the discount rate in appraising an investment project of Tufa Co in the same business area as current operations, for example, an expansion of current business, as business risk is likely to be unchanged in these circumstances.

Similarly, the current WACC can be used as the discount rate in appraising an investment project of Tufa Co if the project is financed in a way that mirrors the current capital structure of the company, as financial risk is then likely to be unchanged.

The required return of the company's investors is likely to change if the investment project is large compared to the size of the company, so the WACC is likely to be an appropriate discount rate providing the investment is small in size relative to Tufa Co.

(c) The following advantages of using convertible loan notes as source of long-term finance could be discussed.

Conversion rather than redemption

If the holders of convertible loan notes judge that conversion into ordinary shares will increase their wealth, conversion of the loan notes will occur on the conversion date and Tufa Co will not need to find the cash needed to redeem the loan notes. This is sometimes referred to as 'self-liquidation'.

Lower interest rate

The option to convert into ordinary shares has value for investors as ordinary shares normally offer a higher return than debt. Investors in convertible loan notes will therefore accept a lower interest rate than on ordinary loan notes, decreasing the finance costs for the issuing company.

Debt capacity

If Tufa Co issued convertible loan notes, its gearing and financial risk will increase and its debt capacity will decrease. When conversion occurs, its gearing and financial risk will decrease and its debt capacity will increase because of the elimination of the loan notes from its capital structure. However, there will a further increase in debt capacity due to the issue of new ordinary shares in order to facilitate conversion.

Attractive to investors

Tufa Co may be able to issue convertible loan notes to raise long-term finance even when investors might not be attracted by an issue of ordinary loan notes, because of the attraction of the option to convert into ordinary shares in the future.

Facilitates planning

It has been suggested than an issue of fixed-interest debt such as convertible loan notes can be attractive to a company as the fixed nature of future interest payments facilitates financial planning.

222 Tin Co

Marking guide		Marks
(a) (i)	Rights issue price	1
	Theoretical ex-rights price	1
		2
(ii)	Increased PBIT	0.5
	Revised PBT	0.5
	Revised PAT	1
	Number of shares	1
	Revised EPS	1
		4
(iii)	Increased interest	1
	Revised PAT	1
	Revised EPS	1
		3
(iv)	Equity share price	0.5
	Debt share price	0.5
		1
(v)	Financial analysis	1
	Gearing	1
	Interest cover	1
	Share price effects	1
		4
(b)	First finance source	4
	Second finance source	4
	Marks Available	8
	Maximum	6
Total		**20**

(a) (i)

Currently	2.5 million shares	@$5	= $12.5 million value
Rights issue	0.5 million shares	@$4	= $2 million
After rights issue	3 million shares		$14.5 million value

TERP = $14.5m/3m = $4.83

(ii) **Revised earnings per share**

	$'000	Notes
Increased PBIT	1,916	Increase of 20% on 1,597
Finance costs (interest)	(315)	
Revised profit before tax	1,601	
Taxation at 22%	(352)	
Revised profit after tax	1,249	
		1 for 5 rights issue, so 500,000 extra shares
Total number of shares	3,000,000	
Total number of shares	0.42 (1,249/3,000)	

(iii) **Revised earnings per share**

	$'000	
Increased PBIT	1,916	
		Extra interest of $2m × 0.06 = $160,000
Finance costs (interest)	(475)	
Revised profit before tax	1,441	
Taxation at 22%	(317)	
Revised profit after tax	1,124	
Total number of shares	2,500,000	
Revised EPS ($/share) using debt	0.45 (1,124/2,500)	

(iv) Revised share prices ($/share)
Using equity = 12.5 × 0.42 = 5.25
Using debt = 12.5 × 0.45 = 5.63

(v) **Gearing**

$'000	Current	Equity finance raised	Debt finance raised
Book value of debt	4,500	4,500	4,500 + 2,000 = **6,500**
Book value of equity	2,500 + 5,488 = **7,988**	7,988 + 2,000 = **9,988**	**7,988**
Debt/equity ratio	4,500/7,988 = **56.3%**	4,500/9,988 = **45.1%**	6,500/7,988 = **81.4%**

Sector average D/E using BV = 60.5%

The gearing of Tin Co at 56.3% is just below the sector average gearing of 60.5%. If equity finance were used, gearing would fall even further below the sector average at 45.1%. If debt finance were used, gearing would increase above the sector average to 84.4%, this may concern shareholders.

Interest cover

$'000	Current	Equity finance raised	Debt finance raised
PBIT	**1,597**	**1,916**	**1,916**
Interest	**315**	**315**	315 + 160 = **475**
Interest cover	1,597/315 = **5.1**	1,916/315 = **6.1**	1,916/475 = **4.0**

Sector average interest cover = 9 times

Interest cover calculations show that raising equity finance would make the interest cover of Tin Co look much safer. When debt finance is used, interest cover of 4.0 times looks quite risky compared to the sector average.

Share price changes

The shareholders of Tin Co experience a capital gain of $0.63 per share compared to the current share price ($5.63 – $5.00) if debt finance is used, compared to a capital gain of $0.42 per share compared to the TERP ($5.25 – $4.83) if equity finance is used.

Although using debt finance looks more attractive, it comes at a price in terms of increased financial risk. It might be decided, on balance, that using equity finance looks to be the better choice.

(b) The forms of Islamic finance equivalent to a rights issue and a loan note issue are mudaraba and sukuk respectively; although Ijara, which is similar to lease finance, might be an alternative to a loan note issue, depending on the nature of the planned business expansion.

Musharaka is similar to venture capital and hence is not seen as equivalent to a rights issue, which is made to existing shareholders.

Mudaraba

A mudaraba contract is between a capital partner and an expertise partner (the manager) for the undertaking of business operations. The business operations must be compliant with Sharia'a law and are run on a day-to-day basis by the manager. The provider of capital has no role in relation to the day-to-day operations of the business. Profits from the business operations are shared between the partners in a proportion agreed in the contract. Losses are borne by the provider of capital alone, as provider of the finance, up to the limit of the capital provided.

Sukuk

Conventional loan notes are not allowed under Sharia'a law because there must be a link to an underlying tangible asset and because interest (riba) is forbidden by the Quran. Sukuk are linked to an underlying tangible asset, ownership of which is passed to the sukuk holders, and do not pay interest.

Since the sukuk holders take on the risks and rewards of ownership, sukuk also has an equity aspect. As owners, sukuk holders will bear any losses or risk from the underlying asset. In terms of rewards, sukuk holders have a right to receive the income generated by the underlying asset and have a right to dismiss the manager of the underlying asset, if this is felt to be necessary.

Ijara

In this form of Islamic finance, the lessee uses a tangible asset in exchange for a regular rental payment to the lessor, who retains ownership throughout the period of the lease contract. The contract may allow for ownership to be transferred from the lessor to the lessee at the end of the lease period.

Major maintenance and insurance are the responsibility of the lessor, while minor or day-to-day maintenance is the responsibility of the lessee. The lessor may choose to appoint the lessee as their agent to undertake all maintenance, both major and minor.

Note. Only two types of finance need to be discussed

OTQ bank – Business valuations

223 The correct answer is: To evaluate a takeover bid by Company X which is offering to buy ML Ltd in exchange for shares in Company X

The first option is only valid if the company is listed.

The second and fourth options are unlikely because both imply that an asset value will be used and this is unlikely for a service company where most of its assets will be intangible.

Syllabus area F1(a)

224 The correct answer is: $2.10 per share

Net asset value (NAV) = 140m – 15m – 20m = $105m

Number of ordinary shares = 25m/0.5 = 50m shares

NAV per share = 105m/50m = $2.10 per share

Syllabus area F2(a)

225 $ 23.41

$$P_0 = \frac{d_0(1 + g)}{r_e - g}$$

(Given on the formula sheet)

Growth 'g' – Dividends grew from ($0.50 – $0.10) = $0.40 to $0.50 in 3 years. This is an average annual growth rate of:

$0.40 (1 + g)^3 = $0.50

$(1 + g) = \sqrt[3]{(0.5/0.4)}$

g = 0.077 = 7.7%

$$P_0 = \frac{0.50(1.077)}{0.1 - 0.077} = \$23.41$$

Syllabus area F2(c)

226 The correct answer is: $6.11

Share price = (0.826 × 0.5)/(0.1 – 0.03) + (0.25 × 0.826) = $6.11 per share

The dividend valuation model states that the ex dividend market value of an ordinary share is equal to the present value of the future dividends paid to the owner of the share. No dividends are to be paid in the current year and in Year 1, so the value of the share does not depend on dividends from these years. The first dividend to be paid is in Year 2 and this dividend is different from the dividend paid in Year 3 and in subsequent years. The present value of the Year 2 dividend, discounted at 10% per year, is (0.25 × 0.826) = $0.2065.

The dividends paid in Year 3 can subsequently be valued using the dividend growth model. By using the formula $P_0 = D_1/(r_e - g)$ we can calculate the present value of the future dividend stream beginning with $0.50 per share paid in Year 3. This present value will be a Year 2 value and will need discounting for two years to make it a Year 0 present value.

P_0 = (0.826 × 0.5)/(0.1 – 0.03) = 0.826 × 7.1429 = $5.90

$5.90 + 0.2065 = $6.11

Syllabus area F2(c)

 BPP

ANSWERS

227 $ 672 million

g = br

g = 0.2 × 0.6 = 0.12

$$P_0 = \frac{d_0(1 + g)}{r_e - g} = \frac{60m \times 1.12}{0.22 - 0.12} = \$672m$$

Syllabus area F2(b)

228 The correct answer is: Gamma Co is a direct competitor of Alpha Co

By eliminating a competitor, there is synergy potential for Alpha meaning they would be prepared to pay more for Gamma than Beta would, therefore this statement is correct.

Notes on incorrect answers:

If Alpha Co used more prudent growth estimates, this would reduce the value of Gamma Co.

If Beta Co could achieve more synergy, this would increase the value that Beta Co has placed on the company.

Negotiation skills will determine the final price paid for Gamma Co, not the initial valuation.

Syllabus area F1(a)

229 The correct answer is: $55

Discounting the interest of $5 per year at a required return of 10% to perpetuity = $5 × 1/0.1 = present value $50.

In addition a payment of $5 is about to be received

So total present value = $50 + $5 = $55.

Notes on incorrect answers:

$50 is obtained if the imminent interest payment is ignored

$76 is obtained if the post-tax cost of debt is used as the discount factor (which is incorrect because we are calculating the market value of the debt to the investor)

$40 is obtained if the post-tax interest ($5 × 0.7 = $3.5) is used, again this is incorrect because we are calculating the market value of the debt to the investor.

Syllabus area F3(a)

230 The correct answer is: $92.67

Discounting the future cash flows at the required return of 9% gives:

$[7 \times AF_{1-7} 9\%] + [105 \times DF_7 9\%]$

$= [7 \times 5.033] + [105 \times 0.547] = 92.67$

∴ current MV = $92.67

Syllabus area E2(b)

231 The correct answer is: $96.94

Market value = (6 × 5.971) + (105 × 0.582) = 35.83 + 61.11 = $96.94

Syllabus area F2(c)

232 The correct answer is: $512,000

The value of next year's dividend has been given, so the share price calculation is:

Share price = D1 / (re − g) = 0.32/(0.12 − 0.02) = $3.20

Seema's shareholding is 800,000 × 20% = 160,000 shares

The value of this shareholding is 160,000 × $3.20 = $512,000

Incorrect answers often incorrectly added growth of 2% to the given dividend figure of $0.32 to get an answer of $522,240.

Syllabus area F2(c)

OTQ bank – Market efficiency

233 The correct answer is: A strong form efficient market

As share price reaction appears to have occurred before the information concerning the new project was made public, this suggests a strong form efficient market (and quite possibly insider dealing) because in a strong form efficient market the share price reflects even privately held information.

Syllabus area F4(a)

234 The correct answers are:

- Share prices fully and fairly represent past information
- Share prices appear to follow a random walk

Notes on incorrect answers:

The second statement would only be true about a strong-form efficient market

The final statement is not true about any form of efficient market

Syllabus area F4(a)

235 The correct answers are:

Share prices	Level of capital market efficiency
$6.05	Semi-strong form
$6.00	Strong form
$6.20	Strong form

In a semi-strong form efficient market the markets value shares based on information relevant to past movements and also published information.

The share price will react to the NPV of Product B today as news is released. The increase will be $160m/800m shares = $0.20 per share, bringing the share price up to $6.20.

In a strong form efficient market the share price reflects historic information, published information and insider information. The share price of $6.00 will already reflect the NPVs of both new products as the decision to launch them was taken two days ago.

Syllabus area F4(a)

236 The correct answer is: The majority of share price reaction to news occurs when it is announced

'Repeating patterns appear to exist' supports the view that markets are completely inefficient.

'Attempting to trade on consistently repeating patterns is unlikely to work' supports the view that markets are weak form efficient.

'The majority of share price reaction to news occurs when it is announced' supports the view that markets are semi-strong form efficient because in such a market share prices reflect publicly available information, but not privately held information. Share price will therefore not reflect information before it is announced.

'Share price reaction occurs before announcements are made public' supports the view that markets are strong form efficient: they reflect all available information including that which is privately held.

Syllabus area F4(a)

BPP

ANSWERS

237 The correct answers are:

- The lack of regulation on use of private information (insider dealing)

- Inability to consistently outperform the market and make abnormal gains

In a strong form efficient market, insider dealing regulations would not be necessary as all private information is reflected in the share price anyway.

The market can still be outperformed by individual investors, but only by luck and not consistently.

Share prices will not react to the public announcement as the private information will already be known as the share price would react to the initial decision instead.

There would be no need for quick announcement as the information will already be known and reflected in the share price.

Syllabus area F4(a)

Section B questions

Bluebell Co

238 The correct answer is: $365.8m

Net realisable value = 1,350 − (768 − 600) − (192 × 0.1) − 30 − 105 − 662 = $365.8m

Syllabus area F2(a)

239 The correct answer is: $1,875m

Earnings yield = 100 × 1/12.5 = 8%

Value = 150/0.08 = $1,875m

Syllabus area F2(b)

240 The correct answer is: An asset-based valuation would be useful for an asset-stripping acquisition

Notes on incorrect answers:

The workforce are an intangible asset cannot be valued.

Cash based valuations discount the value of future cash flows.

Replacement costs do not measure deprival value.

Syllabus area F1(a)

241 The correct answer is: Both 1 and 2

In a perfect market shares are regularly traded, and investors are rational.

Syllabus area F4(a)

242 The correct answer is: Bluebell Co will have to pay a higher price per share to take control of Dandelion Co than if it were buying a minority holding

A control premium will be paid when buying a controlling stake.

Notes on incorrect answers:

Scrip dividends are paid in shares and therefore do not reduce liquidity.

Unlisted company shares are harder to value and generally trade at a discount to a similar listed company's shares.

Syllabus area F4(b)

GWW Co

243    $\boxed{160}$ million

Market capitalisation = number of shares × market value

= ($20m/$0.5) × $4.00 = $160m

Syllabus area F2(b)

244    $\boxed{61.7}$ million

The net realisable value of assets at liquidation = non-current assets + inventory + trade receivables − current liabilities − bonds

= $86m + $4.2m + ($4.5m × 80%) − $7.1m − $25m

= $61.7m

Syllabus area F2(a)

245   The correct answer is: $171.7m

Historic earnings based on 20X2 profit after tax = $10.1m

Average P/E ratio in industry = 17 times

P/E ratio value = 17 × $10.1m = $171.7m

Syllabus area F2(b)

246   The correct answer is: Technical analysis

Technical analysts work on the basis that past price patterns will be repeated, so that future price movements can be predicted from historical patterns.

Syllabus area F4(a)

247   The correct answer is:

Earnings yield of GWW	P/E ratio of GWW
Lower	Higher

For GWW Co, P/E = 15, Earnings yield (= 1/(P/E ratio) = 6.7%.

For its competitor, P/E (= 1/earnings yield) = 16, Earnings yield = 6.25%.

Syllabus area F2(b)

Corhig Co (amended)

248    $\boxed{15}$ million

The value of the company can be calculated using the P/E ratio valuation as:

Expected future earnings × P/E ratio

Using Corhig Co's forecast earnings for Year 1, and taking the average P/E ratio of similar listed companies, Corhig Co can be valued at $3m × 5 = $15m.

Syllabus area F2(b)

249   The correct answers are:

- A P/E valuation using average earnings of $3.63m would be more realistic than the P/E ratio method calculated above - **True**

- Using the average P/E ratio of similar companies is appropriate in this situation - **False**

The valuation above does not take into consideration the fact that earnings are expected to rise by 43% over the next 3 years. Instead of using Year 1 earnings, we could use average

 BPP

expected earnings over the next 3 years of $3.63m. This would give us a more appropriate valuation of $18.15m.

The P/E ratio of 5 is taken from the average of similar listed companies. However, P/E ratios vary from company to company depending on each company's business operations, capital structures, gearing, and markets. The ratio used here is therefore subject to a high degree of uncertainty. An inaccurate P/E ratio would call the valuation into question, as it is so crucial to the calculation.

Corhig Co is listed, so it would be much more appropriate to use the company's own current P/E ratio instead.

Syllabus area F2(b)

250   $ 398,500

PV of Year 2 dividend = 500,000 × 0.797 = **$398,500** (using cost of capital of 12%)

Syllabus area F2(c)

251   10.32 %

After-tax cost of debt = 6 × (1 – 0.2) = 4.8%

Revised after-tax WACC = 14 × 60% + 4.8 × 40% = 10.32%

Syllabus area E2(c)

252   The correct answers are:

- Risk linked to the extent to which the company's profits depend on fixed, rather than variable, costs - **Business Systematic**
- Risk that shareholder cannot mitigate by holding a diversified investment portfolio - **Business Systematic**
- Risk that shareholder return fluctuates as a result of the level of debt the company undertakes - **Financial**

Risk linked to the extent to which the company's profits depend on fixed, rather than variable, costs is business risk.

Risk that shareholder cannot mitigate by holding a diversified investment portfolio is **systematic risk.**

Risk that shareholder return fluctuates as a result of the level of debt the company undertakes is **financial risk.**

Syllabus area E2(a)

Close Co (amended)

253   $ 490 million

Net assets

As no additional information is available, this is based on book values.

Net assets = 720 – 70 – 160 = $490 million

Syllabus area F2(a)

254    $ $\boxed{693}$ million

Dividend growth model

Dividends are expected to grow at 4% per year and the cost of equity is 10%.

$$P_0 = \frac{d_0(1 + g)}{r_e - g}$$

$$P_0 = \frac{40(1.04)}{0.1 - 0.04}$$

= 41.6/0.06

= $693 million

Syllabus area F2(c)

255    $ $\boxed{605.5}$ million

Earnings yield

Earnings are the profit after tax figure of $66.6m and the earnings yield that can be used for the valuation is 11%, ie 66.6/0.11 = $605.5m.

Syllabus area F2(b)

256   The correct answers are:

- It is very sensitive to changes in the growth rate - **True**
- It can only be used if dividends have been paid or are expected to be paid - **True**

The DGM is very sensitive to changes in the growth rate. A 1% change in the growth rate can give a significantly different valuation.

If dividends are expected to be paid at some point in the future, the DGM can be applied at that point to create a value for the shares which can then be discounted to give the current ex dividend share price.

In a situation where dividends are not paid and are not expected to be paid the DGM has no use.

Syllabus area F2(c)

257   The correct answer is: The sum of the present values of the future interest payments + the present value of the bond's conversion value

Syllabus area F3(a)

WAW Co

258 The correct answer is: $7.55

$$g = \left(\frac{3}{2.4}\right)^{1/3} - 1 = 0.0772$$

$$P_0 = \frac{d_0(1 + g)}{r_e - g}$$

$$P_0 = \frac{3m(1.0772)}{0.12 - 0.0772}$$

= $75.5m

Divided by 10 million shares this gives = $7.55/share

Answer A is obtained if you assume that growth has taken place over four years.

Answer B is obtained if you forget to increase the dividend by the growth rate and use four years.

Answer D is obtained if you use the wrong number of shares.

Syllabus area F2(c)

259 The correct answer is: 1, 3 and 4

The cost of equity can be estimated for an unlisted company (for example using CAPM based on the beta of a listed company).

Syllabus area F2(c)

260 The correct answer is: $11.25 per share

Earnings $7.5m × P/E 15 = Value of $112.5m

There are 10 million shares in issue so this is $112.5/10 = $11.25 per share

Syllabus area F2(b)

261 The correct answer is: The company is expected to grow

Assuming an efficient stock market, the high share price indicates confidence in future growth.

Syllabus area F2(b)

262 The correct answer is: 1, 2 and 3

Indifference between dividend and capital growth would be indicated by a more erratic dividend policy. Also, dividend irrelevancy theory assumes no tax, which is not the case here.

Syllabus area E1(e)

Dazvin Co

263 The correct answer is: $7.50m

Cost of preference shares = dividend / share price = 0.08

As the dividend is $0.06 × $0.50 (nominal value) = $0.03 per share, the share price must be 0.03/0.08 = $0.375, so total number of preference shares of 20m ($10m/0.5) have a total value of 20m × $0.375 = $7.50.

The most common error here was to take the nominal value of the preference shares to be $1 and get an answer of $3.75m

Syllabus area F3(a)

264 The correct answer is: $40.8m

Preference dividends = 10.0m x 0.06 = $0.6m

Earnings for equity after preference dividends = 4.0m – 0.6m = $3.4m

Price earnings ratio value = 3.4m x 12 = $40.8m

The most common error here was to not deduct the preference divided before taking the earnings figure and instead using earnings of $4m and getting $48.0m.

Syllabus area F2(b)

265 The correct answer is: $21.0m

Conversion value = 2.00 x 1.06^6 x 40 = $113.48 per loan note

Conversion is higher than nominal value for redemption, so conversion is preferred.

Market value per loan note= (Interest x 6-year annuity factor) + Discounted conversion value = (7.5 x 4.917) + (113.48 x 0.705) = $116.88

Total convertible debt value = 116.88/100 x 18m = $21.0m

A significant number of candidates selected $19.3m, which they would have got by taking the floor value of the loan note rather than the conversion value.

Syllabus area F3(a)

266 The correct answer is: Shares are likely to be mispriced where managers and investors have different levels of information (information asymmetry).

Some candidates selected the option concerning non-release of information not realising that while it may be correct that companies do not release information that undermines their competitive advantage and so are not transparent, there are still benefits from the availability of a wide range of published information which can be used to price shares.

Syllabus area F1

267 The correct answer is: Both 1 and 2

The first statement is correct, as the momentum effect can arise when investors believe that recent share price increases will continue, leading to irrational investment decisions by uninformed investors (noise trading) chasing the trend.

The second statement is correct, as informed investors can make speculative purchases during a stock market bubble with the intention of selling when the price has increased in the future, in the belief that they can realise their gain before the bubble bursts.

Syllabus area F4(c)

OTQ bank – Foreign currency risk

268   The correct answer is: Transaction risk

Transaction risk refers to the fact that the spot rate may move between point of sale (denominated in foreign exchange) and when the customer pays, such that the net domestic receipt differs from expected.

Notes on incorrect answers:

Translation risk is a financial reporting implication of retranslating foreign assets/liabilities and not immediately related to cash.

Economic risk is the impact on business value of long-term exchange rate trends.

Credit risk is the risk that the customer fails to pay.

Syllabus area G1(a)

269   € 417

A strengthening euro means euros are getting more expensive: they will cost more dollars.

The exchange rate becomes €1:$2.40 ($2 × 1.2)

The euro receipt will be $1,000/2.4 = €416.67 (€417 to the nearest euro).

Note that in the exam the exchange rate is normally given to the $, but you need to be prepared to deal with a situation like this where this is not the case.

Syllabus area G1(a)

270   The correct answer is: $2,312

The forward rate for the euro is 0.8500 – 0.8650 to the $.

The rate for buying dollars (selling euros) will be the more expensive/higher rate. Converting into $s will result in there being more dollars than euros. So 2,000/0.8650 = $2,312.

The other answers are a result of using the wrong side of the spread and/or multiplying by the forward rate.

Syllabus area G3(a)

271   The correct answer is: 1 and 2

Derivative hedging instruments that are traded on an exchange or market are standardised in nature. Futures contracts, whether interest rate futures or currency futures, relate to a standard quantity of an underlying asset. Exchange-traded options, by definition, are traded on an exchange and are therefore standardised in nature, whether interest rate options or currency options. A forward rate agreement (FRA) is the interest rate equivalent of a forward exchange contract (FEC). It is an agreement between a bank and a customer to fix an interest rate on an agreed amount of funds for an agreed future period. The FRA is tailored to the customer's needs and so is a bespoke contract rather than a standardised contract. Answers B and C were therefore not correct.

Both currency swaps and interest rate swaps are derivatives that are available to organisations to manage or hedge long-term foreign currency risk and interest rate risk. They are essentially an agreement between two counterparties to exchange interest rate obligations on an agreed amount of funds, whether in the domestic currency or in a foreign currency. A bank will usually act as an intermediary in arranging a swap in exchange for a fee and can even arrange a swap where no counterparty is immediately available. Swaps are therefore tailored to customers' needs and are not standardised in nature. Answers C and D were therefore not correct.

Syllabus area G3(c) & G4(b)

272   The correct answer is: $7,122,195

The US company should borrow US$ immediately and send it to Europe. It should be left on deposit in € for three months then used to pay the supplier.

The amount to put on deposit today = €3.5m × 1/(1 + (0.01/4)) = €3,491,272.

This will cost €3,491,272 × $2 = $6,982,544 today (note $2 is the worst rate for buying €).

Assuming this to be borrowed in US$, the liability in 3 months will be:

$6,982,544 × [1 + (0.08/4)] = $7,122,195.

Syllabus area G3(a)

273   The correct answers are:

- They are only available in a small amount of currencies
- They may be an imprecise match for the underlying transaction

They are only available in a small amount of currencies. They are probably an imprecise match for the underlying transaction.

Statement 1: **False**. Futures contracts are subject to a brokerage fee only (for example there is no spread on the rate) so are relatively cheap.

Statement 2: **True**. It is not possible to purchase futures contracts from every currency to every other currency – there are only limited combinations available.

Statement 3: **False**. Futures contracts can be 'closed out' so if, for example, customers pay early or late, the timing of the futures hedge can accommodate this.

Statement 4: **True**. Futures contracts are for standardised amounts so may not match the size of the transaction being hedged precisely.

Syllabus area G3(a)

274   The correct answer is: $32,500

The borrowing interest rate for 6 months is 8%/2 = 4%.

The company should borrow 500,000 pesos/1.04 = 480,769 today. After 6 months, 500,000 pesos will be repayable, including interest.

These pesos will be converted to $ at 480,769/15 = $32,051. The company must deposit this amount for 6 months, when it will have increased in value with interest.

$32,051 × (1 + (0.03/2)) = $32,532 or $32,500 to the nearest $100.

Syllabus area G3(a)

275 | 1.4718 | euro per $1

Using purchasing power parity:

$S_1 = S_0 \times (1 + h_c)/(1 + h_b)$

The $ is the base currency for the given future spot rate.

Therefore an unknown rate x 1.02 / 1.035 = 1.4505

Rearrange the formula so that Current Spot Rate = Future Spot Rate / (1 + inflation rate in counter currency / 1 + inflation rate in base currency)

Therefore 1.4505 / (1.02 / 1.035) = 1.4718 euro per $1

A common mistake was to switch the inflation rates and instead calculate 1.4505 / (1.035 / 1.02) = 1.4295 euro per $1

Syllabus area G2(b)

276 The correct answer is: Handria has a higher nominal rate of interest than Wengry

The stronger forward value of the $ implies that interest rates are lower in Wengry than in Handria. This will be due to lower inflation in Wengry according to the International Fisher Effect.

Notes on incorrect answers:

The International Fisher Effect assumes that real interest rates are the same.

The 4th option is incorrect according to expectations theory (linked to the International Fisher Effect according to four-way equivalence).

Syllabus area G2(a)

277 The correct answer is: €1.418 per $1

Twelve-month forward rate = 1.415 × (1.02/1.018) = €1.418 per $1

This is the rate that will be offered on the forward market to prevent a risk free gain being made.

Syllabus area G2(b)

OTQ bank – Interest rate risk

278 The correct answers are:

- Enter into a 3 v 9 forward rate agreement
- Sell interest rate futures expiring in three months' time

The forward rate agreement (FRA) to be a purchased by a borrower must reflect the period to the commencement of the borrowing and the cessation of the borrowing. Hence here the appropriate FRA would be a 3 v 9 FRA.

With respect to futures, to hedge against interest rate increases, interest rate futures should be sold now.

Syllabus area G4(a)

279 The correct answers are:

- The debt portfolio will consist of a mixture of fixed and floating rate debt
- Interest payments will still increase if the interest rate rises

Smoothing is holding a balanced mix of both fixed and floating rate debt. This will reduce the effects of an interest rate change but not eliminate it completely, so interest payments will still increase following a rise in rates, therefore statements A and B are correct.

Full benefit will not be obtained from a fall in rates due to the fixed element of the debt portfolio.

Financing fixed cash flow investments with fixed rate debt is a matching strategy, not smoothing.

Syllabus area G4(a)

280   The correct answer is: An inverted yield curve can arise if government policy is to keep short-term interest rates high in order to bring down inflation

The term structure of interest rates suggests that the yield curve normally slopes upwards, so that debt with a longer term to maturity has a higher yield than short-term debt. Occasionally, the yield curve can be inverted, indicating that the yield on short-term debt is higher than the yield on longer-term debt. One of the reasons why this can happen is because government policy has increased short-term interest rates with the objective of reducing inflation, an action which falls in the area of monetary policy.

The incorrect responses are now considered.

Liquidity preference theory suggests that investors want more compensation for short-term lending than for long-term lending.

Liquidity preference theory seeks to explain the shape of the yield curve. It suggests that investors prefer to have cash now, rather than lending cash to borrowers, and that they prefer to have their cash returned to them sooner rather than later. The compensation that investors require for lending their cash increases therefore with the maturity of the debt finance provided. Liquidity preference theory does not therefore suggest that investors want more compensation for short-term lending than for long-term lending, in fact the opposite.

According to expectations theory, the shape of the yield curve gives information on how inflation rates are expected to influence interest rates in the future.

Expectations theory suggests that the shape of the yield curve depends upon the expectations of investors regarding future interest rates. An upward-sloping yield curve indicates an expectation that interest rates will rise in the future, while a downward-sloping yield curve indicates that interest rates are expected to fall in the future. Expectations theory does not therefore provide information on how inflation rates are expected to influence interest rates in the future.

Market segmentation theory suggests long-term interest rates depend on how easily investors can switch between market segments of different maturity.

Market segmentation theory suggests that the borrowing market can be divided into segments, for example the short-term end and the long-term end of the market. Investors in each segment remain in that segment and do not switch segments because of changes in factors influencing particular segments. The shape of the yield curve relating to each segment depends on the balance between the forces of supply and demand in that segment. Market segmentation theory does not therefore suggest that long-term interest rates depend on how easily investors can switch between market segments, since it states that investors do not switch between segments.

Syllabus area G2(c)

281     $ | 5,000 |

The FRA effectively fixes the interest at the upper end of the spread of 3.2%.

The total interest charge is therefore

$10m × 3.2% × 3/12 = $80,000

The actual interest charge on the variable-rate loan is

$10m × 3% × 3/12 = $75,000

Therefore the payment to the financial institution will be the difference of

$80,000 − $75,000 = $5,000

Syllabus area G4(a)

282 The correct answer is: 1 and 3 only

An over-the-counter option is an agreement with a financial institution and an immediate premium is payable on taking out the option. However, it cannot be traded and it is only exercised if actual interest rates are less favourable.

Syllabus area G4(b)

283 The correct answer is: The difference between the amount of interest-sensitive assets and liabilities

This is one way of describing gap exposure. If at any given point in time there is a difference between the value of the (interest-sensitive) assets maturing at that point in time and the value of the (interest sensitive) liabilities maturing at the same point in time then there is gap exposure.

Syllabus area G1(b)

284 The correct answers are:

- Futures contract

- Exchange tradable option

Exchange tradable options and futures contracts are the instruments which have standard contract sizes. All of the other instruments can be tailored to the exact requirements of the hedge.

Syllabus area G3(c), G4(b)

285 $ 73,500

The FRA effectively fixes the interest at the upper end of the spread of 2.85%. This is below the actual rate so the FRA will make an annualised loss of 3.75% - 2.85% = 0.9%. Applied to $14m 7 month loan this is 0.009 x $14m x 7/12 = $73,500.

Syllabus area G4(a)

Section B questions

Rose Co (amended)

286 The correct answer is: Enter into a forward contract to sell €750,000 in 6 months

Rose Co should enter into a forward contract to sell €750,000 in 6 months.

Statement 1 is **incorrect**. Rose Co could use a money market hedge but €750,000 would have to be borrowed, then converted into dollars and then placed on deposit.

Statement 2 is **incorrect**. An interest rate swap swaps one type of interest payment (such as fixed interest) for another (such as floating rate interest). Therefore it would not be suitable.

Statement 4 is not suitable as Rose Co does not have any euro payments to make.

Syllabus area G3(a)

287 The correct answer is: $310,945

Future value = €750,000/2.412 = $310,945.

Syllabus area G3(a)

288 The correct answer is: 4.00%

Rose Co is expecting a euro receipt in six months' time and it can hedge this receipt in the money markets by borrowing euros to create a euro liability. Euro borrowing rate for six months = 8.0%/2 = 4%.

Syllabus area G3(a)

289 The correct answer is: Currency swaps can be used to hedge exchange rate risk over longer periods than the forward market

Statement 1 is **incorrect**. Currency futures have a fixed settlement date, although they can be exercised at any point before then.

Statement 3 is **incorrect**. The bank will make the customer fulfil the contract.

Statement 4 is **incorrect**. Buying a currency option involves paying a premium to the option seller. This is a non-refundable fee which is paid when the option is acquired.

Syllabus area G3(c)

290 The correct answer is: The normal yield curve slopes upward to reflect increasing compensation to investors for being unable to use their cash now

The longer the term to maturity, the higher the rate of interest.

Notes on incorrect answers:

Statement 1 is **incorrect**. This reduces the money supply and could put upward pressure on interest rates.

Statement 3 is **incorrect**. Longer term is considered less certain and more risky. It therefore requires a higher yield.

Statement 4 is **incorrect**. Expectations theory states that future interest rates reflect expectations of future interest rate (not inflation rate) movements.

Syllabus area G1 & G2

Edwen Co

291 The correct answer is: $56,079

Forward market

Net receipt in one month = (240,000 − 140,000) = 100,000 euros

Edwen Co needs to sell euros at an exchange rate of 1.7832 euros = $1

Dollar value of net receipt = 100,000/1.7832 = $56,079

Syllabus area G3(a)

292 The correct answer is: $167,999

Money market hedge

Expected receipt after 3 months = 300,000 euros

Borrowing cost in Europe for 3 months is not given in annual terms and so does not need to be adjusted = 1.35%

Euros to borrow now in order to have 300,000 liability after 3 months = 300,000/1.0135 = 296,004 euros.

Spot rate for selling euros = 1.7822 per $1

Dollar deposit from borrowed euros at spot = 296,004/1.7822 = $166,089

Country C interest rate over 3 months = 1.15%

Value in 3 months of deposit = $166,089 × 1.0115 = $167,999

Syllabus area G3(a)

293 The correct answer is: Both 1 and 2

With a fall in a country's exchange rate Edwen Co's exports will be cheaper (and so be more competitive) and imports will become more expensive. Given imports may include raw materials, this pushes local prices up.

Syllabus area G1(a)

294   The correct answer is: 2 only

'The contracts can be tailored to the user's exact requirements' is false. Futures contracts are standard contracts.

'The exact date of receipt or payment of the currency does not have to be known' is true. The futures contract does not have to be closed out until the actual cash receipt or payment is made.

'Transaction costs are generally higher than other hedging methods' is false. Transaction costs are usually lower than other hedging methods.

Syllabus area G3(c)

295   The correct answer is: Both features relate to forward contracts

Futures contracts are exchange traded and are only available in a limited range of currencies.

Syllabus area G3(b,c)

Zigto Co (amended)

296    $ | 251,256 |

Forward exchange contract

500,000/1.990 = $251,256

Using the 6-month forward rate under the forward exchange contract, Zigto Co will receive $251,256.

Syllabus area G3(a)

297    $ | 248,781 |

Money market hedge

Expected receipt after 6 months = Euro 500,000

Euro interest rate over 6 months = 5%/2 = 2.5%

Euros to borrow now in order to have Euro 500,000 liability after 6 months = Euro 500,000/1.025 = Euro 487,805

Spot rate for selling euros today = 2 euro/$

Dollar deposit from borrowed euros at spot rate = 487,805/2 = $243,903

Dollar deposit rate over 6 months = 4%/2 = 2%

Value of the dollar deposit in 6 months' time = $243,903 × 1.02 = $248,781

Syllabus area G3(a)

298 | Euro 1.971/$ | euro per $

Using purchasing power parity:

$S_1 = S_0 \times (1 + h_c)/(1 + h_b)$

Where:

S_1 = expected spot rate

S_0 = current spot rate

h_c = expected inflation in country c

h_b = expected inflation in country b

$S_1 = 2.00 \times 1.03/1.045 = $ Euro 1.971/$

Syllabus area G2

 BPP

299 The correct answers are:

- Purchasing power parity tends to hold true in the short term - **False**
- Expected future spot rates are based on relative inflation rates between two countries - **True**
- Current forward exchange rates are based on relative interest rates between two countries - **True**

The expected future spot rate is calculated based on the relative inflation rates between two countries. The current forward exchange rates are set based on the relative interest rates between them.

Expectations theory states that there is an equilibrium between relative inflation rates and relative interest rates, so the expected spot rate and the current forward rate would be the same. Realistically, purchasing power parity tends to hold true in the longer term, so is used to forecast exchange rates a number of years into the future. Short-term differences are not unusual.

Syllabus area G2

300 The correct answers are:

- Transaction risk affects cash flows - **True**
- Translation risk directly affects shareholder wealth - **False**
- Diversification of supplier and customer base across different countries reduces economic risk - **True**

However, **investors** may be influenced by the changing values of assets and liabilities so a company may choose to hedge translation risk through, for example, **matching the currency of assets and liabilities**. Statement 3 is true. Economic exposure can be difficult to avoid, although **diversification of the supplier and customer base** across different countries will reduce this kind of exposure to risk.

Syllabus area G1

Marigold Co

301 The correct answer is: Translation

Translation risk is the gain/loss arising from the retranslation of a foreign subsidiary's results.

Syllabus area G1(a)

302 $ 269,663

The appropriate forward rate is 1.1125 MS per $1.

MS 300,000 / 1.1125 = $269,663

Syllabus area G3(a)

303 Amount to borrow: MS297,030

Amount to deposit: $264,027

Borrowing rate pro-rated for three months = 4% × /12 = 1%

Amount to borrow = MS300,000 / 1.01 = MS297,030

Amount to deposit = MS297,030 / MS1.1250 = $264,027

Syllabus area G3(a)

 BPP

304 The correct answers are:

- The option will be more expensive to set up compared with either the forward contract or money market hedge
- If the $ was to strengthen against the MS, Marigold Co is likely to be worse off by using the option compared to either the forward contract or money market hedge

Payment of the option premium upfront will make the option the more expensive means of hedging.

A strengthening of the $ will result in a worse spot rate than the exercise price, forcing exercise of the option. This, along with the premium cost will mean that Marigold Co will be worse off than if they had used the other instruments which offer better rates than even the exercise price.

Standard contract sizes only apply to tradable options, not over-the-counter options which will be tailored to the needs of the customer.

Syllabus area G3(c)

305 The correct answer is: The forward contract will result in Marigold Co receiving the dollar equivalent of the MS receipt in three months' time, whereas the money market hedge will provide Marigold Co with dollar receipts today

A money market hedge will bring the cash translation forward and will therefore provide $ today which could be spent rather than deposited.

The forward contract will not do this, as it will be settled at the set future date.

Syllabus area G3(a)

Peony Co

306 The correct answer is: A kink (discontinuity) in the normal yield curve can be due to differing yields in different market segments

Notes on incorrect answers:

The comment on expectations theory is incorrect because it applies to liquidity preference theory.

Government action to increase long-term borrowing would be likely to increase long-term interest rates (ie a normal upward slope).

Syllabus area G2(c)

307 The correct answer is: Peony Co pays bank $450,000

Company pays bank as interest rate is below the FRA rate.

100m × (9/12) × (7.1 − 6.5)/100 = $450,000

Syllabus area G4(a)

308 The correct answer is: $112.9m

12-month forward rate = 5 × 1.1/1.065 = 5.1643 pesos per $1

6-month forward rate = 5 × 1.05/1.0325 = 5.0848 pesos per $1

Income = (200/5.0848) + (380/5.1643) = $112.9m

Syllabus area G3(a)

309 The correct answer is: Both 1 and 2

Syllabus area G4(a)

310 The correct answer is: Peony Co can hedge interest rate risk on borrowing by selling interest rate futures now and buying them back in the future

Notes on incorrect answers:

Options do not have to be exercised, this is optional.

An interest rate swap only involves swapping the interest payments.

As Peony is borrowing it needs to buy a cap (and sell a floor to create a collar if this is desired).

Syllabus area G4(b)

 BPP

Mock Exams

ACCA

Financial Management (FM)

Mock Exam 1

September 2016

Questions	
Time allowed	3 hours
ALL questions are compulsory and MUST be attempted	

DO NOT OPEN THIS EXAM UNTIL YOU ARE READY TO START
UNDER EXAMINATION CONDITIONS

Section A

ALL 15 questions are compulsory and MUST be attempted

Each question is worth 2 marks.

1   The owners of a private company wish to dispose of their entire investment in the company. The company has an issued share capital of $1m of $0.50 nominal value ordinary shares. The owners have made the following valuations of the company's assets and liabilities.

Non-current assets (book value)	$30m
Current assets	$18m
Non-current liabilities	$12m
Current liabilities	$10m

The net realisable value of the non-current assets exceeds their book value by $4m. The current assets include $2m of accounts receivable which are thought to be irrecoverable.

Required

What is the minimum price per share which the owners should accept for the company (to the nearest $)?

$ [   ]   **(2 marks)**

---

2   Which of the following financial instruments will NOT be traded on a money market?

   O   Commercial paper

   O   Convertible loan notes

   O   Treasury bills

   O   Certificates of deposit   **(2 marks)**

---

3   Andrew Co is a large listed company financed by both equity and debt.

   In which of the following areas of financial management will the impact of working capital management be smallest?

   O   Liquidity management

   O   Interest rate management

   O   Management of relationship with the bank

   O   Dividend policy   **(2 marks)**

---

4   Which TWO of the following are descriptions of basis risk?

   ☐   It is the difference between the spot exchange rate and currency futures exchange rate.

   ☐   It is the possibility that the movements in the currency futures price and spot price will be different.

   ☐   It is the difference between fixed and floating interest rates.

   ☐   It is one of the reasons for an imperfect currency futures hedge.   **(2 marks)**

 BPP

5 Crag Co has sales of $200m per year and the gross profit margin is 40%. Finished goods inventory days vary throughout the year within the following range:

	Maximum	Minimum
Inventory (days)	120	90

All purchases and sales are made on a cash basis and no inventory of raw materials or work in progress is carried.

Crag Co intends to finance permanent current assets with equity and fluctuating current assets with its overdraft.

Required

In relation to finished goods inventory and assuming a 360-day year, how much finance will be needed from the overdraft?

$ [   ] million

(2 marks)

---

6 In relation to an irredeemable security paying a fixed rate of interest, which of the following statements is correct?

○ As risk rises, the market value of the security will fall to ensure that investors receive an increased yield.

○ As risk rises, the market value of the security will fall to ensure that investors receive a reduced yield.

○ As risk rises, the market value of the security will rise to ensure that investors receive an increased yield.

○ As risk rises, the market value of the security will rise to ensure that investors receive a reduced yield.

(2 marks)

---

7 Pop Co is switching from using mainly long-term fixed rate finance to fund its working capital to using mainly short-term variable rate finance.

Which of the following statements about the change in Pop Co's working capital financing policy is true?

○ Finance costs will increase

○ Refinancing risk will increase

○ Interest rate risk will decrease

○ Overcapitalisation risk will decrease

(2 marks)

---

8 Which of the following is NOT an advantage of withholding a dividend as a source of finance?

○ Retained profits are a free source of finance

○ Investment plans need less justification

○ Issue costs are lower

○ It is quick

(2 marks)

9 A company has annual after-tax operating cash flows of $2m per year which are expected to continue in perpetuity. The company has a cost of equity of 10%, a before-tax cost of debt of 5% and an after-tax weighted average cost of capital of 8% per year. Corporation tax is 20%.

What is the theoretical value of the company?

O $20m

O $40m

O $50m

O $25m   (2 marks)

---

10 Which of the following would you expect to be the responsibility of financial management?

O Producing annual accounts

O Producing monthly management accounts

O Advising on investment in non-current assets

O Deciding pay rates for staff   (2 marks)

---

11 Lane Co has in issue 3% convertible loan notes which are redeemable in 5 years' time at their nominal value of $100 per loan note. Alternatively, each loan note can be converted in 5 years' time into 25 Lane Co ordinary shares.

The current share price of Lane Co is $3.60 per share and future share price growth is expected to be 5% per year.

The before-tax cost of debt of these loan notes is 10% and corporation tax is 30%.

What is the current market value of a Lane Co convertible loan note?

O $82.71

O $73.47

O $67.26

O $94.20   (2 marks)

---

12 Country X uses the dollar as its currency and country Y uses the dinar.

Country X's expected inflation rate is 5% per year, compared to 2% per year in country Y. Country Y's nominal interest rate is 4% per year and the current spot exchange rate between the two countries is 1.5000 dinar per $1.

According to the four-way equivalence model, which of the following statements is/are true or false?

	True	False
Country X's nominal interest rate should be 7.06% per year	O	O
The future (expected) spot rate after one year should be 1.4571 dinar per $1	O	O
Country X's real interest rate should be higher than that of country Y	O	O

(2 marks)

 BPP

13 Which TWO of the following government actions would lead to an increase in aggregate demand?

☐ Increasing taxation and keeping government expenditure the same

☐ Decreasing taxation and increasing government expenditure

☐ Decreasing money supply

☐ Decreasing interest rates

(2 marks)

14 Peach Co's latest results are as follows:

	$'000
Profit before interest and taxation	2,500
Profit before taxation	2,250
Profit after tax	1,400

In addition, extracts from its latest statement of financial position are as follows:

	$'000
Equity	10,000
Non-current liabilities	2,500

Required

What is Peach Co's return on capital employed (ROCE)?

O 14%

O 18%

O 20%

O 25%

(2 marks)

15 Drumlin Co has $5m of $0.50 nominal value ordinary shares in issue. It recently announced a 1 for 4 rights issue at $6 per share. Its share price on the announcement of the rights issue was $8 per share.

What is the theoretical value of a right per existing share (to 2 decimal places)?

$ [   ]

(2 marks)

Section B

ALL 15 questions are compulsory and MUST be attempted

Herd Co

This scenario relates to the following five questions

Herd Co is based in a country whose currency is the dollar ($). The company expects to receive €1,500,000 in 6 months' time from Find Co, a foreign customer. The finance director of Herd Co is concerned that the euro (€) may depreciate against the dollar before the foreign customer makes payment and she is looking at hedging the receipt.

Herd Co has in issue loan notes with a total nominal value of $4m which can be redeemed in 10 years' time. The interest paid on the loan notes is at a variable rate. The finance director of Herd Co believes that interest rates may increase in the near future.

The spot exchange rate is €1.543 per $1. The domestic short-term interest rate is 2% per year, while the foreign short-term interest rate is 5% per year.

16 What is the six-month forward exchange rate predicted by interest rate parity (to 3 decimal places)?

$ [   ]   (2 marks)

17 As regards the euro receipt, what is the primary nature of the risk faced by Herd Co?

○ Transaction risk

○ Economic risk

○ Translation risk

○ Business risk   (2 marks)

18 Which of the following hedging methods will NOT be suitable for hedging the euro receipt?

○ Forward exchange contract

○ Money market hedge

○ Currency futures

○ Currency swap   (2 marks)

19 Which of the following statements support the finance director's belief that the euro will depreciate against the dollar?

	Supports the director's belief	Does not support the director's belief
The dollar inflation rate is greater than the euro inflation rate	○	○
The dollar nominal interest rate is less than the euro nominal interest rate	○	○

(2 marks)

20   As regards the interest rate risk faced by Herd Co, which of the following statements is correct?

    ○ In exchange for a premium, Herd Co could hedge its interest rate risk by buying interest rate options.

    ○ Buying a floor will give Herd Co a hedge against interest rate increases.

    ○ Herd Co can hedge its interest rate risk by buying interest rate futures now in order to sell them at a future date.

    ○ Taking out a variable rate overdraft will allow Herd Co to hedge the interest rate risk through matching.
          (2 marks)

(Total = 10 marks)

Ring Co

This scenario relates to the following five questions

Ring Co has in issue ordinary shares with a nominal value of $0.25 per share. These shares are traded on an efficient capital market. It is now 20X6 and the company has just paid a dividend of $0.450 per share. Recent dividends of the company are as follows:

Year	20X6	20X5	20X4	20X3	20X2
Dividend per share	$0.450	$0.428	$0.408	$0.389	$0.370

Ring Co also has in issue loan notes which are redeemable in 7 years' time at their nominal value of $100 per loan note and which pay interest of 6% per year.

The finance director of Ring Co wishes to determine the value of the company.

Ring Co has a cost of equity of 10% per year and a before-tax cost of debt of 4% per year. The company pays corporation tax of 25% per year.

21   Using the dividend growth model, what is the market value of each ordinary share?

    ○ $8.59

    ○ $9.00

    ○ $9.45

    ○ $7.77
          (2 marks)

22   What is the market value of each $100 loan note?

$ [   ]
          (2 marks)

23   The finance director of Ring Co has been advised to calculate the net asset value (NAV) of the company.

Which of the following formulae calculates correctly the NAV of Ring Co?

    ○ Total assets less current liabilities

    ○ Non-current assets plus net current assets

    ○ Non-current assets plus current assets less total liabilities

    ○ Non-current assets less net current assets less non-current liabilities
          (2 marks)

24 Which of the following statements about valuation methods is true?

O The earnings yield method multiplies earnings by the earnings yield.

O The equity market value is number of shares multiplied by share price, plus the market value of debt.

O The dividend valuation model makes the unreasonable assumption that average dividend growth is constant.

O The price/earnings ratio method divides earnings by the price/earnings ratio. **(2 marks)**

---

25 Which of the following statements about capital market efficiency is/are correct?

	Correct	Incorrect
Insider information cannot be used to make abnormal gains in a strong form efficient capital market	O	O
In a weak form efficient capital market, Ring Co's share price reacts to new information the day after it is announced	O	O
Ring Co's share price reacts quickly and accurately to newly released information in a semi-strong form efficient capital market	O	O

(2 marks)

(Total = 10 marks)

Fence Co

This scenario relates to the following five questions

The following information relates to an investment project which is being evaluated by the directors of Fence Co, a listed company. The initial investment, payable at the start of the first year of operation, is $3.9m.

Year	1	2	3	4
Net operating cash flow ($'000)	1,200	1,500	1,600	1,580
Scrap value ($'000)				100

The directors believe that this investment project will increase shareholder wealth if it achieves a return on capital employed greater than 15%. As a matter of policy, the directors require all investment projects to be evaluated using both the payback and return on capital employed methods. Shareholders have recently criticised the directors for using these investment appraisal methods, claiming that Fence Co ought to be using the academically preferred net present value method.

The directors have a remuneration package which includes a financial reward for achieving an annual return on capital employed greater than 15%. The remuneration package does not include a share option scheme.

 BPP

26 What is the payback period of the investment project?

- ○ 2.75 years
- ○ 1.50 years
- ○ 2.65 years
- ○ 1.55 years   (2 marks)

---

27 Based on the average investment method, what is the return on capital employed of the investment project?

- ○ 13.3%
- ○ 26.0%
- ○ 52.0%
- ○ 73.5%   (2 marks)

---

28 Which of the following statements about investment appraisal methods is correct?

- ○ The return on capital employed method considers the time value of money
- ○ Return on capital employed must be greater than the cost of equity if a project is to be accepted
- ○ Riskier projects should be evaluated with longer payback periods
- ○ Payback period ignores the timing of cash flows within the payback period   (2 marks)

---

29 Which of the following statements about Fence Co is/are correct?

	True	False
Managerial reward schemes of listed companies should encourage the achievement of stakeholder objectives	○	○
Requiring investment projects to be evaluated with return on capital employed is an example of dysfunctional behaviour encouraged by performance-related pay	○	○
Fence Co has an agency problem as the directors are not acting to maximise the wealth of shareholders	○	○

(2 marks)

BPP

30   Which of the following statements about Fence Co directors' remuneration package is/are correct?

	True	False
Directors' remuneration should be determined by senior executive directors	O	O
Introducing a share option scheme would help bring directors' objectives in line with shareholders' objectives	O	O
Linking financial rewards to a target return on capital employed will encourage short-term profitability and discourage capital investment	O	O

(2 marks)

(Total = 10 marks)

Section C

BOTH questions are compulsory and MUST be attempted

31 Nesud Co

Nesud Co has credit sales of $45m per year and on average settles accounts with trade payables after 60 days. One of its suppliers has offered the company an early settlement discount of 0.5% for payment within 30 days. Administration costs will be increased by $500 per year if the early settlement discount is taken. Nesud Co buys components worth $1.5m per year from this supplier.

From a different supplier, Nesud Co purchases $2.4m per year of Component K at a price of $5 per component. Consumption of Component K can be assumed to be at a constant rate throughout the year. The company orders components at the start of each month in order to meet demand and the cost of placing each order is $248.44. The holding cost for Component K is $1.06 per unit per year.

The finance director of Nesud Co is concerned that approximately 1% of credit sales turn into irrecoverable debts. In addition, she has been advised that customers of the company take an average of 65 days to settle their accounts, even though Nesud Co requires settlement within 40 days.

Nesud Co finances working capital from an overdraft costing 4% per year. Assume there are 360 days in a year.

Required

(a) Evaluate whether Nesud Co should accept the early settlement discount offered by its supplier.   (4 marks)

(b) Evaluate whether Nesud Co should adopt an economic order quantity approach to ordering Component K.   (6 marks)

(c) Critically discuss how Nesud Co could improve the management of its trade receivables.
                                                                                                        (10 marks)

(Total = 20 marks)

32 Hebac Co

Hebac Co is preparing to launch a new product in a new market which is outside its current business operations. The company has undertaken market research and test marketing at a cost of $500,000, as a result of which it expects the new product to be successful. Hebac Co plans to charge a lower selling price initially and then increase the selling price on the assumption that the new product will establish itself in the new market. Forecast sales volumes, selling prices and variable costs are as follows:

Year	1	2	3	4
Sales volume (units/year)	200,000	800,000	900,000	400,000
Selling price ($/unit)	15	18	22	22
Variable costs ($/unit)	9	9	9	9

Selling price and variable cost are given here in current price terms before taking account of forecast selling price inflation of 4% per year and variable cost inflation of 5% per year.

Incremental fixed costs of $500,000 per year in current price terms would arise as a result of producing the new product. Fixed cost inflation of 8% per year is expected.

The initial investment cost of production equipment for the new product will be $2.5m, payable at the start of the first year of operation. Production will cease at the end of four years because the new product is expected to have become obsolete due to new technology. The production equipment would have a scrap value at the end of 4 years of $125,000 in future value terms.

Investment in working capital of $1.5m will be required at the start of the first year of operation. Working capital inflation of 6% per year is expected and working capital will be recovered in full at the end of four years.

Hebac Co pays corporation tax of 20% per year, with the tax liability being settled in the year in which it arises. The company can claim tax-allowable depreciation on a 25% reducing balance basis on the initial investment cost, adjusted in the final year of operation for a balancing allowance or charge. Hebac Co currently has a nominal after-tax weighted average cost of capital (WACC) of 12% and a real after-tax WACC of 8.5%. The company uses its current WACC as the discount rate for all investment projects.

Required

(a) Calculate the net present value of the investment project in nominal terms and comment on its financial acceptability. **(12 marks)**

(b) Discuss how the capital asset pricing model can assist Hebac Co in making a better investment decision with respect to its new product launch. **(8 marks)**

(Total = 20 marks)

Answers

DO NOT TURN THIS PAGE UNTIL YOU HAVE
COMPLETED THE MOCK EXAM

A PLAN OF ATTACK

Managing your nerves

As you turn the pages to start this mock exam a number of thoughts are likely to cross your mind. At best, examinations cause anxiety so it is important to stay focused on your task for the next three hours! Developing an awareness of what is going on emotionally within you may help you manage your nerves. Remember, you are unlikely to banish the flow of adrenaline, but the key is to harness it to help you work steadily and quickly through your answers.

Working through this mock exam will help you develop the exam stamina you will need to keep going for 3 hours and 15 minutes.

Managing your time

Planning and time management are two of the key skills which complement the technical knowledge you need to succeed. To keep yourself on time, do not be afraid to jot down your target completion times for each question.

Doing the exam

Actually doing the exam is a personal experience. There is not a single **right way**. As long as you submit complete answers to all questions after the three hours are up, then your approach obviously works.

Looking through the exam

Section A has 15 objective test questions. This is the section of the exam where the examining team can test knowledge across the breadth of the syllabus. Make sure you read these questions carefully. The distractors are designed to present plausible, but incorrect, answers. Don't let them mislead you. If you really have no idea – guess. You may even be right.

Section B has three questions, each with a scenario and five objective test questions.

Section C has two longer questions worth 20 marks each, each based on a scenario and featuring a mix of numerical and discussion requirements. These questions are most likely to create time pressure issues. You will need to ensure that you do not spend too long on Section A and B questions because it is hard to rush Section C of the exam.

Allocating your time

BPP's advice is to always allocate your time **according to the marks for the question**. However, **use common sense**. If you're doing a question but haven't a clue how to do part (b), you might be better off reallocating your time and getting more marks on another question, where you can add something you didn't have time for earlier on. Make sure you leave time to recheck the MCQs and make sure you have answered them all.

 BPP

ANSWERS

Section A

1 $ \boxed{14}$

They should not accept less than NRV: (30m + 18m + 4m – 2m – 12m – 10m)/2m = $14 per share

2 The correct answer is: Convertible loan notes

Convertible loan notes are long-term finance and are not traded on a money market.

3 The correct answer is: Dividend policy

Working capital management may have an impact on dividend policy, but the other areas will be more significant.

4 The correct answers are:
- It is the possibility that the movements in the currency futures price and spot price will be different.
- It is one of the reasons for an imperfect currency futures hedge.

Basis risk is the possibility that movements in the currency futures price and spot price will be different. It is one of the reasons for an imperfect currency futures hedge.

5 $ \boxed{10}$ million

$200m × 30/360 × 0.6 = $10m

6 The correct answer is: As risk rises, the market value of the security will fall to ensure that investors receive an increased yield.

7 The correct answer is: Refinancing risk will increase

Pop Co is moving to an aggressive funding strategy which will increase refinancing risk.

8 The correct answer is: Retained profits are a free source of finance

Although free to raise, using retained earnings as a source of finance (by withholding a dividend) is not free to use. It is equity finance and requires the cost of equity to be generated as a return.

Incorrect answers:

Second statement is an advantage. Other forms of finance require up-front justification to be considered by potential investors before funds are made available for investment.

Third statement is an advantage. There are no issue costs.

Fourth statement is an advantage. As the funds are already on hand, availability is essentially instant.

9 The correct answer is: $25m

Theoretical value = 2m/0.08 = $25m. Operating cash flows are before interest so by discounting at the WACC the total value of the company's cash flows to all investors (debt + equity) is obtained.

10 The correct answer is: Advising on investment in non-current assets

This is a key role of financial management.

11 The correct answer is: $82.71

Conversion value = 3.60 × 1.05^5 × 25 = $114.87

Discounting at 10%, loan note value = (3 × 3.791) + (114.87 × 0.621) = $82.71

12 The correct answers are:

- Country X's nominal interest rate should be 7.06% per year - **True**
- The future (expected) spot rate after one year should be 1.4571 dinar per $1 - **True**
- Country X's real interest rate should be higher than that of country Y - **False**

Workings:

(1) (1.04 × 1.05/1.02) − 1 = 7.06%

(2) 1.5 dinar × 1.02/1.05 = 1.4571 dinar/$

(3) Real rates should be the same

13 The correct answers are:

- Decreasing taxation and increasing government expenditure
- Decreasing interest rates

Decreasing taxation and increasing government expenditure would lead to increased aggregate demand. Decreasing interest rates reduces the incentive to save and so would lead to an increase in aggregate demand.

14 The correct answer is: 20%

Operating profit/(D + E) = 100 × 2,500/(10,000 + 2,500) = 20%

15 $ | 0.40 |

TERP = (10m × $8 + 2.5m × $6)/(10m + 2.5m) = $7.60 per share

Value of a right = $7.60 minus $6.00 = $1.60 which becomes $1.60/ 4 shares = $0.40 per existing share

Section B

Herd Co

16   $\$\boxed{1.566}$

Forward rate = 1.543 × (1.025/1.01) = €1.566 per $1

17   The correct answer is: Transaction risk

The euro receipt is subject to transaction risk.

18   The correct answer is: Currency swap

A currency swap is not a suitable method for hedging a one-off transaction.

19   The correct answers are:

- The dollar inflation rate is greater than the euro inflation rate - **Does not support the director's belief**
- The dollar nominal interest rate is less than the euro nominal interest rate - **Supports the director's belief**

If the dollar inflation rate is less than the euro inflation rate, purchasing power parity indicates that the euro will appreciate against the dollar:

If the dollar nominal interest rate is less than the euro nominal interest rate, interest rate parity indicates that the euro will depreciate against the dollar:

20   The correct answer is: In exchange for a premium, Herd Co could hedge its interest rate risk by buying interest rate options.

Ring Co

21   The correct answer is: $9.45

Historical dividend growth rate = 100 × ((0.450/0.370)^0.25 − 1) = 5%

Share price = (0.450 × 1.05)/(0.1 − 0.05) = $9.45

22   $\$\boxed{112.01}$

Market value = (6 × 6.002) + (100 × 0.760) = 36.01 + 76.0 = $112.01

23   The correct answer is: Non-current assets plus current assets less total liabilities

This is the correct formula.

24   The correct answer is: The dividend valuation model makes the unreasonable assumption that average dividend growth is constant.

25   The correct answers are:

- Insider information cannot be used to make abnormal gains in a strong form efficient capital market - **Correct**
- In a weak form efficient capital market, Ring Co's share price reacts to new information the day after it is announced - **Incorrect**
- Ring Co's share price reacts quickly and accurately to newly released information in a semi-strong form efficient capital market - **Correct**

'Insider information cannot be used to make abnormal gains in a strong form efficient capital market' and 'Ring Co's share price reacts quickly and accurately to newly released information in a semi-strong form efficient capital market' are correct.

Fence Co

26 The correct answer is: 2.75 years

Payback period = 2 + (1,200/1,600) = 2.75 years

27 The correct answer is: 26.0%

Average annual accounting profit = (5,880 − 3,800)/4 = $520,000 per year

Average investment = (3,900 + 100)/2 = $2,000,000

ROCE = 100 × 520/2,000 = 26%

28 The correct answer is: Payback period ignores the timing of cash flows within the payback period

29 The correct answers are:

- Managerial reward schemes of listed companies should encourage the achievement of stakeholder objectives - **True**
- Requiring investment projects to be evaluated with return on capital employed is an example of dysfunctional behaviour encouraged by performance-related pay - **True**
- Fence Co has an agency problem as the directors are not acting to maximise the wealth of shareholders - **True**

30 The correct answers are:

- Directors' remuneration should be determined by senior executive directors - **False**
- Introducing a share option scheme would help bring directors' objectives in line with shareholders' objectives - **True**
- Linking financial rewards to a target return on capital employed will encourage short-term profitability and discourage capital investment - **True**

Directors' remuneration should be determined by non-executive directors.

Section C

31 Nesud Co

Marking guide		Marks
(a) Change in trade payables	1	
Increase in finance cost	1	
Administration cost increase	0.5	
Early settlement discount	0.5	
Comment on financial acceptability	1	
		4
(b) Annual demand	1	
Current ordering cost	1	
Current holding cost	1	
EOQ	1	
EOQ ordering cost	0.5	
EOQ holding cost	0.5	
Comment on adopting EOQ approach to ordering	1	
		6
(c) Credit analysis	2	
Credit control	2	

Collection of amounts owed	2
Factoring of trade receivables	2
Other relevant discussion	2
	10
Total	20

(a) Relevant trade payables before discount = 1,500,000 × 60/360 = $250,000

Relevant trade payables after discount = 1,500,000 × 30/360 = $125,000

Reduction in trade payables = 250,000 − 125,000 = $125,000

More quickly, reduction in trade payables = 1,500,000 × (60 − 30)/360 = $125,000

The finance needed to reduce the trade payables will increase the overdraft.

Increase in finance cost = 125,000 × 0.04 = $5,000

Administration cost increase = $500

Discount from supplier = $1,500,000 × 0.005 = $7,500

Net benefit of discount = 7,500 − 5,000 − 500 = $2,000 per year

On financial grounds, Nesud Co should accept the supplier's early settlement discount offer.

(b) Annual demand = 2,400,000/5 = 480,000 units per year

Each month, Nesud Co orders 480,000/12 = 40,000 units

Current ordering cost = 12 × 248.44 = $2,981 per year

Average inventory of Component K = 40,000/2 = 20,000 units

Current holding cost = 20,000 x 1.06 = $21,200 per year

Total cost of current ordering policy = 2,981 + 21,200 = $24,181

Economic order quantity = $(2 \times 248.44 \times 480,000/1.06)^{0.5}$ = 15,000 units per order

Number of orders per year = 480,000/15,000 = 32 orders per year

Ordering cost = 32 × 248.44 = $7,950 per year

Average inventory of Component K = 15,000/2 = 7,500 units

Holding cost = 7,500 × 1.06 = $7,950 per year

Total cost of EOQ ordering policy = 7,950 + 7,950 = $15,900

On financial grounds, Nesud Co should adopt an EOQ approach to ordering Component K as there is a reduction in cost of $8,281.

(c)

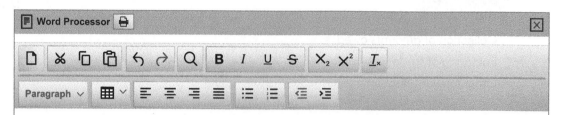

Management of trade receivables can be improved by considering credit analysis, credit control and collection of amounts owing. Management of trade receivables can also be outsourced to a factoring company, rather than being managed in-house.

Credit analysis

Offering credit to customers exposes a company to the risk of bad debts and this should be minimised through credit analysis or assessing creditworthiness. This can be done through collecting and analysing information about potential credit customers. Relevant information includes bank references, trade references, reports from credit reference agencies, records of previous transactions with potential customers, annual reports, and so on. A company might set up its own credit scoring system in order to assess the creditworthiness of potential customers. Where the expected volume of trade justifies it, a visit to a company can be made to gain a better understanding of its business and prospects.

Credit control

The accounts of customers who have been granted credit must be monitored regularly to ensure that agreed trade terms are being followed and that accounts are not getting into arrears. An important monitoring device here is an aged trade receivables analysis, identifying accounts and amounts in arrears, and the extent to which amounts are overdue. A credit utilisation report can assist management in understanding the extent to which credit is being used, identifying customers who may benefit from increased credit, and assessing the extent and nature of a company's exposure to trade receivables.

Collection of amounts owed

A company should ensure that its trade receivables are kept informed about their accounts, amounts outstanding and amounts becoming due, and the terms of trade they have accepted. An invoice should be raised when a sale is made. Regular statements should be sent, for example, on a monthly basis. Customers should be encouraged to settle their accounts on time and not become overdue. Offering a discount for early settlement could help to achieve this.

Overdue accounts should be chased using procedures contained within a company's trade receivables management policy. Reminders of payment due should be sent, leading to a final demand if necessary. Telephone calls or personal visits could be made to a contact within the company. Taking legal action or employing a specialised debt collection agency could be considered as a last resort. A clear understanding of the costs involved is important here, as the costs incurred should never exceed the benefit of collecting the overdue amount.

Factoring of trade receivables

Some companies choose to outsource management of trade receivables to a factoring company, which can bring expertise and specialist knowledge to the tasks of credit analysis, credit control, and collection of amounts owed. In exchange, the factoring company will charge a fee, typically a percentage of annual credit sales. The factoring company can also offer an advance of up to 80% of trade receivables, in exchange for interest.

32 Hebac Co

Marking guide	Marks	
(a) Inflated selling price per unit	1	
Sales revenue	1	
Inflated variable cost	1	
Inflated fixed costs	1	
Tax liabilities	1	
Tax-allowable depreciation benefits Years 1–3	1	
Tax allowable depreciation benefits Year 4	1	
Incremental working capital and recovery	2	
Calculation of present values	1	
Correct initial investment	1	
Comment on financial acceptability	1	
		12
(b) Business risk, financial risk and WACC	2	
Using a proxy company	1	
Systematic risk, business risk and financial risk	1	
Ungearing the equity beta	1	
Regearing the asset beta	1	
Project-specific cost of equity and WACC	2	
		8
Total		20

(a) **Calculation of NPV**

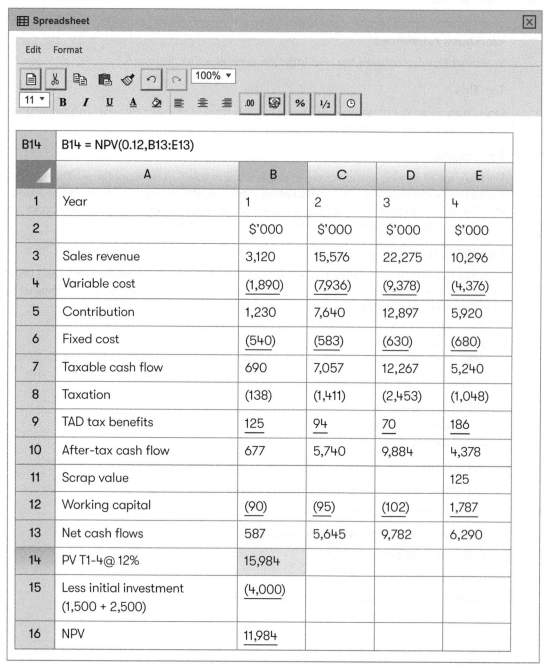

The NPV is strongly positive and so the project is financially acceptable.

Workings

1 **Sales revenue**

Year	1	2	3	4
Selling price ($/unit)	15	18	22	22
Inflated at 4% per year	15.60	19.47	24.75	25.74
Sales volume ('000 units/year)	200	800	900	400
Sales revenue ($'000/year)	3,120	15,576	22,275	10,296

2 Variable cost

Year	1	2	3	4
Variable cost ($/unit)	9	9	9	9
Inflated at 5% per year	9.45	9.92	10.42	10.94
Sales volume ('000 units/year)	200	800	900	400
Variable cost ($'000/year)	1,890	7,936	9,378	4,376

3 Tax benefits of tax-allowable depreciation

Year	1	2	3	4
	$'000	$'000	$'000	$'000
Tax-allowable depreciation	625	469	352	929
Tax benefit	125	94	70	186*

*((2,500 – 125) × 0.2) – 125 – 94 – 70 = $186,000

4 Working capital

Year	0	1	2	3	4
	$'000	$'000	$'000	$'000	$'000
Working capital	1,500				
Inflated at 6%		1,590	1,685	1,787	
Incremental		90	95	102	1,787

5 Alternative calculation of after-tax cash flow

Year	1	2	3	4
	$'000	$'000	$'000	$'000
Taxable cash flow	690	7,057	12,267	5,240
Tax-allowable depreciation	(625)	(469)	(352)	(929)
Taxable profit	65	6,588	11,915	4,311
Taxation	(13)	(1,318)	(2,383)	(862)
After-tax profit	52	5,270	9,532	3,449
Add back TAD	625	469	352	929
After-tax cash flow	677	5,739	9,884	4,378

(b)

A company can use its weighted average cost of capital (WACC) as the discount rate in appraising an investment project as long as the project's business risk and financial risk are similar to the business and financial risk of existing business operations. Where the business risk of the investment project differs significantly from the business risk of existing business operations, a project-specific discount rate is needed.

The capital asset pricing model (CAPM) can provide a project-specific discount rate. The equity beta of a company whose business operations are similar to those of the investment project (a proxy company) will reflect the systematic business risk of the project. If the proxy company is geared, the proxy equity beta will additionally reflect the systematic financial risk of the proxy company.

The proxy equity beta is ungeared to remove the effect of the proxy company's systematic financial risk to give an asset beta which solely reflects the business risk of the investment project.

This asset beta is regeared to give an equity beta which reflects the systematic financial risk of the investing company.

The regeared equity beta can then be inserted into the CAPM formula to provide a project-specific cost of equity. If this cost of capital is used as the discount rate for the investment project, it will indicate the minimum return required to compensate shareholders for the systematic risk of the project. The project-specific cost of equity can also be included in a project-specific WACC. Using the project-specific WACC in appraising an investment project will lead to a better investment decision than using the current WACC as the discount rate, as the current WACC does not reflect the risk of the investment project.

ACCA

Financial Management (FM)

Mock Exam 2

Specimen exam

Questions	
Time allowed	3 hours
ALL questions are compulsory and MUST be attempted	

DO NOT OPEN THIS EXAM UNTIL YOU ARE READY TO START
UNDER EXAMINATION CONDITIONS

Section A

ALL 15 questions are compulsory and MUST be attempted.

Each question is worth 2 marks.

1   The home currency of ACB Co is the dollar ($) and it trades with a company in a foreign country whose home currency is the Dinar. The following information is available:

	Home country	Foreign country
Spot rate	20.00 Dinar per $	
Interest rate	3% per year	7% per year
Inflation rate	2% per year	5% per year

Required

What is the six-month forward exchange rate?

O   20.39 Dinar per $

O   20.30 Dinar per $

O   20.59 Dinar per $

O   20.78 Dinar per $ **(2 marks)**

---

2   The following financial information relates to an investment project:

	$'000
Present value of sale revenue	50,025
Present value of variable costs	25,475
Present value of contribution	24,550
Present value of fixed costs	18,250
Present value of operating income	6,300
Initial investment	5,000
Net present value	1,300

Required

What is the sensitivity of the net present value of the investment project to a change in sales volume?

O   7.1%

O   2.6%

O   5.1%

O   5.3%   **(2 marks)**

 BPP

3   Gurdip plots the historic movements of share prices and uses this analysis to make her investment decisions.

Oliver believes that share prices reflect all relevant information at all times.

Required

Match the level of capital markets efficiency that best reflects each of Gurdip and Oliver's beliefs.

Name		Efficiency
Gurdip		Not efficient at all
Oliver		Weak form efficient
		Semi-strong form efficient
		Strong form efficient

(2 marks)

4   Which of the following statements concerning capital structure theory is correct?

O   In the traditional view, there is a linear relationship between the cost of equity and financial risk.

O   Modigliani and Miller said that, in the absence of tax, the cost of equity would remain constant.

O   Pecking order theory indicates that preference shares are preferred to convertible debt as a source of finance.

O   Business risk is assumed to be constant as the capital structure changes.   **(2 marks)**

5   Which of the following actions is LEAST likely to increase shareholder wealth?

O   The weighted average cost of capital is decreased by a recent financing decision.

O   The financial rewards of directors are linked to increasing earnings per share.

O   The board of directors decides to invest in a project with a positive NPV.

O   The annual report declares full compliance with the corporate governance code.   **(2 marks)**

6   Which TWO of the following statements are features of money market instruments?

☐   A negotiable security can be sold before maturity.

☐   The yield on commercial paper is usually lower than that on treasury bills.

☐   Discount instruments trade at less than face value.

☐   Commercial paper is often issued by companies to fund long-term expenditure   **(2 marks)**

7 The following are extracts from the statement of profit or loss of CQB Co:

	$'000
Sales income	60,000
Cost of sales	50,000
Profit before interest and tax	10,000
Interest	4,000
Profit before tax	6,000
Tax	4,500
Profit after tax	1,500

60% of the cost of sales is variable cost.

Required

What is the operational gearing of CQB Co?

O 5.0 times

O 2.0 times

O 0.5 times

O 3.0 times   **(2 marks)**

8 The management of Lamara Co has annual credit sales of $20m and accounts receivable of $4m. Working capital is financed by an overdraft at 12% interest per year. Assume 365 days in a year.

What is the annual finance cost saving if the management reduces the collection period to 60 days (to the nearest $)?

$ [   ]   **(2 marks)**

9 Are the following statements concerning financial management true or false?

	True	False
It is concerned with investment decisions, financing decisions and dividend decisions	O	O
It is concerned with financial planning and financial control	O	O
It considers the management of risk	O	O
It is concerned with providing information on past plans and decisions	O	O

(2 marks)

 BPP

10 SKV Co has paid the following dividends per share in recent years:

Year	20X4	20X3	20X2	20X1
Dividend ($ per share)	0.360	0.338	0.328	0.311

The dividend for 20X4 has just been paid and SKV Co has a cost of equity of 12%.

Required

Using the geometric average historical dividend growth rate and the dividend growth model, what is the market price of SKV Co shares on an ex dividend basis?

○ $4.67

○ $5.14

○ $5.40

○ $6.97   **(2 marks)**

---

11 'There is a risk that the value of our foreign currency-denominated assets and liabilities will change when we prepare our accounts.'

To which risk does the above statement refer?

○ Translation risk

○ Economic risk

○ Transaction risk

○ Interest rate risk   **(2 marks)**

---

12 The following information has been calculated for A Co:

Trade receivables collection period	52 days
Raw material inventory holding period	42 days
Work in progress inventory holding period	30 days
Trade payables payment period	66 days
Finished goods inventory holding period	45 days

Required

What is the length of the working capital cycle?

[   ] days   **(2 marks)**

13 Which of the following is/are usually seen as benefits of financial intermediation?

(1) Interest rate fixing

(2) Risk pooling

(3) Maturity transformation

○ 1 only

○ 1 and 3 only

○ 2 and 3 only

○ 1, 2 and 3 **(2 marks)**

14 Which TWO of the following statements concerning working capital management are correct?

☐ The twin objectives of working capital management are profitability and liquidity

☐ A conservative approach to working capital investment will increase profitability

☐ Working capital management is a key factor in a company's long-term success

☐ The current ratio is a measure of profitability **(2 marks)**

15 Governments have a number of economic targets as part of their monetary policy.

Which TWO of the following targets relate predominantly to monetary policy?

☐ Increasing tax revenue

☐ Controlling the growth in the size of the money supply

☐ Reducing public expenditure

☐ Keeping interest rates low **(2 marks)**

Section B

ALL 15 questions are compulsory and MUST be attempted

Each question is worth 2 marks.

Par Co

This scenario relates to the following five questions

Par Co currently has the following long-term capital structure:

	$m	$m
Equity finance		
Ordinary shares	30.0	
Reserves	38.4	
		68.4
Non-current liabilities		
Bank loans	15.0	
8% convertible loan notes	40.0	
5% redeemable preference shares	15.0	
		70.0
Total equity and liabilities		138.4

The 8% loan notes are convertible into eight ordinary shares per loan note in seven years' time. If not converted, the loan notes can be redeemed on the same future date at their nominal value of $100. Par Co has a cost of debt of 9% per year.

The ordinary shares of Par Co have a nominal value of $1 per share. The current ex dividend share price of the company is $10.90 per share and share prices are expected to grow by 6% per year for the foreseeable future. The equity beta of Par Co is 1.2.

16 The loan notes are secured on non-current assets of Par Co and the bank loan is secured by a floating charge on the current assets of the company.

Arrange the following sources of finance of Par Co in order of the risk to the investor with the riskiest first.

		Order of risk (1st, 2nd, etc)
Redeemable preference shares		1st
Loan notes		2nd
Bank loan		3rd
Ordinary shares		4th

(2 marks)

17   What is the conversion value of the 8% loan notes of Par Co after seven years (to 2 decimal places)?

$ [   ]   **(2 marks)**

---

18   Assuming the conversion value after 7 years is $126.15, what is the current market value of the 8% loan notes of Par Co?

O $115.20

O $109.26

O $94.93

O $69.00   **(2 marks)**

---

19   Which of the following statements relating to the capital asset pricing model is correct?

O The equity beta of Par Co considers only business risk.

O The capital asset pricing model considers systematic risk and unsystematic risk.

O The equity beta of Par Co indicates that the company is more risky than the market as a whole.

O The debt beta of Par Co is zero.   **(2 marks)**

---

20   Which TWO of the following statements are problems in using the price/earnings ratio method to value a company?

☐ It is the reciprocal of the earnings yield.

☐ It combines stock market information and corporate information.

☐ It is difficult to select a suitable price/earnings ratio.

☐ The ratio is more suited to valuing the shares of listed companies.   **(2 marks)**

(Total = 10 marks)

Zarona Co

This scenario relates to the following five questions

Zarona Co, whose home currency is the dollar, took out a fixed-interest peso bank loan several years ago when peso interest rates were relatively cheap compared to dollar interest rates. Zarona Co does not have any income in pesos. Economic difficulties have now increased peso interest rates while dollar interest rates have remained relatively stable.

Zarona Co must pay interest on the dates set by the bank. A payment of 5,000,000 pesos is due in 6 months' time. The following information is available:

Spot rate	12.500–12.582 pesos per $
Six-month forward rate	12.805–12.889 pesos per $

Interest rates which can be used by Zarona Co:

	Borrow	Deposit
Peso interest rates	10.0% per year	7.5% per year
Dollar interest rates	4.5% per year	3.5% per year

21 What is the dollar cost of a forward market hedge? (to the nearest $)

$ [_____] **(2 marks)**

---

22 Indicate whether the following statements apply to interest rate parity theory, purchasing power parity theory, or both.

	Interest rate parity theory	Purchasing power parity theory	Both
The currency of the country with the higher inflation rate will weaken against the other currency	O	O	O
The theory holds in the long-term rather than in the short-term	O	O	O
The exchange rate reflects the cost of living in the two countries	O	O	O

(2 marks)

---

23 What are the appropriate six-month interest rates for Zarona Co to use if the company hedges the peso payment using a money market hedge?

	Deposit rate	Borrowing rate
O	7.50%	4.50%
O	1.75%	5.00%
O	3.75%	2.25%
O	3.50%	10.00%

(2 marks)

---

24 Which TWO of the following methods are possible ways for Zarona Co to hedge its existing foreign currency risk?

☐ Matching receipts and payments
☐ Currency swaps
☐ Leading or lagging
☐ Currency futures

(2 marks)

 BPP

25   Zarona Co also trades with companies in Europe which use the euro as their home currency. In 3 months' time Zarona Co will receive €300,000 from a customer.

Required

Which of the following is the correct procedure for hedging this receipt using a money market hedge?

- O Step 1 – Borrow an appropriate amount in euro now
     Step 2 – Convert the euro amount into dollars
     Step 3 – Place the dollars on deposit
     Step 4 – Use the customer payment to repay the loan

- O Step 1 – Borrow an appropriate amount in dollars now
     Step 2 – Place the dollars on deposit now
     Step 3 – Convert the dollars into euro in three months' time
     Step 4 – Use the customer payment to repay the loan

- O Step 1 – Borrow an appropriate amount in dollars now
     Step 2 – Convert the dollar amount into euro
     Step 3 – Place the euro on deposit
     Step 4 – Use the customer payment to repay the loan

- O Step 1 – Borrow an appropriate amount in euro now
     Step 2 – Place the euro on deposit now
     Step 3 – Convert the euro into dollars in three months' time
     Step 4 – Use the customer payment to repay the loan

(2 marks)

(Total = 10 marks)

Ridag Co

This scenario relates to the following five questions

Ridag Co operates in an industry which has recently been deregulated as the Government seeks to increase competition in the industry.

Ridag Co plans to replace an existing machine and must choose between two machines. Machine 1 has an initial cost of $200,000 and will have a scrap value of $25,000 after 4 years. Machine 2 has an initial cost of $225,000 and will have a scrap value of $50,000 after 3 years. Annual maintenance costs of the two machines are as follows:

Year	1	2	3	4
Machine 1 ($ per year)	25,000	29,000	32,000	35,000
Machine 2 ($ per year)	15,000	20,000	25,000	

Where relevant, all information relating to this project has already been adjusted to include expected future inflation. Taxation and tax-allowable depreciation must be ignored in relation to Machine 1 and Machine 2.

Ridag Co has a nominal before-tax weighted average cost of capital of 12% and a nominal after-tax weighted average cost of capital of 7%.

26   In relation to Ridag Co, which TWO of the following statements about competition and deregulation are true?

☐ Increased competition should encourage Ridag Co to reduce costs

☐ Deregulation will lead to an increase in administrative and compliance costs for Ridag Co

☐ Deregulation should mean an increase in economies of scale for Ridag Co

☐ Deregulation could lead to a decrease in the quality of Ridag Co's products   **(2 marks)**

---

27   What is the equivalent annual cost of Machine 1?

O $90,412

O $68,646

O $83,388

O $70,609
                                                                          (2 marks)

---

28   Is each of the following statements about Ridag Co using the equivalent annual cost method true or false?

	True	False
Ridag Co cannot use the equivalent annual cost method to compare Machine 1 and Machine 2 because they have different useful lives	O	O
The machine which has the lowest total present value of costs should be selected by Ridag Co	O	O

(2 marks)

---

29   Doubt has been cast over the accuracy of the Year 2 and Year 3 maintenance costs for Machine 2. On further investigation it was found that the following potential cash flows are now predicted:

Year	Cash flow $	Probability
2	18,000	0.3
2	25,000	0.7
3	23,000	0.2
3	24,000	0.35
3	30,000	0.45

What is the expected present value of the maintenance costs for Year 3 (to the nearest $)?

$ [   ]   **(2 marks)**

30　Ridag Co is appraising a different project, with a positive NPV. It is concerned about the risk and uncertainty associated with this other project.

Which of the following statements about risk, uncertainty and the project is true?

○　Sensitivity analysis takes into account the interrelationship between project variables

○　Probability analysis can be used to assess the uncertainty associated with the project

○　Uncertainty can be said to increase with project life, while risk increases with the variability of returns

○　A discount rate of 5% could be used to lessen the effect of later cash flows on the decision　**(2 marks)**

(Total = 10 marks)

Section C

BOTH questions are compulsory and MUST be attempted

31 Vip Co

Vip Co, a large stock exchange listed company, is evaluating an investment proposal to manufacture Product W33, which has performed well in test marketing trials conducted recently by the company's research and development division. Product W33 will be manufactured using a fully automated process which would significantly increase noise levels from Vip Co's factory. The following information relating to this investment proposal has now been prepared:

Initial investment	$2 million
Selling price (current price terms)	$20 per unit
Expected selling price inflation	3% per year
Variable operating costs (current price terms)	$8 per unit
Fixed operating costs (current price terms)	$170,000 per year
Expected operating cost inflation	4% per year

The research and development division has prepared the following demand forecast as a result of its test marketing trials. The forecast reflects expected technological change and its effect on the anticipated life-cycle of Product W33.

Year	1	2	3	4
Demand (units)	60,000	70,000	120,000	45,000

It is expected that all units of Product W33 produced will be sold, in line with the company's policy of keeping no inventory of finished goods. No terminal value or machinery scrap value is expected at the end of four years, when production of Product W33 is planned to end. For investment appraisal purposes, Vip Co uses a nominal (money) discount rate of 10% per year and a target return on capital employed of 30% per year. Ignore taxation.

Required

(a) Calculate the following values for the investment proposal:

    (i)   net present value;   **(5 marks)**

    (ii)   internal rate of return;   **(3 marks)**

    (iii) return on capital employed (accounting rate of return) based on average investment.   **(3 marks)**

(b) Briefly discuss your findings in each section of (a) previously and advise whether the investment proposal is financially acceptable.   **(4 marks)**

(c) Discuss how the objectives of Vip Co's stakeholders may be in conflict if the project is undertaken.

    (5 marks)

    (Total = 20 marks)

32 Froste Co

Froste Co has a dividend payout ratio of 40% and has maintained this payout ratio for several years. The current dividend per share of the company is 50c per share and it expects that its next dividend per share, payable in one year's time, will be 52c per share.

The capital structure of the company is as follows:

	$m	$m
Equity		
Ordinary shares (nominal value $1 per share)	25	
Reserves	35	
		60
Debt		
Bond A (nominal value $100)	20	
Bond B (nominal value $100)	10	
		30
		90

Bond A will be redeemed at nominal value in 10 years' time and pays annual interest of 9%. The cost of debt of this bond is 9.83% per year. The current ex interest market price of the bond is $95.08.

Bond B will be redeemed at nominal value in 4 years' time and pays annual interest of 8%. The cost of debt of this bond is 7.82% per year. The current ex interest market price of the bond is $102.01.

Froste Co has a cost of equity of 12.4%. Ignore taxation.

Required

(a) Calculate the following values for Froste Co:

    (i)   ex dividend share price, using the dividend growth model; **(3 marks)**

    (ii)   capital gearing (debt divided by debt plus equity) using market values; **(2 marks)**

    (iii) market value weighted average cost of capital. **(2 marks)**

(b) Discuss whether a change in dividend policy will affect the share price of Froste Co. **(8 marks)**

(c) Explain why Froste Co's capital instruments have different levels of risk and return. **(5 marks)**

(Total = 20 marks)

Answers

DO NOT TURN THIS PAGE UNTIL YOU HAVE
COMPLETED THE MOCK EXAM

A PLAN OF ATTACK

Managing your nerves

As you turn the pages to start this mock exam a number of thoughts are likely to cross your mind. At best, examinations cause anxiety so it is important to stay focused on your task for the next three hours! Developing an awareness of what is going on emotionally within you may help you manage your nerves. Remember, you are unlikely to banish the flow of adrenaline, but the key is to harness it to help you work steadily and quickly through your answers.

Working through this mock exam will help you develop the exam stamina you will need to keep going for 3 hours and 15 minutes.

Managing your time

Planning and time management are two of the key skills which complement the technical knowledge you need to succeed. To keep yourself on time, do not be afraid to jot down your target completion times for each question.

Doing the exam

Actually doing the exam is a personal experience. There is not a single **right way**. As long as you submit complete answers to all questions after the three hours are up, then your approach obviously works.

Looking through the exam

Section A has 15 objective test questions. This is the section of the exam where the examining team can test knowledge across the breadth of the syllabus. Make sure you read these questions carefully. The distractors are designed to present plausible, but incorrect, answers. Don't let them mislead you. If you really have no idea – guess. You may even be right.

Section B has three questions, each with a scenario and five objective test questions.

Section C has two longer questions worth 20 marks each, each based on a scenario and featuring a mix of numerical and discussion requirements. These questions are most likely to create time pressure issues. You will need to ensure that you do not spend too long on Section A and B questions because it is hard to rush Section C of the exam.

Allocating your time

BPP's advice is to always allocate your time **according to the marks for the question**. However, **use common sense**. If you're doing a question but haven't a clue how to do part (b), you might be better off reallocating your time and getting more marks on another question, where you can add something you didn't have time for earlier on. Make sure you leave time to recheck the MCQs and make sure you have answered them all.

Section A

1   The correct answer is: 20.39 Dinar per $

   20 × (1.035/1.015) = 20.39 Dinar per $

2   The correct answer is: 5.3%

   Sensitivity to a change in sales volume = 100 × 1,300/24,550 = 5.3%

3   The correct answers are:

Name	Efficiency
Gurdip	Not efficient at all
	Weak form efficient
	Semi-strong form efficient
Oliver	Strong form efficient

   Gurdip is basing her investment decisions on technical analysis, which means that she believes the stock market is not efficient at all, not even weak form efficient.

   Oliver believes markets are strong form efficient

4   The correct answer is: Business risk is assumed to be constant as the capital structure changes.

   In the traditional view, there is a curvilinear relationship between the cost of equity and financial risk.

   Modigliani and Miller said that, in the absence of tax, the weighted average cost of capital (not the cost of equity) would remain constant.

   Pecking order theory indicates that any shares are less attractive than debt as a source of finance.

5   The correct answer is: The financial rewards of directors are linked to increasing earnings per share.

   Increases in shareholder wealth will depend on increases in cash flow, rather than increases in earnings per share (ie increases in profit). If the financial rewards of directors are linked to increasing earnings per share, for example, through a performance-related reward scheme, there is an incentive to increase short-term profit at the expense of longer-term growth in cash flows and hence shareholder wealth.

6   The correct answers are:

   • A negotiable security can be sold before maturity.

   • Discount instruments trade at less than face value.

   Commercial paper is a source of short-term finance, it is riskier than Treasury Bills and will therefore carry a higher yield.

7 The correct answer is: 3.0 times

   Operational gearing = Contribution/PBIT

   = [60,000 – (50,000 × 0.6)]/10m = 3 times

8 $ | 85,479 |

   Finance cost saving = 13/365 × 20m × 0.12 = $85,479

9 The correct answers are:

   - It is concerned with investment decisions, financing decisions and dividend decisions - **True**
   - It is concerned with financial planning and financial control - **True**
   - It considers the management of risk - **True**
   - It is concerned with providing information on past plans and decisions - **False**

   The first three statements concerning financial management are correct. However, information about past plans and decisions is a function of financial reporting, not financial management.

10 The correct answer is: $5.40

   The geometric average dividend growth rate is $(36.0/31.1)^{1/3} - 1 = 5\%$

   The ex div share price = $(36.0 \times 1.05)/(0.12 - 0.05) = \$5.40$

11 The correct answer is: Translation risk

12 | 103 | days

   The length of the operating cycle is 52 + 42 + 30 – 66 + 45 = 103 days.

13 The correct answer is: 2 and 3 only

   Risk pooling and maturity transformation are always included in a list of benefits of financial intermediation.

14 The correct answers are:

   - The twin objectives of working capital management are profitability and liquidity
   - Working capital management is a key factor in a company's long-term success

   A conservative approach to working capital investment will involve maintaining high levels of working capital which may well not increase profitability.

   The current ratio is a measure of liquidity, not profitability.

15 The correct answers are:

   - Controlling the growth in the size of the money supply
   - Keeping interest rates low

   The other targets relate to fiscal policy.

Section B

Par Co

16   The correct answers are:

	Order of risk (1st, 2nd, etc)
Ordinary shares	1st
Redeemable preference shares	2nd
Bank loan	3rd
Loan notes	4th

The secured loan notes are safer than the bank loan, which is secured on a floating charge. The redeemable preference shares are above debt in the creditor hierarchy. Ordinary shares are higher in the creditor hierarchy than preference shares.

17    $ 131.12

Future share price after 7 years = 10.90 × 1.06^7= $16.39 per share

Conversion value of each loan note = 16.39 × 8 = $131.12 per loan note

18   The correct answer is: $109.26

Market value of each loan note = (8 × 5.033) + (126.15 × 0.547) = 40.26 + 69.00 = $109.26

19   The correct answer is: The equity beta of Par Co indicates that the company is more risky than the market as a whole.

An equity beta of greater than 1 indicates that the investment is more risky than the market as a whole.

Notes on incorrect answers:

The equity beta of Par Co considers business and financial risk.

The capital asset pricing model only considers systematic risk.

The debt beta of Par Co is zero - this is not an assumption of the CAPM.

20   The correct answers are:

- It is difficult to select a suitable price/earnings ratio.
- The ratio is more suited to valuing the shares of listed companies.

It is correct that the price/earnings ratio is more suited to valuing the shares of listed companies, and it is also true that it is difficult to find a suitable price/earnings ratio for the valuation.

Statements 1 and 2 are true but are not problems.

Zarona Co

21 $ [390,472]

Interest payment = 5,000,000 pesos

Six-month forward rate for buying pesos = 12.805 pesos per $

Dollar cost of peso interest using forward market = 5,000,000/12.805 = $390,472

22 The correct answers are:

- The currency of the country with the higher inflation rate will weaken against the other currency - **Purchasing power parity theory**
- The theory holds in the long-term rather than in the short-term - **Both**
- The exchange rate reflects the cost of living in the two countries - **Purchasing power parity theory**

The correct answer is: All statements relate to purchasing power parity; statement 2 also applies to interest rate parity.

Exchange rates reflecting the different cost of living between two countries is stated by the theory of purchasing power parity.

Both theories hold in the long term rather than the short term (IRP also applies in the short-term).

The currency of the country with the higher inflation rate will be forecast to weaken against the currency of the country with the lower inflation rate in purchasing power parity.

23 The correct answer is:

Deposit rate	Borrowing rate
3.75%	2.25%

Dollars will be borrowed now for 6 months at 4.5 × 6/12 = 2.25%

Pesos will be deposited now for 6 months at 7.5 × 6/12 = 3.75%

24 The correct answers are:

- Currency swaps
- Currency futures

Currency futures and swaps could both be used.

As payment must be made on the date set by the bank, leading or lagging are not appropriate. Matching is also inappropriate as there are no peso income streams.

25 The correct answer is:

Step 1 – Borrow an appropriate amount in euro now

Step 2 – Convert the euro amount into dollars

Step 3 – Place the dollars on deposit

Step 4 – Use the customer payment to repay the loan

The correct procedure is to: Borrow euro now, convert the euro into dollars and place the dollars on deposit for three months, use the customer receipt to pay back the euro loan.

Ridag Co

26   The correct answers are:

- Increased competition should encourage Ridag Co to reduce costs
- Deregulation could lead to a decrease in the quality of Ridag Co's products

Deregulation to increase competition should mean managers act to reduce costs in order to be competitive. The need to reduce costs may mean that quality of products declines.

27   The correct answer is: $90,412

Since taxation and capital allowances are to be ignored, and where relevant all information relating to project 2 has already been adjusted to include future inflation, the correct discount rate to use here is the nominal before-tax weighted average cost of capital of 12%.

	0	1	2	3	4
Maintenance costs		(25,000)	(29,000)	(32,000)	(35,000)
Investment and scrap	(200,000)				25,000
Net cash flow	(200,000)	(25,000)	(29,000)	(32,000)	10,000
Discount at 12%	1.000	0.893	0.797	0.712	0.636
Present values	(200,000)	(22,325)	(23,113)	(22,784)	(6,360)

Present value of cash flows ($274,582)

Cumulative present value factor 3.037

Equivalent annual cost = 274,582/3.037 = $90,412

28   The correct answers are:

- Ridag Co cannot use the equivalent annual cost method to compare Machine 1 and Machine 2 because they have different useful lives - **False**
- The machine which has the lowest total present value of costs should be selected by Ridag Co - **False**

The machine with the lowest equivalent annual cost should be purchased, not the present value of future cash flows alone. The lives of the two machines are different and the equivalent annual cost method allows this to be taken into consideration.

29   $ 18,868

EV of Year 3 cash flow = (23,000 × 0.2) + (24,000 × 0.35) + (30,000 × 0.45) = 26,500

PV discounted at 12% = 26,500 × 0.712 = $18,868

30   The correct answer is: Uncertainty can be said to increase with project life, while risk increases with the variability of returns

Notes on incorrect answers:

Simulation (not sensitivity analysis) takes into account the interrelationship between project variables.

Probability analysis can be used to assess the risk (not uncertainty) associated with the project.

A lower discount rate of 5% would increase the present value of costs incurred in later years and would therefore increase their impact.

Section C

31 Vip Co

Marking guide	Marks	
(a) Inflated income	2	
Inflated operating costs	2	
Net present value	1	
Internal rate of return	3	
Return on capital employed	3	
(b) Discussion of investment appraisal findings	3	
Advice on acceptability of project	1	
		4
(c) Maximisation of shareholder wealth	2	
Conflict from automation of production process	2	
Conflict from additional noise	2	
Marks Available	6	
Maximum		5
Total		20

(a) (i) **Calculation of NPV**

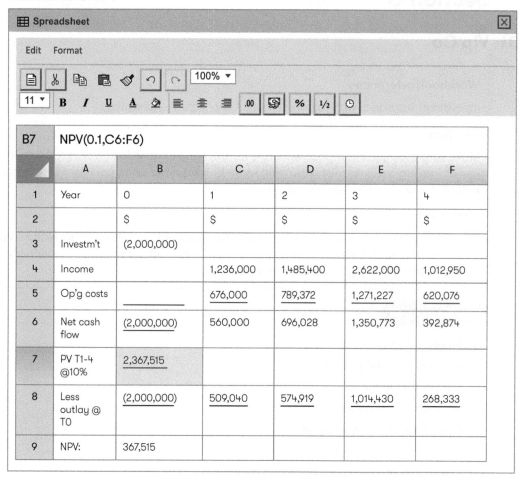

Workings

1 **Calculation of income**

Year	1	2	3	4
Inflated selling price ($/unit)	20.60	21.22	21.85	22.51
Demand (units/year)	60,000	70,000	120,000	45,000
Income ($/year)	1,236,000	1,485,400	2,622,000	1,012,950

2 **Calculation of operating costs**

Year	1	2	3	4
Inflated variable cost ($/unit)	8.32	8.65	9.00	9.36
Demand (units/year)	60,000	70,000	120,000	45,000
Variable costs ($/year)	499,200	605,500	1,080,000	421,200
Inflated fixed costs ($/year)	176,800	183,872	191,227	198,876
Operating costs ($/year)	676,000	789,372	1,271,227	620,076

BPP

3 **Alternative calculation of operating costs**

Year	1	2	3	4
Variables cost ($/unit)	8	8	8	8
Demand (units/year)	60,000	70,000	120,000	45,000
Variable costs ($/year)	480,000	560,000	960,000	360,000
Fixed costs ($/year)	170,000	170,000	170,000	170,000
Operating costs ($/year)	650,000	730,000	1,130,000	530,000
Inflated costs ($/year)	676,000	789,568	1,271,096	620,025

(ii) **Calculation of internal rate of return**

Year	0	1	2	3	4
	$	$	$	$	$
Net cash flow	(2,000,000)	560,000	696,028	1,350,773	392,874
Discount at 20%	1.000	0.833	0.694	0.579	0.482
Present values	(2,000,000)	466,480	483,043	782,098	189,365

Net present value: ($79,014)

$$IRR = \left[a + \frac{NPV_a}{NPV_a - NPV_b} \times (b-a)\right]$$

IRR = 10% + [(366,722/(366,722 + 79,014)](20 − 10) = **18.2%**

Alternatively IRR can be calculated using the IRR spreadsheet function based on these cash flows:

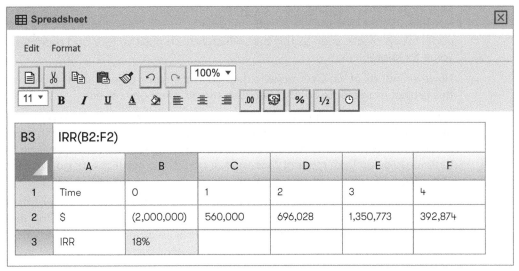

(iii) **Calculation of return on capital employed**

Total cash inflow = 560,000 + 696,028 + 1,350,773 + 392,874 = $2,999,675

Total depreciation and initial investment are the same, as there is no scrap value.

Total accounting profit = 2,999,675 − 2,000,000 = $999,675

Average annual accounting profit = 999,675/4 = $249,919

Average investment = 2,000,000/2 = $1,000,000

Return on capital employed = 100 × 249,919/1,000,000 = 25%

BPP

(b)

The investment proposal has a positive net present value (NPV) of $366,722 and is therefore financially acceptable. The results of the other investment appraisal methods do not alter this financial acceptability, as the NPV decision rule will always offer the correct investment advice.

The internal rate of return (IRR) method also recommends accepting the investment proposal, since the IRR of 18.2% is greater than the 10% return required by Vip Co. If the advice offered by the IRR method differed from that offered by the NPV method, the advice offered by the NPV method would be preferred.

The calculated return on capital employed of 25% is less than the target return of 30% but, as indicated earlier, the investment proposal is financially acceptable as it has a positive NPV. The reason why Vip Co has a target return on capital employed of 30% should be investigated. This may be an out of date hurdle rate which has not been updated for changed economic circumstances.

(c)

As a large listed company, Vip Co's primary financial objective is assumed to be the maximisation of shareholder wealth. In order to pursue this objective, Vip Co should undertake projects, such as this one, which have a positive NPV and generate additional value for shareholders.

However, not all of Vip Co's stakeholders have the same objectives and the acceptance of this project may create conflict between the different objectives.

Due to Product W33 being produced using an automated production process, it will not meet employees' objectives of continuity or security in their employment. It could also mean employees will be paid less than they currently earn. If this move is part of a longer-term move away from manual processes, it could also conflict with government objectives of having a low rate of unemployment.

The additional noise created by the production of Product W33 will affect the local community and may conflict with objectives relating to healthy living. This may also conflict with objectives from environmental pressure groups and government standards on noise levels as well.

32 Froste Co

Marking guide		Marks
(a) Dividend growth rate	1	
Share price using dividend growth model	2	
Capital gearing	2	
Weighted average cost of capital	2	
(b) Dividend irrelevance	4	
Dividend relevance	4	
Marks Available	8	
Maximum		8
(c) Discussion of equity	2	
Debt and recognising business risk is not relevant	2	
Time until maturity of bonds	2	
Different value of bonds	1	
Marks Available	7	
Maximum		5
Total		**20**

(a) (i)   Dividend growth rate = 100 × ((52/50) − 1) = 100 × (1.04 − 1) = 4% per year

Share price using DGM = (50 × 1.04)/(0.124 − 0.04) = 52/0.084 = 619c or $6.19

(ii)   Number of ordinary shares = 25 million

Market value of equity = 25m × 6.19 = $154.75 million

Market value of Bond A issue = 20m × 95.08/100 = $19.016m

Market value of Bond B issue = 10m × 102.01/100 = $10.201m

Market value of debt = $29.217m

Market value of capital employed = 154.75m + 29.217m = $183.967m

Capital gearing = 100 × 29.217/183.967 = 15.9%

(iii)   WACC = ((12.4 × 154.75) + (9.83 × 19.016) + (7.82 × 10.201))/183.967 = 11.9%

 BPP

(b)

Miller and Modigliani showed that, in a perfect capital market, the value of a company depended on its investment decision alone, and not on its dividend or financing decisions. In such a market, a change in dividend policy by Froste Co would not affect its share price or its market capitalisation. They showed that the value of a company was maximised if it invested in all projects with a positive net present value (its optimal investment schedule). The company could pay any level of dividend and, if it had insufficient finance, make up the shortfall by issuing new equity. Since investors had perfect information, they were indifferent between dividends and capital gains. Shareholders who were unhappy with the level of dividend declared by a company could gain a 'home-made dividend' by selling some of their shares. This was possible since there are no transaction costs in a perfect capital market.

Against this view are several arguments for a link between dividend policy and share prices. For example, it has been argued that investors prefer certain dividends now rather than uncertain capital gains in the future (the 'bird in the hand' argument).

It has also been argued that real-world capital markets are not perfect, but semi-strong form efficient. Since perfect information is therefore not available, it is possible for information asymmetry to exist between shareholders and the managers of a company. Dividend announcements may give new information to shareholders and as a result, in a semi-strong form efficient market, share prices may change. The size and direction of the share price change will depend on the difference between the dividend announcement and the expectations of shareholders. This is referred to as the 'signalling properties of dividends'.

It has been found that shareholders are attracted to particular companies as a result of being satisfied by their dividend policies. This is referred to as the 'clientele effect'. A company with an established dividend policy is therefore likely to have an established dividend clientele. The existence of this dividend clientele implies that the share price may change if there is a change in the dividend policy of the company, as shareholders sell their shares in order to reinvest in another company with a more satisfactory dividend policy. In a perfect capital market, the existence of dividend clienteles is irrelevant, since substituting one company for another will not incur any transaction costs. Since real-world capital markets are not perfect, however, the existence of dividend clienteles suggests that if Froste Co changes its dividend policy, its share price could be affected.

(c)

There is a trade-off between risk and return on Froste Co's capital instruments. Investors in riskier assets require a higher return in compensation for this additional risk. In the case of ordinary shares, investors rank behind all other sources of finance in the event of a liquidation so are the most risky capital instrument to invest in. This is partly why Froste Co's cost of equity is more expensive than its debt financing.

Similarly for debt financing, higher-risk borrowers must pay higher rates of interest on their borrowing to compensate lenders for the greater risk involved. Froste Co has two bonds, with Bond A having the higher interest rate and therefore the higher risk. Since both bonds were issued at the same time, business risk is not a factor in the higher level of risk.

Instead, this additional risk is likely to be due to the fact that Bond A has a greater time until maturity, meaning that its cash flows are more uncertain than Bond B's. In particular where interest rates are expected to increase in the future, longer-term debt will have a higher rate of interest to compensate investors for investing for a longer period.

A further factor is that the total nominal value (book value) of Bond A is twice as large as Bond B and therefore may be perceived to be riskier.

ACCA

Financial Management (FM)

Mock Exam 3

December 2016

Questions	
Time allowed	3 hours
ALL questions are compulsory and MUST be attempted	

DO NOT OPEN THIS EXAM UNTIL YOU ARE READY TO START
UNDER EXAMINATION CONDITIONS

 BPP

Section A

QUESTIONS

ALL 15 questions are compulsory and MUST be attempted

Each question is worth 2 marks.

1 Which of the following is an advantage of implementing just-in-time inventory management?

○ Quality control costs will be eliminated

○ Monthly finance costs incurred in holding inventory will be kept constant

○ The frequency of raw materials deliveries is reduced

○ The amount of obsolete inventory will be minimised **(2 marks)**

---

2 Which TWO of the following activities are carried out by a financial intermediary?

☐ Transforming interest rates

☐ Transforming foreign exchange

☐ Transforming maturity

☐ Transforming risk **(2 marks)**

---

3 Frost Co is planning a 1 for 4 rights issue with an issue price at a 10% discount to the current share price.

The EPS is currently $0.50 and the shares of Frost Co are trading on a price/earnings ratio of 20 times. The market capitalisation of the company is $50m.

What is the theoretical ex-rights price per share (to two decimal places)?

$ [   ] **(2 marks)**

---

4 Which of the following statements in relation to business valuation are true or false?

	True	False
The earnings yield method and the dividend growth model should give similar values for a company	○	○
Market capitalisation represents the maximum value for a company	○	○
The price/earnings ratio is the reciprocal of the earnings yield	○	○
The price/earnings ratio should be increased if the company being valued is riskier than the valuing company	○	○

(2 marks)

 BPP

5 Small and medium-sized entities (SMEs) have restricted access to capital markets.

What is the term given to the difference between the finance required to operate an SME and the amount obtained?

○ Forecasted gap

○ Maturity gap

○ Funding gap

○ Asset gap

(2 marks)

---

6 Max Co is a large multinational company which expects to have a $10m cash deficit in one month's time. The deficit is expected to last no more than two months.

Max Co wishes to resolve its short-term liquidity problem by issuing an appropriate instrument on the money market.

Which of the following instruments should Max Co issue?

○ Commercial paper

○ Interest rate futures

○ Corporate loan notes

○ Treasury bills

(2 marks)

---

7 In relation to capital markets, which of the following statements is true?

○ The return from investing in larger companies has been shown to be greater than the average return from all companies

○ Weak form efficiency arises when investors tend not to make rational investment decisions

○ Allocative efficiency means that transaction costs are kept to a minimum

○ Research has shown that, over time, share prices appear to follow a random walk   (2 marks)

---

8 The following data is available:

Country Y currency	Dollar
Country X currency	Peso
Country Y interest rate	1% per year
Country X interest rate	3% per year
Country X expected inflation rate	2% per year
Spot exchange rate in Country Y	1.60 peso per $1

Required

What is the current six-month forward exchange rate in Country Y (to two decimal places)?

(2 marks)

 BPP

9   Green Co, a listed company, had the following share prices during the year ended 31 December 20X5:

At start of 20X5	$2.50
Highest price in the year	$3.15
Lowest price in the year	$2.40
At end of 20X5	$3.00

During the year, Green Co paid a total dividend of $0.15 per share.

Required

What is the total shareholder return for 20X5?

O   26%

O   22%

O   32%

O   36%   **(2 marks)**

---

10   Carp Co has announced that it will pay an annual dividend equal to 55% of earnings. Its earnings per share is $0.80, and it has 10 million shares in issue. The return on equity of Carp Co is 20% and its current cum dividend share price is $4.60.

What is the cost of equity of Carp Co?

O   19.4%

O   20.5%

O   28.0%

O   22.7%   **(2 marks)**

 BPP

11   Mile Co is looking to change its working capital policy to match the rest of the industry. The following results are expected for the coming year:

	$'000
Revenue	20,500
Cost of sales	(12,800)
Gross profit	7,700

Revenue and cost of sales can be assumed to be spread evenly throughout the year. The working capital ratios of Mile Co, compared with the industry, are as follows:

	Mile Co	Industry
Receivable collection period (days)	50	42
Inventory holding period (days)	45	35
Payable payment period (days)	40	35

Assume there are 365 days in each year.

Required

If Mile Co matches its working capital cycle with the industry, what will be the decrease in its net working capital?

O $624,600

O $730,100

O $835,600

O $975,300   (2 marks)

12   Are the following statements true or false?

	True	False
A prospective merger would need to result in a company having a market share greater than 80% before it can be described as a monopoly	O	O
A government may intervene to weaken its country's exchange rate in order to eliminate a balance of payments deficit	O	O
A relatively high rate of domestic inflation will lead to a strengthening currency	O	O
Government fiscal policy involves the management of interest rates	O	O

(2 marks)

BPP

13 Which of the following statements about interest rate risk hedging are correct or incorrect?

	Correct	Incorrect
An interest rate floor can be used to hedge an expected increase in interest rates	O	O
The cost of an interest rate floor is higher than the cost of an interest rate collar	O	O
The premium on an interest rate option is payable when it is exercised	O	O
The standardised nature of interest rate futures means that over- and under-hedging can be avoided	O	O

(2 marks)

14 Which of the following statements is true?

O Value for money is usually taken to mean economy, efficiency and engagement

O Cum dividend means the buyer of the share is not entitled to receive the dividend shortly to be paid

O The dividend payout ratio compares the dividend per share with the market price per share

O The agency problem means that shareholder wealth is not being maximised   **(2 marks)**

15 Swap Co is due to receive goods costing $2,500. The terms of trade state that payment must be received within three months. However, a discount of 1.5% will be given for payment within one month.

Which of the following is the annual percentage cost of ignoring the discount and paying in three months?

O 6.23%

O 9.34%

O 6.14%

O 9.49%   **(2 marks)**

Section B

Park Co

This scenario relates to the following five questions

Park Co is based in a country whose currency is the dollar ($). The company regularly imports goods denominated in euro (€) and regularly sells goods denominated in dinars. Two of the future transactions of the company are as follows:

Three months: Paying €650,000 for imported goods

Six months: Receiving 12 million dinars for exported capital goods

Park Co has the following exchange rates and interest rates available to it:

	Bid	Offer
Spot exchange rate (dinars per $1):	57.31	57.52
Six-month forward rate (dinars per $1):	58.41	58.64
Spot exchange rate (€ per $1):	1.544	1.552
Three-month forward rate (€ per $1):	1.532	1.540

Six-month interest rates:

	Borrow	Deposit
Dinars	4.0%	2.0%
Dollars	2.0%	0.5%

The finance director of Park Co believes that the upward-sloping yield curve reported in the financial media means that the general level of interest rates will increase in the future, and therefore expects the reported six-month interest rates to increase.

16   What is the future dollar value of the dinar receipt using a money market hedge?

    O $197,752

    O $201,602

    O $208,623

    O $210,629   **(2 marks)**

17   In hedging the foreign currency risk of the two transactions, which of the following hedges will Park Co find to be effective?

    (1) Leading the euro payment on its imported goods

    (2) Taking out a forward exchange contract on its future dinar receipt

    (3) Buying a tailor-made currency option for its future euro payment

    O 2 only

    O 1 and 3 only

    O 2 and 3 only

    O 1, 2 and 3   **(2 marks)**

18   Which hedging methods will assist Park Co in reducing its overall foreign currency risk?

(1) Taking out a long-term euro-denominated loan

(2) Taking out a dinar-denominated overdraft

○ 1 only

○ 2 only

○ Both 1 and 2

○ Neither 1 nor 2   (2 marks)

19   Indicate whether the following statements are correct or incorrect.

	Correct	Incorrect
Purchasing power parity can be used to predict the forward exchange rate	○	○
The international Fisher effect can be used to predict the real interest rate	○	○

(2 marks)

20   Which of the following statements is consistent with an upward-sloping yield curve?

○ The risk of borrowers defaulting on their loans increases with the duration of the lending

○ Liquidity preference theory implies that short-term interest rates contain a premium over long-term interest rates to compensate for lost liquidity

○ Banks are reluctant to lend short-term, while government debt repayments have significantly increased the amount of long-term funds available

○ The Government has increased short-term interest rates in order to combat rising inflation in the economy   (2 marks)

(Total = 10 marks)

Coral Co

This scenario relates to the following five questions

The finance director of Coral Co has been asked to provide values for the company's equity and loan notes. Coral Co is a listed company and has the following long-term finance:

	$m
Ordinary shares	7.8
7% convertible loan notes	8.0
	15.8

The ordinary shares of Coral Co have a nominal value of $0.25 per share and are currently trading on an ex dividend basis at $7.10 per share. An economic recovery has been forecast and so share prices are expected to grow by 8% per year for the foreseeable future.

The loan notes are redeemable after 6 years at their nominal value of $100 per loan note, or can be converted after 6 years into 10 ordinary shares of Coral Co per loan note. The loan notes are traded on the capital market.

The before-tax cost of debt of Coral Co is 5% and the company pays corporation tax of 20% per year.

21   What is the equity market value of Coral Co (to two decimal places)?

$ [   ] m   **(2 marks)**

---

22   Assuming conversion, what is the market value of each loan note of Coral Co?

    ○ $110.13

    ○ $112.67

    ○ $119.58

    ○ $125.70   **(2 marks)**

---

23   Which of the following statements about the equity market value of Coral Co is/are true?

    (1) The equity market value will change frequently due to capital market forces.

    (2) If the capital market is semi-strong form efficient, the equity market value will not be affected by the release to the public of insider information.

    (3) Over time, the equity market value of Coral Co will follow a random walk.

    ○ 1 only

    ○ 1 and 3 only

    ○ 2 and 3 only

    ○ 1, 2 and 3   **(2 marks)**

---

24   Indicate whether the following are assumptions made by the dividend growth model.

	Yes	No
Investors make rational decisions	○	○
Dividends show either constant growth or zero growth	○	○
The dividend growth rate is less than the cost of equity	○	○

                                                               (2 marks)

---

25   Why might valuations of the equity and loan notes of Coral Co be necessary?

    (1) The company is planning to go to the market for additional finance.

    (2) The securities need to be valued for corporate taxation purposes.

    (3) The company has received a takeover bid from a rival company.

    ○ 1 and 2 only

    ○ 1 and 3 only

    ○ 3 only

    ○ 1, 2 and 3   **(2 marks)**

                                                                  (Total = 10 marks)

Link Co

This scenario relates to the following five questions

Link Co has been prevented by the competition authorities from buying a competitor, Twist Co, on the basis that this prevents a monopoly position arising. Link Co has therefore decided to expand existing business operations instead and as a result the finance director has prepared the following evaluation of a proposed investment project for the company:

	$m
Present value of sales revenue	6,657
Present value of variable costs	2,777
Present value of contribution	3,880
Present value of fixed costs	1,569
Present value of operating cash flow	2,311
Initial capital investment	1,800
Net present value	511

The project life is expected to be four years and the finance director has used a discount rate of 10% in the evaluation.

The investment project has no scrap value.

The finance director is considering financing the investment project by a new issue of debt.

26   What is the change in sales volume which will make the NPV zero?

○ 7.7%

○ 13.2%

○ 18.4%

○ 22.1%

(2 marks)

---

27   Which of the following statements relating to sensitivity analysis is/are correct?

(1) Although critical factors may be identified, the management of Link Co may have no control over them.

(2) A weakness of sensitivity analysis is that it ignores interdependency between project variables.

(3) Sensitivity analysis can be used by Link Co to assess the risk of an investment project.

○ 1 and 2 only

○ 1 only

○ 2 and 3 only

○ 1, 2 and 3

(2 marks)

---

28   Using the average investment method and assuming operating cash flows of $729,000 per year, what is the return on capital employed of the investment project?

    O 16%

    O 28%

    O 31%

    O 64%   **(2 marks)**

---

29   Which of the following statements relating to debt finance is correct?

    O Link Co can issue long-term debt in the euro currency markets

    O The interest rate which Link Co pays on its new issue of debt will depend on its weighted average cost of capital

    O A new issue of loan notes by Link Co will take place in the primary market

    O Link Co will not be able to issue new debt without offering non-current assets as security   **(2 marks)**

---

30   Which of the following statements relating to competition policy is/are correct?

    (1) Scale economies are an advantage of monopoly and oligopoly

    (2) Social costs or externalities are an example of economic inefficiency arising from market failure

    (3) Monopoly is discouraged because it can lead to inefficiency and excessive profits

    O 1 and 2 only

    O 3 only

    O 2 and 3 only

    O 1, 2 and 3   **(2 marks)**

(Total = 10 marks)

Section C

BOTH questions are compulsory and MUST be attempted

31 Gadner Co

Gadner Co wishes to calculate its weighted average cost of capital. The company has the following sources of finance:

	$'000
Ordinary shares	8,000
10% preference shares	2,000
8% loan notes	6,000
Bank loan	2,000
	18,000

The ordinary shares have a nominal value of $0.20 per share and are currently trading at $6.35 per share. The equity beta of Gadner Co is 1.25.

The preference shares are irredeemable and have a nominal value of $0.50. They are currently trading at $0.55 per share.

The 8% loan notes have a nominal value of $100 per loan note and a market value of $108.29 per loan note. They are redeemable in six years' time at a 5% premium to nominal value.

The bank loan charges fixed interest of 7% per year.

The yield on short-dated UK treasury bills is 4% and the equity risk premium is 5.6% per year. Gadner Co pays corporation tax of 20%.

Required

(a) Calculate the market value weighted average cost of capital of Gadner Co. **(11 marks)**

(b) Explain the meaning of the terms business risk and financial risk. **(4 marks)**

(c) Discuss the key features of a rights issue as a way of raising equity finance. **(5 marks)**

(Total = 20 marks)

32 Dysxa Co

Dysxa Co is looking to expand the capacity of an existing factory in its Alpha Division by 850,000 units per year in order to meet increased demand for one of its products. The expansion will cost $3.2 million.

The selling price of the product is $3.10 per unit and variable costs of production are $1.10 per unit, both in current price terms. Selling price inflation of 3% per year and variable cost inflation of 6% per year are expected. Nominal fixed costs of production have been forecast as follows:

Year	1	2	3	4
Fixed costs ($)	110,000	205,000	330,000	330,000

Dysxa Co has a nominal after-tax weighted average cost of capital of 10% and pays corporation tax of 20% per year one year in arrears. The company can claim 25% reducing balance tax-allowable depreciation on the full cost of the expansion, which you should assume is paid at the start of the first year of operation.

Dysxa Co evaluates all investment projects as though they have a project life of four years and assumes zero scrap value at the end of four years.

 BPP

Dysxa Co has limited the capital investment funds in its Delta Division to $7m. The division has identified five possible investment projects, as follows:

Project	Initial investment	Net present value
A	$3,000,000	$6,000,000
B	$2,000,000	$3,200,000
C	$1,000,000	$1,700,000
D	$1,000,000	$2,100,000
E	$2,000,000	$3,600,000

These projects are divisible and cannot be deferred or repeated. Projects C and E are mutually exclusive.

Required

(a) Calculate the net present value of the investment project and comment on its financial acceptability. **(8 marks)**

(b) Determine the net present value of the optimum investment schedule for Delta Division. **(3 marks)**

(c) Discuss the reasons why hard and soft capital rationing occur. **(5 marks)**

(d) Discuss TWO ways in which the risk of an investment project can be assessed. **(4 marks)**

(Total = 20 marks)

Answers

DO NOT TURN THIS PAGE UNTIL YOU HAVE
COMPLETED THE MOCK EXAM

A PLAN OF ATTACK

Managing your nerves

As you turn the pages to start this mock exam a number of thoughts are likely to cross your mind. At best, examinations cause anxiety so it is important to stay focused on your task for the next three hours! Developing an awareness of what is going on emotionally within you may help you manage your nerves. Remember, you are unlikely to banish the flow of adrenaline, but the key is to harness it to help you work steadily and quickly through your answers.

Working through this mock exam will help you develop the exam stamina you will need to keep going for 3 hours and 15 minutes.

Managing your time

Planning and time management are two of the key skills which complement the technical knowledge you need to succeed. To keep yourself on time, do not be afraid to jot down your target completion times for each question.

Doing the exam

Actually doing the exam is a personal experience. There is not a single **right way**. As long as you submit complete answers to all questions after the three hours are up, then your approach obviously works.

Looking through the exam

Section A has 15 objective test questions. This is the section of the exam where the examining team can test knowledge across the breadth of the syllabus. Make sure you read these questions carefully. The distractors are designed to present plausible, but incorrect, answers. Don't let them mislead you. If you really have no idea – guess. You may even be right.

Section B has three questions, each with a scenario and five objective test questions.

Section C has two longer questions worth 20 marks each, each based on a scenario and featuring a mix of numerical and discussion requirements. These questions are most likely to create time pressure issues. You will need to ensure that you do not spend too long on Section A and B questions because it is hard to rush Section C of the exam.

Allocating your time

BPP's advice is to always allocate your time **according to the marks for the question**. However, **use common sense**. If you're doing a question but haven't a clue how to do part (b), you might be better off reallocating your time and getting more marks on another question, where you can add something you didn't have time for earlier on. Make sure you leave time to recheck the MCQs and make sure you have answered them all.

Section A

1   The correct answer is: The amount of obsolete inventory will be minimised

Inventory should not be held in a JIT environment, and this will be made possible by frequent deliveries from suppliers. Some inspection (quality costs) will still occur.

2   The correct answers are:

- Transforming maturity
- Transforming risk

Maturity is transformed by allowing short-term deposits to be lent out for the long term. Risk is transformed because any losses suffered through default by borrowers or capital losses are effectively pooled and borne as costs by the intermediary allowing money to be deposited at financial institutions without incurring substantial risk.

3   $ 9.80

Current share price = 0.5 × 20 = $10 per share

Rights issue price = 10 × 90/100 = $9 per share

Number of shares to be issued = (50m/10)/4 = 1.25m shares

TERP = (10 × 5 + 9 × 1.25)/6.25 = $9.80 per share

4   The correct answers are:

- The earnings yield method and the dividend growth model should give similar values for a company - **False**
- Market capitalisation represents the maximum value for a company - **False**
- The price/earnings ratio is the reciprocal of the earnings yield - **True**
- The price/earnings ratio should be increased if the company being valued is riskier than the valuing company - **False**

The price/earnings ratio is the reciprocal of the earnings yield (ie P/E = 1 divided by E/P).

Notes on false statements:

Earnings yield and dividend growth will often give different outcomes eg if a company pays zero dividends.

Market capitalisation is the current market value of a company's shares, a company may be worth more than this in an acquisition if synergies could result from the acquisition.

The price/earnings ratio should be **decreased** if the company being valued is riskier than the valuing company.

5   The correct answer is: Funding gap

6   The correct answer is: Commercial paper

Commercial paper will be issued at a discount and then repaid at nominal value on the settlement date. It is short term and traded on the money market. Not interest payments are made.

Notes on incorrect answers:

Interest rate futures are not a type of finance.

Loan notes are a source of long-term finance and are therefore not suitable here.

Treasury bills are a source of finance for governments.

7 The correct answer is: Research has shown that, over time, share prices appear to follow a random walk

Notes on incorrect answers:

The **risk** from investing in larger companies has been shown to be **lower** than the average for all companies. The relationship between risk and return suggests that this will translate into lower returns.

Zero form efficiency arises when investors tend not to make rational investment decisions.

Operational efficiency means that transaction costs are kept to a minimum.

8 1.62

Forward rate = 1.60 × (1.015/1.005) = 1.62 pesos per $

9 The correct answer is: 26%

TSR = 100 × (3.00 − 2.50 + 0.15)/2.50 = 26%

10 The correct answer is: 20.5%

Dividend to be paid = 0.80 × 0.55 = $0.44 per share

Retention ratio = 100% − 55% = 45%

Dividend growth rate = 45% × 20% = 9% per year

K_e = (0.44 × 1.09)/(4.60 − 0.44) + 0.09 = 20.5%

11 The correct answer is: $624,600

Reduced receivables = 8/365 × 20,500 = $449,300

Net inventory/payables effect = (10 − 5)/365 × 12,800 = $175,300

Total net working capital effect = 449.3 + 175.3 = $624,600

12 The correct answers are:

- A prospective merger would need to result in a company having a market share greater than 80% before it can be described as a monopoly - **False**
- A government may intervene to weaken its country's exchange rate in order to eliminate a balance of payments deficit - **True**
- A relatively high rate of domestic inflation will lead to a strengthening currency - **False**
- Government fiscal policy involves the management of interest rates - **False**

This is because the effect of a weaker exchange rate is to reduce the price of exports and increase the cost of imports.

Notes on false statements:

A prospective merger would normally need to result in a company having a market share greater than 25% before regulatory authorities would be concerned about monopoly power. Strictly a monopolist has 100% market share.

A relatively high rate of domestic inflation will lead to a **weakening** currency according to purchasing power parity theory.

Government fiscal policy involves the management of tax and spending policies, not interest rates.

13 The correct answers are:

- An interest rate floor can be used to hedge an expected increase in interest rates - **Incorrect**
- The cost of an interest rate floor is higher than the cost of an interest rate collar - **Correct**
- The premium on an interest rate option is payable when it is exercised - **Incorrect**
- The standardised nature of interest rate futures means that over- and under-hedging can be avoided - **Incorrect**

This is because a floor involves buying a call option, whereas a collar involves selling a put option as well (which offsets the cost of buying a call).

Notes on incorrect statements:

An interest rate cap (not floor) can be used to hedge an expected increase in interest rates.

The premium on an interest rate option is payable when it is purchased not when it is exercised.

The standardised nature of interest rate futures means that over- and under-hedging occurs because a company is often unable to hedge exactly the amount that it requires.

14 The correct answer is: The agency problem means that shareholder wealth is not being maximised

Notes on incorrect answers:

Value for money is usually taken to mean economy, efficiency and effectiveness (not engagement).

Ex (not cum) dividend means the buyer of the share is not entitled to receive the dividend shortly to be paid.

The dividend payout ratio compares the dividend per share with the earnings per share.

15 The correct answer is: 9.49%

If the discount is accepted, the company must pay $2,462.50 at the end of one month.

Alternatively, the company can effectively borrow the $2,462.50 for an additional 2 months at a cost of $37.50.

The 2-month rate of interest is therefore $37.50/2,462.5 \times 100 = 1.5228\%$

The annual equivalent rate (AER) = $(1 + 0.015228)6 - 1 = 0.0949$ or 9.49%

Section B

Park Co

16 The correct answer is: $201,602

Dollar value = (12m × 1.005)/(1.04 × 57.52) = $201,602

17 The correct answer is: 1, 2 and 3

All three hedges will allow Park Co to hedge its foreign currency risk.

18 The correct answer is: 2 only

Only the dinar-denominated overdraft will be effective, by matching assets and liabilities. The long-term euro-denominated loan will increase payments to be made in euros and hence increase foreign currency risk.

19 The correct answers are:

- Purchasing power parity can be used to predict the forward exchange rate - **Incorrect**
- The international Fisher effect can be used to predict the real interest rate - **Incorrect**

Purchasing power parity predicts the future spot rate, not the forward exchange rate. The international Fisher effect does not predict 'real' interest rates.

20 The correct answer is: The risk of borrowers defaulting on their loans increases with the duration of the lending

If default risk increases with duration, compensation for default risk increases with time and hence the yield curve will slope upwards.

Notes on incorrect answers:

Liquidity preference theory implies that **long-term** interest rates contain a premium over **short-term** interest rates to compensate for lost liquidity.

If government debt repayments have significantly increased the amount of long-term funds available this will decrease the cost of borrowing in the long-term.

If the Government has increased short-term interest rates in order to combat rising inflation in the economy this may lead to a downward sloping yield curve.

Coral Co

21 $ 221.52 m

Equity market value = 7.10 × (7.8m/0.25) = $221.52m

22 The correct answer is: $119.58

Conversion value = 7.10 × 1.086 × 10 = $112.67 per loan note

Market value = (7 × 5.076) + (112.67 × 0.746) = 35.53 + 84.05 = $119.58

23 The correct answer is: 1 and 3 only

If the capital market is semi-strong form efficient, newly released insider information will quickly and accurately be reflected in share prices. The other statements are true.

24 The correct answers are:

- Investors make rational decisions - **Yes**
- Dividends show either constant growth or zero growth - **Yes**
- The dividend growth rate is less than the cost of equity - **Yes**

25 The correct answer is: 1 and 3 only

A valuation for corporate taxation purposes is not necessary.

 BPP

Link Co

26 The correct answer is: 13.2%

100 × 511/3,880 = 13.2%

27 The correct answer is: 1 and 2 only

Sensitivity Analysis assesses the **uncertainty** of a project, not the risk (probability analysis does this).

28 The correct answer is: 31%

The total operating cash flow = 4 × (2,311/3.170) = $2,916,088

The average annual accounting profit = (2,916,088 – 1,800,000)/4 = $279,022

Average investment = 1,800,000/2 = $900,000

ROCE = 100 × 279,022/900,000 = 31%

29 The correct answer is: A new issue of loan notes by Link Co will take place in the primary market

Notes on incorrect answers:

Link Co can issue **short-term** debt in the euro currency markets.

The interest rate which Link Co pays on its new issue of debt will depend factors such as risk and the duration of the debt, not on its weighted average cost of capital.

Link Co will be able to issue new debt using debt covenants or floating charges on its asset base as a whole.

30 The correct answer is: 1, 2 and 3

Section C

31 Gadner Co

Marking guide	Marks	
(a) Cost of equity	2	
Cost of preference shares	1	
After-tax loan note interest cost	1	
Setting up Kd calculation	1	
After-tax Kd of loan notes	1	
Cost of debt of bank loan	1	
Market value of equity	0.5	
Market value of preference shares	0.5	
Market value of loan notes	0.5	
Total market value of sources of finance	0.5	
Calculation of WACC	2	
		11
(b) Nature of business risk	2	
Nature of financial risk	2	
		4
(c) One mark per relevant point	5	
Maximum		5
Total		**20**

(a) **Cost of equity**

Using the CAPM, $K_e = 4 + (1.25 \times 5.6) = 11.0\%$

Cost of capital of 10% irredeemable preference shares

Preference share dividend = $0.1 \times 0.5 = \$0.05$ per share

Cost of preference shares = $100 \times 0.05/0.55 = 9.1\%$

Cost of debt of loan notes

After-tax interest cost = $8 \times 0.8 = \$6.40$ per $100 loan note

Year	Cash flow	$	5% discount	PV $	6% discount	PV $
0	Market value	(108.29)	1.000	(108.29)	1.000	(108.29)
1–6	Interest	6.40	5.076	32.49	4.917	31.47
6	Redemption	105.00	0.746	78.33	0.705	74.03
				2.53		(2.79)

After-tax Kd = IRR = 5 + (1 × 2.53)/(2.53 + 2.79) = 5 + 0.5 = 5.5%

Alternatively IRR can be calculated using the =IRR spreadsheet function based on these cash flows:

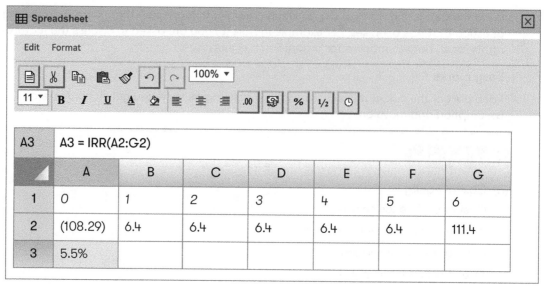

This approach also gives an IRR of 5.5%

Cost of debt of bank loan

The after-tax interest cost can be used as Kd, ie 7 × 0.8 = 5.6%.

Alternatively, the after-tax cost of debt of the loan notes can be used as a substitute.

Appropriate values of the sources of finance

	$'000
Market value of equity = $6.35 ×(8m/0.2) =	254,000
Market value of preference shares = 0.55 × (2m/0.5) =	2,200
Market value of loan notes = $108.29 × (6m/100) =	6,497
Book value of debt	2,000
Total market value of sources of finance	264,697

Calculation of WACC

WACC = [(11 × 254,000) + (9.1× 2,200) + (5.5 × 6,497) + (5.6 × 2,000)]/264,697 = 10.8%

(b)

Business risk in financial management relates to the variability of shareholder returns which arises from business operations. It can be measured from a statement of profit or loss perspective by operational gearing, which considers the relative importance of fixed and variable operating costs in relation to operating profit (PBIT). One definition of operational gearing is contribution/profit before interest and tax or PBIT. Business risk is not influenced by the way in which a company is financed; that is, it is not influenced by the capital structure of a company.

Financial risk relates to the variability of shareholder returns which arises from the way in which a company finances itself; that is, from its capital structure. It can be measured from a balance sheet perspective by gearing (financial gearing, debt/equity ratio, debt ratio) and from a statement of profit or loss perspective by interest cover and income gearing.

The combination of business risk and financial risk is referred to as total risk.

(c)

Pre-emptive right of shareholders

In order to preserve the balance of ownership and control in a company, existing shareholders have a right to be offered new shares before they are offered to other buyers. This is known as the pre-emptive right and an offer of new shares to existing shareholders is consequently referred to as a rights issue.

Rights issue price and cum rights price

The price at which the new shares are offered to existing shareholders is called the rights issue price. The share price following the announcement of the rights issue is called the cum rights price and the rights issue price is at a discount to this price.

Theoretical ex-rights price

The share price after the rights issue has taken place is called the theoretical ex-rights price. This is a weighted average of the cum rights price and the rights issue price. The weighting arises from what is called the form of the rights issue, eg a 1 for 5 issue would allow an existing shareholder to buy 1 new share for every 5 shares already held.

Neutral effect on shareholder wealth

If issue costs and the use or application of the rights issue funds is ignored then, theoretically, rights issues have a neutral effect on shareholder wealth. The rights issue transfers cash from existing shareholders to the company in exchange for shares, so the shareholder will see cash wealth replaced by ordinary share wealth. The theoretical ex-rights price, rather than the cum rights price, is therefore a benchmark for assessing the effect on shareholder wealth of the use or application to which the rights issue funds are put.

Balance of ownership and control

Providing existing shareholders buy the shares to which they are entitled, there is no change in the balance of ownership and control in a company. Relative voting rights are therefore preserved.

Underwriting

In order to ensure that a company receives the funds it needs, rights issues are underwritten as a form of insurance. Shares which are not taken up by existing shareholders will be taken up, for a fee, by the underwriters.

32 Dysxa Co

Workbook references

Investment appraisal with tax and inflation is covered in Chapter 6, risk in Chapter 7 and capital rationing in Chapter 8.

Top tips

Make sure that you show your workings for this type of question (in part (a)) to minimise the risk of making careless mistakes. If you get stuck in part (b) then quickly move on to parts (c) and (d) which are worth almost half of the total marks for this question.

Easy marks

Part (a), for eight marks, asked for a net present value (NPV) in nominal terms. This featured the normal elements of an NPV calculation – tax, capital allowances, inflation etc. This question should have been an area of strength for any well-prepared candidate.

Marking guide		Marks
(a)	Inflated sales revenue	1
	Inflated variable cost	1
	Tax liabilities	1
	Tax-allowable depreciation benefits Years 1–3	1
	Tax-allowable depreciation benefit Year 4	1
	Timing of tax liabilities and depreciation benefits	1
	Calculation of present values	1
	Comment on financial acceptability	1
		8
(b)	Calculating profitability indexes	1
	Formulating optimum investment schedule	1
	NPV of optimum investment schedule	1
		3
(c)	Soft capital rationing	2
	Hard capital rationing	2
	Additional detail	1
		5
(d)	Risk assessment method 1	2
	Risk assessment method 2	2
		4
Total		**20**

(a) **NPV calculation**

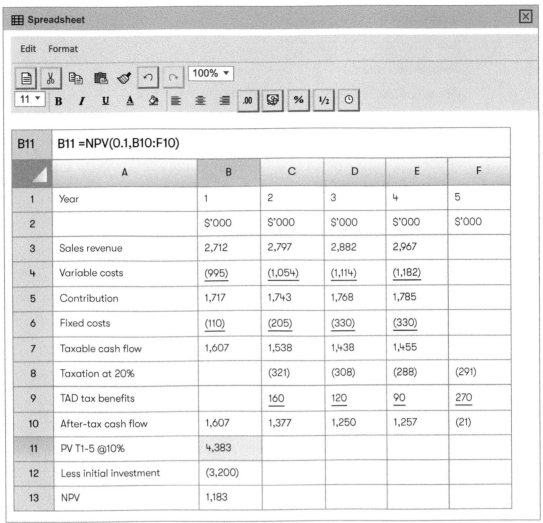

	A	B	C	D	E	F
		B11 =NPV(0.1,B10:F10)				
1	Year	1	2	3	4	5
2		$'000	$'000	$'000	$'000	$'000
3	Sales revenue	2,712	2,797	2,882	2,967	
4	Variable costs	(995)	(1,054)	(1,114)	(1,182)	
5	Contribution	1,717	1,743	1,768	1,785	
6	Fixed costs	(110)	(205)	(330)	(330)	
7	Taxable cash flow	1,607	1,538	1,438	1,455	
8	Taxation at 20%		(321)	(308)	(288)	(291)
9	TAD tax benefits		160	120	90	270
10	After-tax cash flow	1,607	1,377	1,250	1,257	(21)
11	PV T1-5 @10%	4,383				
12	Less initial investment	(3,200)				
13	NPV	1,183				

Comment

The NPV is positive and so the investment project is financially acceptable.

Workings

1 ***Sales revenue***

Year	1	2	3	4
Selling price ($/unit)	3.1	3.1	3.1	3.1
Inflated at 3% per year	3.19	3.29	3.39	3.49
Sales volume ('000 units/year)	850	850	850	850
Sales revenue ($'000/year)	2,712	2,797	2,882	2,967

 BPP

ANSWERS

2 **Variable cost**

Year	1	2	3	4
Variable cost ($/unit)	1.1	1.1	1.1	1.1
Inflated at 6% per year	1.17	1.24	1.31	1.39
Sales volume ('000 units/year)	850	850	850	850
Variable cost ($'000/year)	995	1,054	1,114	1,182

Year	1	2	3	4
TAD ($'000)	800	600	450	1,350
Tax benefits ($'000)	160	120	90	270*

*(3,200 × 0.2) − 160 − 120 − 90 = $270,000

Alternative calculation of after-tax cash flow

Year	1	2	3	4	5
	$'000	$'000	$'000	$'000	$'000
Taxable cash flow	1,607	1,538	1,438	1,455	
TAD	(800)	(600)	(450)	(1,350)	
Taxable profit	807	938	988	105	
Taxation at 20%		(161)	(188)	(198)	(21)
After-tax profit	807	777	800	(93)	(21)
Add back TAD	800	600	450	1,350	
After-tax cash flow	1,607	1,377	1,250	1,257	(21)

(b) **Analysis of profitability indexes**

Project	Initial investment	Net present value	Profitability index*	Rank
A	$3,000,000	$6,000,000	2.0	2nd
B	$2,000,000	$3,200,000	1.6	4th
C	$1,000,000	$1,700,000	1.7	Excluded
D	$1,000,000	$2,100,000	2.1	1st
E	$2,000,000	$3,600,000	1.8	3rd

*NPV divided by initial investment (note that it is also acceptable to calculate the profitability index as the PV of future cash flows/initial investment).

Optimum investment schedule

Project	Initial investment	Rank	Net present value	
D	$1,000,000	1st	$2,100,000	
A	$3,000,000	2nd	$6,000,000	
E	$2,000,000	3rd	$3,600,000	
B	$1,000,000	4th	$1,600,000	($3.2m x $1m/$2m)
	$7,000,000		$13,300,000	

The NPV of the optimum investment schedule for Delta Division is $13.3 million.

(c)

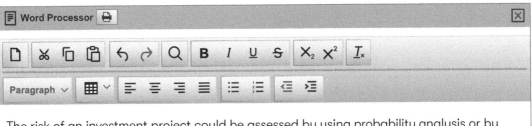

Capital rationing can be divided into hard capital rationing, which is externally imposed, or soft capital rationing, which is internally imposed.

Soft capital rationing

Investment capital may be limited internally because a company does not want to take on a commitment to increased fixed interest payments; for example, if it expects future profitability to be poor. A company may wish to avoid diluting existing earnings per share or changing existing patterns of ownership and control by issuing new equity. A company may limit investment funds because it wishes to pursue controlled growth rather than rapid growth. Given the uncertainty associated with forecasting future cash flows, a company may limit investment funds in order to create an internal market where investment projects compete for finance, with only the best investment projects being granted approval.

Hard capital rationing

External reasons for capital rationing can be related to risk and to availability of finance. Providers of finance may see a company as too risky to invest in, perhaps because it is highly geared or because it has a poor record or poor prospects in terms of profitability or cash flow. Long-term finance for capital investment may have limited availability because of the poor economic state of the economy, or because there is a banking crisis.

(d)

The risk of an investment project could be assessed by using probability analysis or by using the capital asset pricing model (CAPM).

Probability analysis

Project risk can be assessed or quantified by attaching probabilities to expected investment project outcomes. At an overall level, this could be as simple as attaching probabilities to two or more expected scenarios, for example, associated with different economic states. Key project variables might then take different values depending on the economic state.

At the level of individual project variables, probability distributions of values could be found through expert analysis, and the probability distributions and relationships between variables then built into a simulation model. This model could then be used to generate a probability distribution of expected project outcomes in terms of net present values. Project risk could then be measured by the standard deviation of the expected net present value.

CAPM

The systematic business risk of an investment project can be assessed by identifying a proxy company in a similar line of business. The equity beta of the proxy company can then be ungeared to give the asset beta of the company, which reflects systematic business risk alone as the effect of the systematic financial risk of the proxy company is removed by the ungearing process. The asset beta can then be regeared to reflect the systematic financial risk of the investing company, giving an equity beta which reflects the systematic risk of the investment project.

ACCA

Financial Management (FM)

Mock Exam 4

(including ACCA September/December 2022 Section C exam questions)

Questions	
Time allowed	3 hours
ALL questions are compulsory and MUST be attempted	

DO NOT OPEN THIS EXAM UNTIL YOU ARE READY TO START
UNDER EXAMINATION CONDITIONS

 BPP

Section A

ALL 15 questions are compulsory and MUST be attempted

Each question is worth 2 marks.

1 Which TWO of the following are roles of the money market?

☐ Allows investors to sell loan notes that they have purchased

☐ Allows companies to manage foreign currency risk

☐ Provides a less regulated market for small companies to trade their shares

☐ Enables companies to raise new short-term finance (2 marks)

---

2 Wallace Co manufactures and sells mid-range sports-wear in S-land. Wallace Co has high financial gearing, and all of its debt is paid at a fixed rate. Wallace Co is not currently planning to raise any new debt finance.

The government in S-land have adopted a contractionary monetary policy.

How would a contractionary monetary policy affect Wallace Co?

(1) Lower demand for its products

(2) Higher tax rates on profits

(3) Increased interest rates on its debt finance

○ 1 and 2

○ 1 only

○ 2 and 3

○ 3 only (2 marks)

---

3 DD Co's P/E ratio is 12. Its competitor's earnings yield is 10%.

When comparing DD Co to its competitor, which of the following is correct?

	Earnings yield	P/E ratio
○	DD's is higher	DD's is higher
○	DD's is higher	DD's is lower
○	DD's is lower	DD's is higher
○	DD's is lower	DD's is lower

(2 marks)

4 KEW Co is planning an investment of $10 million for a six-month period starting in three months' time.

KEW Co is worried about interest rates falling and hedges the risk using an appropriate forward rate agreement (FRA).

Details of the FRAs available to KEW Co are as follows:

6-9 FRA 2.80%–3.10%

3-9 FRA 3.00%–3.20%

Assume that in three-months' time, interest rates are 3.50%.

Which of the following shows the correct impact on cashflow for KEW to settle the FRA?

O KEW receives $50,000 from the bank

O KEW pays the bank $30,000

O KEW receives $40,000 from the bank

O KEW pays the bank $25,000

(2 marks)

---

5 PXP Co is an ungeared company and has a weighted average cost of capital of 14%. The company is about to introduce long-term debt into its capital structure.

This is expected to increase PXP Co's cost of equity, but to increase the overall market value of the company.

This is consistent with which TWO theories?

☐ Modigliani & Miller's theory with tax

☐ Modigliani & Miller's theory without tax

☐ Pecking order theory

☐ Traditional theory of capital structure

(2 marks)

---

6 Max Co is appraising a project with the following financial information:

	$m
Investment in depreciable non-current assets	10
Residual value of non-current assets at end of 4 years	2
Profit in years 1–3	1
Profit in year 4	5

Straight-line depreciation has been used in the calculation of the profit figures.

Required

What is the payback period of the project?

O 3.11 years

O 3.14 years

O 3.20 years

O 4.00 years

(2 marks)

7 JC Co decides to offer an 4% early settlement discount that half of all customers take up. They pay in one month instead of the usual two. JC Co pays interest on its overdraft facility at 12% per year.

What impact will this have?

	Reduce	Increase
Cash operating cycle	O	O
Accounting profit	O	O

(2 marks)

8 PP Co is a public listed provider of healthcare and operates a number of privately-run hospitals. NH Co is a state-controlled and -owned healthcare provider, it also operates a number of hospitals which are funded by the government.

Which TWO of the following are valid differences between the objectives of PP Co and NH Co?

☐ PP Co will aim to maximise shareholder wealth whereas NH Co won't

☐ NH Co will not have financial objectives but PP Co will

☐ NH Co will be most concerned about value for money whereas PP Co will prioritise the maximisation of shareholder wealth

☐ NH Co will focus of satisfying a wide range of stakeholders whereas PP Co will only focus on satisfying shareholders (2 marks)

9 Giblin Co has annual sales of $15 million. 30% of sales are for cash and the rest are on credit. Giblin Co finances its working capital with an overdraft at an annual interest rate of 10%.

Giblin Co's receivables are currently $1 million.

Assume a 360-day year.

What is the finance cost saving if the receivables collection period is reduced to 30 days?

O $13,699

O $12,500

O $87,500

O $62,500 (2 marks)

10 A company has created an interest rate floor by purchasing an interest rate call option, in order to manage its interest rate exposure.

Which of the following statements concerning the company are true?

O It will receive a payment if the market rate exceeds the floor rate

O It will receive a payment if the market rate is less than the floor rate

O It will be required to make a payment if the market rate exceeds the floor rate

O It will be required to make a payment if the market rate is less than the floor rate (2 marks)

 BPP

11 Which TWO of the following are benefits of the ROCE method of investment appraisal?

☐ It considers the whole project

☐ It is cash flow based

☐ It produces information that is easy to understand for a non-finance person

☐ It will not be impacted by a change in accounting policies   **(2 marks)**

---

12 Cham Co is planning to issue a loan note with a coupon rate of 5%.

At redemption each $100 nominal value loan note is either redeemable in five years' time or convertible into five ordinary shares.

The share price of Cham Co is expected to grow at a rate of 3% per year from its current level of $18.98.

Corporation tax is payable by the company at a rate of 20%.

Investors expect a yield of 6%.

What is the current market value of each loan note?

O $99.02

O $95.76

O $103.23

O $112.21   **(2 marks)**

---

13 Which TWO of the following are limitations of using the dividend valuation method to value an unlisted company?

☐ The valuation fails to take account the premium required to obtain a controlling interest

☐ The model cannot cope with periods of non-constant growth

☐ It is based on profit not cash flow

☐ It involves an unreliable estimate of the cost of equity   **(2 marks)**

---

14 The following information relates to the ordinary shares of G Co.

Share price	$5.00
Dividend cover	2.5
Published dividend yield	4.8%

Required

What is the earnings per share of G Co (to 2 decimal places)?

$ [   ]   **(2 marks)**

 BPP

15   An issue of a 9% redeemable loan note in ATV Co is planned. This loan note is due to mature in five years' time at a premium of 15%, or convertible into 25 ordinary shares at that point. The current share price is $4, expected to grow at 10% per year. ATV pays corporation tax at a rate of 30%.

Which TWO of the following factors will cause the cost of this debt to increase?

☐   An increase in the rate of corporation tax

☐   An increase in the expected growth rate of the share price

☐   An increase in the market value of debt

☐   An increase in the conversion ratio   **(2 marks)**

 BPP

Section B

ALL 15 questions are compulsory and MUST be attempted

Each question is worth 2 marks.

TGA CO

This scenario relates to the following five questions

TGA Co's sales are exported to a European country and are invoiced in euros.

TGA Co expects to receive €500,000 from export sales at the end of three months. A forward rate of €1.680–€1.687 per $1 has been offered by the company's bank and the spot rate is €1.670–€1.675 per $1.

Other relevant financial information is as follows:

Short-term dollar borrowing rate: 5% per year

Short-term dollar deposit rate: 4% per year

TGA Co can borrow short term in the euro at 9% per year.

Assume there are 365 days in each year.

16 Which of the following are valid courses of action for TGA Co to reduce the risk of the euro value dropping relative to the dollar before the €500,000 is received?

(1) Deposit €500,000 immediately

(2) Enter into a forward contract to sell €500,000 in three months

(3) Enter into an interest rate swap for three months

○ 1 or 2 only

○ 2 only

○ 3 only

○ 1, 2 or 3 **(2 marks)**

---

17 What is the dollar value of a forward market hedge (to the nearest whole number) in three months' time?

$ _____ **(2 marks)**

---

18 What is the dollar value of a money market hedge in three months' time?

$ _____ **(2 marks)**

---

19 TGA Co is considering futures contracts.

Which of the following statements are true of futures contracts?

	True	False
Transactions costs are lower than other hedging methods	○	○
They can be tailored to TGA Co's exact requirements	○	○

(2 marks)

---

20   The following statements refer to types of foreign currency risk.

   (1)   The risk that TGA Co will make exchange losses when the accounting results of its foreign branches are expressed in the home currency

   (2)   The risk that exchange rate movements will affect the international competitiveness of TGA Co

   What types of risk do the statements refer to?

	Economic	Translation	Transaction
Statement 1	O	O	O
Statement 2	O	O	O

(2 marks)

(Total = 10 marks)

IML Co

This scenario relates to the following five questions

IML Co is an all-equity financed listed company. Nearly all its shares are held by financial institutions.

IML has recently appointed a new finance director who advocates using the capital asset pricing model as a means of evaluating risk and interpreting stock market reaction to the company.

The following initial information has been put forward by the finance director for a rival company operating in the same industry:

	Equity beta
AZT Co	0.7

The finance director notes that the risk-free rate is 5% each year and the expected rate of return on the market portfolio is 15% each year.

21   Calculate, using the capital asset pricing model, the required rate of return on equity of AZT Co (give your answer to the nearest whole number).

      [   ] %   (2 marks)

22   At the end of the year IML Co paid a dividend of 15c per share. At the year-end share price was $3.30 cum div. Share price was $2.50 at the start of the year.

   What is the total shareholder return over the period (give your answer to the nearest whole number)?

      [   ] %   (2 marks)

23   Calculate the equity beta of IML Co, assuming its required annual rate of return on equity is 17% and the stock market uses the capital asset pricing model to calculate the equity beta (give your answer to one decimal place).

      [   ]   (2 marks)

24   Which TWO of the following statements are true?

☐ If IML Co's share price generally moved at three times the market rate, its equity beta factor would be 3.0

☐ The beta factor of IML Co indicates the level of unsystematic risk

☐ The higher the level of systematic risk, the lower the required rate of return by IML Co

☐ IML Co will expect the return on a project to exceed the risk-free rate   **(2 marks)**

---

25   Are the following statements true or false?

	True	False
The CAPM model assumes that investors hold a fully diversified portfolio	O	O
If IML Co has a low price/earnings ratio, it will have a low cost of equity	O	O

(2 marks)

(Total = 10 marks)

Phobis Co

This scenario relates to the following five questions

Phobis Co is considering a bid for Danoca Co. Both companies are stock market listed and are in the same business sector. Financial information on Danoca Co, which is shortly to pay its annual dividend, is as follows:

Number of ordinary shares	5 million
Ordinary share price (ex div basis)	$3.30
Earnings per share	40.0c
Dividend payout ratio	60%
Dividend per share one year ago	23.3c
Dividend per share two years ago	22.0c
Average sector earnings yield	10%

26   Calculate the value of Danoca Co using the earnings yield method.
    O $2m
    O $5m
    O $16.5m
    O $20m   **(2 marks)**

---

27 Are the following statements true or false?

	True	False
If the P/E ratio of Danoca Co is lower than the average sector P/E ratio then the market does not view the growth prospects of Danoca very favourably	O	O
If the P/E ratio of Danoca Co is higher than the average sector ratio then an acquisition by Phobis Co could result in improved financial performance of Danoca Co	O	O

(2 marks)

28 Using a cost of equity of 13% and a dividend growth rate of 4.5%, calculate the value of Danoca Co using the dividend growth model.

O $14.75m

O $5.00m

O $2.95m

O $16.50m   (2 marks)

29 Calculate the market capitalisation of Danoca Co.

O $14.75m

O $16.50m

O $5.00m

O $20.00m   (2 marks)

30 Which TWO of the following are true?

☐ Under weak form hypothesis of market efficiency, share prices reflect all available information about past changes in share price

☐ If a stock market displays semi-strong efficiency then individuals can beat the market

☐ Behavioural finance aims to explain the implications of psychological factors on investor decisions

☐ Random walk theory is based on the idea that past share price patterns will be repeated   (2 marks)

(Total = 10 marks)

Section C

BOTH questions are compulsory and MUST be attempted

31 Purdy Co

Purdy Co uses 5 million litres of chemical X per year in its plastic manufacturing business. Chemical X costs Purdy Co $2.50 per litre per year to store and each order requires a quality check that costs Purdy Co $400 per order to perform.

Purdy Co currently purchases chemical X from a local supplier at a cost of $3.00 per litre. It uses the economic order quantity (EOQ) model to determine order size and carries a safety inventory of five days' usage to protect against variations in lead time demand.

Purdy Co has recently been approached by a company offering to supply chemical X at a cost of $2.25 per litre, if it will order in quantities of 1 million litres. The new supplier's credit terms are the same as the current supplier. Purdy Co estimates that its storage cost per litre and its quality check cost per order will be unchanged if it accepts this offer and that it will have sufficient storage space to cope with larger orders. However, it will need to increase its safety inventory to 15 days' usage if it accepts the new supplier's offer.

Purdy Co is under pressure from its bank to reduce its overdraft and its finance director is interested in the effect of the new supplier's offer on chemical X costs, working capital investment and the cash operating cycle.

Purdy Co operates for 365 days per year.

Required

(a) In relation to Purdy Co's potential change of supplier:

    (i) Calculate the total annual costs relating to Chemical X for both the current and potential suppliers; **(7 marks)**

    (ii) Calculate the value of the average investment in Chemical X inventory for both the current and potential suppliers; and **(2 marks)**

    (iii) Recommend, with justification, whether Purdy Co should change its supplier. **(1 mark)**

(b) Discuss the conflict that exists between the objectives of liquidity and profitability in the management of working capital. **(5 marks)**

(c) Explain the cash operating cycle and its relationship with the level of investment in working capital. **(5 marks)**

(Total = 20 marks)

32 Clover Co

Clover Co must replace a machine which is essential to its production process. The company has identified two machines of identical capacity, but different technology, which would be suitable. Only one machine would be purchased in this mutually exclusive investment decision.

Machine 1

This machine would cost $2,000,000 and would need replacing after three years, when its residual value would be $200,000. Maintenance costs would be $52,000 per year in the first year of operation, increasing by 8% per year in each subsequent year. Annual operating costs, expected to be $300,000 in the first year of operation, would increase by 10% per year in each subsequent year.

Machine 2

This machine would cost $2,500,000 and would need replacing after five years, when its residual value would be $150,000. Maintenance costs are forecast to be $39,000 per year in the first year of operation, increasing by 6% per year in each subsequent year. Annual operating costs, expected to be $248,000 in the first year of operation, would increase by 12% per year in each subsequent year.

Other information

Clover Co believes that whether Machine 1 or Machine 2 is selected, future replacement machines would, in each case, be more advanced versions of the machines, with identical life cycles. Buying Machine 1 would therefore commit the company to a three-year replacement cycle, while buying Machine 2 would commit the company to a five-year replacement cycle.

The residual value of Machine 1 is a buyback price from the machine's seller that would be included in the contract of sale. The residual value of Machine 2 is an estimate made by Clover Co based on existing market information.

The technology used in each machine is expected to continue to develop in the future. While Clover Co thinks it is unlikely that Machine 1 would become obsolescent during its three-year life, the company thinks it is likely that Machine 2 could be affected by obsolescence towards the end of its life.

For both machines, all increases in costs are due to increasing age.

Clover Co uses a discount rate of 13% to appraise investment projects. Ignore taxation.

Required

(a) (i) Calculate the equivalent annual cost of each machine's replacement cycle.   **(10 marks)**

(ii) Discuss which machine should be selected by Clover Co.   **(4 marks)**

(b) Discuss why discounted cash flow (DCF) investment appraisal methods are considered to be superior to non-DCF methods.   **(6 marks)**

Note. Calculations have been done using a spreadsheet, rounding differences may occur in candidates' answers, for example, relating to discount factors.

(Total = 20 marks)

Answers

DO NOT TURN THIS PAGE UNTIL YOU HAVE
COMPLETED THE MOCK EXAM

A PLAN OF ATTACK

Managing your nerves

As you turn the pages to start this mock exam a number of thoughts are likely to cross your mind. At best, examinations cause anxiety so it is important to stay focused on your task for the next three hours! Developing an awareness of what is going on emotionally within you may help you manage your nerves. Remember, you are unlikely to banish the flow of adrenaline, but the key is to harness it to help you work steadily and quickly through your answers.

Working through this mock exam will help you develop the exam stamina you will need to keep going for 3 hours and 15 minutes.

Managing your time

Planning and time management are two of the key skills which complement the technical knowledge you need to succeed. To keep yourself on time, do not be afraid to jot down your target completion times for each question.

Doing the exam

Actually doing the exam is a personal experience. There is not a single **right way**. As long as you submit complete answers to all questions after the three hours are up, then your approach obviously works.

Looking through the exam

Section A has 15 objective test questions. This is the section of the exam where the examining team can test knowledge across the breadth of the syllabus. Make sure you read these questions carefully. The distractors are designed to present plausible, but incorrect, answers. Don't let them mislead you. If you really have no idea – guess. You may even be right.

Section B has three questions, each with a scenario and five objective test questions.

Section C has two longer questions worth 20 marks each, each based on a scenario and featuring a mix of numerical and discussion requirements. These questions are most likely to create time pressure issues. You will need to ensure that you do not spend too long on Section A and B questions because it is hard to rush Section C of the exam.

Allocating your time

BPP's advice is to always allocate your time **according to the marks for the question**. However, **use common sense**. If you're doing a question but haven't a clue how to do part (b), you might be better off reallocating your time and getting more marks on another question, where you can add something you didn't have time for earlier on. Make sure you leave time to recheck the MCQs and make sure you have answered them all.

Section A

1 The correct answers are:

- Allows companies to manage foreign currency risk
- Enables companies to raise new short-term finance

The money market is a section of the financial market where financial instruments with short-term maturities are traded. It is used as a way of borrowing and lending for the short term and for hedging risk (through the use of derivatives).

The Capital market enables companies to raise and sell new long term finance instruments such as loan notes. The Alternative Investment market (AIM) provides a less regulated market for small companies to trade their shares.

2 The correct answer is: 1 only

A contractionary monetary policy involves increasing interest rates. Due to increased debt repayments, consumers have less disposable income resulting in decreased demand for products.

A contractionary **monetary** policy will increase interest rates on debt finance but this will not impact on Wallace Co's debt repayments, which are at a fixed rate.

3 The correct answer is:

Earnings yield	**P/E ratio**
DD's is lower	DD's is higher

For DD Co, P/E = 12, Earnings yield (= 1/(P/E ratio) = 0.0833 = 8.3%.

For competitor, P/E (= 1/earnings yield) = 10, Earnings yield = 10%.

4 The correct answer is: KEW pays the bank $25,000

The FRA guarantees a net interest receipt of 3.0% (the lower end of the spread for an FRA starting in three months' time and ending six months later, ie a 3-9 FRA).

As the interest rate is above this (at 3.5%) , KEW Co will need to pay the bank 0.5% × $10 million × (6/12) = $25,000.

5 The correct answers are:

- Modigliani & Miller's theory with tax
- Traditional theory of capital structure

Both M&M with tax and the traditional theory of gearing suggest that WACC will fall as the level of debt is initially increased (thereby increasing the market value of the company). Both accept that increased gearing will increase the financial risk of equity and will lead to an increase in the cost of equity.

M&M suggested that the WACC would continue to fall as the level of gearing is steadily increased but the traditional theory suggests that at an optimum point of gearing the WACC would start to rise again.

6   The correct answer is: 3.14 years

Depreciation = ($10m-$2m)/4= $2.0m per year

Cash received after 3 years = year 1 $1m profit + $2m depreciation + year 2 $1m profit + $2m depreciation + year 3 $1m profit + $2m depreciation = $9m

This leaves $1m to payback during year 4 where cash flows are 5 + 2 = $7m so 1/7 = 0.14 of year 4 cash flows are needed to payback. The payback period is therefore 3.14 years.

Incorrectly basing the $1m required to payback during year 4 on the total cash in year 4 including the residual value gives payback of 3.11 years.

Incorrectly basing the $1m required to payback during year 4 on the profit in year 4 gives payback of 3.20 years.

Incorrectly using profit to calculate payback gives 4 years. Remember that payback is based on cash flows.

7   The correct answers are:

*   Cash operating cycle - **Reduce**
*   Accounting profit - **Reduce**

Receivables paying sooner will reduce the receivables collection period and hence reduce the length of the cash operating cycle. The cost of the discount (approximately 4% per month as they pay a month earlier than usual) outweighs the interest saved on the overdraft (at 12% per year this is 1% per month) hence the net effect will be reduced profit.

8   The correct answers are:

*   PP Co will aim to maximise shareholder wealth whereas NH Co won't
*   NH Co will be most concerned about value for money whereas PP Co will prioritise the maximisation of shareholder wealth

The key objective of a listed entity will be to maximise shareholder wealth whereas the key objective of a state owned entity will be value for money.

Notes on incorrect answers:

NH Co will not have financial objectives but PP Co will – while NH Co's objectives may not be profit focussed it will still have financial objectives.

NH Co will focus of satisfying a wide range of stakeholders whereas PP Co will only focus on satisfying shareholders – PP's key objective will focus on shareholders but it will also need to meet the needs of a wide range of stakeholders.

9   The correct answer is: $12,500

$15m × 0.7 = $10.5m credit sales x 30/360 = $875,000 new receivables. Existing receivables are $1m therefore receivables reduce by $125,000 saving interest at 10% = $12,500.

Notes on incorrect answers:

$13,699 – incorrectly using 365 days

$87,500 – calculating interest saving on new receivables instead of the change in receivables.

$62,500 – using credit sales of $4.5m ($15m × 0.3)

 BPP

10　The correct answer is: It will receive a payment if the market rate is less than the floor rate

An interest rate floor protects an investor from a fall in the market rate below the floor rate. The company will therefore receive a payment if the market rate is below the floor rate.

11　The correct answers are:

- It considers the whole project
- It produces information that is easy to understand for a non-finance person

ROCE considers the whole project as there is no 'cut-off' point (unlike the payback period calculation). ROCE is a percentage which is more meaningful to non-finance professionals than more complex DCF based methods.

Incorrect answers: ROCE is not cash based – it is based on profit. ROCE will be affected by a change in accounting policy that impacts on annual profit.

12　The correct answer is: $103.23

In five years' time the share price is estimated as $18.98 \times 1.03^5 = \$22$.

The bond would be converted as the MV of shares exceeds the nominal value on redemption 5 shares @ $22 = $110 conversion value

Time	CF $	DF@6%	PV
1–5	$5	4.212	21.06
5	$110	0.747	82.17
			103.23

Notes on incorrect answers:

$99.02 – incorrectly includes tax saving on interest

$95.76 – using par value for redemption

$112.21 – uses $6 as the interest and 5% as discount factor

13　The correct answers are:

- The valuation fails to take account the premium required to obtain a controlling interest
- It involves an unreliable estimate of the cost of equity

Explanation

No adjustment is made for achieving a controlling interest, it is mainly useful for valuing minority holdings.

An unlisted company's cost of equity is hard to estimate, basing it on an equivalent listed company is often used but this relies on finding an equivalent listed company which is unlikely.

Notes on incorrect answers:

Periods of non-constant growth can be adjusted for.

It is based on cash – as the dividend is cash.

14 $ 0.60

Step 1 Calculate the dividend amount using dividend yield

Dividend yield = Dividend per share / share price

∴ 0.048 = dividend per share / $5

∴ $5 × 0.048 = Dividend per share = $0.24

Step 2 Calculate the EPS share using dividend cover

Dividend cover = Earnings per share / Dividend per share

∴ 2.5 = Earnings per share / 0.24

∴ 2.5 × $0.24 = Earnings per share = $0.60

15 The correct answers are:

- An increase in the expected growth rate of the share price
- An increase in the conversion ratio

Explanation

A higher share price and a higher conversion ratio (the number of shares per $100 of debt) will increase the cost of redeeming the debt.

Notes on incorrect answers

Higher corporation tax increases the tax shield on debt and therefore reduces the cost of debt.

A higher market value increases the finance raised for a given coupon interest repayment and redemption cost. This therefore reduces the cost of debt.

BPP

Section B

TGA CO

16   The correct answer is: 2 only

TGA Co should enter into a forward contract to sell €500,000 in 3 months. Statement 1 is incorrect. TGA Co could use a money market hedge but €500,000 would have to be borrowed, then converted into dollars and then placed on deposit. Statement 3 is incorrect. An interest rate swap swaps one type of interest payment (such as fixed interest) for another (such as floating rate interest). Therefore it would not be suitable.

17    $ | 296,384 |

Forward market hedge

The higher rate should be used (the least favourable to TGA Co)

Receipt from forward contract = €500,000/1.687 = $296,384

18    $ | 294,858 |

Money market hedge

3-month euro borrowing rate = 9% × 3/12 = 2.25%

3-month dollar deposit rate = 4% × 3/12 = 1%

Borrow euros now 500,000/1.0225 = €488,998

Convert to $ now 488,998/1.675 = $291,939

Again the higher rate should be used (the least favourable to TGA Co)

$ after investing $291,939 × 1.01 = $294,858

19   The correct answers are:

- Transactions costs are lower than other hedging methods - **True**
- They can be tailored to TGA Co's exact requirements - **False**

One of the advantages of futures contracts is that the transaction costs are lower than other hedging methods. One of the disadvantages is that they cannot be tailored to the user's requirements. So statement 1 is true and statement 2 is false.

20   The correct answers are:

- Statement 1 - **Translation**
- Statement 2 - **Economic Transaction**

IML Co

21 | 12 | %

The required rate of return on equity can be found using the capital asset pricing model:

$E(r_j) = R_f + \beta i(E(r_m - R_f)$

AZT Co

$E(r_j) = 5\% + 0.7(15\% - 5\%)$

$= 12\%$

 BPP

22 | 32 | %

Ex div share price = $3.30 - $0.15 = $3.15

Total shareholder return =

$$\frac{315 - 250 + 15}{250} = 0.32 = 32\%$$

23 | 1.2 |

The equity beta for IML Co can be found using the same expression:

17% = 5% + β(15% − 5%)

β = (17 − 5) / (15 − 5)

The equity beta factor = 1.2

24 The correct answers are:

- If IML Co's share price generally moved at three times the market rate, its equity beta factor would be 3.0

- IML Co will expect the return on a project to exceed the risk-free rate

The equity beta factor is a measure of the volatility of the return on a share relative to the stock market. If for example a share price moved at 3 times the market rate, its equity beta factor would be 3.0.

The beta factor indicates the level of systematic risk, which is the risk of making an investment that cannot be diversified away.

It is used in the capital asset pricing model to determine the level of return required by investors; the higher the level of systematic risk, the **higher** the required level of return.

It is true that companies want a return on a project to exceed the risk-free rate.

25 The correct answers are:

- The CAPM model assumes that investors hold a fully diversified portfolio - **True**

- If IML Co has a low price/earnings ratio, it will have a low cost of equity - **False**

Under the CAPM, the return required from a security is related to its systematic risk rather than its total risk. Only the risks that cannot be eliminated by diversification are relevant. The assumption is that investors will hold a fully diversified portfolio and therefore deal with the unsystematic risk themselves.

A low cost of equity would discount future earnings at a low rate – leading to a high market value and a high P/E ratio.

Phobis Co

26   The correct answer is: $20m

Earnings yield = EPS/Price which is the same as 1 ÷ P/E ratio

So the P/E ratio = 10

Price/earnings ratio method of valuation

Market value = P/E ratio × EPS

EPS = 40.0c

Average sector P/E ratio = 10

Value of shares = 40.0 × 10 = $4.00 per share

(Alternatively 40.0 cents divided by earnings yield of 0.1)

Number of shares = 5 million

Value of Danoca Co = $20 million

27   The correct answers are:

- If the P/E ratio of Danoca Co is lower than the average sector P/E ratio then the market does not view the growth prospects of Danoca very favourably - **True**

- If the P/E ratio of Danoca Co is higher than the average sector ratio then an acquisition by Phobis Co could result in improved financial performance of Danoca Co - **False**

The current share price of Danoca Co is $3.30 which equates to a P/E ratio of 8.25 (3.30/0.4). This is lower than the average sector P/E ratio of 10 which suggests that the market does not view the growth prospects of Danoca Co as favourably as an average company in that business sector.

If Danoca Co has a **lower** P/E ratio, this would imply that an acquisition by Phobis could result in improved financial performance of Danoca Co.

28   The correct answer is: $14.75m

Dividend growth model method of valuation

$$P_0 = \frac{d_0(1 + g)}{r_e - g}$$

D_0 can be found using the proposed payout ratio of 60%.

$D_0 = 60\% \times 40c = 24c$

Value of shares =

$$P_0 = \frac{0.24(1 + 0.045)}{0.13 - 0.045}$$

= $2.95

Value of Danoca Co = $2.95 × 5 million shares = $14.75 million

29   The correct answer is: $16.50m

Market capitalisation of Danoca Co is $3.30 × 5m = $16.5m.

30   The correct answers are:

- Under weak form hypothesis of market efficiency, share prices reflect all available information about past changes in share price
- Behavioural finance aims to explain the implications of psychological factors on investor decisions

'If a stock market displays semi-strong efficiency then individuals can beat the market' is not true. Individuals cannot beat the market because all information publicly available will already be reflected in the share price.

'Random walk theory is based on the idea that past share price patterns will be repeated' is not true. Chartists believe that past share price patterns will be repeated.

Section C

31 Purdy Co

> **Workbook references**
>
> Inventory management and the working capital cycle are both covered in Chapter 3.
>
> **Top tips**
>
> Make sure your spreadsheet contains clear headings and workings so that your calculations can be followed by the marker.
>
> **Easy marks**
>
> The discussion areas of the question should be straightforward as long as your answer addresses the question's requirements.

Marking guide			Marks	
(a)	(i)	Current EOQ calculation	1	
		Current safety inventory	1	
		Current total Co/year	0.5	
		Current total Ch/year	1	
		Current purchase cost	0.5	
		New safety inventory	1	
		New total Co/year	0.5	
		New total Ch/year	1	
		New purchase cost	0.5	
				7
	(ii)	Average inventories	2	
				2
	(iii)	Overall recommendation	1	
				1
(b)		Discussion on conflict	3	
		Further illustration	2	
				5
(c)		Explanation of cycle	2	
		Link to investment in working capital	3	
				5
Total				**20**

(a) (i) **Total annual costs relating to Chemical X for current and potential suppliers**

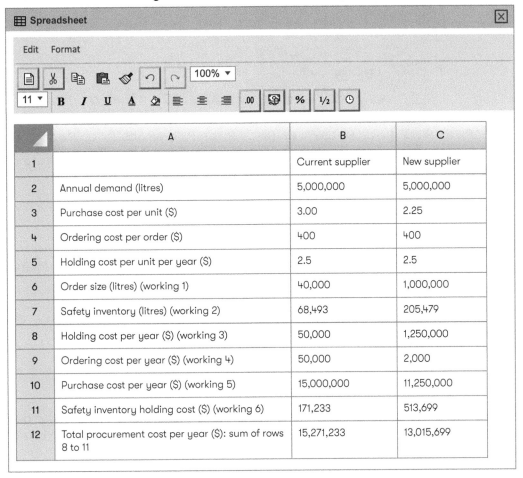

	A	B	C
		Current supplier	New supplier
1			
2	Annual demand (litres)	5,000,000	5,000,000
3	Purchase cost per unit ($)	3.00	2.25
4	Ordering cost per order ($)	400	400
5	Holding cost per unit per year ($)	2.5	2.5
6	Order size (litres) (working 1)	40,000	1,000,000
7	Safety inventory (litres) (working 2)	68,493	205,479
8	Holding cost per year ($) (working 3)	50,000	1,250,000
9	Ordering cost per year ($) (working 4)	50,000	2,000
10	Purchase cost per year ($) (working 5)	15,000,000	11,250,000
11	Safety inventory holding cost ($) (working 6)	171,233	513,699
12	Total procurement cost per year ($): sum of rows 8 to 11	15,271,233	13,015,699

Switching to the new supplier will reduce procurement costs by $2,255,534 ($15,271,233 – $13,015,699) which is equal to 15% of current purchasing cost.

Workings

1 EOQ for current supplier = $((2 \text{ Co D})/\text{Ch})^{0.5}$ = $((2 \times \$400 \times 5,000,000)/\$2.50)^{0.5}$ = 40,000 litres

2 5,000,000/365 days x 5 days = 68,493 litres

   5,000,000/365 days x 15 days = 205,479 litres

3 40,000 litres/2 x $2.5 = $50,000

   1,000,000 litres/2 x $2.5 = $1,250,000

4 5,000,000 litres/40,000 litres x $400 = $50,000

   5,000,000 litres/1,000,000 litres x $400 = $2,000

5 5,000,000 litres x $3 = $15,000,000

   5,000,000 litres x $2.25 = $11,250,000

6 68,493 litres x $2.50 = $171,233

   205,479 litres x $2.50 = $513,698

(ii) **Value of the average investment in Chemical X inventory for current suppliers**

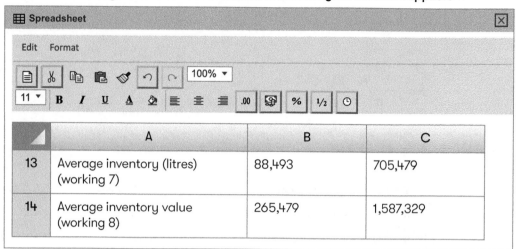

	A	B	C
13	Average inventory (litres) (working 7)	88,493	705,479
14	Average inventory value (working 8)	265,479	1,587,329

Switching supplier would increase average inventory and require an investment in inventory of $1,321,850 ($1,587,329 – $265,479).

Workings

1   40,000 litres/2 + 68,493 litres = 88,493 litres

1,000,000 litres/2 + 205,479 litres = 705,479 litres

2   88,493 litres x $3.00 = $265,479

705,479 litres x $2.25 = $1,587,328

(iii) Although switching suppliers would reduce cost, it is not recommended because of the large investment in working capital it would require and the increase in overdraft which this would entail.

(b)

Working capital management involves the management of a company's current assets and current liabilities, principally inventory, accounts receivable, cash and accounts payable. When managing working capital, a company faces twin objectives. One objective is to earn profits in order to provide satisfactory returns for its investors and contribute towards the maximisation of shareholder wealth.

Another is to generate enough cash to allow the business to meet its financial commitments, such as wages, salaries, accounts payable, interest and tax.

These two objectives can often conflict. For example, to increase profitability, a firm may increase its inventory levels in order to be able to offer customers prompt delivery. In theory, this will be attractive to customers and sales and profits should increase. However, by increasing inventory levels the company ties up more cash in inventory, thus decreasing its ability to meet its short-term commitments.

On the other hand, a company which pressurises customers for payment by aggressive management of accounts receivable may find that its cash resources increase as customers pay more promptly, but at the same time its sales and profits may fall as customers turn to other suppliers who offer more generous credit terms.

 BPP

Cash management involves a similar trade off. Cash is often regarded as 'an idle asset' as it earns no return. Companies often invest their cash resources to earn some return and increase profitability. By doing so, they usually have to tie up the cash for a fixed amount of time (otherwise the interest earned would be very small), and hence damage their liquidity.

Finally, companies which take long periods of credit from suppliers may find their liquidity improves but this can be to the detriment of profits as settlement discounts may be lost and supplier relationships damaged.

When managing working capital, firms need to be aware of the conflict between the twin objectives. A sensible approach is to see the need for sufficient liquidity as a constraint on working capital management and then to seek to maximise profits subject to this constraint.

(c)

The cash operating cycle (sometimes known as the working capital cycle) measures the interval between the company paying out cash at the start of its production process (in manufacturing, this is normally paying suppliers for raw materials) and receiving cash from customers when products are sold and paid for.

The cash operating cycle for a company can be calculated by adding inventory days (for raw materials, work in progress and finished goods) to accounts receivable days and then deducting accounts payable days.

The length of a company's cash operating cycle has two major drivers. First the type of industry a company operates in. House construction companies often have very long cash operating cycles. Their business involves buying land, gaining permission to build, building houses and infrastructure, selling and then collecting cash from sales. This whole process often takes more than a year.

Large supermarket chains on the other hand often have very short cash operating cycles. Their buying power allows them to enjoy long credit periods from suppliers, whilst inventory holding periods and accounts receivables are very short. Often, they have negative cash operating cycles.

The efficiency of a company's working capital management will also affect the length of the cycle. A company which has poor control of inventory and accounts receivable, yet which pays its suppliers promptly will find that it has a longer cash operating cycle than competitors who manage their working capital well.

The longer a company's cash operating cycle, the greater its investment in net working capital will be. If inventory is held for a large amount of days, physical inventory, and the amount of money invested in it will be high.

Similarly the longer it takes accounts receivable to be settled, the more money the company will have invested.

Finally, a short accounts payable period will mean that the company takes little credit from suppliers and hence fails to reduce its net working capital investment.

32 Clover Co

Marking guide			Marks
(a)	(i)	Initial investment	1
		Residual values	1
		Machine 1 maintenance costs	1
		Machine 1 operating costs	1
		Machine 1 PVs	1
		Machine 1 EAC	1
		Machine 2 maintenance costs	1
		Machine 2 operating costs	1
		Machine 2 PVs	1
		Machine 2 EAC	1
			10
	(ii)	Financial decision on EAC	1
		Uncertainty	1
		Obsolescence	1
		Other relevant points	1
			4
(b)		Time value of money	2
		Cash flow basis	2
		Whole project considered	1
		Other relevant points	1
			6
Total			20

(a) (i) **Equivalent annual cost of Machine 1 (three-year cycle)**

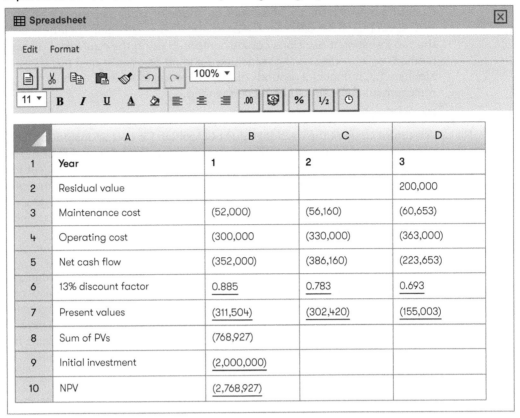

	A	B	C	D
1	**Year**	1	2	3
2	Residual value			200,000
3	Maintenance cost	(52,000)	(56,160)	(60,653)
4	Operating cost	(300,000	(330,000)	(363,000)
5	Net cash flow	(352,000)	(386,160)	(223,653)
6	13% discount factor	0.885	0.783	0.693
7	Present values	(311,504)	(302,420)	(155,003)
8	Sum of PVs	(768,927)		
9	Initial investment	(2,000,000)		
10	NPV	(2,768,927)		

EAC = (2,768,927)/2.361 = ($1,172,777)

Equivalent annual cost of Machine 2 (five-year cycle)

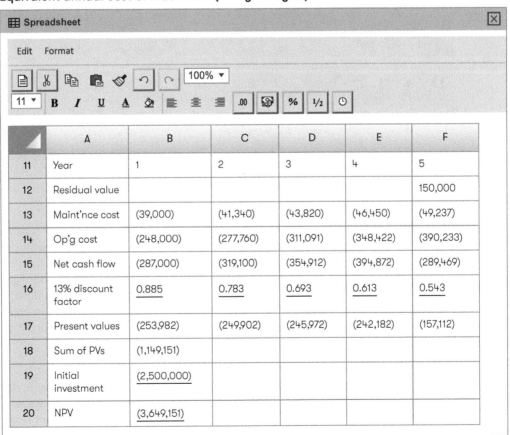

	A	B	C	D	E	F
11	Year	1	2	3	4	5
12	Residual value					150,000
13	Maint'nce cost	(39,000)	(41,340)	(43,820)	(46,450)	(49,237)
14	Op'g cost	(248,000)	(277,760)	(311,091)	(348,422)	(390,233)
15	Net cash flow	(287,000)	(319,100)	(354,912)	(394,872)	(289,469)
16	13% discount factor	0.885	0.783	0.693	0.613	0.543
17	Present values	(253,982)	(249,902)	(245,972)	(242,182)	(157,112)
18	Sum of PVs	(1,149,151)				
19	Initial investment	(2,500,000)				
20	NPV	(3,649,151)				

EAC = (3,649,151)/3.517 = ($1,037,575)

ANSWERS

(ii) Financial acceptability

Choosing between the two machines on financial grounds cannot be achieved using NPV, since they have different replacement cycles, reflecting their unequal lives. However, the two investment decisions can be compared using the equivalent annual cost (EAC) method, which indicates that Machine 2 should be chosen as it has a lower EAC than Machine 1. On financial grounds alone, therefore, Machine 2 with its five-year replacement cycle should be recommended.

Uncertainty

The future value of the residual value of Machine 1 is certain insofar as it will be a contractual commitment by the selling company. The future value of the residual value of Machine 2 is an estimate made by Clover Co and is therefore subject to uncertainty. The three-year replacement cycle might therefore be chosen, even though it has a higher EAC, because its residual value is more certain than that of the five-year replacement cycle. However, even if the residual value of Machine 2 were zero, Machine 2 would still have the lower EAC.

Obsolescence

Purchasing Machine 1 and committing to a three-year replacement cycle looks to carry little risk of Clover Co suffering from obsolescence due to technological advances. By contrast, purchasing Machine 2 and committing to a five-year replacement cycle appears to lead to significant obsolescence risk late in the life of the machine. The three-year replacement cycle might therefore be chosen, even though it has a higher EAC, because Clover Co believes it carries significantly less obsolescence risk.

Flexibility

Purchasing Machine 1 may give Clover Co greater flexibility in that its shorter replacement cycle could facilitate a more rapid response to changing technology through investment in other machines than the two under consideration, if such were to become available.

(b)

Discounted cash flow (DCF) investment appraisal methods, such as net present value (NPV) and internal rate of return (IRR), are considered superior to non-DCF investment appraisal methods, such as payback and return on capital employed (ROCE), for a variety of reasons, as follows.

Time value of money

DCF investment appraisal methods are seen as superior to non-DCF methods because DCF methods take account of the time value of money by discounting future cash flows to their present values, while non-DCF methods ignore the time value of money. While DCF methods therefore give more weight in an investment appraisal to cash flows in the near future compared to cash flows in the distant future, payback ignores the amount and timing of cash flows within the payback period, while ROCE averages profit over the life of the project.

Cash flow basis

DCF investment appraisal methods are seen as superior to non-DCF methods because DCF methods use cash flows. Cash flows are not distorted by company-specific factors such as depreciation policy and amortisation decisions which can affect profit, for example, the average annual accounting profit used by ROCE. From this point of view, DCF methods can be seen as more objective than non-DCF methods.

Whole project considered

DCF investment appraisal methods consider cash flows over the whole life of an investment project, whereas payback ignores cash flows after the payback period. Investment decisions using payback period may therefore be sub-optimal in relation to the financial management objective of maximising shareholder wealth, because a project with a higher NPV might be rejected in favour of a project with a lower NPV but a shorter payback period.

Formulae, ratios and mathematical tables

Appendices

Appendix A: Formulae and ratios that you need to learn

Profitability ratios:

$$\text{ROCE} = \frac{\text{Profit from operations (before interest and tax)}}{\text{Capital employed}}$$

Debt ratios include:

$$\text{Gearing} = \frac{\text{Value of debt}}{\text{Value of equity (or debt + equity)}}$$

$$\text{Interest cover} = \frac{\text{Profit from operations}}{\text{Interest}}$$

Liquidity ratios:

$$\text{Current ratio} = \frac{\text{Current assets}}{\text{Current liabilities}}$$

Shareholder investor ratios include:

$$\text{Dividend yield} = \frac{\text{Dividend per share}}{\text{Share price}} \times 100$$

$$\text{Earnings per share (EPS)} = \frac{\text{Profits after tax - preference dividend}}{\text{Number of ordinary shares}}$$

$$\text{Price to earnings ratio (P/E)} = \frac{\text{Share price}}{\text{EPS}}$$

Working capital ratios

Operating cycle = inventory holding period + receivable collection period – payables payment period

Inventory holding period = inventory/cost of sales × 365

Receivables collection period = trade receivables/(credit) sales × 365

Payables payment period = trade payables/(credit) purchases × 365

Sales to net working capital ratio = sales/net working capital (excl cash)

Cost of capital formulae:

$$K_d = \frac{I(1-t)}{P_0}$$

$$K_p = \frac{d}{p}$$

Other useful formulae to learn:

$$IRR = a\% + \left[\frac{NPV_a}{NPV_a - NPV_b} \times (b\% - a\%)\right]$$

$$\text{Total shareholder return} = \frac{\text{dividend gain} + \text{capital}}{\text{share price at start year}}$$

$$EAC = \frac{\text{NPV of costs}}{\text{Annuity factor for life of the project}}$$

$$\text{Profitability index} = \frac{\text{Present value of cash inflows (or NPV of the project)}}{\text{Present value of cash outflows}}$$

Appendix B: Mathematical tables

Present Value Table

Present value of $1, that is $(1+r)^{-n}$ where r = interest rate; n = number of periods until payment or receipt.

Periods (n)	Interest rates (r)									
	1%	2%	3%	4%	5%	6%	7%	8%	9%	10%
1	0.990	0.980	0.971	0.962	0.952	0.943	0.935	0.926	0.917	0.909
2	0.980	0.961	0.943	0.925	0.907	0.890	0.873	0.857	0.842	0.826
3	0.971	0.942	0.915	0.889	0.864	0.840	0.816	0.794	0.772	0.751
4	0.961	0.924	0.888	0.855	0.823	0.792	0.763	0.735	0.708	0.683
5	0.951	0.906	0.863	0.822	0.784	0.747	0.713	0.681	0.650	0.621
6	0.942	0.888	0.837	0.790	0.746	0705	0.666	0.630	0.596	0.564
7	0.933	0.871	0.813	0.760	0.711	0.665	0.623	0.583	0.547	0.513
8	0.923	0.853	0.789	0.731	0.677	0.627	0.582	0.540	0.502	0.467
9	0.914	0.837	0.766	0.703	0.645	0.592	0.544	0.500	0.460	0.424
10	0.905	0.820	0.744	0.676	0.614	0.558	0.508	0.463	0.422	0.386
11	0.896	0.804	0.722	0.650	0.585	0.527	0.475	0.429	0.388	0.350
12	0.887	0.788	0.701	0.625	0.557	0.497	0.444	0.397	0.356	0.319
13	0.879	0.773	0.681	0.601	0.530	0.469	0.415	0.368	0.326	0.290
14	0.870	0.758	0.661	0.577	0.505	0.442	0.388	0.340	0.299	0.263
15	0.861	0.743	0.642	0.555	0.481	0.417	0.362	0.315	0.275	0.239

Periods (n)	Interest rates (r)									
	11%	12%	13%	14%	15%	16%	17%	18%	19%	20%
1	0.901	0.893	0.885	0.877	0.870	0.862	0.855	0.847	0.840	0.833
2	0.812	0.797	0.783	0.769	0.756	0.743	0.731	0.718	0.706	0.694
3	0.731	0.712	0.693	0.675	0.658	0.641	0.624	0.609	0.593	0.579
4	0.659	0.636	0.613	0.592	0.572	0.552	0.534	0.516	0.499	0.482
5	0.593	0.567	0.543	0.519	0.497	0.476	0.456	0.437	0.419	0.402
6	0.535	0.507	0.480	0.456	0.432	0.410	0.390	0.370	0.352	0.335
7	0.482	0.452	0.425	0.400	0.376	0.354	0.333	0.314	0.296	0.279
8	0.434	0.404	0.376	0.351	0.327	0.305	0.285	0.266	0.249	0.233
9	0.391	0.361	0.333	0.308	0.284	0.263	0.243	0.225	0.209	0.194
10	0.352	0.322	0.295	0.270	0.247	0.227	0.208	0.191	0.176	0.162
11	0.317	0.287	0.261	0.237	0.215	0.195	0.178	0.162	0.148	0.135
12	0.286	0.257	0.231	0.208	0.187	0.168	0.152	0.137	0.124	0.112
13	0.258	0.229	0.204	0.182	0.163	0.145	0.130	0.116	0.104	0.093
14	0.232	0.205	0.181	0.160	0.141	0.125	0.111	0.099	0.088	0.078
15	0.209	0.183	0.160	0.140	0.123	0.108	0.095	0.084	0.079	0.065

Annuity Table

Present value of an annuity of 1 ie $\dfrac{1-(1+r)^{-n}}{r}$

Where r = discount rate; n = number of periods

Periods (n)	Discount rate (r)									
	1%	2%	3%	4%	5%	6%	7%	8%	9%	10%
1	0.990	0.980	0.971	0.962	0.952	0.943	0.935	0.926	0.917	0.909
2	1.970	1.942	1.913	1.886	1.859	1.833	1.808	1.783	1.759	1.736
3	2.941	2.884	2.829	2.775	2.723	2.673	2.624	2.577	2.531	2.487
4	3.902	3.808	3.717	3.630	3.546	3.465	3.387	3.312	3.240	3.170
5	4.853	4.713	4.580	4.452	4.329	4.212	4.100	3.993	3.890	3.791
6	5.795	5.601	5.417	5.242	5.076	4.917	4.767	4.623	4.486	4.355
7	6.728	6.472	6.230	6.002	5.786	5.582	5.389	5.206	5.033	4.868
8	7.652	7.325	7.020	6.733	6.463	6.210	5.971	5.747	5.535	5.335
9	8.566	8.162	7.786	7.435	7.108	6.802	6.515	6.247	5.995	5.759
10	9.471	8.983	8.530	8.111	7.722	7.360	7.024	6.710	6.418	6.145
11	10.368	9.787	9.253	8.760	8.306	7.887	7.499	7.139	6.805	6.495
12	11.255	10.575	9.954	9.385	8.863	8.384	7.943	7.536	7.161	6.814
13	12.134	11.348	10.635	9.986	9.394	8.853	8.358	7.904	7.487	7.103
14	13.004	12.106	11.296	10.563	9.899	9.295	8.745	8.244	7.786	7.367
15	13.865	12.849	11.938	11.118	10.380	9.712	9.108	8.559	8.061	7.606

(n)	11%	12%	13%	14%	15%	16%	17%	18%	19%	20%
1	0.901	0.893	0.885	0.877	0.870	0.862	0.855	0.847	0.840	0.833
2	1.713	1.690	1.668	1.647	1.626	1.605	1.585	1.566	1.547	1.528
3	2.444	2.402	2.361	2.322	2.283	2.246	2.210	2.174	2.140	2.106
4	3.102	3.037	2.974	2.914	2.855	2.798	2.743	2.690	2.639	2.589
5	3.696	3.605	3.517	3.433	3.352	3.274	3.199	3.127	3.058	2.991
6	4.231	4.111	3.998	3.889	3.784	3.685	3.589	3.498	3.410	3.326
7	4.712	4.564	4.423	4.288	4.160	4.039	3.922	3.812	3.706	3.605
8	5.146	4.968	4.799	4.639	4.487	4.344	4.207	4.078	3.954	3.837
9	5.537	5.328	5.132	4.946	4.772	4.607	4.451	4.303	4.163	4.031
10	5.889	5.650	5.426	5.216	5.019	4.833	4.659	4.494	4.339	4.192
11	6.207	5.938	5.687	5.453	5.234	5.029	4.836	4.656	4.486	4.327
12	6.492	6.194	5.918	5.660	5.421	5.197	4.988	4.793	4.611	4.439
13	6.750	6.424	6.122	5.842	5.583	5.342	5.118	4.910	4.715	4.533
14	6.982	6.628	6.302	6.002	5.724	5.468	5.229	5.008	4.802	4.611
15	7.191	6.811	6.462	6.142	5.847	5.575	5.324	5.092	4.876	4.675

Formula Sheet

Economic Order Quantity

$$= \sqrt{\frac{2C_0D}{C_H}}$$

Miller-Orr Model

Return point $=$ Lower limit $+ \left(\frac{1}{3} \times \text{spread}\right)$

$$\text{Spread} = 3\left[\frac{\frac{3}{4} \times \text{transaction cost} \times \text{variance of cash flows}}{\text{Interest rate}}\right]^{\frac{1}{3}}$$

The Capital Asset Pricing Model

$$E(n) = R_f + \beta_i(E(r_m) - R_f)$$

The asset beta formula

$$\beta_a = \left[\frac{V_e}{(V_e + V_d(1-T))}\beta_e\right] + \left[\frac{V_d(1-T)}{(V_e + V_d(1-T))}\beta_d\right]$$

The Growth Model

$$P_0 = \frac{D_0(1 + g)}{(r_e - g)} \qquad r_e = \frac{D_0(1 + g)}{P_0} + g$$

Note: $D_0(1+g)$ may be replaced by D_1

Gordon's Growth Approximation

$g = br$

The weighted average cost of capital

$$\text{WACC} = \left[\frac{V_e}{V_e + V_d}\right]k_e + \left[\frac{V_d}{V_e + V_d}\right]k_d(1 - T)$$

The Fisher formula

$$(1 + i) = (1 + r)(1 + h)$$

Purchasing Power Parity and Interest Rate Parity

$$S_1 = S_0 \times \frac{(1 + h_c)}{(1 + h_b)} \qquad F_0 = S_0 \times \frac{(1 + i_c)}{(1 + i_b)}$$

Tell us what you think

Got comments or feedback on this book? Let us know.
Use your QR code reader:

Or, visit:
https://bppgroup.fra1.qualtrics.com/jfe/form/SV_9TrxTtw8jSvO7Pv

Need to get in touch with customer service?

www.bpp.com/request-support

Spotted an error?

www.bpp.com/learningmedia/Errata